The Complete

BIBLICAL

LIBRARY

HARMONY
OF THE
GOSPELS

The Complete BIBLICAL LIBRARY

The Complete Biblical Library, part 1, a 16-volume study series on the New Testament.
Volume 1: HARMONY OF THE GOSPELS.
World Copyright © 1986, 1994 Dagengruppen AB, Stockholm, Sweden.
© Published 1986, 1990, 1991, 1994 by World Library Press, Inc., Springfield, Missouri, 65804, U.S.A.

Printed in the United States of America 1994 by R.R. Donnelley and Sons Company, Chicago, Illinois 60606. Library of Congress Catalog Card Number 86-070454. International Standard Book Number 0-88243-361-X.

INTERNATIONAL EDITOR
THORALF GILBRANT

Executive Editor: Ralph W. Harris, M.A.

NATIONAL EDITORS

U.S.A.
Stanley M. Horton, Th.D.

SWEDEN
Bertil E. Gartner, D.D.
Thorsten Kjall, M.A.
Stig Wikstrom, Th.M.

HOLLAND
Herman ter Welle, pastor

NORWAY
Erling Utnem, Bishop
Arthur Berg, B.D.

DENMARK
Jorgen Glenthoj, Th.M.

FINLAND
Valter Luoto, pastor
Matti Liljequist, B.D.

STAFF

Editing and Research: Patrick Alexander, M.A.; Gary Leggett, M.A.; Dorothy B. Morris; Gayle A. Seaver, J.D.; **Graphic Design:** Chuck Clore, Terry Van Someren; **Secretarial and Stenographic:** Faye Faucett, Sonja Jensen, Nancy Salzer, Rachel Wisehart, Kathy Wootton.

PROJECT COORDINATOR
William G. Eastlake

HARMONY OF THE GOSPELS

Concerning the Greatest Life Ever Lived

THE FOUR GOSPELS IN PARALLEL COLUMNS

together with

Jesus—His Story

an interwoven account from all four Gospels

by Robert Shank, D.H.L.

In full color: 118 photos of the Holy Land, from the *Pictorial Archive*, Jerusalem and other sources; satellite maps of Palestine; and 25 paintings by the British artist, William Hole, depicting the life of Christ.

WORLD LIBRARY PRESS, INC.
Springfield, Missouri, U.S.A.

Acknowledgements

Photographic Credits

The many photographs and maps of the Holy Land are a valuable feature of the HARMONY OF THE BIBLE. We are indebted to NASA for providing maps from space which afford unique views of the land where Jesus lived. For the most part the photos and sections of the maps have been located where they can illustrate and identify the events described in the Gospels. Following are the names of those whose photos enhance this book. The numerals indicate the pages where their pictures appear.

Raymond Cox—54, 85, 92; **Garo Photographic**—65, 80, 91, 108, 113, 117, 120, 142, 147, 155, 161, 162, 183, 197, 203, 204, 222, 232B, 236, 245, 270, 272, 299; **Ralph W. Harris**—51, 59A, 66, 69, 73, 74, 77, 83A, 83B, 95, 122, 123, 128, 134. 141, 144, 145, 156, 165, 168, 173, 176, 180, 185, 200, 207, 209, 211, 212, 215, 216, 221, 224, 227, 230, 241, 247, 249, 250, 253, 254, 256, 260, 263, 265A, 265B, 268, 283, 286, 290, 293, 297, 313, 328, 338, 341; **E. I. Moore**—194; **Roloc Color Slides**—56, 60, 72, 119, 160, 232A, 315, 334; **Everett Stenhouse**—327.

Contributors

The Editors of THE COMPLETE BIBLICAL LIBRARY are greatly indebted to the many people whose talents and skills have helped to make this set of volumes a reality. They have come from various backgrounds but all have shown their dedication to the purpose of making the Word of God more understandable.

The names which follow represent those who have assisted in producing the entire set. Although their contributions have been made in the *Study Bible* and the *Bible Dictionary*, it seemed fitting to pay tribute to them in this first volume of the entire *Library* also. They are listed alphabetically by countries.

United States

Abshier, Carolyn, B.A.
Aker, Benny C., Ph.D.
Albrecht, Daniel E., M.A.
Alexander, Donald L., Ph.D.
Alexander, Patrick, M.A.
Anderson, Carl, B.D.
Anderson, Gordon, M.A.
Arrington, French L., Ph.D.
Autry, Arden C., Ph.D.
Bailey, Gary D., M.A.
Bailey, Mark, Th.M.
Baker, Carmen, B.A.
Baldwin, Donald, Ph.D.
Ballantyne, Jeff K., B.A.
Barlow, John, M.Div.
Barton, Freeman, Ph.D.
Beacham, A. D., Jr., D.Min.
Beaty, James M., Ph.D.
Bechtle, John D., D.Min.
Bibb, Charles W., B.A.
Bicket, Zenas, Th.D.
Bishop, Richard W., D.Min.
Black, Daniel L., Th.D.
Black, David Alan, D.Theo.
Boonstra, Gerald D., B.A.
Broadus, Steve, B.A.
Brock, Raymond T., Ed.D.
Brookman, William R., Ph.D.
Brown, William K., Ph.D.
Brubaker, Malcolm, M.Div.
Bundrick, David R., M.Div.
Buswell, Robert C., D.Min.
Cargal, Eric Michael, B.A.
Carlson, G. Raymond, D.D.
Carlson, John, B.A.
Castleberry, Joseph L., B.A.
Chamberlain, Ernest H., B.D.
Clyde, Terese, B.A.
Cohen, Gary G., Th.D.
Cole, Greg, B.A.
Collins, Oral, Ph.D.

Cornet, R. Dale, M.Div.
Cotton, Roger D., Th.D.
Crabtree, Dan, B.A.
Darnell, Lonnie L., II, M.A.
Dayton, Wilber T., Th.D.
Dean, David A., Th.D.
Deisher, John, M.Div.
Dippold, David, M.A.
Doerksen, Vernon D., Th.D.
Drury, Rodney A., B.A.
Dusing, Michael, M.Div.
Dyce, Shelley L., M.A.
Elliott, William E., Th.D.
Esposito, David, B.A.
Estridge, Charles A., D.Min.
Eustler, Steve, B.A.
Faber, Charles H., M.Div.
Fettke, Steven M., Th.M.
Fiensy, David, Ph.D.
Fisher, Robert E., Ph.D.
Flokstra, Gerard, Jr., M.T.S.
Flower, Joseph, B.A.
Flower, John, M.A.
Ford, Joseph Michael, M.A.
Foreman, Kenneth K., Th.D.
Franklin, Karen, M.Div.
Franklyn, Paul, Ph.D.
Fransisco, John C., M.Div.
Freeman, Ernest R., Ph.D.
Friskney, Thomas E., B.D.
Gause, R. Hollis, Ph.D.
Gerlicher, John, Th.M.
Gilley, Bobby Lee, M.Ed.
Gilman, Tom, M.A.
Glandon, Arvin W., D.Min.
Good, Sanford, M.Th.
Grabill, Paul, Th.M.
Graves, Robert W., M.A.
Hackett, Gregory A., B.A.
Haight, Larry L., M.A.
Haltom, Michael F., D.Min.

Hammock, Hoyt, Jr., B.A.
Hampton, Ralph C., Jr., M.Div.
Hancock, Trey, B.A.
Hands, Greg, Th.M.
Hansen, Wesley, B.A.
Hardman, Samuel G., B.S.
Harris, Ralph W., M.A.
Hartman, Dawn, B.A.
Hatchner, Walter, B.A.
Heady, Jerry, M.A.
Henes, Kenneth E., M.Div.
Hernando, James D., M.Div.
Heuser, Roger, Ph.D.
Hewett, James Allen, Ph.D.
Hillis, David P., B.A.
Holman, Charles L., Ph.D.
Horne, Edward S., B.A.
Horner, Jerry W., Th.D.
Horton, Stanley, Th.D.
Indest, Michael, M.A.
Israel, Richard D., M.Div.
Jackson, Bill, M.Div.
Jenkins, James D., Ph.D.
Jenney, Timothy P., M.A.
Johns, Donald A., Ph.D.
Johnson, Dave, B.A.
Johnson, Fred R., Ph.D.
Jones, Randall Wayne, B.A.
Kath, Gerald, M.Div.
Kerkeslager, Allen, B.A.
Kiehl, Erich H., Th.D.
Kime, Harold A., M.Th.
Klaus, Byron D., M.R.E.
Koffarnus, Richard A., M.Div.
Krause, Mark, M.Div.
Kyser, Winston, M.A.
LaBelle, Lisa, B.A.
Linderman, Albert, M.A.T.S.
Lohr, Philip K., B.A.
Lowen, A. Wayne, M.Div.

5

Acknowledgements (continued)

Lucas, Howard, M.Div.
Macy, David C., Th.M.
Maempa, John, M.A.
Mainse, Ronald, B.A.
Manley, Grady W., Sr., M.A.
Mansfield, M. Robert, Ph.D.
Markham, Thomas E., M.Div.
Martin, Phil, B.A.
Mattingly, Gerald L., Ph.D.
McCaslin, Keith, M.Div.
McMahan, Oliver, D.Min.
McNaughton, Daniel, B.A.
McReynolds, Paul, Ph.D.
Melton, Terri L. C., B.A.
Menken, Debbie L., M.Div.
Menzies, Robert P., B.A.
Menzies, William W., Ph.D.
Meyer, Don, M.A.
Millard, Amos D., D.Min.
Miller, Johnny V., Th.D.
Miller, Kevin, M.A.
Miller, Steven E., M.Div.
Molina, John, M.Div.
Moyer, Dale, B.A.
Nash, Fred D., M.A.
Neal, Jeff, B.B.A.
Nelson, G. Edward, M.Div.
Neumann, Matthew L., B.A.
Newman, John, B.A.
Nicholaides, Stasie T., M.Div.
Nichols, Larry, B.A.
O'Grady, Brian, B.A.
Olsen, Wesley A., D.Ed.
Paris, Andrew, M.A.
Paschal, R. Wade, Ph.D.
Perrin, Jac, B.A.
Penchansky, David, M.A.
Peterson, Eugene H., M.Th.
Pettis, Bob, B.A.
Phillipps, John P., D.D.
Picirilli, Robert E., Ph.D.

Pledge, Joel K., M.Div.
Plummer, Hubert Lee, B.A.
Powell, Timothy, Ph.D.
Pratt, Thomas D., S.T.M.
Price, James D., Ph.D.
Quinn, Christopher L., B.A.
Railey, James H., Jr., Th.M.
Ray, Randall, B.A.
Reid, Garnett H., M.A.
Reinhard, David L., B.A.
Reynolds, Steven R., M.A.
Richardson, James E., M.Div.
Rossier, Bernard, Ed.S.
Rymer, David D., Minister
Saglimbeni, Dan, M.Div.
Sanderson, Dave, B.A.
Schatzmann, Siegfried, Ph.D.
Shaner, Danny L., M.Div.
Shelton, James B., Ph.D.
Sherrer, Stormy, B.A.
Shuert, Norman, M.Div.
Simkins, Ron, M.A.T.S.
Smith, David E., M.A.
Sonia, John, B.A.
Starner, Roger, M.A.
Steward, Stan, Th.M.
Stockton, Greg, B.A.
Stout, Maury, Th.M.
Stronstad, Roger, M.C.S.
Stroud, Robert, M.Th.
Stuart, Streeter S., Jr., Ph.D.
Suthers, Edwin B., B.A.
Swanson, Mary, B.A.
Tharp, Stan, M.A.
Tedeschi, Edmund L., M.A.
Terrell, Terry L., B.A.
Thee, Francis, C. R., Ph.D.
Thomas, John Christopher,
  Th.M.
Thomas, Mark S., B.A.
Tourville, Robert E., M.A.

Tracy, Brian, B.A.
Tunstall, Frank G., B.A.
Van Doren, Michael, D.Min.
Walker, Paul, Ph.D.
Warren, Virgil, Ph.D.
Williams, Don, B.A.
Williams, Larry, M.A.
Williams, Marjorie
Williams, William C., Ph.D.
Williamsen, Kelleen, B.A.
Wilser, Joseph, Th.D.
Wilson, Doug, M.A.
Wilson, Ralph F., D.Min.
Wimer, Barney, Ph.D.
Wisehart, Russell, M.Div.
Wittstock, Peter A., B.A.
Wretlind, Dennis O., Th.M.
Wright, Paul O., Th.D.
Yantz, Buddy, B.A.
Young, Richard A., Ph.D.
York, Gary, M.Div.

Norway

Almaas, Ragnhild, B.D.
Andersen, Hakon E., Dean
Andersen, Oivind, B.D.
Aske, Sigurd, D.D.
Berg, Arthur, B.D.
Berg, Marie, B.D.
Bjerkrheim, Trygve, B.D.
Breen, Hakon Fred, B.D.
Danbolt, Erling, D.D.
Dordal, Ole, B.D.
Fjeld, Bjorn Oyvind, B.D.
Gilbrant, Tor Inge,
  Computer specialist
Hauge, Dagfinn, Bishop
Hove, Odd Sverre, B.D.
Jensen, Sonja Lie, Secretary
Kjelle, Edvard, Editor
Kvalbein, Hans, D.D.
Kvarme, Ole Chr. M., B.D.
Lunde, Age, B.D.
Maeland, Jens Olav, B.D.
Nilsen, Oddvar, Editor
Reigstad, Leif, B.D.
Ruud, Erling, Pastor
Rudd, Kjell, B.D.
Solli, Einar, Professor
Strand, Egil, Editor
Saugstad, Anne Margrete,
  B.D.
Utnem, Erling, Bishop
Senstad, Magne Valen, B.D.
Saeveras, Olav, D.D.
Vik, Jofrid, B.D.
Wisloff, Carl Fr., D.D.
Wisloff, Fredrik, B.D.
With, Thor, Bishop
Yri, Norvald, B.D.

Sweden

Abrahamsson, Stig, General
  Superintendent
Bernspang, Erik, Pastor
Corell, Alf, D.D.
Djurfeldt, Olof, LL.D.
Giertz, Bo, D.D.
Gartner, Bertil E., D.D.
Heinerborg, Karl Erik, Pastor
Johansson, Carlo, Pastor
Josephsson, Torsten, B.D.
Kjall, Thorsten, B.D.
Lindholm, Hans, B.D.
Mangs, Frank,
  National evangelist
Norlander, Agne, D.D.
Olingdahl, Gote, B.D.
Paulson, Berthil,
  National evangelist
Svensson, Samuel, B.D.
Termen, David, B.D.
Wigholm, Anders,
  Salvation Army officer
Wikstrom, Stig, B.D.

Denmark

Bech, Robert, Dr. Jur.
Behrens, Carl Peter, B.D.
Berno, Aage, B.D.
Christiansen, Henrik, Bishop
Frokjaer-Jensen, Flemming,
  Pastor
Geil, Georg S., B.D.
Glenthoj, Jorgen, B.D.
Hansen, K. Robert, B.D.
Haystrup, Helge, B.D.
Hoffman, Poul, J.D.
Kjaer-Hansen, Kai, B.D.
Langagergaard, Poul, B.D.
Legarth, Peter V., B.D.
Lorenzen, Alfred,
  Superintendent

Nissen, Hans Erik, B.D.
Paaske, Oluf E., B.D.
Prenter, Regin, D.D.
Rasmussen, Leif, B.D.
Ruager, Soren, B.D.
Svendsen, Flemming Kofoed,
  B.D.
Wagner, Hartvig, B.D.

Finland

Koilo, Toivo, M.Div.
Liljeqvist, Matti, B.D.
Luoto, Walter, Pastor
Saarisalo, Aapeli, Ph.D.

Holland

Van den Brink, Gys, Ph.D.
Courtz, Henk, Ph.D.

Canada

Du Pont, Dennis E., M.Div.
Hayward, David R., M.A.T.S.
Przybylski, Benno, Ph.D.
Pugerude, Dan, M.Phil.
Ruthven, Jon, Ph.D.

France

Bachke, Gerard A., M.A.
Stotts, George R., Ph.D.

New Zealand

Williams, S.J., Gen. Supt.

West Germany

Herron, Robert W. Jr., M.A.

Table of Contents

Introduction

A Harmony of the Gospels is the first volume in a set of 16 study books on the New Testament, *The Complete Biblical Library.* The original concept was developed in Norway by Thoralf Gilbrant, a leading theologian of that country. The five-volume set received a warm reception and was translated into two other Scandinavian languages.

In the early 1980's Gilbrant approached the Gospel Publishing House, the literature arm of the Assemblies of God, about producing a much-expanded English version. After more than two years of strenuous preparation, *A Harmony of the Gospels* was completed, and a schedule was established for producing the other books.

The Complete Biblical Library

The set is composed of three divisions: *A Harmony of the Gospels,* a 9-volume *Study Bible* and a 6-volume *Bible Dictionary.* The latter two are very closely interrelated.

The term *Library* is appropriate, for the set contains all the information one needs for a basic understanding of the New Testament. The *Study Bible* provides an interlinear of the Greek text, with the pronunciation and meaning of each word, a verse-by-verse commentary, a *textual apparatus* and a verse-by-verse listing of various ways phrases or words have been translated. The *Bible Dictionary* provides a list of all the Greek words in their alphabetical order, a Greek-English concordance showing every place each word occurs in the New Testament and an article showing its use in the classical Greek literature, the *Septuagint Version* and the New Testament context itself.

A special genius of *The Complete Biblical Library* is the numbering system. Each of the nearly 5,000 Greek words found in the New Testament has been assigned a number, according to its Greek alphabetical order. For example, the first word, *alpha,* bears the numeral 1. Each time a word occurs in the interlinear of the *Study Bible,* its number is placed by it. It also appears with the word in the *Bible Dictionary.* If a student wishes to know more about a particular word, in moments he can find that word in the *Bible Dictionary,* by using either the numerical or alphabetical order.

A bridge from the island of the theologian to the mainland of the layman is one way *The Complete Biblical Library* has been described. It serves the scholar by shortening his research time. It blesses the lay student by revealing the rich treasures of the Greek language found in the New Testament.

A Unique Book

Most grammarians agree that the adjective *unique* should be used with great care. However, this word seems the best way to describe *A Harmony of the Gospels.* Its many features make it different from any similar volume ever produced.

For example, the addition of a *diatessaron* provides a fifth narrative for comparing the Gospel accounts.

Several charts add to the value of the book. The *Prophecies Fulfilled in the New Testament;* the *Parables of Jesus;* and *Dates and Data of the New Testament Era* offer informative insights.

The *Gospels and the Gospel* section provides helpful knowledge on how the first four books of the New Testament came into being.

The book contains two other fascinating features. *A Biographical Panorama* provides an overview of Jesus' life, and *A Pictorial Panorama* tells His story in 25 beautiful paintings by the British artist William Hole.

The Diatessaron

A special feature of the *Harmony* section is a *diatessaron* by the well-known scholar and writer Robert Shank, from his book *Jesus— His Story.* It is his own translation, combining all four Gospels in one interwoven account.

He states that he has drawn upon the work done by Broadus, Kerr and Robertson, with some differences based on his own research.

Shank does not include every word of the four Gospels. It was not his purpose, he says, "to present an exhaustive harmony," but rather a quick survey of Jesus' life "for easy, pleasant reading." For that reason, when incidents are recorded by more than one writer he has usually selected the fullest account. However, he has presented certain major events as composites from the Gospels in which they appear.

View of Inspiration

The editors of *The Complete Biblical Library* are committed to a strong view of Biblical inspiration. It is our purpose that all interpretations shall be based on an inviolate position that protects the inerrancy of all Scripture.

It is a basic conviction for us that God was the motivator, not man. It is not that men decided what to write, and then God inspired them. Men did not select the words they wrote. God used the author's personality and background in determining the exact words to be used. Yet, in all this God did not exclude the author's personality. He worked through it, using words and illustrations from the man's own background.

Problems of Harmony

At first, it may seem easy to prepare a harmony of the Gospels, but it is one of the most difficult tasks a scholar can undertake. Since four different men wrote these books without collaboration, the accounts are somewhat different at times, though all were inspired by the same divine Author, the Holy Spirit.

One of the greatest problems is that of determining the sequence of events. When two or more Gospel writers report the same incident they sometimes differ as to the exact time it occurred. Add to this the fact that Jesus possibly made the same statements on more than one occasion, and you have some idea of the difficulty in reaching an agreement on the sequence of events in His life.

In one instance conflicting viewpoints have been left unchanged. The *Biographical Panorama* presents a slightly different sequence of events from that found in the *Harmony*. Since each of the differing views is held by qualified scholars, it seemed best to include both viewpoints.

Providing special helps added to the problems. The *Dates and Data of the New Testament Era* section is a case in point. There is no broad consensus among scholars on the date of Jesus' birth. We have fixed it as 6 B.C. There is also much disagreement as to the chronology of Paul's life and writings.

No system can—or should—claim infallibility. We have researched the facts carefully and have consulted well qualified people. We believe the views which appear in this volume represent those of a majority of reputable scholars.

*In conclusion...*It has been our purpose and aim to be accurate to the utmost degree in preparing *A Harmony of the Gospels,* but experience has taught us that 100% accuracy is an almost unreachable goal. The multifaceted material, the interweaving of a mass of details, the difficulty of matching the Scripture passages, the task of determining sequences—these add up to an assignment that strains human abilities. We have asked God for His assistance; we now ask for your indulgence.

We have probably fulfilled the first part of the adage, "To err is human"; we ask you to fulfill the latter, "to forgive is divine."

Ralph W. Harris
Executive Editor

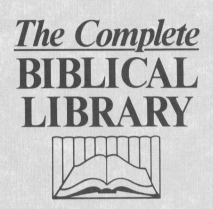

The Complete
BIBLICAL
LIBRARY

DATES AND DATA
OF THE NEW
TESTAMENT ERA

PROPHECIES
FULFILLED
IN THE
NEW TESTAMENT

PARABLES
OF JESUS

Dates and Data of the New Testament

In some cases the date is approximate. The names of Roman Emperors appear in capital letters (e.g. AUGUSTUS); procurators of Palestine with an asterisk (e.g. *Coponius).

B.C.	BIBLE EVENTS	ROMAN RULERS
7 or 6	Birth of John the Baptist	AUGUSTUS CAESAR, 31 B.C. to A.D. 14
6	Birth of Jesus; He is presented in the Temple.	Herod the Great, king of all Palestine, 37 to 4 B.C.
Winter, 5	Visit of the Wise Men; flight to Egypt; murder of Bethlehem children	
4		Herod the Great dies. His kingdom divided among his three sons: (a) Archelaus, tetrarch in Samaria, Judea and Idumea, 4 B.C. to A.D. 6 (b) Herod Antipas, tetrarch in Galilee and Perea, 4 B.C. to A.D. 39 (c) Philip II, tetrarch in Iturea and Trachonitis 4 B.C. to A.D. 34
4 or 3	Joseph returns to Nazareth.	

A.D.		
6		Archelaus is exiled; his land becomes a Roman province.
6-9		*Coponius
7 or 8	Jesus in Temple, 12 years old	
9-12		*Marcus Ambibulus
12		TIBERIUS, co-regent
12-15		*Annius Rufus
14		AUGUSTUS dies, August 19.
14-37		TIBERIUS
15-26		*Valerius Gratus
18-36	Caiaphas, high priest	
Summer, 26	John the Baptist begins ministry.	
26	Baptism of Jesus	
26-36		*Pontius Pilate
Easter, 27	Jesus purifies the Temple (John 2:13 ff), starts His Judean ministry, about 8 months (John 3:22).	
Winter, 28	Jesus starts His Galilean ministry, about 22 months (Matthew 4:12-25).	
Easter, 28	Jesus visits Jerusalem (John 5:1).	
Summer, 28	Jesus chooses 12 apostles. The Sermon on the Mount	

A.D.	BIBLE EVENTS	ROMAN RULERS
Easter, 29	Jesus feeds 5,000 (John 6:4 ff).	
Fall, 29	Jesus visits Jerusalem (John 7:2, 10); end of Galilean ministry (Luke 9:51).	
Winter, 29, 30	Jesus back in Jerusalem (John 10:22). Ministers in Judea and Perea (about 6 months).	
Easter, 30	Jesus' Triumphal Entry, Sunday Passover meal, Thursday Crucifixion, Friday Resurrection, Sunday	
30	Jesus' Ascension Day of Pentecost	
31	Death of Ananias and Sapphira; apostles before the Sanhedrin (Acts 5)	
32	Stephen martyred (Acts 7) Gospel preached in Samaria (Acts 8)	
32 or 33	Conversion of Saul of Tarsus (Acts 9)	
34	Paul in Arabia and Damascus (Galatians 1:17)	Philip II dies; his land added to Syria
36	Paul visits Jerusalem (Acts 9:26; Galatians 1:18).	Pilate exiled by Vitellius, governor of Syria; *Marcellus succeeds him.
37	Paul in Tarsus Conversion of Cornelius (Acts 10)	TIBERIUS dies. Herod Agrippa I gets Iturea, Trachonitis and Abilene.
37-41		CALIGULA
39		Herod Antipas exiled; Herod Agrippa I takes over his territory.
41	Gospel spreads to Antioch and Syria (Acts 11).	CALIGULA dies, January 24.
41-44		Herod Agrippa I, king of all Palestine
41-54		CLAUDIUS
42	Barnabas brings Paul from Tarsus to Antioch. Followers of Jesus called Christians there (Acts 11:25, 26).	
44	Barnabas and Paul bring relief to the churches in Judea (Acts 11:30). James martyred; Peter miraculously delivered (Acts 12).	Herod Agrippa I dies

13

Dates and Data of the New Testament (continued)

A.D.	BIBLE EVENTS	ROMAN RULERS
44-46		*Cuspius Fadus
46-48		*Tiberius Alexander
47	Paul and Barnabas' first missionary journey. On Cyprus (Acts 13:4-12)	
47-48	Epistle of James written.	
48	Paul and Barnabas in Asia Minor (Acts 13:13, 14, 25). They return to Antioch (Acts 14:26-28).	Theudas executed. *Ventidius Cumanus. Herod of Chalcis dies.
48-53		Herod Agrippa II king in Chalcis.
49	Jews exiled from Rome. Jerusalem Council (Acts 15) Paul writes Galatians. Paul's second missionary journey, in Asia Minor and Macedonia (Acts 15:40-18:22)	
Summer, 50, to Spring, 52	Paul spends 18 months in Corinth; meets Aquila and Priscilla (Acts 18).	
50 or 51	Paul writes First Epistle to the Thessalonians.	
51	Paul before Gallio (Acts 18:12-16) Paul writes Second Epistle to the Thessalonians.	
52	Paul travels from Corinth to Antioch.	Herod Agrippa II takes over territory of Philip II.
52-56	Paul's third missionary journey (Acts 18:23 ff); goes to Ephesus (Acts 19).	
52-58		*Antonius Felix
54-68		NERO
55	Paul writes First Epistle to Corinthians.	
Spring or Summer, 55	Paul leaves Ephesus (1 Corinthians 16:8).	
Summer and Fall, 55	Paul in Macedonia (Acts 20:2; 2 Corinthians 7:5); writes Second Corinthians.	
Winter, 55, 56	Paul 3 months in Corinth (Acts 20:2, 3); writes Epistle to the Romans.	
Spring, 56	Paul sails from Philippi (Acts 20:6); arrives in Jerusalem (Acts 21:15).	
56-58	Paul a prisoner in Caesarea (Acts 24-26)	
58-62		*Porcius Festus
Winter, 58, 59	Paul's voyage to Rome (Acts 27, 28)	

A.D.	BIBLE EVENTS	ROMAN RULERS
59-61	Paul a prisoner in Rome; writes the Epistles to the Colossians, Ephesians, Philemon and the Philippians. Luke finishes the Acts in Rome.	
61	Paul probably travels to Spain.	
62, 63	Paul visits the churches of Crete, Asia Minor, Macedonia and Greece. Writes the First Epistle to Timothy and the Epistle to Titus.	
62-64		*Florus Albinus
63	Peter writes his Epistles.	
64	Great fire of Rome; persecution of Christians	
64, 65	Paul's second imprisonment in Rome; writes Second Epistle to Timothy. Paul dies as a martyr in Rome. Peter dies as a martyr in Rome.	
64-66		*Gessius Florus
66		Jewish revolt against Rome begins.
67		*Marcus Antonius Julianus
68	Epistle to Hebrews written.	NERO commits suicide.
68, 69		GALBA, OTHO and VITELLIUS
69-79		VESPASIAN
70		Titus conquers Jerusalem.
79-81		TITUS
81-96		DOMITIAN; severe persecution of Christians
ca. 90	John the apostle writes his Gospel and Epistles.	
ca. 95	John writes the Book of Revelation.	
96-98		NERVA
98	Death of John	
98-117		TRAJAN
100		Herod Agrippa II dies in Rome.

Prophecies Fulfilled in the New Testament

One of the most important features of the Bible is the close relationship between the Old and New Testaments. And nothing shows this more emphatically than the many Old Testament prophecies which foretell details of the life and ministry of Jesus Christ. The following list is not exhaustive (one scholar claimed to have found more than 300 such references), but these highlight major aspects of Jesus' sojourn on earth.

Prophecy	Old Testament References	New Testament Fulfillment
The seed of the woman	Genesis 3:15	Galatians 4:4
From Abraham's family	Genesis 12:3; 18:18	Matthew 1:1 Luke 3:34 Galatians 3:16
From Isaac's family	Genesis 17:19	Matthew 1:2 Luke 3:34
From Jacob's family	Genesis 28:14 Numbers 24:17	Matthew 1:2 Luke 3:34
Of the tribe of Judah	Genesis 49:10 Micah 5:2	Matthew 1:2, 3 Luke 3:33 Hebrews 7:14 Revelation 5:5
Of the family of David and heir to his throne	2 Samuel 7:12 Psalm 132:11 Isaiah 9:6, 7 Jeremiah 23:5, 6	Matthew 1:1-16 Luke 1:32, 33 John 7:42 Revelation 22:16
Birthplace: Bethlehem	Micah 5:2	Matthew 2:1-6 Luke 2:4 John 7:42
The time for his birth	Daniel 9:25	Luke 2:1-7 Galatians 4:4
Born of a virgin	Isaiah 7:14	Matthew 1:18, 23 Luke 1:26-35
The slaughter of the children	Jeremiah 31:15	Matthew 2:16-18
The flight to Egypt	Hosea 11:1	Matthew 2:15
The ministry of Jesus in Galilee	Isaiah 9:1, 2	Matthew 4:12-16
His ministry as a prophet	Deuteronomy 18:15	John 6:14; 7:40 Acts 3:22; 7:37
His ministry as a priest	Psalm 110:4	Hebrews 5:6; 6:20; 7:17, 21
The purification of the Temple	Psalm 69:10	Matthew 21:12, 13 John 2:17
Rejected by the Jews and Gentiles	Psalm 2:2, 3 Isaiah 53:3	Luke 17:25; 23:18 John 1:11 Acts 4:25-28 1 Corinthians 2:8

Prophecy	Old Testament References	New Testament Fulfillment
Spiritual qualities of His character	Psalm 45:7, 8 Isaiah 11:2-5	Luke 2:52
The Triumphal Entry	Isaiah 6:11 Zechariah 9:9	Matthew 21:4-11 John 12:12-15
Betrayed by a friend	Psalm 41:9	Matthew 26:14-16, 47-50 Mark 14:10, 11, 43-45
For thirty pieces of silver	Zechariah 11:12, 13	Matthew 26:15; 27:3-10 Mark 14:10, 11
Judas' place given to another	Psalm 109:8	Acts 1:18-20
False witnesses	Psalm 35:11	Matthew 26:59-61
Silence when accused	Psalm 38:13-15 Isaiah 53:7	Matthew 26:62, 63; 27:12-14
Beaten and spit upon	Isaiah 50:6	Matthew 26:67 Mark 14:65
Hated without reason	Psalm 69:4; 109:3-5	John 15:23-25
Substitutional suffering	Isaiah 53:4-12	Matthew 8:17 Romans 4:25 1 Corinthians 15:3 2 Corinthians 5:21 1 Peter 2:22-24
Counted among the transgressors	Isaiah 53:12	Matthew 27:38 Mark 15:27, 28 Luke 23:33
Hands and feet pierced	Psalm 22:16 Zechariah 12:10	John 19:34, 37; 20:25-27
Scorned and scoffed at	Psalm 22:7-9; 69:20; 109:25	Matthew 27:39-44 Mark 15:29-32
Given wine mixed with gall	Psalm 69:21	Matthew 27:34
Praying for His enemies	Psalm 109:4 Isaiah 53:12	Luke 23:34
Casting of lots for His garments	Psalm 22:18	John 19:24
His bones not to be broken	Exodus 12:46 Psalm 34:20	John 19:33
His tomb with the rich	Isaiah 53:9	Matthew 27:57-60
His resurrection	Psalm 16:10	Matthew 28:6 Mark 16:6 Luke 24:6 1 Corinthians 15:4
His exaltation	Psalm 68:19; 110:1	Luke 24:50, 51 Acts 1:9; 2:33-35 Ephesians 4:8-10 Colossians 2:15

Parables of Jesus

There is some difference of opinion as to which comments of Jesus should be considered as parables. This listing presents a broader view. Also, to provide a fuller understanding, in some cases the context of the parables is given.

Description	Matthew	Mark	Luke	John
The Candle on the Candlestick	5:14-16			
The Houses on the Rock and Sand	7:24-27			
A New Piece on an Old Cloth	9:16	2:21	5:36	
New Wine in Old Bottles	9:17	2:22	5:37-39	
Evil Spirit and Empty House	12:43-45		11:24-26	
Loving Because Forgiven			7:36-50	
The Sower	13:1-23	4:1-20	8:4-15	
How a Seed Grows		4:26-29		
The Tares Among the Wheat	13:24-30, 36-43			
The Mustard Seed	13:31, 32	4:30-32	13:18, 19	
The Leaven	13:33		13:20, 21	
The Treasure in the Field	13:44			
The Pearl of Great Price	13:45, 46			
The Net	13:47-50			
The Wicked Servant	18:21-35			
The Good Samaritan			10:25-37	
The Importunate Friend			11:5-8	
The Rich Fool			12:16-21	
Watchful Servants			12:35-40	
The Unfaithful Servant	24:45-51		12:41-48	
The Unfruitful Fig Tree			13:6-9	
The Narrow Gate	7:13, 14, 21-23		13:22-30	
Taking the Low Place			14:7-11	
The Great Supper			14:15-24	
Counting the Cost			14:25-33	
The Lost Sheep	18:10-14		15:1-7	
The Lost Coin			15:8-10	
The Lost Son			15:11-32	
The Shrewd Steward			16:1-13	
The Rich Man and Lazarus			16:19-31	
The Correct Attitude in Service			17:7-10	
The Unjust Judge and the Widow			8:1-8	
The Pharisee and the Publican			18:9-14	
The Workers in the Vineyard	20:1-16			
Investing Wisely			19:11-27	
The Good Shepherd				10:1-16
The Two Sons	21:28-32			
The Vineyard	21:33-46	12:1-12	20:9-19	
The Wedding of the King's Son	22:1-14			
Sign of the Fig Tree	24:32-35	13:28-31	21:29-33	
The Ten Virgins	25:1-13			
The Talents	25:14-30			
The Sheep and the Goats	25:31-46			
The Vine and the Branches				15:1-8

THE
GOSPELS
AND THE
GOSPEL

The Gospels and the Gospel

That there is only one gospel is a truth which the New Testament emphasizes very strongly. This does not apply only to the false gospel which Paul calls "another gospel" (2 Corinthians 11:4; Galatians 1:6-9). The first-century Christians very carefully avoided the plural number, which we so often use when, for instance, we refer to the four Gospels. They never spoke of the Gospel of Matthew, the Gospel of Mark, etc. They used the terms "the Gospel according to Matthew," or "the Gospel according to Mark." To them it was always the one and the same gospel, brought into being by different authors.

All things considered, the word *gospel* was never used in a literary sense of a Gospel writing; instead, it always designated the Christian message of salvation. It was about the year A. D. 150 that the word was first used in the sense of a Gospel writing.

The English word *gospel* comes from the Middle English word *godspel*, literally "good spell," with the idea being a "good tale," "good news." The Greek behind the concept is *euangelion*, "good news." This gospel is "the power of God unto salvation to everyone that believeth" (Romans 1:16). It was preached and received "not as the word of men, but as it is in truth the word of God, which effectually worketh also in you that believe" (1 Thessalonians 2:13). It is "words whereby thou and all thy house shall be saved" (Acts 11:14).

This message of salvation does not consist of religious philosophy or human ideas. It is something more than a collection of commandments and rules for living. It is a historical account of a series of events which took place in Palestine when Tiberius was the ruler of the Roman Empire. Standing at the center of these events is the person of Jesus Christ. The importance of the gospel, its relevance throughout the ages, is firmly rooted in the truth and reality of such history.

Initially the message of salvation was proclaimed orally. Acts affords us with the earliest examples of such oral preaching. Two distinguishing features marked the ancient preaching of the gospel by the apostles. First, it was a personal witness of "what we have seen and heard," an eyewitness testimony of Jesus Christ's ministry, His life, death, and resurrection. Second, the apostles interpreted this Christ-event. Jesus' life and death were a fulfillment of the messianic prophecies of the Old Testament. The witness of the apostles was part and parcel of their teaching. They were not only able to proclaim that Jesus had died and risen again, but that this was, in fact, for our sins. They, therefore, not only witnessed to His resurrection, they knew that through the

> *The central message of the gospel is the preaching of the forgiveness of sins as the result of the atoning sacrifice of another.*

Resurrection we have been justified (Romans 4:25) and regenerated to a new and living hope (1 Peter 1:3).

The gospel does not attempt to satisfy the curiosity of man with philosophical explanations of the "mysteries" of life. And it is not limited to proclaiming a series of ethical propositions in response to man's suffering. Christianity proclaims salvation, "good news." The central message of the gospel is the preaching of the forgiveness of sins as a result of the atoning sacrifice of another. The gospel declares when and where this took place. Thus its effectiveness depends upon the historical reality of the message. The earliest Christian preachers were keenly aware of this, as Paul demonstrates in 1 Corinthians 15 in his description of his gospel message. In 15:2 he assures his readers that those who consider themselves "saved" have been redeemed only through the gospel.

Paul proceeds to outline what he considers "essential" or basic to the gospel message. He is so committed to the historical reality of the message that he admits if the message were not true the entire Christian faith is utterly useless. "If Christ be not risen, then is our preaching vain, and your faith is also vain.... If Christ be not raised, your faith is vain; ye are yet in your sins. Then they also which are fallen asleep in Christ are perished" (1 Corinthians 15:14-19). It cannot be emphasized enough how much the effectiveness of the gospel depends upon its truthfulness.

In such a respect we see the first gospel preachers could assert that they themselves had witnessed what they preached, or they could point to other eyewitnesses. Paul does this in reference to Christ's resurrection. He lists those who have encountered the Risen One. He recalls, among other things, that "more than five hundred brethren, of these the most are still alive" did, indeed, witness the Resurrection. These eyewitnesses assumed key roles in the earliest Christian churches. As long as this first generation of believers lived they closely guarded the testimony of Jesus Christ and kept it from being twisted or falsified in any way. Although some maintain that Jesus' gospel message was a creation of the Early Church, it is obvious that it would have been virtually impossible to introduce fabricated stories about Jesus which would have been accepted by the early churches.

The Scriptures suggest that the early Christians were extremely careful to distinguish between Jesus' words and their interpretations of these words (cf. 1 Corinthians 7:10-12). That is not to say, however, that knowledge of Jesus Christ was in any way "secret knowledge" which had been entrusted to the Church. Peter could remind his listeners on the Day of Pentecost that they themselves had a knowledge of Jesus of Nazareth (Acts 2:22). Paul reminded King Agrippa that the life and death of Jesus had not taken place in a "corner," but the king knew of its reality (Acts 26:26). Even the enemies of Christianity could not deny its historical reality. The proclaimers of the faith protected their testimony against any incorrect teaching, since any deviation would be targeted and attacked by its opponents.

The oral proclamation of the gospel was principally carried out by those who "from the beginning were eyewitnesses, and ministers of the word" (Luke 1:2). Nevertheless, these eyewitnesses could not personally be in every Christian church. Consequently, controlling the oral tradition became an almost impossible task. Furthermore, a need to defend the gospel against the attacks of its opponents led to the

The Gospel literary form represents something completely unique in the ancient world. The Christ-event resulted in an entirely new kind of literature.

need to put in writing the gospel message. This is one reason we possess the New Testament Scriptures today. At the same time, the gospel—the "good news"—remained one. The four Gospels are thus four forms of the one gospel—the "good news of Jesus Christ." Thus the word gospel stands for the message of the books rather than as a title.

The Gospel literary form represents something completely unique in the ancient world. The Christ-event resulted in an entirely new kind of literature. The Gospels do not intend to give a historical, chronological biography of the life of Jesus. Instead, one might say that the Gospels are concerned to present the passion and resurrection of Jesus from different points of view. From the birth of Jesus the accounts advance quickly and silently through the first 30 years of Jesus' life. And then, after reading uniquely selected events in Jesus' ministry, we are given a detailed discussion of the final week of His life. This clearly demonstrates that the Gospels were never intended to be a "biography" in the normal sense of that term. The Gospels have an evangelistic and missionary aim.

> *...the greatest portion of the New Testament, both Epistles and Gospels, was written within about 30 years of Jesus' death and resurrection.*

We cannot be certain when the oral apostolic preaching acquired its present written form, but it happened very early. When Luke undertook to write his Gospel, many had already attempted "to set forth in order a declaration of those things which are most surely believed among us" (Luke 1:1). Perhaps the Gospels we possess were not the first attempts to "tell the story of Jesus." Many others who came in contact with Christianity and who had perhaps personally seen and heard Jesus had attempted to write it down. Apparently Luke knew of such documents. It is possible that more fragmented apostolic writings existed even during Jesus' lifetime.

Apparently Jesus began His ministry about the year A.D. 26; His crucifixion probably occurred in early A.D. 30. Within a few decades the Christian faith had spread throughout large areas of the Roman Empire. The Gospels were not the first New Testament writings, for while the gospel was spreading in these early years Paul wrote many of his letters to early Christian churches. Galatians was written shortly after the Jerusalem Council which occurred in A.D. 49, and First and Second Thessalonians were composed about A.D. 50 and 51. In A.D. 55 Paul sent the two letters to the church at Corinth, and a few months later, in the winter of A.D. 55-56, wrote to the saints at Rome. While a prisoner in Rome, A.D. 59-61, he wrote the Epistles to the Colossians, Ephesians, Philemon, and Philippians. Finally, shortly before his martyrdom in A.D. 64, Paul wrote his letters to Timothy and Titus. Thus most of the Pauline epistles were written 20 to 30 years after Jesus' ascension.

Closely related to this the Gospels followed. With regard to the Gospel of Luke, its date of composition can be fixed with relative certainty. Actually Luke's Gospel is the first part of a two-volume work which included Acts as well. Acts closes with the account of Paul's 2-year imprisonment in Rome which can be fixed with some certainty around A.D. 59-61. Thus the first volume was written before that time. Luke, who had accompanied Paul in Palestine as well as on a voyage to Rome, possibly made good use of his time (while Paul was imprisoned) to write both volumes.

Several factors indicate that the Gospel of Mark was written before Luke's, possibly sometime shortly after A.D. 60. The traditions, however, do vary. Clement and Origen maintain that the Gospel was written during Peter's lifetime and under his supervision. Irenaeus, however, contends that it was written after the death of Peter in the year A.D. 65.

Concerning Matthew's Gospel we should note that Matthew records Jesus' prediction of the destruction of Jerusalem (chapter 24). But the text does not indicate any knowledge that the prediction was fulfilled: consequently, we may conclude that this Gospel was written prior to the fall of Jerusalem, which occurred in A.D. 70. This corresponds with statements of the early church fathers. Irenaeus declares that Matthew wrote his Gospel "while Peter and Paul preached the gospel in Rome." Some evidence suggests that Peter and Paul were in Rome simultaneously in the early sixties. If Irenaeus is correct, we may assume that Matthew was written before 65 but not earlier than A.D. 60. It should be noted, then, that rather strong arguments exist for dating the writing of the Synoptic Gospels between the years A.D. 60 and 70, perhaps in the early sixties.

Such information shows that the greatest portion of the New Testament, both Epistles and Gospels, was written within about 30 years of Jesus' death and resurrection, in other words while the first generation of believers were still alive and were able to control and insure the reliability of what was written.

John's Gospel seems to have been composed much later than the Synoptics, perhaps around the year 90. Nonetheless, John's Gospel is still the work of an eyewitness who recalls events without any intermediate dependency. The date of this Gospel is of no dispute when one acknowledges its author. At an earlier period it was rather popular to deny that the apostle John could have been the author of the Gospel bearing his name. It was supposed instead that it was written by an unknown person in the middle of the second century.

Some suggested that the date of composition was as late as A.D. 170; however, in 1935 it was discovered that a papyrus fragment found in Egypt 15 years earlier contained portions of the Gospel of John text. This fragment was dated at A.D. 130, proving that the fourth Gospel was known in Egypt only 30 to 40 years after John wrote it in Ephesus.

As we have observed, the Gospels were written only a short time after the events they record. Other non-Biblical sources from both Jewish and pagan authors confirm the historical Jesus. In his description of the fire in Rome, the Roman historian Tacitus mentions Christians. He notes that their name comes from a "Chrestus" whom the governor Pontius Pilate, who served under Tiberius the emperor, had crucified. Another Roman historian, Suetonius, records that the Emperor Claudius "expelled the Jews from Rome because they under the direction of one Chrestus constantly caused trouble" (cf. Acts 11:27, 28). In both instances these historians refer to Christ as a proper name.

The Jewish historian Josephus tells his readers in one of his volumes of the execution of James and calls him the "brother of Jesus, the so-called Christ." Moreover, there are numerous sections in Josephus whose details are identical to Gospel accounts. Jesus is mentioned in the Jerusalem Talmud. There—as one might expect from Jewish rabbis who were at enmity with Christianity—He is not referred to in the most positive terms. Nonetheless, the historical reality of His life is confirmed.

By and large, however, the secular historians of the ancient world have little to say about Jesus of Nazareth. What might have been said is lost. God would not desire our portrait of Jesus to be drawn by irreligious historians; He chose His witnesses himself.

The Gospels are more than biography, but they do proclaim the most wonderful biography ever written. The Gospels are history and more, and the story of the Son of God they tell is a true and reliable account. Much of our knowledge of the ancient history of the world depends upon one individual. Such is not the case, however, of the Gospel "history." Here we can draw from four separate witnesses who join with other New Testament authors to give their testimony. Luke was correct when he wrote: "That thou mightest know the certainty of those things, wherein thou hast been instructed."

There is probably nothing from the ancient world which has as much historical support as the gospel. First, the original "autographs" of the New Testament were written by persons who lived when the events took place. The thousands of manuscripts which perpetuate the original autographs are made up of some that are so old they might have been contemporaneous with the original documents.

Secular histories, such as that by the "father of history," Herodotus, or the historian Thucydides, are only attested secondarily, through a few manuscripts which were copied more than a thousand years after the death of the original author. The oldest manuscript telling of Caesar's Gallic War is from the 9th century, almost a thousand years after Caesar.

The immense quantity of Greek manuscripts and early versions assures us that the New Testament text has been preserved and is wholly reliable.

Tacitus' "History" is attested by only two manuscripts, one from the 9th and the other from the 11th century—once more a thousand years after the original. Despite such tenuous evidence not one historian would ever dream of denying these important historical documents.

It is evident that the New Testament witness to history is infinitely more reliable since it is backed not by a few manuscripts, as was the case with the secular histories, but by no less than five thousand manuscripts containing portions or all of the New Testament.

Among the oldest parchment manuscripts are the Codex Sinaiticus and Codex Vaticanus (from around the 4th century), and Codex Alexandrinus and Codex Ephraemi from the 5th century. More than 70 parchment manuscripts have been discovered within the last two centuries. Many of these can be dated as early as the year A.D. 200. These ancient manuscripts are naturally of tremendous value in the task of reconstructing the New Testament text. What must be emphasized here is that these manuscripts essentially conform to the text of the New Testament that has served the Church throughout its history. A comparison of the variations reveals that most cases are of little or no importance. The immense quantity of Greek manuscripts and early versions assure us that the New Testament text has been preserved and is wholly reliable.

One of the foremost authorities on textual criticism in our time, Frederic Kenyon, wrote that the interval between the time these Scriptures were believed to have been originally written and the earliest handwritten copies we have is so little that it practically means nothing. Because of this there is little doubt we have an accurate collection of the sacred writings as they were first written. Ryland's Professor of Biblical Criticism and Exegesis at the University of Manchester, the well-known F. F. Bruce, is reported to have stated: "The testimonies concerning the early existence of our New Testament are much more than what is the fact concerning the classical authors,...If the New Testament had been a collection of profane epistles, their genuineness would have been considered beyond all doubt. It is also a puzzling fact that historians often have been more inclined to believe the New Testament than many theologians."

A surprising feature of the New Testament is that the Gospel history comes to us in four different forms. Some have questioned why the evangelists did not instead give us a single, but jointly authored document. Undoubtedly such a thought was far from their minds. Moreover, it should be apparant that to possess the Gospel account through four independent witnesses has a tremendous advantage of breadth. Their testimonies do correspond. But at the same time each Gospel is uniquely worthwhile as an independent witness.

A single authoritative Gospel writing was

never the objective of either the Church or the authors of the New Testament. The immediacy of a situation within the larger Church is what prompted these Spirit-directed men to write. They wrote to meet a need. Just as the early Epistles were designed to meet the needs of certain readers, each of the Gospels was addressed to unique churches or groups within the Church. These holy writings became integral to the worship services of the Church, valuable both in public reading and church doctrine. Later they were included in the canon of the New Testament.

Shortly after the last of the four Gospels had been written they were all collected in one codex. This volume was then distributed among the churches under the title "The Gospel," not "The Gospels." This stressed that there is only one gospel. The different accounts of the "one story" were distinguished by the term *kata*, "according to." As early as the year A.D. 115 Ignatius referred to the gospel as a writing. It is possible that he is referring to the book of the gospel containing the four Gospels.

The ancient church did not try to bring about unity by eliminating supposedly conflicting Gospels; instead, they created harmonious unity by grouping them. The New Testament Gospels' repetition of material was not in itself unique. The same circumstance occurs in the Old Testament, which often gives two or more accounts of the same incident (e.g. the books of Kings and Chronicles).

Because the Gospels are four in number this led to early attempts to harmonize their accounts into one. The first known Gospel harmony, the Diatessaron (literally meaning "through four") is credited to Tatian around the year A.D. 170. This harmony endured in the Syrian church for a long period as the most popular Gospel book. It acquired almost official status until it was eventually replaced by the Peshitta (meaning "the plain, unchanged") in the fifth century.

The similarities as well as the differences of various Gospels have always been a subject of great interest. The subject matter of the four Gospels falls naturally under three basic headings: 1) the story of the life and ministry of Jesus; 2) the record of Jesus' words and teaching; 3) the Passion narrative.

The first three Gospels of Matthew, Mark and Luke share much material and much the same interests. As a result they overlap one another. This condition has led to their being called "synoptic," that is, they can be "seen together" (Griesbach, 1742-1812). Whereas the Synoptic Gospels primarily recount Jesus' ministry in Galilee, the Gospel of John expands our insight into the life of Jesus by offering some unique stories of Jesus' visits to Jerusalem on the feast days. This is graphically evident in a synopsis which gathers the parallel texts of the first three Gospels and places them alongside one another in columns. The arrangement of John falls largely in between the common sections of the Synoptic Gospels.

The relationship among the first three Gospels is intriguing. Until the 18th century scholars were primarily concerned to explain and harmonize the differences between the three accounts. Later, and to this day, scholarship is fascinated by their similarities. How can their relationship be explained? The expression "Synoptic problem" characterizes the discussion; the Gospel of John is only of secondary importance for resolving the seeming dilemma. Some became so obsessed with the "problem" that they almost inadvertently threw out the proverbial "baby with the bathwater" when they exaggerated the significance of the problem. That is not to say that the Synoptic problem does not raise serious theological questions. The resolution of the Synoptic problem centers around one's attitude toward the reliability of Scripture, its nature as inspired, and from these the interpretation of Jesus' words and work. What stands out is that the similarities attest to the evangelists' independence of each other.

With regard to the similarities among the Synoptic witnesses three characteristics emerge:

The Gospels and the Gospel

1) their shared material; 2) their common arrangement; 3) their close verbal similarities. This latter includes entire sentences as well as individual words.

The similarity of the Gospels as a whole is undeniable; most of the material in Mark occurs in Matthew and Luke. Of the 661 verses in Mark only 31 do not in part or in total have parallels in the other Gospels. No less than 606 verses of Mark are repeated in Matthew, either almost word for word or in an abbreviated

---

Of the 661 verses in Mark only 31 do not in part or in total have parallels in the other Gospels.

---

form. Three hundred and eighty verses from Mark recur in Luke.

While practically all of Mark occurs in Matthew and Luke, that material comprises only about half of Matthew's contents (1068 verses) and only about one-third of Luke (1149 verses).

In comparing Matthew and Luke, one discovers that they have material in common which does not appear in Mark, approximately 250 verses. This leaves about 300 verses in Matthew and about 500 in Luke which are unique to these evangelists. This is truly striking since there are only 31 verses unique to Mark.

A calculation such as the one above is, of course, only approximate; it will vary from book to book depending upon the author. Nevertheless, it is of possible interest to examine the above in terms of percentages. According to Westcott the Gospel of John's material is 92 percent unique to him. Mark has only 7 percent of unshared material; 93 percent is in common with the other Synoptics. Forty-two percent of

Matthew's material is unique to him; the remaining 58 percent is found either in Mark or Luke or both. Luke has 59 percent of his material without parallel, with the remaining 41 percent being found in either Matthew, Mark, or both.

Furthermore, the Synoptic Gospels share a basic pattern of arrangement. Each has the same historical structure: following an introduction each recounts the baptism of Jesus and then proceeds to describe Jesus' ministry in Galilee and His instruction of the disciples. Then follows a climax at Caesarea Philippi where Peter confesses his faith in Jesus as the Son of God. Next comes the story of Jesus' final journey to Jerusalem. Finally the Passion story and the disciples' encounter with the Risen Lord closes each Gospel.

The similarities in vocabulary and in sentence construction, as a glance at a synopsis will confirm and which this work will demonstrate, are noteworthy. A striking note here is that the similarities are greater in the sentences containing Jesus' words than in the narrative material.

In spite of all the similarities and the common material, it is still evident that the evangelists have not copied one another. First, there are differences in their views. Historical context as well as the choice of words is, at times, very different. A problem such as this is not resolvable in every aspect and detail; however, recent investigation has thrown interesting light upon what had previously seemed puzzling and almost without solution. We can be sure that a resolution of the Synoptic problem would afford insight into the origin of the Gospels. Differences as well as similarities demand explanation, and the parts cannot be solved apart from the whole. If the issue of similarities is explained, so too, the variations in the accounts will be understandable.

Generally, the different attempts to resolve the Synoptic problem can be broken down into three groups: the *Tradition Hypothesis*, the *Borrowing Hypothesis* and the *Source Hypothesis*.

1. The *Tradition Hypothesis* originated in 1796 with J. G. Herder. This theory proposes that the three Synoptic Gospels draw from a common oral tradition, which has to some degree been maintained and perpetuated by the apostles. This theory is reflected by statements of the church fathers to some extent. They seem to assume either that the authors of the Gospels had personal knowledge of Jesus' ministry and His words, or that they acquired the material from other apostolic authority. Thus it is supposed that Mark drew from the preaching of Peter; Irenaeus terms the Gospel of Luke a recollection from the preaching of Paul.

The underlying assumption of this theory is that a record of Jesus' life existed in a rather fixed form, perhaps originally oral. Some facts support this hypothesis. First, it is clear that the gospel was preached orally before it was written. If the work and person of Jesus were to become known it would depend upon those who were with Him and familiar with His ministry to pass it on. Thus the message of Jesus was proclaimed repeatedly; gradually it assumed a more or less fixed form, a typical consequence of repetition.

Paul mentions on more than one occasion that he has "received" certain instruction (1 Corinthians 11:23; 15:3). He does this in such a way that he indicates the message/instruction consisted of certain teaching which was not to be changed. He does not mention any written sources of this teaching. Indeed, he does mention "books and parchments" in 2 Timothy 4:13, but we cannot be certain of the contents.

The *Tradition Hypothesis* does appear to explain to some extent the phenomenon that two or three of the Synoptics share common words and phrases that could not possibly be coincidental. This old theory, which had for a long time been overshadowed by a theory of literary sources, has returned in a modified form in the so-called *form-critical method*. In contrast to the traditional historical method, which asserts that a genuine transmission of Jesus' words and His life took place under apostolic supervision, radical form criticism maintains that the gospel account as we have it did not in the truest sense of the word become tradition in the period between Jesus' ministry and the actual writing down of the Gospel accounts. Instead, this theory asserts that the preaching of the ancient church actually created the gospel message in this interim period.

Instead of regarding the oral tradition as a unified, consistent report of the life of Jesus that

In spite of all the similarities and the common material, it is still evident that the evangelists have not copied one another.

is based upon the testimony of eyewitnesses who are intending to provide a historically reliable account, the radical form critics contend that the oral tradition is an unrelated collection of fragments. The form critic further believes that individual stories have not derived their meaning from a historical basis. Rather, it is believed that the needs of the churches caused the material to evolve.

Thus form criticism not only attempts to analyze the form of the Gospel material, it also tries to explain the background and origin of the underlying tradition. This theory claims that the sources are composed of smaller units about Jesus and fragments of His sermons which had circulated among His followers. Accordingly it is believed that a wide variety of unknown preachers and storytellers of the ancient church shaped these unrelated fragments in response to congregational needs.

The Gospels and the Gospel (continued)

Thus the gospel story was not "passed on" but was, in actuality, "created" by the *kerugma* of the ancient church. The radical form critic would (in varying degrees) hold that a multitude of these isolated fragments, given form according to the needs of ancient preaching and liturgy, were then gathered by the Gospel authors or their predecessors. The author then set these stories in a framework of a larger story. These became the Gospels as we know them or an early source for the Gospels.

If form criticism is correct in supposing that the sermons of the ancient churches contributed in determining which parts of the Jesus tradition would survive, a point is to be conceded. It might also be added that form criticism has rendered scholarship a valuable service by demonstrating that a hypothesis of literary sources behind the Gospels is both unprovable and improbable. Nevertheless, in itself form criticism is nothing less than a theological dead end. It is difficult to imagine that the stories about Jesus—unrelated accounts—should have been collected through anonymous, popular sources into a unified whole. Such an event would be unprecedented in ancient history and literature. It is so unreasonable that it deserves no comment. The old saying "one needs a Jesus to invent a Jesus" says enough. Hugo Odeberg says in this connection: "The view concerning Jesus which is expressed in the Gospels, cannot reasonably be explained in any other way than that it originates from such people who have lived under the immediate impression of an overwhelming personality."

Furthermore, the time factor makes form-critical methodology doubtful. As long as a late dating for time of composition is held, those who favor the evolutionary idea of form criticism will continue to see insertions of historical traditions and "contrived" stories. But when one considers the likelihood that the Gospels were written while the first generation of believers remained—the eyewitnesses who had seen and heard Jesus—the form-critical

method appears impossible.

F. G. Kenyon writes concerning this: "There is simply no time for the circumstantial processes which are necessary for Dibelius' *Formgesohichte*, which has won such a surprising popularity, but which supposes first the expansion of the stories from Jesus' life and teaching, then their collection and classification in groups corresponding with their character, and then the formation of connected stories where they are used."

In reaction to radical form criticism Harald Riesenfeld has characterized it as typical of rationalistic hypotheses which have their "day" and then gradually fade away or are removed in order not to impede the progress of further investigation. He points out the fact that the words of Jesus had a holy character to the early believers. He traces the origins of the gospel tradition back to Jesus himself. Moreover, Riesenfeld advances the theory that Jesus, following contemporary rabbinic practice, encouraged His disciples to memorize His instruction.

Within Judaism very rigid laws regarding oral transmission of holy tradition were enforced. The legal experts and their followers developed precise methods for transmitting the "instruction of the elders." This highly revered material dated back several hundred years. Judaism regarded tradition to be holy; in practice it was placed on a par with the written Word of God, the Law of Moses which was so closely followed. The tradition of the elders was passed on orally from generation to generation. It was written down for the first time in the Mishna about A.D. 200.

Passing on tradition was not the practice of ordinary synagogue members. Instead, this responsibility was entrusted to a chosen, authorized group of legal experts. They were responsible to memorize carefully the tradition. They were not to add or omit a single word. Here we encounter a carefully controlled passing on of tradition from one person authorized to do so to another person chosen specifically to learn the tradition which he would later pass on. The ideal is reflected in the rabbinic statement: ''I have not spoken a word which I have not heard from the mouth of my teacher.'' One was to be like a water jar—not a drop was to be lost.

Jesus is described as a teacher and a rabbi. Like other teachers and rabbis He had disciples. From the larger group of followers Jesus chose ''the Twelve.'' These were chosen not only to continue Jesus' ministry, they were supposed to bring to the Church the holy Word of God, the revealed word which God spoke through Jesus.

> *Jesus is described as a teacher and a rabbi. Like other teachers and rabbis He had disciples. From the larger group of followers Jesus chose "the Twelve."*

Jesus apparently followed the practice of the rabbis in order to preserve faithfully and to transmit His words. He himself apparently wrote nothing. Neither are we told that the disciples initially wrote down what they heard. God's final, eschatological word through His Son, however, was not given in any careless or unreliable way. It was not as some argue, that the disciples wrote down only fragments they remembered. Neither was this then united with stories created by the later church. No, we probably see here the rabbinic practice of passing on doctrine, ethical teaching, and words of wisdom in condensed form being carried on by Jesus' disciples. Jesus probably preached the material in various forms at various times.

Then His disciples may have received private instruction for memorizing the essential content of His messages. The ''sermons'' of Jesus are obviously not ''sermons'' in the ordinary sense of that word; rather, they are collections of Jesus' sayings, each of which represents a miniature expression of His teaching.

There are several indications that this is indeed the case. Through a style-critical analysis the sayings of Jesus appear to have been formed intentionally in a succinct, rhythmic form for easy memorization. Even in their Greek form (Jesus spoke Aramaic) this is evident. In the Aramaic form this was probably so to an even higher degree.

Attempts have been made to recreate the Aramaic sayings of Jesus as they must have been. Of course a reconstruction like that would have elements of uncertainty; nevertheless, the words of Jesus according to an Aramaic form would have a poetic quality in each of the four Gospels. The poetic symmetry found in the Old Testament, both in the Psalms and in prophetic writings, recurs in the sayings of Jesus even in a Greek form. But when they are reconstructed in Aramaic one sees even more clearly poetic rhythm. At times even rhymes occur. C. F. Burney has investigated this phenomenon in a study entitled ''The Poetry of Our Lord.''

Undeniably the extent of Jesus' collected sayings was limited. Moreover, the Epistles clearly indicate that in the ancient church the highest degree of authority was afforded Jesus' sayings. They were apparently passed on orally. Their authority equalled that of the apostles.

Paul distinguishes between his own words and those of the Lord Jesus, which he knows according to an oral form (e.g. 1 Corinthians 7:10, 25, 40; 9:14; 11:23-25; 14:37). Other texts in the New Testament reflect the same technical words for ''receiving'' and ''passing on'' the tradition that occurs in rabbinic writings (Luke 1:1; 1 Corinthians 15:1ff; 1 Thessalonians 4:1ff). Apparently what Jesus regarded as important for the Church He taught the disciples to memorize.

The Gospels and the Gospel (continued)

Jesus' words have, in a restricted sense of the word, been understood as "divine-words," words of the Lord which carry an authority above every other. Naturally the disciples of Jesus viewed His words as more authoritative and revered than the rabbinic disciples. Thus we can boldly declare that hardly any other doctrine of the Early Church was passed on with such care and certainty by the original authors as the words of Jesus were.

One of the most important responsibilities of the apostles was to guard the tradition and to recite it in the Church. In reference to Peter's statement that the apostles should not neglect the "Word of God," this is not a reference to preaching but to passing on the tradition about Jesus. When the apostles are called "ministers of the Word" (Luke 1:2), it seems likely this is the same idea. When the Church is said to be devoting itself to the apostles' teaching (Acts 2:42), we can detect a faithful following of the apostolic Jesus tradition, which would have been considered complementary to the Old Testament—indeed, its fulfillment.

The ancient church also recognized the apostles as chosen "pillars" in the temple of the new people of God. As such they received special promises from Jesus that they would be responsible for passing on His instruction. Jesus had said, "The Comforter, which is the Holy Ghost, whom the Father will send in my name, he shall teach you all things, and bring all things to your remembrance, whatsoever I have said unto you" (John 14:26). "When he, the Spirit of truth is come, he will guide you into all truth" (John 16:13). These promises were essentially directed to the Twelve. The unique teaching Jesus gave the Twelve, coupled with the supernatural assistance of the Holy Spirit, uniquely enabled the apostles to pass on Jesus' words and teaching in the historical, trust-worthy gospel story.

The evangelists, therefore, were not the "authors" of the material, but the "editors" who gathered and arranged it, although each one was personally and uniqely affected by it.

We can be extremely certain that the oral tradition the apostles carried was written down at an early date. Undoubtedly there was a written collection of Jesus' parables (cf. Matthew 13 and Mark 4) as well as collections of Jesus' sayings about life and the end times. Collections of miracle and healing stories must also have been gathered. The Passion story was in all likelihood recorded very early. This story raises some of the more puzzling chronological questions. As the Church expanded its borders, a need to have the Jesus tradition in written form increased; oral preaching simply could not fill the gap. At that point the Gospels came into being.

That the teaching of Jesus is among the most uniformly parallelled material in the Gospels is solid support for the traditional historical hypothesis. If we are right about Jesus' patterning His instruction of His disciples after the rabbis, this is exactly what one would expect to encounter.

2. The *Borrowing Hypothesis* was introduced in 1789 by J. J. Griesbach. He drew from Augustine, who maintained that the evangelists had known and had depended upon one another. Six variations of this theory are possible, and all have had their spokesmen. It is often termed, the *Marcan Hypothesis*. The fundamental assumption of this theory is that two of the evangelists borrowed their material from a third. The Gospel considered to be the most probable is Mark, from which Matthew and Luke draw much of their material. In this relationship it is stressed that if any literary dependence is recognized at all, it is most likely Mark was used and not vice versa.

In a sense this is not far removed from the Tradition Hypothesis outlined above. One distinction, however, is that Mark is viewed as having only written down the oral tradition of the apostles. We note in the early chapters of Acts that Peter had a prominent place as preacher; perhaps it was he more than anyone else who helped collect the Jesus tradition. Papias, an early church father and an important witness to such matters, writes that Mark was the interpreter of Peter and that he wrote precisely, although not chronologically, what he remembered. Justin Martyr, picking up on this, calls the Gospel of Mark the "memoirs of Peter."

We can conclude that Mark wrote down the essential aspects of Jesus' ministry. As a result Mark set a precedent which the later evangelists Matthew and Luke followed. Of course, this is not to say that Mark only repeats the apostolic tradition. Although Peter may have been responsible most for this line of tradition, the material itself differs in its intent from Matthew and Luke. They too, however, were influenced by oral tradition just as Mark was. Not every proponent of the Borrowing Hypothesis, thus making the evangelists dependent upon one another, believes that the Gospel of Mark plays a fundamental role.

Still others advocate that Matthew is the oldest of the Gospels and that it is the source for Mark and Luke. Luke, according to this theory, depends upon both Matthew and Mark. The fact that Biblical interpreters and scholars have arrived at such a wide variety of conclusions should tell us how little we actually know about these matters.

At the same time, there is a principle invovled which is more important than the question of authorial dependency. What seems more crucial in this matter is whether or not the evangelists continue to be independent witnesses to Jesus if they are indebted to one another. To have a proper grasp of the situation one must first consider the nature of the evangelists' authorship. In light of that one must concede that all the authors are "copyists" to some extent. They are not trying to be "original" in the usual sense of the word.

Each of the Synoptic writers repeats a tradition. They have studied the tradition closely; it would be unimaginable to think they would have ignored other writings known to them. It would also be odd for them to omit a part of a tradition simply because it was repeated elsewhere. Such a position does not affect their status as historically sensitive authors and preachers of the gospel. What does contribute strongly to their integrity and value as witnesses is that each one of the Synoptic Gospels is an independent work which differs from the others in a thousand details. The authors were not interested in conforming to one another's style; neither did they adjust their material to make it identical, any more than they struggled to be original.

The Gospels in their present form exclude the possibility of any slavish dependence among the various authors. They are in fact unique in their handling of common material. In addition they individually have material unique to themselves. This is true not only in Matthew and Luke, but also in Mark. Although 606 out of the 661 verses in Mark appear in Matthew, Mark is more complete in his presentation. A comparison of the Synoptics reveals clearly that the *Borrowing Hypothesis* contains some correct conclusions as long as it is properly understood.

3. The *Source Hypothesis*. This is a third attempt to explain the Synoptic problem. This theory argues, in contrast to the Traditional Historical method, that the evangelists relied upon literary sources for their work. The *Source Hypothesis* was introduced by G. E. Lessing in 1778 as a theory for reconstructing an original Gospel, an ancient Gospel in Aramaic. Later, J. G. Eichorn presented his ideas that there were immediate links. He said that there were no less than nine different gospels behind the present canonical Gospels. In 1817 F. Schleiermacher began his section hypothesis in which he maintained that the Gospels did not originate from an "original gospel," but from countless brief fragments collected by the evangelists.

The point of departure, as with the Marcan Hypothesis, continues to see Mark as a primary source for the other Synoptics; however, the theory also supposes other written documents. In that respect one must distinguish between the Two Document (source) Hypothesis and the Four Document Hypothesis. Since there are so many other opinions within these regarding details, it will be impossible to give a balanced treatment of these variations. A short summary of the two basic options must suffice.

(a) The *Two-Document Hypothesis*. This is a reconstruction which has enjoyed wide favor over the past few years. These scholars, or most of them who favor it, follow the Marcan Hypothesis inasmuch as they recognize that most of Mark is contained in the other two Gospels. Matthew and Luke generally follow Mark's order, and when they do differ it is rarely in the same place. They never together contradict the order of Mark. Furthermore, the advocates of this position contend that the added material of Matthew and Luke is largely teaching material, fragments from Jesus' instruction.

Matthew and Luke share much of this "fragmentary" material. At this point the *Two-Document Hypothesis* states that this material was derived by the evangelists from a common source. In scholarly literature this hypothetical document is called "Q"—from the German *Quelle* ("source"). Even scholars who do not agree that such a document exists usually refer to the material that Matthew and Luke have in common as Q-material. The *Two-Document Hypothesis* fundamentally asserts that the two chief sources for Matthew and Luke are the Gospel of Mark and Q.

Some scholars have reacted against this. They claim Q is wholly fictitious and its presence is purely speculation. A more plausible explanation of the similarity between the two Synoptics is that Luke knew the Gospel of Matthew. If this is the case any need to postulate a common source disappears. The argument against Q is that it is easier to accept the use of a known source (Matthew) than one that is unknown (Q). "It is possible that Q after all is nothing else but something created by modern imagination" (D. Guthrie).

Those who "believe in" Q are not easily shaken from their position. From the common material of Matthew and Luke, several attempts have been made to reconstruct Q (e.g. A. von Harnack, 1908: A. M. Hunter, 1950). J. Moffat mentions 16 different arrangements—at least indicative of the wide variety of possibilities.

However, the *Two-Document Hypothesis* is perhaps not totally without historical support, if one is willing to equate Q with a document mentioned by Papias. Papias states: "Matthew gathered logia [sayings] in the Hebrew language, and translated each one as well as he could." This "forerunner" of the Gospel of Matthew mentioned by Papias is probably a collection of Jesus-sayings. The New Testament use of *logia* especially concerns God's word through the Old Testament prophets. Those scholars who wish to identify Q with the *logia* of Matthew usually speak of Q as a "sayings source." It can only be self-evident that Matthew used his sayings source in writing his Gospel. Whether Luke acquired this material from the *logia* of Matthew or from Matthew's finished product is a secondary question if Matthew is in both cases his source.

But another question remains. Is it correct to limit the *logia* to the Q material that Matthew and Luke have, in addition to Mark? If there was such a *logia/sayings* source this is potentially true according to the words of Papias—it seems likely that Mark also knew and used it. Furthermore, all five sermonic sections in Matthew appear in Mark. Except for the Sermon on the Mount, these are just as intact in Mark as they are in Luke. If Matthew collected the sayings source it seems probable that the sermons would have been a part of that document. Consequently, it seems unlikely that the *logia* of Matthew equals the document Q of source criticism.

(b) The *Four-Document Hypothesis*. Although one may agree with the Two Document Hypothesis in one form or another, there is a serious drawback to it: it fails to explain where the material unique to Matthew and Luke came from. This involves a rather significant portion of these documents. According to Westcott's estimates of similarities and differences, 42 percent of Matthew and 59 percent of Luke is unique. In terms of quantity almost one-third of Matthew is unique, while an even larger portion of Luke is not repeated.

The uniquely Lucan material includes the early childhood of Jesus, chapters 1 and 2, and the large travel narrative in chapters 9:51 to 18:14, which, among other things, includes 16 parables which Luke alone records.

In order to resolve this "difficulty" two new sources are postulated: M for Matthew's unique material and L for Luke's distinctive accounts (B. H. Streeter). The existence of these hypothetical sources has never been demonstrated, but it is imagined that M was the private source of Matthew and that it originated in Jerusalem. The private information of Luke is supposed to have its origin in Caesarea. According to this explanation, Matthew supposedly used Mark, Q, and M as his chief sources. Luke, it is imagined, employed Mark, Q, and L to write his Gospel.

Such a reconstruction of sources that are not only unknown but not precise presents on one hand a much too complicated system. On the other hand, it implies an unacceptable oversimplification of the situation of the evangelists. The scholarly contribution and gathering traditionally ascribed to the inspired evangelists is, in this theory, eliminated. We are left with anonymous "sources" which were never a recognized part of the community. We then must assume that the evangelists almost without discretion copied these sources.

But neither Matthew nor Luke can be explained by asserting the existence of three distinct records. Their situation was quite distinctly characterized by Luke when he tells us that he "set out to write an orderly account" (Luke 1:3). Matthew, as a member of the Twelve, was one of the same witnesses who was entrusted with the passing on of the Jesus tradition. He is infinitely more qualified—an eyewitness and apostle—to be a "servant of the Word" and "bearer of tradition" than some anonymous "source." The idea of an unknown intermediate link is therefore a threat to the trustworthiness of the Gospel.

If one accepts the late dating of the Gospels, then it is possible to see where such an intermediate link might be a necessity. However, when we acknowledge that there was only a short interval between the ministry of Jesus and the writing of the Gospels, it becomes unnecessary to resort to complicated theories to solve problems which no longer exist.

With regard to the Synoptic problem itself, one must acknowledge that after centuries of debate no unanimously accepted answer has been presented. The same proposed solutions we find in the early history of the Church still exist today. This leads us to conclude that none of these attempts have succeeded in solving the Synoptic problem. At the same time it is apparent that each view has a measure of merit.

That Gospel stories were originally oral in form is almost certain; consequently, it is also true that the tradition of Jesus was passed on through the preaching of the apostles at a very early time. We can also be sure that the holy tradition was written down. Luke confirms this in his opening words. And since he indicates that he knows these writings, it is hard to dispute that he did not use them as sources for his Gospel, in conjunction with the oral tradition which he knew so well, as well as his firsthand, eyewitness testimony. The three principal hypotheses for resolving the Synoptic problem are in no way at odds with one another. Rather, each supplements another to provide a fuller, more accurate picture of what took place.

Each of the theories has served as a basis for attacks on the reliability of the Gospels. But it must be stressed that this is not, in itself, inherent in the methodology. If scholarship was unable to solve satisfactorily the dilemmas posed, neither could it raise unanswerable questions.

The Gospels and the Gospel (continued)

There are certainly difficulties in the Synoptic Gospels in reference to the disparities; yet much can be explained. When accounts are found in different contexts it is usually to be admitted that they are not intended to provide a strict chronological order of events. Whenever Jesus' words occur in different contexts and in different form it must be remembered that Jesus may have repeated His sayings under different circumstances with different intent. Related to this factor is that the New Testament was written in Greek, while Jesus spoke Aramaic. It has been observed that if Jesus' words were translated back into Aramaic (which the evangelists may have worded differently) one might see a common Aramaic original as the basis for the various Greek forms.

The similarities among the Synoptics also pose problems, but these are not insurmountable. Any acceptable solution of the synoptical problem must make room for oral tradition as well as written sources. If one accepts the idea of previously written records, much is simplified.

With regard to the similarities in arrangement in the Synoptics, it naturally follows that the story-line should follow the life of Jesus. As to the relationship between the incidents told, one must remember that the writers were probably in close contact with one another. For example, we see from Philemon 24 that Mark and Luke were both in Rome at the time when they probably wrote their Gospels. Despite the fact that they were close co-workers with Paul, and though they wrote their Gospels after Paul's most significant correspondence, they did not impose later theological insights and language upon their recollections. This strongly testifies to the care the evangelists employed to keep the gospel record historically intact.

The Gospels testify to their own integrity. They stand distinctly unique from the other New Testament documents. Only in the Gospels do we have an understanding of Jesus as the Son of Man (except in Acts 7:56, Stephen). Only in the Gospels do we encounter Jesus' parables. This itself is adequate proof that the Jesus tradition could not possibly have evolved out of the Church. This teaching method is not found in the rest of the New Testament nor in other early Christian literature. If the apostolic era had created this masterly method of instruction, other writings from that period would also contain the same method, but they do not. The Early Church maintained an understanding of the difference between Jesus' teaching methods and their own ideas and methods.

The Gospel writers were not influenced by a "theology of the Church," nor were they obligated to conform to *kerugma*. They did follow their sources carefully; this includes both the Synoptics and John, who testifies of what he has seen and heard. Together they confirm and complement one another and give us a unified picture of Jesus Christ. A Johannine tone can be heard in the Matthean note, for example: "All things are delivered unto me of my Father: and no man knoweth the Son, but the Father; neither knoweth any man the Father, save the Son, and he to whomsoever the Son will reveal him" (Matthew 11:27).

The Gospels come to us as Holy Scriptures, just as they came to and were received by the Early Church. This does not prevent us from investigating their background. At the same time it would be totally inappropriate and misguided to try to discover a "historical Jesus" over against the Jesus who is revealed in the Gospels. In our present earthly existence we cannot draw any closer to the real and true Jesus Christ than we do in the Word of God. The Gospels are more than a collection of sources; mystery will always surround their origin until perfect knowledge comes in eternity. They are inspired by the Holy Spirit who has kept the "deposit" entrusted to us (cf. 2 Timothy 1:14).

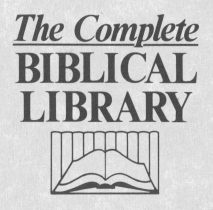

A

SYNOPSIS

OF THE

GOSPELS

A Synopsis of the Gospels

EVENT	REF	MATTHEW	MARK	LUKE	JOHN	PAGE
BEGINNING OF HIS STORY	Dia.				1:1-18	49
	KJV			1:1-4	1:1-18	
JESUS' GENEALOGY	Dia.					50
	KJV	1:1-17		3:23-38		
THE BIRTH OF JOHN PROMISED	Dia.			1:5-25		51
	KJV			1:5-25		
GABRIEL'S ANNOUNCEMENT TO MARY	Dia.			1:26-38		54
	KJV			1:26-38		
MARY'S VISIT TO ELISABETH	Dia.			1:39-56		55
	KJV			1:39-56		
THE BIRTH OF JOHN THE BAPTIST	Dia.			1:57-80		56
	KJV			1:57-80		
THE ANGEL'S ANNOUNCEMENT TO JOSEPH	Dia.	1:18-25				58
	KJV	1:18-25				
THE BIRTH OF JESUS	Dia.			2:1-7		60
	KJV			2:1-7		
THE STORY OF THE SHEPHERDS	Dia.			2:8-20		61
	KJV			2:8-20		
THE DEDICATION OF JESUS	Dia.			2:21-39		62
	KJV			2:2l-38		
THE COMING OF THE WISE MEN	Dia.	2:1-12				64
	KJV	2:1-12				
TRAVELING TO EGYPT	Dia.	2:13-15				66
	KJV	2:13-15				
MURDER OF BETHLEHEM BABIES	Dia.	2:16-18				67
	KJV	2:16-18				
THE FAMILY SETTLES IN NAZARETH	Dia.	2:19-23		2:40		67
	KJV	2:19-23		2:39-40		
JESUS' BOYHOOD VISIT TO JERUSALEM	Dia.			2:41-52		68
	KJV			2:4l-52		
JOHN THE BAPTIST'S MINISTRY	Dia.	3:4-10		3:1-6, 10-18		70
	KJV	3:1-12	1:1-8	3:1-18		
THE BAPTISM OF JESUS	Dia.	3:13-17		3:23a		72
	KJV	3:13-17	1:9-11	3:21-22		
THE TEMPTATION OF JESUS	Dia.	4:1-11				73
	KJV	4:1-11	1:12-13	4:1-13		
JESUS' DEITY DECLARED	Dia.				1:19-34	75
	KJV				1:19-36	
FIRST DISCIPLES OF JESUS	Dia.				1:35-51	76
	KJV				1:35-51	
JESUS' FIRST MIRACLE	Dia.				2:1-12	77
	KJV				2:1-12	
JESUS CLEANSES THE TEMPLE	Dia.				2:13-25	79
	KJV				2:13-25	
JESUS TALKS WITH NICODEMUS	Dia.				3:1-21	80
	KJV				3:1-21	
JOHN TESTIFIES ABOUT JESUS	Dia.				3:22-36	82

A Synopsis of the Gospels (continued)

A Synopsis of the Gospels (continued)

EVENT	REF	MATTHEW	MARK	LUKE	JOHN	PAGE
JESUS LEAVES GALILEE	Dia.			9:51-56		190
	KJV			9:51-56		
COST OF DISCIPLESHIP	Dia.			9:57-62		191
	KJV	8:18-22		9:57-62		
JESUS AT THE FEAST OF TABERNACLES	Dia.				7:2-9, 11-52	191
	KJV				7:1-53	
JESUS DECLARES HIS DEITY	Dia.				8:12-59	195
	KJV				8:12-59	
JESUS HEALS THE MAN BORN BLIND	Dia.				9:1-41	199
	KJV				9:1-41	
JESUS, THE GOOD SHEPHERD	Dia.				10:1-21	202
	KJV				10:1-21	
MISSION OF THE SEVENTY	Dia.	11:21-24		10:1-12, 16-20		205
	KJV	11:20-24		10:1-24		
PARABLE OF THE GOOD SAMARITAN	Dia.			10:25-37		206
	KJV			10:25-37		
JESUS VISITS MARY AND MARTHA	Dia.			10:38-42		208
	KJV			10:38-42		
JESUS TEACHES ABOUT PRAYER	Dia.			11:1-13		210
	KJV			11:1-13		
JESUS DENOUNCES HYPOCRISY	Dia.			11:37-54		211
	KJV			11:37-54		
GREAT TEACHINGS OF THE MASTER	Dia.			12:1-9, 13-21, 49-53		213
	KJV			12:1-59		
JESUS' WARNING TO REPENT	Dia.			13:1-9		216
	KJV			13:1-9		
JESUS HEALS ON THE SABBATH	Dia.			13:10-21		217
	KJV			13:10-21		
JESUS TEACHES AS HE TRAVELS	Dia.			13:22-33		218
	KJV			13:22-33		
JESUS TELLS SOME POINTED PARABLES	Dia.			14:1-24		220
	KJV			14:1-24		
THE COST OF TRUE DISCIPLESHIP	Dia.			14:25-35		222
	KJV			14:25-35		
JESUS MEETS THE JEW'S CHALLENGE	Dia.				10:22-42	223
	KJV	19:1-2	10:1		10:22-42	
LOST: A SHEEP, SILVER, A SON	Dia.			15:1-32		225
	KJV			15:1-32		
THE PROPER USE OF WEALTH	Dia.			16:1-15		227
	KJV			16:1-17		
THE RICH MAN AND LAZARUS	Dia.			16:19-31		229
	KJV			16:19-31		
FORGIVENESS, FAITH AND DUTY	Dia.					230
	KJV			17:1-10		

A Synopsis of the Gospels (continued)

EVENT	REF	MATTHEW	MARK	LUKE	JOHN	PAGE
THE WOMAN TAKEN	Dia.				8:2-11	273
IN ADULTERY	KJV				8:1-11	
ATTACKS BY	Dia.	22:15-33				274
RELIGIOUS LEADERS	KJV	22:15-33	12:13-27	20:20-40		
THE GREATEST COMMANDMENT	Dia.	22:34-40				276
	KJV	22:34-40	12:28-34			
JESUS' UNANSWERABLE	Dia.	22:41-46				277
QUESTION	KJV	22:41-46	12:35-40	20:41-47		
JESUS DENOUNCES SIN	Dia.	23:1-39				278
	KJV	23:1-39		13:34-35		
JESUS PREVIEWS HISTORY	Dia.	24:1-14, 21-51	13:33-37	21:12-24, 34-36		281
	KJV	24:1-51	13:1-37	21:5-38		
PARABLE OF THE VIRGINS	Dia.	25:1-13				289
	KJV	25:1-13				
PARABLE OF THE TALENTS	Dia.	25:14-30				289
	KJV	25:14-30				
THE COMING JUDGMENT	Dia.	25:31-46				292
	KJV	25:31-46				
JUDAS' CONSPIRACY	Dia.	26:1-5, 14-16				294
	KJV	26:1-5, 14-16	14:1-2, 10-11	22:1-6		
PREPARING FOR PASSOVER	Dia.		14:12-17			295
	KJV	26:17-20	14:12-17	22:7-18	13:1-2	
CONTENDING FOR	Dia.			22:24-27		297
THE HIGHEST PLACE	KJV			22:24-30		
JESUS TEACHES HUMILITY	Dia.				13:3-20	298
	KJV				13:3-20	
EVENTS AT	Dia.	26:21-29		22:15-16	13:22-30	299
THE LAST SUPPER	KJV	26:21-29	14:18-25	22:19-23	13:21-30	
JESUS TO BE FORSAKEN,	Dia.	26:30-35		22:31-38	13:31-38	301
DENIED	KJV	26:30-35	14:26-31	22:31-38	13:31-38	
JESUS COMFORTS	Dia.				14:1-31	302
HIS DISCIPLES	KJV				14:1-31	
THE TRUE VINE	Dia.				15:1-27	304
	KJV				15:1-27	
PROMISE OF	Dia.				16:1-33	307
THE HOLY SPIRIT	KJV				16:1-33	
JESUS PRAYS	Dia.				17:1-26	309
FOR HIS DISCIPLES	KJV				17:1-26	
PRAYING IN GETHSEMANE	Dia.	26:36-46				311
	KJV	26:36-46	14:32-42	22:39-46	18:1	
JESUS' BETRAYAL	Dia.	26:47-56				314
AND ARREST	KJV	26:47-56	14:43-52	22:47-53	18:2-11	
TRIAL BEFORE	Dia.	26:59-68; 27:1-2			18:12-13, 19-24	316
JEWISH AUTHORITIES	KJV	26:57,	14:53,	22:54,	18:12-14,	

EVENT	REF	MATTHEW	MARK	LUKE	JOHN	PAGE
		59-68	55-65	63-71	19-24	
PETER'S DENIAL	Dia.	26:58, 69-74		22:61-62		318
	KJV	26:58, 69-75	14:54, 66-72	22:55-62	18:15-18, 25-27	
JESUS BROUGHT BEFORE PILATE	Dia.	27:1-2	15:3-5	23:2,5-7	18:28-38	319
	KJV	27:1-2, 11-14	15:1-7	23:1-5	18:28-38	
JESUS APPEARS BEFORE HEROD	Dia.			23:8-12		321
	KJV			23:8-12		
BEFORE PILATE AGAIN	Dia.	27:17-26	15:6-7	23:13-16		322
	KJV	27:15-26	15:6-15	23:13-25	18:39-40	
JESUS MOCKED	Dia.	27:27-30				324
	KJV	27:27-30	15:16-19		19:1-3	
JESUS DELIVERED FOR CRUCIFIXION	Dia.				19:4-16	324
	KJV				19:4-16	
JUDAS' REMORSE AND DEATH	Dia.	27:3-10				325
	KJV	27:3-10				
JESUS LED TO CALVARY	Dia.	27:31-32		23:27-32	19:17	326
	KJV	27:31-34	15:20-23	23:26-32	19:17	
THE CRUCIFIXION	Dia.	27:39-54	15:22-27	23:34-49	19:19-37	328
	KJV	27:35-56	15:24-41	23:33-49	19:18-37	
THE BURIAL OF JESUS	Dia.	27:57,60	15:42-47	23:50	19:38-41	332
	KJV	27:57-61	15:42-47	23:50-56	19:38-42	
GUARDS STATIONED AT THE TOMB	Dia.	27:62-66				333
	KJV	27:62-66				
JESUS RISES FROM THE DEAD	Dia.	28:2-4,8	16:1-7	24:1-11	20:2	334
	KJV	28:1-8	16:1-8	24:1-11	20:1-2	
PETER AND JOHN RUN TO THE TOMB	Dia.				20:3-10	336
	KJV			24:12	20:3-10	
THE WOMEN SEE JESUS	Dia.	28:9-10	16:11		20:11-18	336
	KJV	28:9-10	16:9-11		20:11-18	
THE REPORT OF THE GUARDS	Dia.	28:11-15				339
	KJV	28:11-15				
THE EMMAUS ROAD APPEARANCE	Dia.			24:13-35		339
	KJV		16:12-13	24:13-35		
JESUS APPEARS TO THE DISCIPLES	Dia.			24:36-49	20:21-23	342
	KJV		16:14	24:36-49	20:19-23	
THOMAS SEES JESUS AND BELIEVES	Dia.				20:24-31	343
	KJV				20:24-31	
JESUS APPEARS BY GALILEE	Dia.				21:1-23	344
	KJV				21:1-23	
JESUS COMMISSIONS HIS DISCIPLES	Dia.	28:16-20	16:15-18			347
	KJV	28:16-20	16:15-18			
JESUS' ASCENSION	Dia.			24:50-53	ACTS	348
	KJV		16:19-20	24:50-53	1:3-11	
JOHN'S EPILOGUE	KJV				21:24-25	348

Satellite Map of Palestine

Palestine from Space

It seems fitting to view the Holy Land from the heavens. The United States space program has given the science of photography a new dimension. This HARMONY OF THE GOSPELS contains maps which give more detailed and accurate information than before possible.

The view shown on this page was taken by U. S. astronauts while in earth orbit aboard the Apollo spacecraft, using a 70 mm Hasselbad camera. The crew was Thomas P. Stafford, commander; Donald K. Slayton, docking module pilot; and Vance D. Brand, command module pilot.

It also seems appropriate that they were the first astronauts to rendezvous with a Russian spacecraft, the Soyuz—on July 17, 1975.

Other maps placed throughout this HARMONY are Landsat photos taken by satellites whirling around the earth. For better viewing some maps have an eastern orientation. This is not a new concept. Ancient maps often used this perspective, for the east was considered the most important direction.

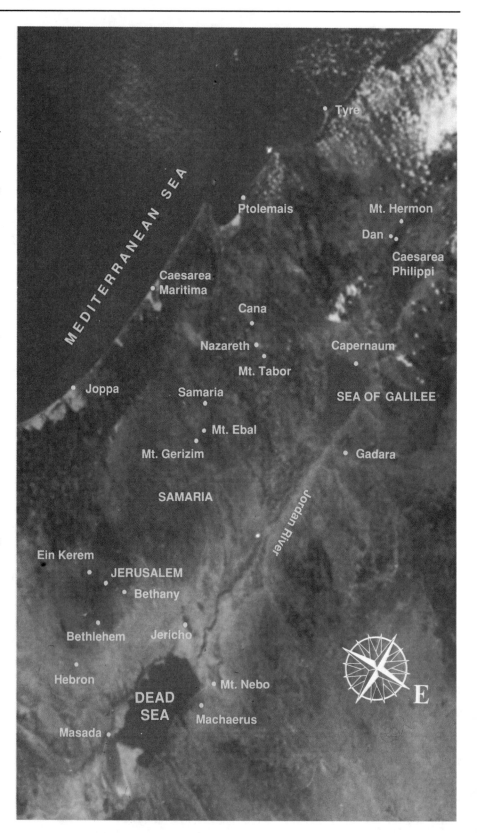

Jerusalem as It Was in the Time of Christ

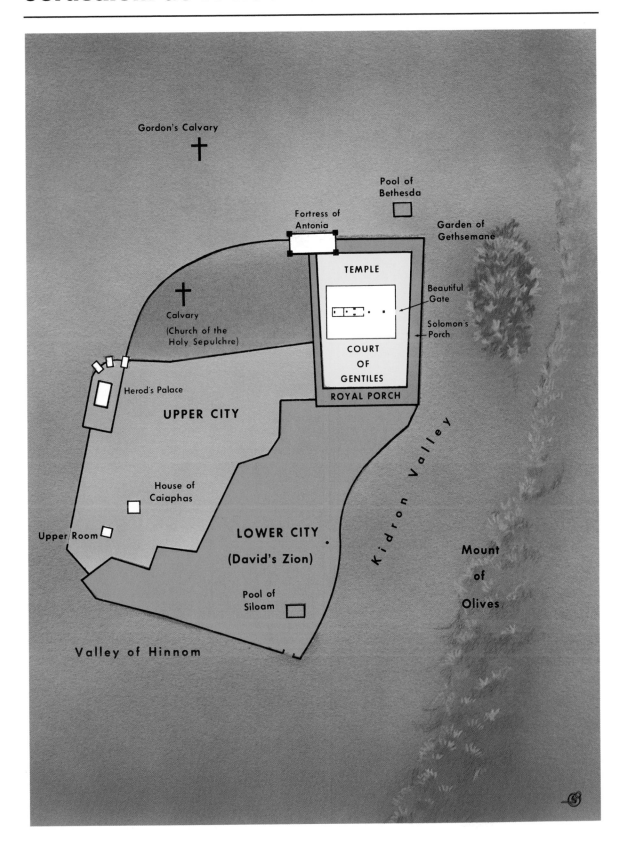

The Complete
BIBLICAL
LIBRARY

HARMONY

OF THE

GOSPELS

Introduction to the Harmony of the Gospels

This *Harmony of the Gospels* is unique: (1) It is in full color. (2) It is illustrated by recent pictures of Holy Land sites and scenes. (3) It contains maps to pinpoint locations where events took place. (4) In addition to parallel columns of the four Gospels, there is an interwoven account of Jesus' life from all four Gospels, a *diatessaron* (Greek, "through four").

A *Harmony* is of great value in studying the Gospels by comparing the accounts. Some have thought that each Gospel had a different target audience: that Matthew wrote for the Jews, Mark for the Romans, Luke for the Greeks, and John for believers of all nationalities. If this is true, it would require a different approach and choice of subject matter. Also some events and teachings would be stressed more than others.

The first attempt to provide a harmony system was by Tatian, a student of Justin Martyr, about A.D. 175. In more recent times the work of the theologian Dr. John Broadus in the late 1800s has exerted a strong influence upon modern-day efforts. Until his time, scholars used the feasts mentioned in the Gospels to determine the sequence of events. He led the way in departing from this system, and his work became the standard which has been followed almost universally since that time. John Kerr (1903) and A. T. Robertson (1923) have also become recognized leaders in this field.

In the *Preface* of his work Kerr presents interesting facts which explain why it is difficult to provide a Harmony with which all agree. In the 168 different sections of his book which outline Jesus' life, the following divisions occur among the evangelists:

76 are provided by just *one* Gospel writer
28 are provided by *two*
49 are provided by *three*
15 are provided by all *four*

According to Kerr, Mark has only *one* section found in no other Gospel; Matthew *11,* John *27,* and Luke *37.*

Robert Shank's *diatessaron* is a welcome addition to the *Harmony.* It provides, as he states, "the four Gospels as one narrative in language for today." This interwoven story offers an interesting comparison with the other accounts.

Shank expresses his guiding principles forthrightly: "(1) to be faithful to the meaning of the Greek text; (2) to present a simple and reverent translation that commends itself to the reader for clarity and pure pleasure of reading; and (3) to stay close to the *King James Version* to retain a sense of familiarity for readers well acquainted with the classic English version, especially when dealing with the most familiar passages."

Notice the easy-to-use system for identifying the five different accounts. The headings for Matthew in yellow, for Mark in green, for Luke in blue and for John in red. The *diatessaron* is overprinted on a cream background and in a larger type size.

With the four Gospels arranged in parallel columns for ease of comparison and the *diatessaron* alongside to provide continuity, the user of this *Harmony of the Gospels* should find in it a lifetime of pleasurable reading and stimulating study.
—*The Editors*

Beginning of His Story

John 1:1-18

In the beginning was the Word, and the Word was with God, and the Word was in fact God. He was present with God in the beginning, and through him all things came into being. Apart from him was nothing made of all that was created. In him was life, and the life was the light of men. And the light shines on in the darkness, and the darkness has not overcome it.

There was a man sent from God whose name was John. He came as a witness, to bear witness to the Light, that through him all might believe. He was not the Light, but came to bear witness to the Light. The true Light that enlightens every man was always there, coming into the world: he was in the world, and the world was made by him; but the world did not know him.

He came to the things of his own creation, and his own people did not accept him. But as many as received him, to them he gave the right to become sons of God, to those who trust in his name, who are born—not of bloods nor of the desire of the flesh or of man, but of God.

And the Word became flesh and dwelt among us, full of grace and truth. And we saw his glory—the glory of the only begotten Son from the Father.

John bore witness to him and cried, "This is he of whom I said, 'He who comes after me is greater than I, for he was before me.' "

And from his fulness have we all received, grace upon grace. For the law was given through Moses, but grace and truth came through Jesus Christ. No one has ever seen God; but the only begotten Son, who is in the presence of the Father, has made him known.

LUKE 1:1-4

1 Forasmuch as many have taken in hand to set forth in order a declaration of those things which are most surely believed among us,

2 Even as they delivered them unto us, which from the beginning were eye-witnesses, and ministers of the word;

3 It seemed good to me also, having had perfect understanding of all things from the very first, to write unto thee in order, most excellent Theophilus,

4 That thou mightest know the certainty of those things, wherein thou hast been instructed.

JOHN 1:1-18

1 In the beginning was the Word, and the Word was with God, and the Word was God.

2 The same was in the beginning with God.

3 All things were made by him; and without him was not any thing made that was made.

4 In him was life; and the life was the light of men.

5 And the light shineth in darkness; and the darkness comprehended it not.

6 There was a man sent from God, whose name *was* John.

7 The same came for a witness, to bear witness of the Light, that all *men* through him might believe.

8 He was not that Light, but *was sent* to bear witness of that Light.

9 *That* was the true Light, which lighteth every man that cometh into the world.

10 He was in the world, and the world was made by him, and the world knew him not.

11 He came unto his own, and his own received him not.

12 But as many as received him, to them gave he power to become the sons of God, *even* to them that believe on his name:

13 Which were born, not of blood, nor of the will of the flesh, nor of the will of man, but of God.

14 And the Word was made flesh, and dwelt among us, (and we beheld his glory, the glory as of the only begotten of the Father,) full of grace and truth.

15 John bare witness of him, and cried, saying, This was he of whom I spake, He that cometh after me is preferred before me; for he was before me.

16 And of his fulness have all we received, and grace for grace.

17 For the law was given by Moses, *but* grace and truth came by Jesus Christ.

18 No man hath seen God at any time; the only begotten Son, which is in the bosom of the Father, he hath declared *him*.

Jesus' Genealogy

MATTHEW 1:1-17

1 The book of the generation of Jesus Christ, the son of David, the son of Abraham.

2 Abraham begat Isaac; and Isaac begat Jacob; and Jacob begat Judah and his brethren;

3 And Judah begat Pharez and Zerah of Tamar; and Pharez begat Hezrom; and Hezrom begat Ram;

4 And Ram begat Amminadab; and Amminadab begat Nahshon; and Nahshon begat Salmon;

5 And Salmon begat Boaz of Rachab; and Boaz begat Obed of Ruth; and Obed begat Jesse;

6 And Jesse begat David the king. And David the king begat Solomon of her that had been the wife of Uriah;

7 And Solomon begat Rehoboam; and Rehoboam begat Abijah; and Abijah begat Asa;

8 And Asa begat Jehoshaphat; and Jehoshaphat begat Jehoram; and Jehoram begat Uzziah;

9 And Uzziah begat Jotham; and Jotham begat Ahaz; and Ahaz begat Hezekiah;

10 And Hezekiah begat Manasseh; and Manasseh begat Amon; and Amon begat Josiah;

11 And Josiah begat Jeconiah and his brethren, about the time they were carried away to Babylon:

12 And after they were brought to Babylon, Jeconiah begat Shealtiel; and Shealtiel begat Zerubbabel;

13 And Zerubbabel begat Abiud; and Abiud begat Eliakim; and Eliakim begat Azor;

14 And Azor begat Zadoc; and Zadoc begat Achim; and Achim begat Eliud;

15 And Eliud begat Eleazar; and Eleazar begat Matthan; and Matthan begat Jacob;

16 And Jacob begat Joseph the husband of Mary, of whom was born Jesus, who is called Christ.

17 So all the generations from Abraham to David are fourteen generations; and from David until the carrying away into Babylon are fourteen generations; and from the carrying away into Babylon unto Christ are fourteen generations.

LUKE 3:23-38

23 And Jesus himself began to be about thirty years of age, being (as was supposed) the son of Joseph, which was *the son* of Heli,

24 Which was *the son* of Matthat, which was *the son* of Levi, which was *the son* of Melchi, which was *the son* of Janna, which was *the son* of Joseph,

25 Which was *the son* of Mattathias, which was *the son* of Amos, which was *the son* Nahum, which was *the son* of Esli, which was *the son* of Naggai,

26 Which was *the son* of Maath, which was *the son* of Mattathias, which was *the son* of Semei, which was *the son* of Joseph, which was *the son* of Judah,

27 Which was *the son* of Joanna, which was *the son* of Rhesa, which was *the son* of Zerubbabel, which was *the son* of Shealtiel, which was *the son* of Neri,

28 Which was *the son* of Melchi, which was *the son* of Addi, which was *the son* of Cosam, which was *the son* of Elmodam, which was *the son* of Er,

29 Which was *the son* of Jose, which was *the son* of Eliezer, which was *the son* of Jorim, which was *the son* of Matthat, which was *the son* of Levi,

30 Which was *the son* of Simeon, which was *the son* of Judah, which was *the son* of Joseph, which was *the son* of Jonan, which was *the son* of Eliakim,

31 Which was *the son* of Melea, which was *the son* of Menan, which was *the son* of Mattatha, which was *the son* of Nathan, which was *the son* of David,

32 Which was *the son* of Jesse, which was *the son* of Obed, which was the son of Boaz, which was *the son* of Salmon, which was *the son* of Nahshon,

33 Which was *the son* of Amminadab, which was *the son* of Ram, which was *the son* of Hezron, which was *the son* of Pharez, which was *the son* of Judah,

34 Which was *the son* of Jacob, which was *the son* of Isaac, which was *the son* of Abraham, which was *the son* of Terah, which was *the son* of Nahor,

35 Which was *the son* of Serug, which was *the son* of Reu, which was *the son* of Peleg, which was *the son* of Eber, which was *the son* of Salah,

36 Which was *the son* of Cainan, which was *the son* of Arphaxad, which was *the son* of Shem, which was *the son* of Noah, which was *the son* of Lamech,

37 Which was *the son* of Methuselah, which was *the son* of Enoch, which was *the son* of Jared, which was *the son* of Mahalaleel, which was *the son* of Cainan,

38 Which was *the son* of Enos, which was *the son* of Seth, which was *the son* of Adam, which was *the son* of God.

The Birth of John Promised

Home of Zechariah and Elisabeth. *Luke 1:39,40 states that it was in "the hill country" of Judea the parents of John the Baptist lived. A small village called Ein Kerem is now identified as the place of their residence.*

Luke 1:5-25

In the days of Herod, king of Judea, there was a priest of the division of Abijah named Zacharias whose wife Elisabeth was of the daughters of Aaron. They were both righteous before God, walking in all the commandments and ordinances of the Lord blameless. And they had no child, because Elisabeth was barren, and they were both advanced in years.

And it came to pass that while Zacharias was serving as priest before God during the time when his division was on duty, it fell to him by lot, according to the custom of the priesthood, to go into the sanctuary of the Lord in the temple to burn incense. All the people were praying in the court of the temple, outside the sanctuary, at the time of the burning of incense. And there appeared to him an angel of the Lord, standing

LUKE 1:5-25

5 There was in the days of Herod, the king of Judea, a certain priest named Zechariah, of the course of Abijah: and his wife *was* of the daughters of Aaron, and her name *was* Elisabeth.

6 And they were both righteous before God, walking in all the commandments and ordinances of the Lord blameless.

7 And they had no child, because that Elisabeth was barren; and they both were *now* well stricken in years.

8 And it came to pass, that, while he executed the priest's office before God in the order of his course,

9 According to the custom of the priest's office, his lot was to burn incense when he went into the temple of the Lord.

10 And the whole multitude of the people were praying without at the time of incense.

11 And there appeared unto him an angel of the Lord standing on the right side of the altar of incense.

The Birth of John Promised (continued)

to the right of the altar of incense. Now when Zacharias saw him, he was startled and became afraid. But the angel said,

"Do not be afraid, Zacharias, for your prayer has been heard. Your wife Elisabeth will bear you a son, and you are to call him John. You will have joy and gladness, and many will rejoice over his birth. He will be great in the sight of the Lord. He will drink neither wine nor strong drink, and will be filled with the Holy Spirit, even from his mother's womb. He will turn many of the sons of Israel to the Lord their God, for he will go before Him in the spirit and power of Elijah, to turn the hearts of the fathers to the children, and the disobedient to walk in the wisdom of the righteous, to make ready a people prepared for the Lord."

"How can I be sure of this?" said Zacharias, "for I am an old man, and my wife is advanced in years."

"I am Gabriel," answered the angel, "who stand in the presence of God. I was sent to speak to you and to announce to you these good tidings. And now, because you did not believe my words, which surely will be fulfilled in the appointed time, you will be silent and unable to speak until the day this comes to pass."

Now the people were waiting for Zacharias, and they wondered why he remained so long in the sanctuary. But when he came out and was unable to speak to them, they knew that he had seen a vision in the sanctuary; for he made signs to them, and remained unable to speak.

When the days of his service were ended, Zacharias returned to his home; and after those days his wife Elisabeth conceived. And she remained in seclusion five months, saying, "This is what the Lord has done for me, now that he has looked on me with favor, to take away my disgrace among the people."

LUKE 1:5-25

12 And when Zechariah saw *him,* he was troubled, and fear fell upon him.

13 But the angel said unto him, Fear not, Zechariah: for thy prayer is heard; and thy wife Elisabeth shall bear thee a son, and thou shalt call his name John.

14 And thou shalt have joy and gladness; and many shall rejoice at his birth.

15 For he shall be great in the sight of the Lord, and shall drink neither wine nor strong drink; and he shall be filled with the Holy Ghost, even from his mother's womb.

16 And many of the children of Israel shall he turn to the Lord their God.

17 And he shall go before him in the spirit and power of Elijah, to turn the hearts of the fathers to the children, and the disobedient to the wisdom of the just; to make ready a people prepared for the Lord.

18 And Zechariah said unto the angel, Whereby shall I know this? for I am an old man, and my wife well stricken in years.

19 And the angel answering said unto him, I am Gabriel, that stand in the presence of God; and am sent to speak unto thee, and to show thee these glad tidings.

20 And, behold, thou shalt be dumb, and not able to speak, until the day that these things shall be performed, because thou believest not my words, which shall be fulfilled in their season.

21 And the people waited for Zechariah, and marveled that he tarried so long in the temple.

22 And when he came out, he could not speak unto them: and they perceived that he had seen a vision in the temple; for he beckoned unto them, and remained speechless.

23 And it came to pass, that, as soon as the days of his ministration were accomplished, he departed to his own house.

24 And after those days his wife Elisabeth conceived, and hid herself five months, saying,

25 Thus hath the Lord dealt with me in the days wherein he looked on *me,* to take away my reproach among men.

Mary Visits Elisabeth. *After Gabriel told Mary she would be the mother of the Messiah she went to visit her elderly cousin Elisabeth and tell her the wonderful news.*

53

Gabriel's Announcement to Mary

Luke 1:26-38

Now in the sixth month the angel Gabriel was sent from God to a city of Galilee named Nazareth, to a virgin betrothed to a man named Joseph, a descendant of David; and the maiden's name was Mary. And the angel came to her and said, "Hail, O favored one, the Lord is with you!"

But she was greatly troubled at the saying and wondered what such a greeting could mean.

"Do not be afraid, Mary," said the angel, "for you have found favor with God. Behold, you will conceive in your womb and bear a son, and you are to call his name Jesus. He will be great, and will be called the Son of the Most High. The Lord God will give to him the throne of his father David; he will reign over the house of Jacob for ever, and of his kingdom there will be no end."

"How can this be," said Mary, "since I have no husband?"

"The Holy Spirit will come upon you," said the angel, "and the power of the Most High will overshadow you. Therefore the Holy One who is to be born will be called the Son of God. Behold, your kinswoman Elisabeth has also conceived a son in her old age, and this is the sixth month with her who was called barren. For with God nothing will be impossible."

And Mary said, "Behold, I am the handmaid of the Lord; let it be to me according to your word."

And the angel departed from her.

LUKE 1:26-38

26 And in the sixth month the angel Gabriel was sent from God unto a city of Galilee, named Nazareth,

27 To a virgin espoused to a man whose name was Joseph, of the house of David; and the virgin's name *was* Mary.

28 And the angel came in unto her, and said, Hail, *thou that art* highly favored, the Lord *is* with thee: blessed *art* thou among women.

29 And when she saw *him,* she was troubled at his saying, and cast in her mind what manner of salutation this should be.

30 And the angel said unto her, Fear not, Mary: for thou hast found favor with God.

31 And, behold, thou shalt conceive in thy womb, and bring forth a son, and shalt call his name JESUS.

32 He shall be great, and shall be called the Son of the Highest; and the Lord God shall give unto him the throne of his father David:

33 And he shall reign over the house of Jacob for ever; and of his kingdom there shall be no end.

34 Then said Mary unto the angel, How shall this be, seeing I know not a man?

35 And the angel answered and said unto her, The Holy Ghost shall come upon thee, and the power of the Highest shall overshadow thee: therefore also that holy thing which shall be born of thee shall be called the Son of God.

36 And, behold, thy cousin Elisabeth, she hath also conceived a son in her old age; and this is the sixth month with her, who was called barren.

37 For with God nothing shall be impossible.

38 And Mary said, Behold the handmaid of the Lord; be it unto me according to thy word. And the angel departed from her.

Mary's Well. *Nazareth contains many sites claiming to be the place Mary was told she would become the mother of the Messiah. One such location is the one shown here.*

Mary's Visit to Elisabeth

Luke 1:39-56

And in those days Mary rose and went with haste into the hill country to a city of Judah, and entered the house of Zacharias and greeted Elisabeth. And when Elisabeth heard Mary's greeting, the babe leaped in her womb, and she was filled with the Holy Spirit and cried,

"Blessed are you among women, and blessed is the fruit of your womb! But why is such an honor mine, that the mother of my Lord should come to me? For behold, when the voice of your greeting came to my ears, the babe in my womb leaped for joy. Blessed is she who believed, for there shall be brought to pass all that was told her from the Lord."

And Mary said,

"My soul magnifies the Lord, and my spirit rejoices in God my Saviour; for he has looked with favor upon the humble estate of his handmaid. Behold, henceforth all generations will call me blessed, for he who is mighty has done great things for me, and holy is his name. His mercy is on those who fear him from generation to generation. He has shown strength with his arm, and has scattered the proud. He has cast down the mighty from their thrones and exalted the lowly. The hungry he has filled with good things, and the rich he has sent away empty. He has helped Israel his servant, remembering mercy, even as he promised to our fathers, to Abraham and to his posterity for ever."

And Mary remained with her about three months, and returned to her own home.

LUKE 1:39-56

39 And Mary arose in those days, and went into the hill country with haste, into a city of Judah;

40 And entered into the house of Zechariah, and saluted Elisabeth.

41 And it came to pass, that, when Elisabeth heard the salutation of Mary, the babe leaped in her womb; and Elisabeth was filled with the Holy Ghost:

42 And she spake out with a loud voice, and said, Blessed *art* thou among women, and blessed *is* the fruit of thy womb.

43 And whence *is* this to me, that the mother of my Lord should come to me?

44 For, lo, as soon as the voice of thy salutation sounded in mine ears, the babe leaped in my womb for joy.

45 And blessed *is* she that believed: for there shall be a performance of those things which were told her from the Lord.

46 And Mary said, My soul doth magnify the Lord,

47 And my spirit hath rejoiced in God my Saviour.

48 For he hath regarded the low estate of his handmaiden: for, behold, from henceforth all generations shall call me blessed.

49 For he that is mighty hath done to me great things; and holy *is* his name.

50 And his mercy *is* on them that fear him from generation to generation.

51 He hath showed strength with his arm; he hath scattered the proud in the imagination of their hearts.

52 He hath put down the mighty from *their* seats, and exalted them of low degree.

53 He hath filled the hungry with good things; and the rich he hath sent empty away.

54 He hath holpen his servant Israel, in remembrance of *his* mercy;

55 As he spake to our fathers, to Abraham, and to his seed for ever.

56 And Mary abode with her about three months, and returned to her own house.

The Birth of John the Baptist

Luke 1:57-80

Now the time came for Elisabeth to be delivered, and she brought forth a son. And her neighbors and kinsfolk heard how the Lord had shown great mercy to her, and they rejoiced with her. And on the eighth day they came to circumcise the child, and they were calling him Zacharias, after his father. But his mother said, "No, he is to be called John."

"None of your kin is called by that name," they said. And they made signs to his father, asking what he wanted him to be called; and he beckoned for a writing tablet and wrote, "His name is John." And they all marveled, and immediately Zacharias' mouth was opened and his tongue loosed, and he began to speak, praising God.

And great wonder and fear came on all who lived round about them, and all these things were talked about throughout all the hill country of Judea. And all who heard it took it to heart, saying, "What, indeed, will this child be?" And the hand of the Lord was with him.

LUKE 1:57-80

57 Now Elisabeth's full time came that she should be delivered; and she brought forth a son.

58 And her neighbors and her cousins heard how the Lord had showed great mercy upon her; and they rejoiced with her.

59 And it came to pass, that on the eighth day they came to circumcise the child; and they called him Zechariah, after the name of his father.

60 And his mother answered and said, Not so; but he shall be called John.

61 And they said unto her, There is none of thy kindred that is called by this name.

62 And they made signs to his father, how he would have him called.

63 And he asked for a writing table, and wrote, saying, His name is John. And they marveled all.

64 And his mouth was opened immediately, and his tongue *loosed,* and he spake, and praised God.

65 And fear came on all that dwelt round about them: and all these sayings were noised abroad throughout all the hill country of Judea.

66 And all they that heard *them* laid *them* up in their hearts, saying, What manner of child shall this be? And the hand of the Lord was with him.

Birthplace of John the Baptist. *Ein Kerem, on the western outskirts of modern-day Jerusalem, is in the area where John's parents lived. This church was erected to commemorate his birth and ministry.*

The Birth of John the Baptist (continued)

The Holy Land is divided into four different geographical areas: the coastal plain, the mountain region, the Jordan Valley and the eastern plateau. John's birthplace was in hilly area near Jerusalem.

And Zacharias, his father, was filled with the Holy Spirit and prophesied, saying,

"Blessed be the Lord God of Israel, for he has visited and redeemed his people, and has raised up a horn of salvation for us in the house of his servant David, as he spoke by the mouth of his holy prophets from of old, that we should be saved from our enemies, and from the hand of all who hate us; to perform the mercy promised to our fathers, and to remember his holy covenant, the oath which he swore to our father Abraham, to grant us that, being delivered out of the hand of our enemies, we might serve him without fear, in holiness and righteousness before him all the days of our life.

"And you, child, will be called the prophet of the Most High. For you will go before the Lord to prepare the way, to give knowledge of salvation to his people in the forgiveness of their sins through the tender mercy of our God, whereby the Dayspring from on high will visit us, to give light to those who sit in darkness and in the shadow of death, to guide our feet into the way of peace."

And the child grew and became strong in spirit, and lived in the wilderness until the day of his manifestation to Israel.

LUKE 1:57-80

67 And his father Zechariah was filled with the Holy Ghost, and prophesied, saying,

68 Blessed *be* the Lord God of Israel; for he hath visited and redeemed his people,

69 And hath raised up a horn of salvation for us in the house of his servant David;

70 As he spake by the mouth of his holy prophets, which have been since the world began:

71 That we should be saved from our enemies, and from the hand of all that hate us;

72 To perform the mercy *promised* to our fathers, and to remember his holy covenant;

73 The oath which he sware to our father Abraham,

74 That he would grant unto us, that we, being delivered out of the hand of our enemies, might serve him without fear,

75 In holiness and righteousness before him, all the days of our life.

76 And thou, child, shalt be called the prophet of the Highest: for thou shalt go before the face of the Lord to prepare his ways;

77 To give knowledge of salvation unto his people by the remission of their sins,

78 Through the tender mercy of our God; whereby the dayspring from on high hath visited us,

79 To give light to them that sit in darkness and *in* the shadow of death, to guide our feet into the way of peace.

80 And the child grew, and waxed strong in spirit, and was in the deserts till the day of his showing unto Israel.

The Angel's Announcement to Joseph

Matthew 1:18-25

Now the birth of Jesus Christ happened in this way. After his mother Mary had been betrothed to Joseph, before they came together she was found with child by the Holy Spirit. And Joseph her husband, being a righteous man, and yet unwilling to make her a public example, planned to divorce her privately.

But while he was considering the matter, behold, an angel of the Lord appeared to him in a dream and said, "Joseph, son of David, do not fear to take Mary your wife, for that which is conceived in her is of the Holy Spirit. She will bear a son, and you are to call his name Jesus, for he will save his people from their sins."

Now all this took place to fulfill the word of the Lord through the prophet,

Behold, the virgin shall conceive and bear a son, and they shall call his name Emmanuel —which means "God with us."

And Joseph rose from his sleep and did as the angel of the Lord had commanded him, and took to him his wife, but was not intimate with her until she had borne a son. And he called his name Jesus.

MATTHEW 1:18-25

18 Now the birth of Jesus Christ was on this wise: When as his mother Mary was espoused to Joseph, before they came together, she was found with child of the Holy Ghost.

19 Then Joseph her husband, being a just man, and not willing to make her a public example, was minded to put her away privily.

20 But while he thought on these things, behold, the angel of the Lord appeared unto him in a dream, saying, Joseph, thou son of David, fear not to take unto thee Mary thy wife: for that which is conceived in her is of the Holy Ghost.

21 And she shall bring forth a son, and thou shalt call his name Jesus: for he shall save his people from their sins.

22 Now all this was done, that it might be fulfilled which was spoken of the Lord by the prophet, saying,

23 Behold, a virgin shall be with child, and shall bring forth a son, and they shall call his name Immanuel, which being interpreted is, God with us.

24 Then Joseph being raised from sleep did as the angel of the Lord had bidden him, and took unto him his wife:

25 And knew her not till she had brought forth her firstborn son: and he called his name Jesus.

In Jesus' time on earth the land west of the Jordan River was divided into 3 regions, Judea in the south, Samaria in the center and Galilee in the north. Nazareth was a city in Galilee. The other provinces were the Decapolis mainly east of the Jordan, and Perea.

The Shepherds Visit the Baby Jesus. *Humble shepherds were the first to hear of the Saviour's birth. They came and found Him lying in a manger, just as the angel had promised them.*

The Birth of Jesus

Shepherds Fields. *To shepherds in fields near Bethlehem, angels appeared with the wonderful announcement that a Saviour had been born.*

Luke 2:1-7

Now it came to pass in those days that a decree went out from Caesar Augustus that a census should be taken of all the world. This was the first census, when Quirinius was governor of Syria. And all went to be registered, each to his own city. And because he was of the house and lineage of David, Joseph went up from Galilee and the city of Nazareth to Judea, to the city of David which is called Bethlehem, to be registered with Mary, his espoused wife, who was with child. And it came to pass that, while they were there, the time came for her to be delivered. And she brought forth her firstborn son, and wrapped him in swaddling clothes and laid him in a manger, because there was no room for them in the inn.

LUKE 2:1-7

1 And it came to pass in those days, that there went out a decree from Caesar Augustus, that all the world should be taxed.

2 (*And* this taxing was first made when Cyrenius was governor of Syria.)

3 And all went to be taxed, every one into his own city.

4 And Joseph also went up from Galilee, out of the city of Nazareth, into Judea, unto the city of David, which is called Bethlehem, (because he was of the house and lineage of David,)

5 To be taxed with Mary his espoused wife, being great with child.

6 And so it was, that, while they were there, the days were accomplished that she should be delivered.

7 And she brought forth her firstborn son, and wrapped him in swaddling clothes, and laid him in a manger; because there was no room for them in the inn.

The Story of the Shepherds

Luke 2:8-20

And there were in the same country shepherds abiding in the field, keeping watch over their flock by night. And, lo! an angel of the Lord appeared to them, and the glory of the Lord shone round about them, and they were much afraid. And the angel said to them,

"Fear not; for behold, I bring you good tidings of great joy which shall be to all people. For to you is born this day in the city of David a Saviour, who is Christ the Lord. And this will be the sign to you: you will find a babe wrapped in swaddling clothes, lying in a manger."

And suddenly there was with the angel a multitude of the heavenly host praising God and saying, "Glory to God in the highest, and on earth peace among men of good will."

And it came to pass when the angels had departed from them into heaven, the shepherds said one to another, "Let us go to Bethlehem and see this thing which has come to pass, which the Lord has made known to us."

And they came with haste and found Mary and Joseph, and the babe lying in a manger. And when they saw it, they made known the things which had been told them concerning this child. And all who heard it wondered at the things the shepherds told them. But Mary treasured all these things, pondering them in her heart. And the shepherds returned, glorifying and praising God for all the things they had heard and seen, just as it had been told them.

LUKE 2:8-20

8 And there were in the same country shepherds abiding in the field, keeping watch over their flock by night.

9 And, lo, the angel of the Lord came upon them, and the glory of the Lord shone round about them; and they were sore afraid.

10 And the angel said unto them, Fear not: for, behold, I bring you good tidings of great joy, which shall be to all people.

11 For unto you is born this day in the city of David a Saviour, which is Christ the Lord.

12 And this *shall be* a sign unto you; Ye shall find the babe wrapped in swaddling clothes, lying in a manger.

13 And suddenly there was with the angel a multitude of the heavenly host praising God, and saying,

---

...unto you is born this day in the city of David a Savior, which is Christ the Lord.

---

14 Glory to God in the highest, and on earth peace, good will toward men.

15 And it came to pass, as the angels were gone away from them into heaven, the shepherds said one to another, Let us now go even unto Bethlehem, and see this thing which is come to pass, which the Lord hath made known unto us.

16 And they came with haste, and found Mary and Joseph, and the babe lying in a manger.

17 And when they had seen *it*, they made known abroad the saying which was told them concerning this child.

18 And all they that heard *it* wondered at those things which were told them by the shepherds.

19 But Mary kept all these things, and pondered *them* in her heart.

20 And the shepherds returned, glorifying and praising God for all the things that they had heard and seen, as it was told unto them.

The Dedication of Jesus

Luke 2:21-39

At the end of eight days, the child was circumcised and given the name Jesus, which he was called by the angel before he was conceived in the womb. And when the time was fulfilled for their purification according to the law of Moses, they brought him to Jerusalem to present him to the Lord, as it is written in the law of the Lord,

Every male that opens the womb shall be called holy to the Lord

and to offer a sacrifice according to what is commanded in the law of the Lord,

a pair of turtledoves, or two young pigeons.

Now there was in Jerusalem a man named Simeon, and this man was righteous and devout, looking for the consolation of Israel, and the Holy Spirit was upon him. And it had been revealed to him by the Holy Spirit that he should not see death before he had seen the Lord's Messiah. And he came, led by the Spirit, into the temple. And when the parents brought in the child Jesus to do for him according to the custom of the law, he took him up in his arms and praised God, saying,

"Now, O Lord, you will let your servant depart in peace, according to your word; for my eyes have seen your salvation which you have prepared before the face of all peoples, a light to shine upon the Gentiles, and the glory of your people Israel."

21 And when eight days were accomplished for the circumcising of the child, his name was called JESUS, which was so named of the angel before he was conceived in the womb.

22 And when the days of her purification according to the law of Moses were accomplished, they brought him to Jerusalem, to present *him* to the Lord;

23 (As it is written in the law of the Lord, Every male that openeth the womb shall be called holy to the Lord;)

24 And to offer a sacrifice according to that which is said in the law of the Lord, A pair of turtledoves, or two young pigeons.

25 And, behold, there was a man in Jerusalem, whose name *was* Simeon; and the same man *was* just and devout, waiting for the consolation of Israel: and the Holy Ghost was upon him.

26 And it was revealed unto him by the Holy Ghost, that he should not see death, before he had seen the Lord's Christ.

27 And he came by the Spirit into the temple: and when the parents brought in the child Jesus, to do for him after the custom of the law,

28 Then took he him up in his arms, and blessed God, and said,

29 Lord, now lettest thou thy servant depart in peace, according to thy word:

30 For mine eyes have seen thy salvation,

31 Which thou hast prepared before the face of all people;

32 A light to lighten the Gentiles, and the glory of thy people Israel.

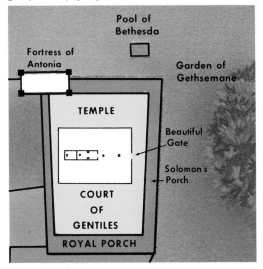

Jerusalem and Bethlehem are not far apart, only about 5 miles distant. The parents of Jesus made the short trip to have Him dedicated in the Temple.

And his father and mother marveled at the things said about him. And Simeon blessed them and said to Mary his mother,

"Behold, this child is set for the fall and rising of many in Israel, and for a sign that is spoken against (and a sword will pierce your soul, too!) that the thoughts and intentions of many hearts may be revealed."

And there was a prophetess named Anna, the daughter of Phanuel of the tribe of Asher. She was very old, having lived with a husband seven years from her maidenhood, and as a widow until she was eighty-four. She was continually in the temple, worshipping with fastings and prayers night and day. And coming up at that moment, she gave thanks to God, and spoke of the child to all who were looking for the redemption of Jerusalem.

And when Joseph and Mary had performed all things according to the law of the Lord, they returned [to Bethlehem].

LUKE 2:21-38

33 And Joseph and his mother marveled at those things which were spoken of him.

34 And Simeon blessed them, and said unto Mary his mother, Behold, this *child* is set for the fall and rising again of many in Israel; and for a sign which shall be spoken against;

35 (Yea, a sword shall pierce through thy own soul also;) that the thoughts of many hearts may be revealed.

36 And there was one Anna, a prophetess, the daughter of Phanuel, of the tribe of Asher: she was of a great age, and had lived with a husband seven years from her virginity;

37 And she *was* a widow of about fourscore and four years, which departed not from the temple, but served *God* with fastings and prayers night and day.

38 And she coming in that instant gave thanks likewise unto the Lord, and spake of him to all them that looked for redemption in Jerusalem.

Simeon Prophesies about Jesus. *When Joseph and Mary brought Jesus to the temple to be dedicated, a godly man, Simeon, led by the Holy Spirit, met them. Taking the infant in his arms he praised God and foretold the child's future ministry.*

The Coming of the Wise Men

Matthew 2:1-12

Now after Jesus was born in Bethlehem of Judea in the days of Herod the king, behold, there came wise men from the East to Jerusalem, saying, "Where is he who has been born king of the Jews? We have seen his star in the East and have come to worship him."

Now when Herod the king heard this, he was troubled, and all Jerusalem with him. And having called together all the chief priests and scribes among the people, he inquired of them where the Messiah was to be born.

"In Bethlehem of Judea," they replied, "for thus it is written by the prophet, 'And you, Bethlehem, in the land of Judah, are in no wise least among the principalities of Judah, for out of you shall come forth a ruler who will be a shepherd to my people Israel.' "

Then Herod summoned the wise men privately and learned from them what time the star appeared. And he sent them to Bethlehem, saying, "Go and search carefully for the young child; and when you have found him, bring me word, that I, too, may come and worship him."

And when they had heard the king, they went their way. And lo! the star which they had seen in the East went before them until it came and stood over the place where the young child was. When they saw the star, they rejoiced with great joy. And they entered the house and saw the young child with Mary his mother, and fell down and worshipped him. And they opened their treasures and presented gifts to him of gold, frankincense, and myrrh. And being warned of God in a dream not to return to Herod, they returned to their own country by another way.

MATTHEW 2:1-12

1 Now when Jesus was born in Bethlehem of Judea in the days of Herod the king, behold, there came wise men from the east to Jerusalem,

2 Saying, Where is he that is born King of the Jews? for we have seen his star in the east, and are come to worship him.

3 When Herod the King had heard *these things,* he was troubled, and all Jerusalem with him.

4 And when he had gathered all the chief priests and scribes of the people together, he demanded of them where Christ should be born.

5 And they said unto him, In Bethlehem of Judea: for thus it is written by the prophet,

6 And thou Bethlehem, *in* the land of Judah, art not the least among the princes of Judah: for out of thee shall come a Governor, that shall rule my people Israel.

7 Then Herod, when he had privily called the wise men, inquired of them diligently what time the star appeared.

8 And he sent them to Bethlehem, and said, Go and search diligently for the young child; and when ye have found *him,* bring me word again, that I may come and worship him also.

> *When they saw the star, they rejoiced with exceeding great joy.*

9 When they had heard the king, they departed; and, lo, the star, which they saw in the east, went before them, till it came and stood over where the young child was.

10 When they saw the star, they rejoiced with exceeding great joy.

11 And when they were come into the house, they saw the young child with Mary his mother, and fell down, and worshipped him: and when they had opened their treasures, they presented unto him gifts; gold, and frankincense, and myrrh.

12 And being warned of God in a dream that they should not return to Herod, they departed into their own country another way.

Bell Tower at Bethlehem. *Joy was the dominant emotion at the birth of Jesus, and the ringing of the bells reminds us over and over of that wonderful event.*

65

Traveling to Egypt

Matthew 2:13-15

Now when the wise men had departed, behold, an angel of the Lord appeared to Joseph in a dream, saying, "Rise, take the young child and his mother and flee to Egypt and remain there until I tell you; for Herod will search for the child to destroy him."

And Joseph rose and took the young child and his mother by night and departed to Egypt, and remained there until the death of Herod, in fulfillment of the word spoken by the Lord through the prophet,

Out of Egypt have I called my son.

MATTHEW 2:13-15

13 And when they were departed, behold, the angel of the Lord appeareth to Joseph in a dream, saying, Arise, and take the young child and his mother, and flee into Egypt, and be thou there until I bring thee word: for Herod will seek the young child to destroy him.

14 When he arose, he took the young child and his mother by night, and departed into Egypt:

15 And was there until the death of Herod: that it might be fulfilled which was spoken of the Lord by the prophet, saying, Out of Egypt have I called my son.

The Great Pyramid. *The symbol of Egypt, where Joseph, Mary and Jesus fled from the murderous plans of Herod. One of the "Seven Wonders" of the ancient world, it is 450 feet high, covers 13 acres at its base.*

Murder of Bethlehem Babies

Matthew 2:16-18

Then Herod, when he saw that he had been disregarded by the wise men, was furious. And he sent and killed all the little boys in Bethlehem and the surrounding countryside who were two years old or under, according to the time which he had determined from the wise men. Then was fulfilled the word spoken by the prophet Jeremiah,

A voice was heard in Ramah,
wailing and great lamentation—
Rachel weeping for her children;
she refused to be comforted,
because they were no more.

MATTHEW 2:16-18

16 Then Herod, when he saw that he was mocked of the wise men, was exceeding wroth, and sent forth, and slew all the children that were in Bethlehem, and in all the coasts thereof, from two years old and under, according to the time which he had diligently inquired of the wise men.

17 Then was fulfilled that which was spoken by Jeremy the prophet, saying,

18 In Ramah was there a voice heard, lamentation, and weeping, and great mourning, Rachel weeping *for* her children, and would not be comforted, because they are not.

The Family Settles in Nazareth

Matthew 2:19-23, Luke 2:40

And when Herod was dead, behold, and angel of the Lord appeared in a dream to Joseph in Egypt, saying, "Rise, and take the young child and his mother and go into the land of Israel, for they who sought the child's life are dead."

Then Joseph rose and took the young child and his mother, and went into the land of Israel. But when he heard that Archelaus reigned in Judea in the place of his father Herod, he was afraid to go there; and being warned of God in a dream, he turned aside into Galilee. And he came and dwelt in a city called Nazareth, that the word of the prophets might be fulfilled,

He shall be called a Nazarene.

And the child grew and became strong and full of wisdom, and the favor of God was upon him.

MATTHEW 2:19-23

19 But when Herod was dead, behold, an angel of the Lord appeareth in a dream to Joseph in Egypt,

20 Saying, Arise, and take the young child and his mother, and go into the land of Israel: for they are dead which sought the young child's life.

21 And he arose, and took the young child and his mother, and came into the land of Israel.

22 But when he heard that Archelaus did reign in Judea in the room of his father Herod, he was afraid to go thither: notwithstanding, being warned of God in a dream, he turned aside into the parts of Galilee:

23 And he came and dwelt in a city called Nazareth: that it might be fulfilled which was spoken by the prophets, He shall be called a Nazarene.

LUKE 2:39-40

39 And when they had performed all things according to the law of the Lord, they returned into Galilee, to their own city Nazareth.

40 And the child grew, and waxed strong in spirit, filled with wisdom; and the grace of God was upon him.

Jesus' Boyhood Visit to Jerusalem

Luke 2:41-52

Now his parents went to Jerusalem every year at the Feast of the Passover. And when he was twelve years old, they went up at the time of the feast, according to custom. And after the days of the feast were ended, when they started home, the boy Jesus remained behind in Jerusalem. Now his parents did not know it, and supposing him to be in the caravan, they traveled a day's journey, all the while seeking him among their kinsfolk and acquaintances. And when they did not find him, they returned to Jerusalem, anxiously searching for him.

After three days, they found him in the temple sitting among the teachers, listening to them and asking them questions. And all who heard him were amazed at his understanding and his answers. When Joseph and Mary saw him, they were astonished, and his mother said,

"Child, why have you treated us so? Behold, your father and I have been searching for you in sorrow and anguish."

"Why did you need to search for me?" replied Jesus. "Did you not know that I must be in my Father's house?" But they did not understand the meaning of what he said.

And he went with them back to Nazareth and was obedient to them, and his mother treasured all these things in her heart. And Jesus increased in wisdom and stature, and in the favor of God and men.

41 Now his parents went to Jerusalem every year at the feast of the passover.

42 And when he was twelve years old, they went up to Jerusalem after the custom of the feast.

43 And when they had fulfilled the days, as they returned, the child Jesus tarried behind in Jerusalem; and Joseph and his mother knew not *of it.*

44 But they, supposing him to have been in the company, went a day's journey; and they sought him among *their* kinsfolk and acquaintance.

45 And when they found him not, they turned back again to Jerusalem, seeking him.

46 And it came to pass, that after three days they found him in the temple, sitting in the midst of the doctors, both hearing them, and asking them questions.

47 And all that heard him were astonished at his understanding and answers.

48 And when they saw him, they were amazed: and his mother said unto him, Son, why hast thou thus dealt with us? behold, thy father and I have sought thee sorrowing.

49 And he said unto them, How is it that ye sought me? wist ye not that I must be about my Father's business?

50 And they understood not the saying which he spake unto them.

51 And he went down with them, and came to Nazareth, and was subject unto them: but his mother kept all these sayings in her heart.

52 And Jesus increased in wisdom and stature, and in favor with God and man.

A 12-year-old boy would enjoy the hilly hike to and from Jerusalem.

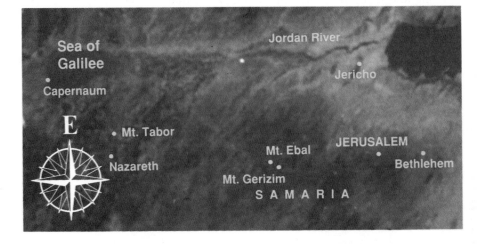

Herod's Temple. *Part of a model of first-century Jerusalem, located in West Jerusalem. Erected on a scale of 1 to 50. Provides an idea of how beautiful the Temple was in Jesus' time on earth.*

John the Baptist's Ministry

Luke 3:1-6, Matthew 3:4-10, Luke 3: 10-18

In the fifteenth year of the reign of Tiberius Caesar, when Pontius Pilate was governor of Judea, and Herod was tetrarch of Galilee and his brother Philip tetrarch of Iturea and Trachonitis, and Lysanias tetrarch of Abilene; in the time when Annas and Caiaphas were High Priests, the word of God came to John, the son of Zacharias, in the wilderness. And he went through all the valley of the Jordan, preaching a baptism of repentance for the forgiveness of sins, as it is written in the book of the prophet Isaiah,

The voice of one crying in the wilderness:
Prepare the way of the Lord,
make his paths straight.
Every valley shall be filled,
and every mountain and hill shall be brought
    low;
the crooked shall be made straight,
and the rough ways shall be made smooth;
and all flesh shall see the salvation of God.

John wore a garment of camel's hair with a leather girdle about his waist, and his food was locusts and wild honey. Multitudes from Jerusalem and all Judea and all the region of the Jordan went out to him and were baptized by John in the river Jordan, confessing their sins.

But when John saw many of the Pharisees and Sadducees coming for baptism, he said to them,

"You brood of snakes, who warned you to flee from the wrath to come? Show by your actions that you are really repenting, and do not think to excuse yourselves by telling yourselves, 'We have Abraham as our father!' For I say to you,

God is able from these stones to raise up children to Abraham. Even now the axe is laid to the root of the trees; every tree which does not bring forth good fruit will be cut down and thrown into the fire."

"Then what shall we do?" asked the multitudes.

"He who has two coats, let him give one to him who has none," replied John, "and he who has food, let him likewise share."

Some tax collectors also came to be baptized, and they asked him, "Master, what shall we do?"

"Collect no more than the amount appointed you," said John.

Some soldiers also asked him, "And what about us, what shall we do?"

"Do not extort money from people by violence or bring false charges against men, and be satisfied with your wages," said John.

Now as all the people were in expectation and wondering about John, whether he might possibly be the Messiah, John answered them, saying,

"I baptize you with water; but one mightier than I is coming, the strap of whose sandals I am not worthy to unfasten. He will baptize you with the Holy Spirit and with fire. His winnowing fork is in his hand, and he will thoroughly clean his threshing floor. He will gather the wheat into his barn, but the chaff he will burn with unquenchable fire."

And with many other exhortations, John preached the gospel to the people.

MATTHEW 3:1-12	MARK 1:1-8	LUKE 3:1-18
1 In those days came John the Baptist, preaching in the wilderness of Judea, 2 And saying, Repent ye: for the kingdom of heaven is at hand. 3 For this is he that was spoken of by the prophet Isaiah, saying, The voice of one crying in the wilderness,	1 The beginning of the gospel of Jesus Christ, the Son of God. 2 As it is written in the prophets, Behold, I send my messenger before thy face, which shall prepare thy way before thee. 3 The voice of one crying in the wilderness, Prepare	1 Now in the fifteenth year of the reign of Tiberius Caesar, Pontius Pilate being governor of Judea, and Herod being tetrarch of Galilee, and his brother Philip tetrarch of Ituraea and of the region of Trachonitis, and Lysanias the tetrarch of Abilene, 2 Annas and Caiaphas being the high priests, the word of God came unto John the son of Zechariah in the wilderness. 3 And he came into all the country about

John the Baptist's Ministry (continued)

Prepare ye the way of the Lord, make his paths straight.

4 And the same John had his raiment of camel's hair, and a leathern girdle about his loins; and his meat was locusts and wild honey.

5 Then went out to him Jerusalem, and all Judea, and all the region round about Jordan,

6 And were baptized of him in Jordan, confessing their sins.

7 But when he saw many of the Pharisees and Sadducees come to his baptism, he said unto them, O generation of vipers, who hath warned you to flee from the wrath to come?

8 Bring forth therefore fruits meet for repentance:

9 And think not to say within yourselves, We have Abraham to *our* father: for I say unto you, that God is able of these stones to raise up children unto Abraham.

10 And now also the axe is laid unto the root of the trees: therefore every tree which bringeth not forth good fruit is hewn down, and cast into the fire.

11 I indeed baptize you with water unto repentance: but he that cometh after me is mightier than I, whose shoes I am not worthy to bear: he shall baptize you with the Holy Ghost, and *with* fire:

12 Whose fan *is* in his hand, and he will thoroughly purge his floor, and gather his wheat into the garner; but he will burn up the chaff with unquenchable fire.

ye the way of the Lord, make his paths straight.

4 John did baptize in the wilderness, and preach the baptism of repentance for the remission of sins.

5 And there went out unto him all the land of Judea, and they of Jerusalem, and were all baptized of him in the river of Jordan, confessing their sins.

The voice of one crying in the wilderness, Prepare ye the way of the Lord, make his paths straight.

6 And John was clothed with camel's hair, and with a girdle of a skin about his loins; and he did eat locusts and wild honey;

7 And preached, saying, There cometh one mightier than I after me, the latchet of whose shoes I am not worthy to stoop down and unloose.

8 I indeed have baptized you with water: but he shall baptize you with the Holy Ghost.

Jordan, preaching the baptism of repentance for the remission of sins;

4 As it is written in the book of the words of Isaiah the prophet, saying, The voice of one crying in the wilderness, Prepare ye the way of the Lord, make his paths straight.

5 Every valley shall be filled, and every mountain and hill shall be brought low; and the crooked shall be made straight, and the rough ways *shall be* made smooth;

6 And all flesh shall see the salvation of God.

7 Then said he to the multitude that came forth to be baptized of him, O generation of vipers, who hath warned you to flee from the wrath to come?

8 Bring forth therefore fruits worthy of repentance, and begin not to say within yourselves, We have Abraham to *our* father: for I say unto you, That God is able of these stones to raise up children unto Abraham.

9 And now also the axe is laid unto the root of the trees: every tree therefore which bringeth not forth good fruit is hewn down, and cast into the fire.

10 And the people asked him, saying, What shall we do then?

11 He answereth and saith unto them, He that hath two coats, let him impart to him that hath none; and he that hath meat, let him do likewise.

12 Then came also publicans to be baptized, and said unto him, Master, what shall we do?

13 And he said unto them, Exact no more than that which is appointed you.

14 And the soldiers likewise demanded of him, saying, And what shall we do? And he said unto them, Do violence to no man, neither accuse *any* falsely; and be content with your wages.

15 And as the people were in expectation, and all men mused in their hearts of John, whether he were the Christ, or not;

16 John answered, saying unto *them* all, I indeed baptize you with water; but one mightier than I cometh, the latchet of whose shoes I am not worthy to unloose: he shall baptize you with the Holy Ghost and with fire:

17 Whose fan *is* in his hand, and he will thoroughly purge his floor, and will gather the wheat into his garner; but the chaff he will burn with fire unquenchable.

18 And many other things in his exhortation preached he unto the people.

The Baptism of Jesus

Matthew 3:13-17, Luke 3:23a

Then Jesus came from Galilee to the Jordan, to John, to be baptized by him. But John protested, saying, "I need to be baptized by you, and do you come to me?"

But Jesus answered, "Let it be so now, for it is right for us to fulfill all the obligations of righteousness."

Then John consented. And after he had been baptized, Jesus immediately went up from the water; and behold, the heavens were opened, and he saw the Spirit of God descending like a dove and alighting on him. And lo, a voice out of the heavens said, "This is my beloved Son, in whom I am well pleased."

And Jesus, when he began his ministry, was about thirty years of age.

MATTHEW 3:13-17

13 Then cometh Jesus from Galilee to Jordan unto John, to be baptized of him.

14 But John forbade him, saying, I have need to be baptized of thee, and comest thou to me?

15 And Jesus answering said unto him, Suffer *it to be so* now: for thus it becometh us to fulfil all righteousness. Then he suffered him.

16 And Jesus, when he was baptized, went up straightway out of the water: and, lo, the heavens were opened unto him, and he saw the Spirit of God descending like a dove, and lighting upon him:

17 And lo a voice from heaven, saying, This is my beloved Son, in whom I am well pleased.

MARK 1:9-11

9 And it came to pass in those days, that Jesus came from Nazareth of Galilee, and was baptized of John in Jordan.

10 And straightway coming up out of the water, he saw the heavens opened, and the Spirit like a dove descending upon him:

11 And there came a voice from heaven, *saying,* Thou art my beloved Son, in whom I am well pleased.

LUKE 3:21-22

21 Now when all the people were baptized, it came to pass, that Jesus also being baptized, and praying, the heaven was opened,

22 And the Holy Ghost descended in a bodily shape like a dove upon him, and a voice came from heaven, which said, Thou art my beloved Son; in thee I am well pleased.

Jordan River. The traditional site of Jesus' baptism is located 6 to 8 miles east of Jericho. It was here also that Israel crossed into the Promised Land under the leadership of Joshua.

The Temptation of Jesus

Matthew 4:1-11

Then Jesus was led by the Spirit into the wilderness to be tempted by the devil. And he fasted forty days and nights, and afterward was hungry. Then the tempter came and said to him, "If you really are the Son of God, command these stones to become bread."

But Jesus answered, "It is written, 'Man shall not live by bread alone, but by every word that goes forth out of the mouth of God.'"

Then the devil took him to the holy city and set him on a pinnacle of the temple and said to him, "If you are actually the Son of God, throw yourself down; for it is written, 'He will give his angels charge over you; they will bear you up on their hands, lest you strike your foot against a stone.'"

"But it is also written, 'You shall not tempt the Lord your God,'" replied Jesus.

Again, the devil took him up on a very high mountain and showed him all the kingdoms of the world and their glory and said, "All these things will I give you, if you will fall down and worship me."

Then said Jesus, "Begone, Satan! For it is written, 'You shall worship the Lord your God, and him only shall you serve.'"

Then the devil left him, and behold, angels came and ministered to him.

MATTHEW 4:1-11

1 Then was Jesus led up of the Spirit into the wilderness to be tempted of the devil.

2 And when he had fasted forty days and forty nights, he was afterward ahungered.

3 And when the tempter came to him, he said, If thou be the Son of God, command that these stones be made bread.

4 But he answered and said, It is written, Man shall not live by bread alone, but by every word that proceedeth out of the mouth of God.

MARK 1:12-13

12 And immediately the Spirit driveth him into the wilderness.

13 And he was there in the wilderness forty days tempted of Satan; and was with the wild beasts; and the angels ministered unto him.

LUKE 4:1-13

1 And Jesus being full of the Holy Ghost returned from Jordan, and was led by the Spirit into the wilderness,

2 Being forty days tempted of the devil. And in those days he did eat nothing: and when they were ended, he afterward hungered.

3 And the devil said unto him, If thou be the Son of God, command this stone that it be made bread.

4 And Jesus answered him, saying, It is written, That man shall not live by bread alone, but by every word of God.

Judean Wilderness.

This is a forbidding region, lying between the hilly central part of the country and the Jordan Valley. It is unusual to see it covered with grass like this. It was in this desolate area that Jesus was tempted for 40 days.

The Temptation of Jesus (continued)

Mount of Temptation.
From the archaeological
"dig" at ancient Jericho one
can view the mountain
where Jesus was tempted to
bow down and worship
Satan.

MATTHEW 4:1-11

5 Then the devil taketh him up into the holy city, and setteth him on a pinnacle of the temple,

6 And saith unto him, If thou be the Son of God, cast thyself down: for it is written, He shall give his angels charge concerning thee: and in *their* hands they shall bear thee up, lest at any time thou dash thy foot against a stone.

7 Jesus said unto him, It is written again, Thou shalt not tempt the Lord thy God.

8 Again, the devil taketh him up into an exceeding high mountain, and showeth him all the kingdoms of the world, and the glory of them;

9 And saith unto him, All these things will I give thee, if thou wilt fall down and worship me.

10 Then saith Jesus unto him, Get thee hence, Satan: for it is written, Thou shalt worship the Lord thy God, and him only shalt thou serve.

11 Then the devil leaveth him, and, behold, angels came and ministered unto him.

MARK 1:12-13

LUKE 4:1-13

5 And the devil, taking him up into a high mountain, showed unto him all the kingdoms of the world in a moment of time.

6 And the devil said unto him, All this power will I give thee, and the glory of them: for that is delivered unto me; and to whomsoever I will, I give it.

7 If thou therefore wilt worship me, all shall be thine.

8 And Jesus answered and said unto him, Get thee behind me, Satan: for it is written, Thou shalt worship the Lord thy God, and him only shalt thou serve.

9 And he brought him to Jerusalem, and set him on a pinnacle of the temple, and said unto him, If thou be the Son of God, cast thyself down from hence:

10 For it is written, He shall give his angels charge over thee, to keep thee:

11 And in *their* hands they shall bear thee up, lest at any time thou dash thy foot against a stone.

12 And Jesus answering said unto him, It is said, Thou shalt not tempt the Lord thy God.

13 And when the devil had ended all the temptation, he departed from him for a season.

Jesus' Deity Declared

John 1:19-34

Now this was the testimony of John when the Jews sent priests and Levites from Jerusalem to ask him, "Who are you?" He frankly acknowledged, "I am not the Messiah."

"Then are you Elijah?" they asked.

"I am not," said John.

"Are you the Prophet?"

"No," replied John.

"Then who are you?" they asked. "We must give an answer to those who sent us. What do you say about yourself?"

John answered, "I am a voice crying in the wilderness, 'Make straight the way of the Lord,' as the prophet Isaiah said."

Then the messengers, who were Pharisees, asked, "Why then are you baptizing, if you are not the Messiah, nor Elijah, nor the Prophet?"

"I baptize with water," replied John, "but among you stands one whom you do not know—the one who follows me, the strap of whose sandal I am not worthy to unfasten."

These things took place at Bethany beyond the Jordan, where John was baptizing.

The next day John saw Jesus coming toward him and said, "Behold, the Lamb of God who will bear away the sin of the world! This is he of whom I said, 'After me will come a man who is greater than I, for he was before me.' And I did not know him; but in order that he might be revealed to Israel, I have come baptizing with water."

And John also bore witness, saying, "I saw the Spirit descend as a dove out of heaven, and it rested on him and remained. And I did not know him; but he who sent me to baptize with water told me, 'On whom you see the Spirit descend and remain, he it is who baptizes with the Holy Spirit.' And I have seen and have borne witness that this is the Son of God."

19 And this is the record of John, when the Jews sent priests and Levites from Jerusalem to ask him, Who art thou?

20 And he confessed, and denied not; but confessed, I am not the Christ.

21 And they asked him, What then? Art thou Elijah? And he saith, I am not. Art thou that Prophet? And he answered, No.

22 Then said they unto him, Who art thou? that we may give an answer to them that sent us. What sayest thou of thyself?

23 He said, I *am* the voice of one crying in the wilderness, Make straight the way of the Lord, as said the prophet Isaiah.

24 And they which were sent were of the Pharisees.

25 And they asked him, and said unto him, Why baptizest thou then, if thou be not that Christ, nor Elijah, neither that Prophet?

26 John answered them, saying, I baptize with water: but there standeth one among you, whom ye know not;

27 He it is, who coming after me is preferred before me, whose shoe-latchet I am not worthy to unloose.

28 These things were done in Bethabara beyond Jordan, where John was baptizing.

29 The next day John seeth Jesus coming unto him, and saith, Behold the Lamb of God, which taketh away the sin of the world!

30 This is he of whom I said, After me cometh a man which is preferred before me; for he was before me.

31 And I knew him not: but that he should be made manifest to Israel, therefore am I come baptizing with water.

32 And John bare record, saying, I saw the Spirit descending from heaven like a dove, and it abode upon him.

33 And I knew him not: but he that sent me to baptize with water, the same said unto me, Upon whom thou shalt see the Spirit descending, and remaining on him, the same is he which baptizeth with the Holy Ghost.

34 And I saw, and bare record that this is the Son of God.

First Disciples of Jesus

John 1:35-51

Again the next day, John was standing with two of his disciples. And seeing Jesus pass by, he exclaimed, ''Behold, the Lamb of God!'' And the two disciples heard him, and followed Jesus.

Then Jesus turned and, seeing them following him, said, ''What do you want?''

''Rabbi,'' they said (which means Teacher), ''where are you staying?''

''Come, and you shall see,'' said Jesus.

They came and saw where he was staying, and remained with him that day, for it was about the tenth hour. One of the two who heard John's exclamation and followed Jesus was Andrew, Simon Peter's brother. He first found his brother Simon and said, ''We have found the Messiah!'' (which means Christ). And he brought him to Jesus.

Jesus looked at him intently and said, ''You are Simon, the son of John. You shall be called Cephas'' (which means Peter).

The next day Jesus determined to go into Galilee, and he found Philip and said to him, ''Follow me.'' Now Philip was from Bethsaida, the city of Andrew and Peter. Philip found Nathanael and said, ''We have found him of whom Moses wrote in the law and of whom the prophets wrote—Jesus of Nazareth, the son of Joseph.''

''Can anything good come out of Nazareth?'' replied Nathanael.

''Come and see!'' said Philip.

When he saw Nathanael coming to him, Jesus said, ''Behold, a true son of Israel, in whom is no guile!''

''How can you know anything about me?'' asked Nathanael.

''Before Philip called you, when you were under the fig tree, I saw you,'' answered Jesus.

''Rabbi,'' exclaimed Nathanael, ''you are the Son of God! You are the King of Israel!''

''Do you believe in me because I said, 'I saw you under the fig tree'? You will see greater things than that,'' said Jesus. ''I tell you truly, you will all see heaven opened, and the angels of God ascending and descending upon the Son of Man.''

JOHN 1:35-51

35 Again the next day after, John stood, and two of his disciples;

36 And looking upon Jesus as he walked, he saith, Behold the Lamb of God!

37 And the two disciples heard him speak, and they followed Jesus.

38 Then Jesus turned, and saw them following, and saith unto them, What seek ye? They said unto him, Rabbi, (which is to say, being interpreted, Master,) where dwellest thou?

39 He saith unto them, Come and see. They came and saw where he dwelt, and abode with him that day: for it was about the tenth hour.

40 One of the two which heard John *speak,* and followed him, was Andrew, Simon Peter's brother.

41 He first findeth his own brother Simon, and saith unto him, We have found the Messias, which is, being interpreted, the Christ.

42 And he brought him to Jesus. And when Jesus beheld him, he said, Thou art Simon the son of Jona: thou shalt be called Cephas, which is by interpretation, A stone.

43 The day following Jesus would go forth into Galilee, and findeth Philip, and saith unto him, Follow me.

44 Now Philip was of Bethsaida, the city of Andrew and Peter.

45 Philip findeth Nathanael, and saith unto him, We have found him, of whom Moses in the law, and the prophets, did write, Jesus of Nazareth, the son of Joseph.

46 And Nathanael said unto him, Can there any good thing come out of Nazareth? Philip saith unto him, Come and see.

47 Jesus saw Nathanael coming to him, and saith of him, Behold an Israelite indeed, in whom is no guile!

48 Nathanael saith unto him, Whence knowest thou me? Jesus answered and said unto him, Before that Philip called thee, when thou wast under the fig tree, I saw thee.

49 Nathanael answered and saith unto him, Rabbi, thou art the Son of God; thou art the King of Israel.

50 Jesus answered and said unto him, Because I said unto thee, I saw thee under the fig tree, believest thou? thou shalt see greater things than these.

51 And he saith unto him, Verily, verily, I say unto you, Hereafter ye shall see heaven open, and the angels of God ascending and descending upon the Son of man.

Jesus' First Miracle

John 2:1-12

. Now on the third day there was a marriage at Cana in Galilee, and Jesus' mother was there. Jesus was invited to the marriage, too, and his disciples. And when the supply of wine failed, Jesus' mother said to him, "They have no wine."

"Woman, what have you to do with me?" said Jesus. "My hour has not yet come."

His mother said to the servants, "Do whatever he tells you."

Now there were six stone jars standing there, for use in the purification rites of the Jews, each holding twenty or thirty gallons.

"Fill the jars with water," said Jesus, and they filled them to the brim. "Now draw some out," said Jesus, "and take it to the master of the feast."

Now when the master of the feast tasted the water which now had become wine, not knowing where it came from (though the servants who had drawn the water knew) he called the bridegroom and said to him, "Every man serves the good wine first, and the poorer wine after men have drunk generously, but you have kept the good wine till now."

This, the beginning of his miracles, Jesus performed at Cana in Galilee, and manifested his glory; and his disciples believed in him. After this, he went down to Capernaum with his mother and brothers and his disciples, and they remained there only a few days.

1 And the third day there was a marriage in Cana of Galilee; and the mother of Jesus was there:

2 And both Jesus was called, and his disciples, to the marriage.

3 And when they wanted wine, the mother of Jesus saith unto him, They have no wine.

4 Jesus saith unto her, Woman, what have I to do with thee? mine hour is not yet come.

5 His mother saith unto the servants, Whatsoever he saith unto you, do *it.*

6 And there were set there six waterpots of stone, after the manner of the purifying of the Jews, containing two or three firkins apiece.

7 Jesus saith unto them, Fill the waterpots with water. And they filled them up to the brim.

8 And he saith unto them, Draw out now, and bear unto the governor of the feast. And they bare *it.*

9 When the ruler of the feast had tasted the water that was made wine, and knew not whence it was, (but the servants which drew the water knew,) the governor of the feast called the bridegroom,

10 And saith unto him, Every man at the beginning doth set forth good wine; and when men have well drunk, then that which is worse: *but* thou hast kept the good wine until now.

11 This beginning of miracles did Jesus in Cana of Galilee, and manifested forth his glory; and his disciples believed on him.

12 After this he went down to Capernaum, he, and his mother, and his brethren, and his disciples; and they continued there not many days.

Water Jug. *Scholars say the jars Jesus used in performing His first miracle were about this size. What a spectacular way to begin His public ministry. John says it awakened the faith of His disciples.*

Jesus' First Miracle. *Jesus began His miracle ministry at a wedding in Cana, about 10 miles from Nazareth, by turning water into wine. He must have been acquainted with the bride and the groom.*

78

Jesus Cleanses the Temple

John 2:13-25

Now the Passover of the Jews was at hand, and Jesus went up to Jerusalem. And he found in the temple those who were selling oxen and sheep and doves, and the money-changers sitting at their tables. And having made a whip of cords, he drove them all out of the temple, both the sheep and the oxen; and he poured out the money-changers' coins and overturned their tables. And to those who sold doves he said, "Take these things out of here! Do not make my Father's house a market place!"

And his disciples remembered that it was written,

Zeal for your house will consume me.

Then the Jews demanded of Jesus, "What sign can you show us for your authority to do these things?"

"Destroy this temple, and in three days I will raise it up," answered Jesus.

Then said the Jews, "This temple took forty-six years to build, and will you indeed rebuild it in three days?"

But Jesus was speaking of the temple of his body. When therefore he was raised from the dead, his disciples remembered that he had said this, and believed the scripture and the word which Jesus had spoken.

Now while he was in Jerusalem during the Feast of the Passover, many believed in his name when they saw the miracles he was performing. But Jesus did not commit himself to them, because he knew what they were like. He had no need for anyone to tell him what any man was like, for he always knew what was in a man.

13 And the Jews' passover was at hand, and Jesus went up to Jerusalem,

14 And found in the temple those that sold oxen and sheep and doves, and the changers of money sitting:

15 And when he had made a scourge of small cords, he drove them all out of the temple, and the sheep, and the oxen; and poured out the changers money, and overthrew the tables;

16 And said unto them that sold doves, Take these things hence; make not my Father's house a house of merchandise.

17 And his disciples remembered that it was written, The zeal of thine house hath eaten me up.

...when he was in Jerusalem at the passover, in the feast day, many believed in his name, when they saw the miracles which he did.

---

18 Then answered the Jews and said unto him, What sign showest thou unto us, seeing that thou doest these things?

19 Jesus answered and said unto them, Destroy this temple, and in three days I will raise it up.

20 Then said the Jews, Forty and six years was this temple in building, and wilt thou rear it up in three days?

21 But he spake of the temple of his body.

22 When therefore he was risen from the dead, his disciples remembered that he had said this unto them; and they believed the Scripture, and the word which Jesus had said.

23 Now when he was in Jerusalem at the passover, in the feast *day*, many believed in his name, when they saw the miracles which he did.

24 But Jesus did not commit himself unto them, because he knew all *men*,

25 And needed not that any should testify of man; for he knew what was in man.

Jesus Talks with Nicodemus

John 3:1-21

There was a man of the Pharisees named Nicodemus, a ruler of the Jews, who came to Jesus by night and said, "Rabbi, we know that you are a teacher who has come from God, for no man can do these miracles that you are doing unless God is with him."

"I tell you truly," replied Jesus, "unless a man is born anew, he cannot see the kingdom of God."

"How can a man be born when he is old?" asked Nicodemus. "Can he enter a second time into his mother's womb and be born?"

"I tell you truly," replied Jesus, "unless a man is born of water and the Spirit, he cannot enter the kingdom of God. That which is born of the flesh is flesh, and that which is born of the Spirit is spirit. Do not marvel that I said to you, 'You must be born anew.' The wind blows where it wills, and you hear the sound of it, but you do not know where it comes from, or where it goes. So it is with everyone who is born of the Spirit."

JOHN 3:1-21

1 There was a man of the Pharisees, named Nicodemus, a ruler of the Jews:

2 The same came to Jesus by night, and said unto him, Rabbi, we know that thou art a teacher come from God: for no man can do these miracles that thou doest, except God be with him.

3 Jesus answered and said unto him, Verily, verily, I say unto thee, Except a man be born again, he cannot see the kingdom of God.

4 Nicodemus saith unto him, How can a man be born when he is old? can he enter the second time into his mother's womb, and be born?

5 Jesus answered, Verily, verily, I say unto thee, Except a man be born of water and *of* the Spirit, he cannot enter into the kingdom of God.

6 That which is born of the flesh is flesh; and that which is born of the Spirit is spirit.

7 Marvel not that I said unto thee, ye must be born again.

8 The wind bloweth where it listeth, and thou hearest the sound thereof, but canst not tell whence it cometh, and whither it goeth: so is every one that is born of the Spirit.

Jerusalem at Night.
Even at night this renowned city affords a spectacular view. Nicodemus came to the Master by night, perhaps to insure having privacy as he bared his heart to Jesus.

Jesus Talks with Nicodemus (continued)

"How can these things be?" asked Nicodemus.

"Do you presume to be a teacher of Israel," replied Jesus, " and yet do not understand this? I tell you truly, we are speaking of something we know and testifying of something we have seen; but you do not accept our testimony. If I have told you of earthly things and you do not believe, how will you believe if I tell you of heavenly things? No one has ascended into heaven but he who came down from heaven, the Son of Man. And as Moses lifted up the serpent in the wilderness, even so must the Son of Man be lifted up, that whoever believes in him may not perish, but have eternal life.

"For God so loved the world that he gave his only begotten Son, that whoever believes in him should not perish, but have eternal life. For God did not send his Son into the world to condemn it, but that the world through him might be saved. He who believes in him is not condemned but he who does not believe stands condemned, because he has not put his trust in the name of the only begotten Son of God. And this is why men stand condemned: the light has come into the world, but men loved darkness rather than light, because their deeds were evil. For everyone who practices evil hates the light and refuses to come to it, lest his deeds should be exposed, but he who seeks to live the truth comes to the light, that it may be shown that his deeds have been done in the fear of God."

JOHN 3:1-21

9 Nicodemus answered and said unto him, How can these things be?

10 Jesus answered and said unto him, Art thou a master of Israel, and knowest not these things?

11 Verily, verily, I say unto thee, We speak that we do know, and testify that we have seen; and ye receive not our witness.

12 If I have told you earthly things, and ye believe not, how shall ye believe, if I tell you *of* heavenly things?

13 And no man hath ascended up to heaven, but he that came down from heaven, *even* the Son of man which is in heaven.

14 And as Moses lifted up the serpent in the wilderness, even so must the son of man be lifted up:

15 That whosoever believeth in him should not perish, but have eternal life.

16 For God so loved the world, that he gave his only begotten Son, that whosoever believeth in him should not perish, but have everlasting life.

17 For God sent not his Son into the world to condemn the world; but that the world through him might be saved.

...he that doeth truth cometh to the light, that his deeds may be made manifest, that they are wrought in God.

---

18 He that believeth on him is not condemned: but he that believeth not is condemned already, because he hath not believed in the name of the only begotten Son of God.

19 And this is the condemnation, that light is come into the world, and men loved darkness rather than light, because their deeds were evil.

20 For every one that doeth evil hateth the light, neither cometh to the light, lest his deeds should be reproved.

21 But he that doeth truth cometh to the light, that his deeds may be made manifest, that they are wrought in God.

John Testifies About Jesus

John 3:22-36

After these things, Jesus went into the countryside of Judea with his disciples and remained there a while, baptizing. John, too, was baptizing at Aenon, near Salim, because there was much water there, and people were coming and being baptized. (John had not yet been put in prison.)

Now there arose a controversy between some disciples of John and a Jew over the matter of ceremonial cleansing. And they came to John and said, "Rabbi, he who was with you beyond the Jordan, to whom you have borne witness, is now baptizing, and all men are coming to him."

"A man can receive nothing except what is given him from heaven," replied John. "You yourselves bear me witness that I said, 'I am not the Messiah, but only his forerunner.' It is the bridegroom who receives the bride; but the bridegroom's friend, who stands and listens to him, rejoices greatly as he hears the voice of the bridegroom. And so my joy is now complete. He must increase, but I must decrease.

"He who came from above is above all others, but he who is only from earth is earthly, and speaks of earthly things. He who came from heaven is above all others; and he is bearing witness to what he has seen and heard, but men are not accepting his testimony. But whoever accepts his testimony affirms that God is true, for he whom God has sent is giving voice to the words of God. For to him, God gives the Spirit without limit. The Father loves the Son, and has given all things into his hand. He who trusts in the Son has eternal life; but he who refuses to obey the Son shall not see life, but the wrath of God will remain upon him."

JOHN 3:22-36

22 After these things came Jesus and his disciples into the land of Judea; and there he tarried with them, and baptized.

23 And John also was baptizing in Aenon near to Salim, because there was much water there: and they came, and were baptized.

The Father loveth the Son, and hath given all things into his hand.

24 For John was not yet cast into prison.

25 Then there arose a question between *some* of John's disciples and the Jews about purifying.

26 And they came unto John, and said unto him, Rabbi, he that was with thee beyond Jordan, to whom thou barest witness, behold, the same baptizeth, and all *men* come to him.

27 John answered and said, A man can receive nothing, except it be given him from heaven.

28 Ye yourselves bear me witness, that I said, I am not the Christ, but that I am sent before him.

29 He that hath the bride is the bridegroom: but the friend of the bridegroom, which standeth and heareth him, rejoiceth greatly because of the bridegroom's voice: this my joy therefore is fulfilled.

30 He must increase, but I *must* decrease.

31 He that cometh from above is above all: he that is of the earth is earthly, and speaketh of the earth: he that cometh from heaven is above all.

32 And what he hath seen and heard, that he testifieth; and no man receiveth his testimony.

33 He that hath received his testimony hath set to his seal that God is true.

34 For he whom God hath sent speaketh the words of God: for God giveth not the Spirit by measure *unto him*.

35 The Father loveth the Son, and hath given all things into his hand.

36 He that believeth on the Son hath everlasting life: and he that believeth not the Son shall not see life; but the wrath of God abideth on him.

Mt. Gerizim *(top). A sacred site for the Samaritans who had a temple there. The woman referred to "this mountain" when talking with Jesus.*
Mt. Ebal *(center). Across the narrow valley from Gerizim. Sychar was located on its lower slopes.*

(Bottom) The Jacob's Well area is at the heart of the land. It is about 35 miles north of Jerusalem.

83

The Woman at Jacob's Well

JOHN 4:1-42

John 4:1-42

Now when Jesus knew that the Pharisees had heard that he was winning and baptizing more disciples than John (though Jesus himself did not baptize, but rather his disciples) he left Judea and departed again to Galilee, passing through Samaria. And he came to a village of Samaria called Sychar, near the field which Jacob gave to his son Joseph. Now Jacob's well was there, and Jesus, being tired from his journey, sat down beside the well. It was about the sixth hour.

There came a Samaritan woman to draw water. Jesus said to her, "Give me a drink." (His disciples had gone into the village to buy food.)

The Samaritan woman said, "How is it that you, a Jew, ask a drink of me—a Samaritan woman?" For the Jews have no dealings with Samaritans.

"If you knew about the gift of God and who it is that is saying to you, 'Give me a drink,' " replied Jesus, "you would have asked him, and he would have given you living water."

"Sir," said the woman, "you have nothing to draw with, and the well is deep. Where do you get that living water? Are you greater than our father Jacob, who gave us the well and drank from it himself, and his sons and his cattle?"

"Everyone who drinks of this water will thirst again," said Jesus, "but whoever drinks of the water that I shall give him will never thirst, but the water that I shall give him will be a fountain of water within him springing forth into life eternal."

"Sir," said the woman, "give me this water, that I may not thirst again nor come here to draw water."

JOHN 4:1-42

1 When therefore the Lord knew how the Pharisees had heard that Jesus made and baptized more disciples than John,

2 (Though Jesus himself baptized not, but his disciples,)

3 He left Judea, and departed again into Galilee.

4 And he must needs go through Samaria.

5 Then cometh he to a city of Samaria, which is called Sychar, near to the parcel of ground that Jacob gave to his son Joseph.

6 Now Jacob's well was there. Jesus therefore, being wearied with *his* journey, sat thus on the well: *and* it was about the sixth hour.

7 There cometh a woman of Samaria to draw water: Jesus saith unto her, Give me to drink.

8 (For his disciples were gone away unto the city to buy meat.)

9 Then saith the woman of Samaria unto him, How is it that thou, being a Jew, askest drink of me, which am a woman of Samaria? for the Jews have no dealings with the Samaritans.

10 Jesus answered and said unto her, If thou knewest the gift of God, and who it is that saith to thee, Give me to drink; thou wouldest have asked of him, and he would have given thee living water.

11 The woman saith unto him, Sir, thou hast nothing to draw with, and the well is deep: from whence then hast thou that living water?

12 Art thou greater than our father Jacob, which gave us the well, and drank thereof himself, and his children, and his cattle?

13 Jesus answered and said unto her, Whosoever drinketh of this water shall thirst again:

14 But whosoever drinketh of the water that I shall give him shall never thirst; but the water that I shall give him shall be in him a well of water springing up into everlasting life.

15 The woman saith unto him, Sir, give me this water, that I thirst not, neither come hither to draw.

The Woman at Jacob's Well (continued)

"Go call your husband and come back," said Jesus.

"I have no husband," replied the woman.

"You were right in saying 'I have no husband,' " said Jesus, "for you have had five husbands, and you are not married to the man with whom you are now living. You told the truth when you said you have no husband."

"Sir," said the woman, "I see that you are a prophet! Our fathers worshipped on this mountain, but you Jews say that in Jerusalem is the place where men should worship."

"Woman," replied Jesus, "believe me, the time is coming when you will worship the Father neither on this mountain nor in Jerusalem. You Samaritans worship without knowing what you worship; but we know what we worship, for salvation is to come through the Jews. But the time is coming, indeed it has already come, when the true worshippers will worship the Father in spirit and in truth, for the Father seeks those who will truly worship him. God is a spirit, and those who worship him must worship in spirit and truth."

JOHN 4:1-42

16 Jesus saith unto her, Go, call thy husband, and come hither.

17 The woman answered and said, I have no husband. Jesus said unto her, thou hast well said, I have no husband:

18 For thou hast had five husbands; and he whom thou now hast is not thy husband: in that saidst thou truly.

19 The woman saith unto him, Sir, I perceive that thou art a prophet.

20 Our fathers worshipped in this mountain; and ye say, that in Jerusalem is the place where men ought to worship.

21 Jesus saith unto her, Woman, believe me, the hour cometh, when ye shall neither in this mountain, nor yet at Jerusalem, worship the Father.

22 Ye worship ye know not what: we know what we worship; for salvation is of the Jews.

23 But the hour cometh, and now is, when the true worshippers shall worship the Father in spirit and in truth: for the Father seeketh such to worship him.

24 God *is* a Spirit: and they that worship him must worship *him* in spirit and in truth.

Jacob's Well (interior). Almost 4,000 years old, still flowing today. About 110 feet deep, with depth of water about 40 feet.

The Woman at Jacob's Well (continued)

"I know that Messiah is coming," said the woman, "and when he comes, he will tell us all things."

"I who speak to you am he," said Jesus.

At that moment his disciples appeared and were astonished to find him talking with a woman, but no one said, "What do you want?" or, "Why are you talking with her?"

Then the woman left her waterpot and hurried into the village and said to the people, "Come see a man who told me everything I have done! Is he not the Messiah?" And they left the village and hurried to him.

Meanwhile, the disciples kept insisting, "Rabbi, eat something."

But Jesus said, "I have food to eat of which you are not aware."

Then the disciples said one to another, "Did someone bring him something to eat?"

"My food," said Jesus, "is to do the will of him who sent me, and to finish his work. Do you not say, 'There are yet four months, and then will come the harvest'? Behold, I say to you, open your eyes and look at the fields, for they are already ripe for the harvest. And he who reaps receives wages and gathers fruit for life eternal, so that he who sows and he who reaps may rejoice together. For in this harvest, the proverb indeed is true, 'One sows, and another reaps.' I sent you to reap a harvest for which you did not toil; others have toiled, and you have reaped the fruit of their labor."

And many of the Samaritans of that village believed in him because of the testimony of the woman who said, "He told me everything I have done!" And when they came to Jesus, they begged him to stay with them, and he remained there two days. And many more believed because of his words and said to the woman, "Now we believe, not because of your report, but because we have heard him ourselves, and we know that he is indeed the Saviour of the world."

JOHN 4:1-42

25 The woman saith unto him, I know that Messiah cometh, which is called Christ: when he is come, he will tell us all things.

26 Jesus saith unto her, I that speak unto thee am *he*.

27 And upon this came his disciples, and marveled that he talked with the woman: yet no man said, What seekest thou? or, Why talkest thou with her?

28 The woman then left her waterpot, and went her way into the city, and saith to the men,

29 Come, see a man, which told me all things that ever I did: is not this the Christ?

30 Then they went out of the city, and came unto him.

31 In the mean while his disciples prayed him, saying, Master, eat.

32 But he said unto them, I have meat to eat that ye know not of.

33 Therefore said the disciples one to another, Hath any man brought him *aught* to eat?

34 Jesus saith unto them, My meat is to do the will of him that sent me, and to finish his work.

35 Say not ye, There are yet four months, and *then* cometh harvest? behold, I say unto you, Lift up your eyes, and look on the fields; for they are white already to harvest.

36 And he that reapeth receiveth wages, and gathereth fruit unto life eternal: that both he that soweth and he that reapeth may rejoice together.

37 And herein is that saying true, One soweth, and another reapeth.

38 I sent you to reap that whereon ye bestowed no labor: other men labored, and ye are entered into their labors.

39 And many of the Samaritans of that city believed on him for the saying of the woman, which testified, He told me all that ever I did.

40 So when the Samaritans were come unto him, they besought him that he would tarry with them: and he abode there two days.

41 And many more believed because of his own word;

42 And said unto the woman, Now we believe, not because of thy saying: for we have heard *him* ourselves, and know that this is indeed the Christ, the Saviour of the world.

John the Baptist Imprisoned

Luke 3:19-20

But Herod the tetrarch, having been rebuked by John for taking his brother's wife, Herodias, and for all the wicked things he had done, added to all his evil doings by putting John in prison.

LUKE 3:19-20

19 But Herod the tetrarch, being reproved by him for Herodias his brother Philip's wife, and for all the evils which Herod had done,

20 Added yet this above all, that he shut up John in prison.

Jesus Goes to Galilee

Luke 4:14-15, Matthew 4:13-17

And Jesus returned to Galilee in the power of the Spirit, and news of him spread through all the region round about. And he taught in their synagogues, and was acclaimed on every hand.

And leaving Nazareth, Jesus came and dwelt in Capernaum by the sea in the country of Zebulun and Naphtali, that the word spoken by the prophet Isaiah might be fulfilled,

The land of Zebulun and the land of Naphtali, toward the sea, beyond the Jordan, Galilee of the Gentiles, the people who sat in darkness have seen a great light: a light has dawned on those who sat in the land and shadow of death.

From that time Jesus began to preach, saying, "Repent, for the kingdom of heaven is at hand."

MATTHEW 4:12-17

12 Now when Jesus had heard that John was cast into prison, he departed into Galilee;

13 And leaving Nazareth, he came and dwelt in Capernaum, which is upon the seacoast, in the borders of Zebulun and Naphtali:

14 That it might be fulfilled which was spoken by Isaiah the prophet, saying,

15 The land of Zebulun, and the land of Naphtali, *by* the way of the sea, beyond Jordan, Galilee of the Gentiles;

16 The people which sat in darkness saw great light; and to them which sat in the region and shadow of death light is sprung up.

17 From that time Jesus began to preach, and to say, Repent: for the kingdom of heaven is at hand.

MARK 1:14-15

14 Now after that John was put in prison, Jesus came into Galilee, preaching the gospel of the kingdom of God,

15 And saying, The time is fulfilled, and the kingdom of God is at hand: repent ye, and believe the gospel.

LUKE 4:14-15

14 And Jesus returned in the power of the Spirit into Galilee: and there went out a fame of him through all the region round about.

15 And he taught in their synagogues, being glorified of all.

JOHN 4:43-45

43 Now after two days he departed thence, and went into Galilee.

44 For Jesus himself testified, that a prophet hath no honor in his own country.

45 Then when he was come into Galilee, the Galileans received him, having seen all the things that he did at Jerusalem at the feast: for they also went unto the feast.

Jesus Heals a Nobleman's Son

John 4:46-54

Jesus came again to Cana in Galilee, where he made the water wine. Now there was a nobleman at Capernaum whose son was ill. When he heard that Jesus had come from Judea to Galilee, he hurried to him and began to beg him to come down and heal his son, for he was at the point of death.

"Unless you see signs and wonders," said Jesus, "you will not believe."

"Sir," said the nobleman, "please come down, before my child dies!"

"Go your way," said Jesus, "your son will live."

And the man believed the word Jesus had spoken and went his way. And as he was returning, his servants met him and reported that his son was alive and well. Then he asked them the hour when he began to mend, and they replied, "Yesterday at the seventh hour the fever left him." Then the father knew that it was the very hour in which Jesus had said to him, "Your son will live." And he and all his household believed. This is the second miracle that Jesus performed in Galilee, after he returned from Judea.

JOHN 4:46-54

46 So Jesus came again into Cana of Galilee, where he made the water wine. And there was a certain nobleman, whose son was sick at Capernaum.

47 When he heard that Jesus was come out of Judea into Galilee, he went unto him, and besought him that he would come down, and heal his son: for he was at the point of death.

48 Then said Jesus unto him, Except ye see signs and wonders, ye will not believe.

49 The nobleman saith unto him, Sir, come down ere my child die.

50 Jesus saith unto him, Go thy way; thy son liveth. And the man believed the word that Jesus had spoken unto him, and he went his way.

51 And as he was now going down, his servants met him, and told *him*, saying, Thy son liveth.

52 Then inquired he of them the hour when he began to amend. And they said unto him, Yesterday at the seventh hour the fever left him.

53 So the father knew that *it was* at the same hour, in the which Jesus said unto him, Thy son liveth: and himself believed, and his whole house.

54 This *is* again the second miracle *that* Jesus did, when he was come out of Judea into Galilee.

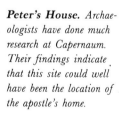

Peter's House. Archaeologists have done much research at Capernaum. Their findings indicate that this site could well have been the location of the apostle's home.

Jesus' Rejection at Nazareth

Luke 4:16-30

And he came to Nazareth, where he had been brought up. And as his custom was, he went to the synagogue on the Sabbath day. And he stood up to read, and the book of the prophet Isaiah was handed to him. He opened the book and found the place where it is written,

The Spirit of the Lord is upon me,
because he has anointed me to preach the gospel to the poor.
He has sent me to proclaim release to the captives
and recovering of sight to the blind;
to set at liberty those who are bruised,
to proclaim the year of the Lord's gracious favor.

And he closed the book and gave it back to the attendant, and sat down. And the eyes of everyone in the synagogue were fixed on him. And he began to speak to them, saying, "Today has this scripture been fulfilled in your hearing."

And as he continued to speak, everyone commented favorably about him and marveled at the gracious words which poured from his lips. But then they began to say, "But after all, isn't this only the son of Joseph?"

Then Jesus said to them, "You will doubtless quote this proverb to me, 'Physician, heal yourself; do here in your own country the things we have heard that you did at Capernaum.' I tell you truly, no prophet is accepted in his own country. I tell you the truth, there were many widows in Israel in the days of Elijah, when the heaven was shut up three years and six months and there came a great famine throughout all the land; but Elijah was sent to none of them, but rather to a widow in Zarephath, in the land of Sidon. And there were many lepers in Israel in the time of the prophet Elisha, and none of them was cleansed, but rather Naaman the Syrian."

And when they heard this, everyone in the synagogue was furious. And they rose up and thrust him out of the town and led him to the brow of the hill on which their town stood, intending to throw him down headlong. But passing through the midst of them, he went his way.

16 And he came to Nazareth, where he had been brought up: and, as his custom was, he went into the synagogue on the sabbath day, and stood up for to read.

17 And there was delivered unto him the book of the prophet Isaiah. And when he had opened the book, he found the place where it was written,

18 The Spirit of the Lord *is* upon me, because he hath anointed me to preach the gospel to the poor; he hath sent me to heal the broken-hearted, to preach deliverance to the captives, and recovering of sight to the blind, to set at liberty them that are bruised,

19 To preach the acceptable year of the Lord.

20 And he closed the book, and he gave *it* again to the minister, and sat down. And the eyes of all them that were in the synagogue were fastened on him.

21 And he began to say unto them, This day is this Scripture fulfilled in your ears.

22 And all bare him witness, and wondered at the gracious words which proceeded out of his mouth. And they said, Is not this Joseph's son?

23 And he said unto them, Ye will surely say unto me this proverb, Physician, heal thyself: whatsoever we have heard done in Capernaum, do also here in thy country.

24 And he said, Verily I say unto you, No prophet is accepted in his own country.

25 But I tell you of a truth, many widows were in Israel in the days of Elijah, when the heaven was shut up three years and six months, when great famine was throughout all the land;

26 But unto none of them was Elijah sent, save unto Zarephath, *a city* of Sidon, unto a woman *that was* a widow.

27 And many lepers were in Israel in the time of Elisha the prophet; and none of them was cleansed, saving Naaman the Syrian.

28 And all they in the synagogue, when they heard these things, were filled with wrath,

29 And rose up, and thrust him out of the city, and led him unto the brow of the hill whereon their city was built, that they might cast him down headlong.

30 But he, passing through the midst of them, went his way,

The Call of Four Disciples

Matthew 4:18-22, Luke 5:1-11

And walking by the Sea of Galilee, he saw two brothers, Simon (called Peter) and Andrew, casting a net into the sea; for they were fishermen. And he said, ''Follow me, and I will make you fishers of men.'' And they immediately left their nets and followed him.

And going on from there, he saw two other brothers, James and John, in a boat with their father Zebedee, mending their nets. And he called them, and they immediately left the boat and their father and followed him.

Now it came to pass that while Jesus was standing on the shore of the Lake of Gennesaret, a throng of people crowded close about him to hear the word of God. And seeing two boats tied at the water's edge (the fishermen had left them and were washing their nets) he got into one of the boats, which was Simon's, and asked him to push off a little from the shore. Then he sat down and taught the people from the boat.

And when he had finished speaking, he said to Simon, ''Now shove out into the deep water and let down your nets for a catch.''

''Master,'' said Peter, ''we have toiled all night and caught nothing. Nevertheless, at your word, I will let down the nets.''

And when they had done so, they caught such a great school of fish that the nets began to break. And they beckoned to their partners in the other boat to come and help them, and they came and filled both boats so full that they were about to sink.

When Simon Peter saw all this, he fell on his knees before Jesus and exclaimed, ''Depart from me, for I am a sinful man, Lord!'' For he was astonished at the catch of fish they had taken, as were all those with him, and his partners, James and John, the sons of Zebedee.

But Jesus said to Simon, ''Do not be afraid. From now on, you will be catching men.''

And when they brought their boats to shore, they left everything and followed him.

MATTHEW 4:18-22	MARK 1:16-20	LUKE 5:1-11
18 And Jesus, walking by the sea of Galilee, saw two brethren, Simon called Peter, and Andrew his brother, casting a net into the sea: for they were fishers.	16 Now as he walked by the sea of Galilee, he saw Simon and Andrew his brother casting a net into the sea: for they were fishers.	1 And it came to pass, that, as the people pressed upon him to hear the word of God, he stood by the lake of Gennesaret,
19 And he saith unto them, Follow me, and I will make you fishers of men.	17 And Jesus said unto them, Come ye after me, and I will make you to become fishers of men.	2 And saw two ships standing by the lake: but the fishermen were gone out of them, and were washing *their* nets.
20 And they straightway left *their* nets, and followed him.	18 And straightway they forsook their nets, and followed him.	3 And he entered into one of the ships, which was Simon's, and prayed him that he would thrust out a little from the land. And he sat down, and taught the people out of the ship.
21 And going on from thence, he saw other two brethren, James *the son of* Zebedee, and John his brother, in a ship with Zebedee their father, mend-	19 And when he had gone a little further thence, he saw James the *son* of Zebedee, and John his brother, who also were in the ship mending their nets.	4 Now when he had left speaking, he said unto Simon, Launch out into the deep, and let down your nets for a draught.
		5 And Simon answering said unto him, Master, we have toiled all the night, and have taken nothing: nevertheless at thy word I will let down the net.
		6 And when they had this done, they inclosed a great multitude of fishes: and their net brake.

The Call of Four Disciples (continued)

ing their nets; and he called them.

22 And they immediately left the ship and their father, and followed him.

20 And straightway he called them: and they left their father Zebedee in the ship with the hired servants, and went after him.

7 And they beckoned unto *their* partners, which were in the other ship, that they should come and help them. And they came, and filled both the ships, so that they began to sink.

8 When Simon Peter saw *it*, he fell down at Jesus' knees, saying, Depart from me; for I am a sinful man, O Lord.

9 For he was astonished, and all that were with him, at the draught of the fishes which they had taken:

10 And so *was* also James, and John, the sons of Zebedee, which were partners with Simon. And Jesus said unto Simon, Fear not; from henceforth thou shalt catch men.

11 And when they had brought their ships to land, they forsook all, and followed him.

Fishermen on the Sea of Galilee (below). *In our present time the Sea yields many tons of fish each night.*

91

A Day of Miracles in Capernaum

Mark 1:21-34

They went into Capernaum, and on the Sabbath, Jesus entered the synagogue and began to teach. And they were astonished at his teaching, for he taught them as one having authority, and not as the scribes.

Suddenly, a man with an evil spirit entered the synagogue shouting, "What have you to do with us, Jesus of Nazareth? Have you come to destroy us? I know who you are, you're the Holy One of God!"

But Jesus rebuked him, saying, "Hold your peace, and come out of him!"

After throwing the man into convulsions and loud screaming, the evil spirit departed from him. And the people were so astonished that they all began to exclaim, "What is this? Here is a new teaching with real authority! He even commands the evil spirits, and they obey him."

And his fame quickly spread throughout all Galilee.

Jesus left the synagogue and entered the house of Simon and Andrew, with James and John. Now Simon's mother-in-law lay sick with a fever, and they told Jesus about her at once. He came and took her by the hand and lifted her up; and the fever left her, and she began to attend to their comfort.

Now in the evening, when the sun had set, they began bringing to him all who were sick or demon possessed, until it seemed that the whole city was crowded about the door of Simon's house. And he healed many who were sick with various diseases, and cast out many demons. But he would not permit the demons to speak, because they knew who he was.

Miracles at Capernaum.
Much of Jesus' ministry took place in Capernaum. He healed many who were afflicted.

A Day of Miracles in Capernaum (continued)

14 And when Jesus was come into Peter's house, he saw his wife's mother laid, and sick of a fever.

15 And he touched her hand, and the fever left her: and she arose, and ministered unto them.

16 When the even was come, they brought unto him many that were possessed with devils: and he cast out the spirits with *his* word, and healed all that were sick:

17 That it might be fulfilled which was spoken by Isaiah the prophet, saying, Himself took our infirmities, and bare *our* sicknesses.

21 And they went into Capernaum; and straightway on the sabbath day he entered into the synagogue, and taught.

22 And they were astonished at his doctrine: for he taught them as one that had authority, and not as the scribes.

23 And there was in their synagogue a man with an unclean spirit; and he cried out,

24 Saying, Let *us* alone; what have we to do with thee, thou Jesus of Nazareth? art thou come to destroy us? I know thee who thou art, the Holy One of God.

25 And Jesus rebuked him, saying, Hold thy peace, and come out of him.

26 And when the unclean spirit had torn him, and cried with a loud voice, he came out of him.

27 And they were all amazed, insomuch that they questioned among themselves, saying, What thing is this? what new doctrine *is* this? for with authority commandeth he even the unclean spirits, and they do obey him.

28 And immediately his fame spread abroad throughout all the region round about Galilee.

29 And forthwith, when they were come out of the synagogue, they entered into the house of Simon and Andrew, with James and John.

30 But Simon's wife's mother lay sick of a fever; and anon they tell him of her.

31 And he came and took her by the hand, and lifted her up; and immediately the fever left her, and she ministered unto them.

32 And at even, when the sun did set, they brought unto him all that were diseased, and them that were possessed with devils.

33 And all the city was gathered together at the door.

34 And he healed many that were sick of divers diseases, and cast out many devils; and suffered not the devils to speak, because they knew him.

31 And came down to Capernaum, a city of Galilee, and taught them on the sabbath days.

32 And they were astonished at his doctrine: for his word was with power.

33 And in the synagogue there was a man, which had a spirit of an unclean devil, and cried out with a loud voice,

34 Saying, Let *us* alone; what have we to do with thee, *thou* Jesus of Nazareth? art thou come to destroy us? I know thee who thou art; the Holy One of God.

35 And Jesus rebuked him, saying, Hold thy peace, and come out of him. And when the devil had thrown him in the midst, he came out of him, and hurt him not.

36 And they were all amazed, and spake among themselves, saying, What a word *is* this! for with authority and power he commandeth the unclean spirits, and they come out.

37 And the fame of him went out into every place of the country round about.

38 And he arose out of the synagogue, and entered into Simon's house. And Simon's wife's mother was taken with a great fever; and they besought him for her.

39 And he stood over her, and rebuked the fever; and it left her: and immediately she arose and ministered unto them.

40 Now when the sun was setting, all they that had any sick with divers diseases brought them unto him; and he laid his hands on every one of them, and healed them.

41 And devils also came out of many, crying out, and saying, Thou art Christ the Son of God. And he rebuking *them* suffered them not to speak: for they knew that he was Christ.

Jesus Preaches in Galilee

Mark 1:35-39, Matthew 4:25

In the early morning hours, long before daybreak, Jesus rose and went out to a solitary place, and there he prayed. And Simon and his companions began searching for him; and when they found him, they said, "Everyone is looking for you."

But Jesus replied, "Let us go on to the neighboring towns, that I may preach there, too; for that is why I have come."

And he went throughout all Galilee, preaching in their synagogues and casting out demons. And great crowds followed him from Galilee and the Decapolis, and from Jerusalem and Judea and beyond the Jordan.

MATTHEW 4:23-25	MARK 1:35-39	LUKE 4:42-44
23 And Jesus went about all Galilee, teaching in their synagogues, and preaching the gospel of the kingdom, and healing all manner of sickness and all manner of disease among the people. 24 And his fame went throughout all Syria: and they brought unto him all sick people that were taken with divers diseases and torments, and those which were possessed with devils, and those which were lunatic, and those that had the palsy; and he healed them. 25 And there followed him great multitudes of people from Galilee, and *from* Decapolis, and *from* Jerusalem, and *from* Judea, and *from* beyond Jordan.	35 And in the morning, rising up a great while before day, he went out, and departed into a solitary place, and there prayed. 36 And Simon and they that were with him followed after him. 37 And when they had found him, they said unto him, All *men* seek for thee. 38 And he said unto them, Let us go into the next towns, that I may preach there also: for therefore came I forth. 39 And he preached in their synagogues throughout all Galilee, and cast out devils.	42 And when it was day, he departed and went into a desert place: and the people sought him, and came unto him, and stayed him, that he should not depart from them. 43 And he said unto them, I must preach the kingdom of God to other cities also: for therefore am I sent. 44 And he preached in the synagogues of Galilee.

Jesus Heals a Leper

Mark 1:40-45

A leper came to Jesus begging help and, kneeling before him, said, "If you will, you can make me clean."

Jesus, moved with compassion, reached out his hand and touched him, saying, "I will; be clean."

Immediately the leprosy left him, and he was clean.

"See that you do not speak to anyone about this," said Jesus, "but go show yourself to the priest and offer for your cleansing the things which Moses commanded, as an evidence to the people."

Having sternly admonished him, Jesus sent him away at once. But he went out and began to tell it everywhere, so that Jesus was no longer able to enter the town openly, but was obliged to remain out in the countryside. But the people continued to come to him from every quarter.

Sea of Galilee. *This small body of water, more a lake than a sea, figured much in Jesus' ministry. It was sometimes called the Sea of Chinnereth (harp) because it is shaped like that instrument.*

Jesus Heals a Leper (continued)

MATTHEW 8:2-4

2 And, behold, there came a leper and worshipped him, saying, Lord, if thou wilt, thou canst make me clean.

3 And Jesus put forth *his* hand, and touched him, saying, I will; be thou clean. And immediately his leprosy was cleansed.

4 And Jesus saith unto him, See thou tell no man; but go thy way, show thyself to the priest, and offer the gift that Moses commanded, for a testimony unto them.

MARK 1:40-45

40 And there came a leper to him, beseeching him, and kneeling down to him, and saying unto him, If thou wilt, thou canst make me clean.

41 And Jesus, moved with compassion, put forth *his* hand, and touched him, and saith unto him, I will; be thou clean.

42 And as soon as he had spoken, immediately the leprosy departed from him, and he was cleansed.

43 And he straitly charged him, and forthwith sent him away;

44 And saith unto him, See thou say nothing to any man: but go thy way, show thyself to the priest, and offer for thy cleansing those things which Moses commanded, for a testimony unto them.

45 But he went out, and began to publish *it* much, and to blaze abroad the matter, insomuch that Jesus could no more openly enter into the city, but was without in desert places: and they came to him from every quarter.

LUKE 5:12-16

12 And it came to pass, when he was in a certain city, behold a man full of leprosy; who seeing Jesus fell on *his* face, and besought him, saying, Lord, if thou wilt, thou canst make me clean.

13 And he put forth *his* hand, and touched him, saying, I will: be thou clean. And immediately the leprosy departed from him.

14 And he charged him to tell no man: But go, and show thyself to the priest, and offer for thy cleansing, according as Moses commanded, for a testimony unto them.

15 But so much the more went there a fame abroad of him: and great multitudes came together to hear, and to be healed by him of their infirmities.

16 And he withdrew himself into the wilderness, and prayed.

Jesus Heals a Paralytic

Mark 2:1-12

Some days later, Jesus returned to Capernaum, and it was reported that he was at home. A crowd gathered—so many that there was no more room, not even about the door—and Jesus began to preach the word to them. And they brought a paralytic, carried by four men; and when they could not get near Jesus because of the crowd, they removed a section of the roof above him and let down the pallet on which the paralytic was lying. When Jesus saw their faith, he said to the paralytic, "Son, your sins are forgiven."

Now some of the scribes were sitting there, reasoning in their hearts, "Why does this man say such things? He is blaspheming! Who can forgive sins but God alone?"

Then Jesus, knowing what they were thinking, said to them, "Why are you thinking such things in your hearts? Which is easier, to say to the paralytic, 'Your sins are forgiven,' or to say, 'Rise, pick up your pallet and walk'? But that you may know that the Son of Man has authority on earth to forgive sins, I say to you, (he was speaking to the paralytic) Rise, pick up your pallet and go home."

And the man immediately rose, picked up his pallet, and walked away before them all. And they were all amazed and praised God, saying, "We never saw anything like it!"

Jesus Heals a Paralytic (continued)

1 And he entered into a ship, and passed over, and came into his own city.

2 And, behold, they brought to him a man sick of the palsy, lying on a bed: and Jesus seeing their faith said unto the sick of the palsy; Son, be of good cheer; thy sins be forgiven thee.

3 And, behold, certain of the scribes said within themselves, This *man* blasphemeth.

But when the multitudes saw it, they marveled, and glorified God, which had given such power unto men.

---

4 And Jesus knowing their thoughts said, Wherefore think ye evil in your hearts?

5 For whether is easier, to say, *Thy* sins be forgiven thee; or to say, Arise, and walk?

6 But that ye may know that the Son of man hath power on earth to forgive sins, (then saith he to the sick of the palsy,) Arise, take up thy bed, and go unto thine house.

7 And he arose, and departed to his house.

8 But when the multitudes saw *it,* they marveled, and glorified God, which had given such power unto men.

1 And again he entered into Capernaum after *some* days; and it was noised that he was in the house.

2 And straightway many were gathered together, insomuch that there was no room to receive *them,* no, not so much as about the door: and he preached the word unto them.

3 And they come unto him, bringing one sick of the palsy, which was borne of four.

4 And when they could not come nigh unto him for the press, they uncovered the roof where he was: and when they had broken *it* up, they let down the bed wherein the sick of the palsy lay.

5 When Jesus saw their faith, he said unto the sick of the palsy, Son, thy sins be forgiven thee.

6 But there were certain of the scribes sitting there, and reasoning in their hearts,

7 Why doth this *man* thus speak blasphemies? who can forgive sins but God only?

8 And immediately, when Jesus perceived in his spirit that they so reasoned within themselves, he said unto them, Why reason ye these things in your hearts?

9 Whether is it easier to say to the sick of the palsy, *Thy* sins be forgiven thee; or to say, Arise, and take up thy bed, and walk?

10 But that ye may know that the Son of man hath power on earth to forgive sins, (he saith to the sick of the palsy,)

11 I say unto thee, Arise, and take up thy bed, and go thy way into thine house.

12 And immediately he arose, took up the bed, and went forth before them all; insomuch that they were all amazed, and glorified God, saying, We never saw it on this fashion.

17 And it came to pass on a certain day, as he was teaching, that there were Pharisees and doctors of the law sitting by, which were come out of every town of Galilee, and Judea, and Jerusalem: and the power of the Lord was *present* to heal them.

18 And, behold, men brought in a bed a man which was taken with a palsy: and they sought *means* to bring him in, and to lay *him* before him.

19 And when they could not find by what *way* they might bring him in because of the multitude, they went upon the housetop, and let him down through the tiling with *his* couch into the midst before Jesus.

20 And when he saw their faith, he said unto him, Man, thy sins are forgiven thee.

21 And the scribes and the Pharisees began to reason, saying, Who is this which speaketh blasphemies? Who can forgive sins, but God alone?

22 But when Jesus perceived their thoughts, he answering said unto them, What reason ye in your hearts?

23 Whether is easier, to say, Thy sins be forgiven thee; or to say, Rise up and walk?

24 But that ye may know that the Son of man hath power upon earth to forgive sins, (he said unto the sick of the palsy,) I say unto thee, Arise, and take up thy couch, and go into thine house.

25 And immediately he rose up before them, and took up that whereon he lay, and departed to his own house, glorifying God.

26 And they were all amazed, and they glorified God, and were filled with fear, saying, We have seen strange things today.

The Call of Matthew

Mark 2:13-17

Jesus went out by the sea again, and all the crowd gathered about him, and he continued teaching them. Now as he passed by, he saw Levi, the son of Alphaeus, sitting at the tax office, and he said to him, "Follow me." And he rose and followed him.

And it came to pass that, as Jesus sat at dinner in Levi's house, many tax collectors and sinners sat down with Jesus and his disciples, for there were many who were following him. Now when the scribes and Pharisees saw him eating with sinners and tax collectors, they said to his disciples, "Why does he eat with tax collectors and sinners?"

When Jesus heard it, he said to them, "Those who are well have no need of a physician, but those who are sick. I did not come to call the 'righteous,' but sinners."

MATTHEW 9:9-13

9 And as Jesus passed forth from thence, he saw a man, named Matthew, sitting at the receipt of custom: and he saith unto him, Follow me. And he arose, and followed him.

10 And it came to pass, as Jesus sat at meat in the house, behold, many publicans and sinners came and sat down with him and his disciples.

11 And when the Pharisees saw *it,* they said unto his disciples, Why eateth your master with publicans and sinners?

12 But when Jesus heard *that,* he said unto them, They that be whole need not a physician, but they that are sick.

13 But go ye and learn what *that* meaneth, I will have mercy, and not sacrifice: for I am not come to call the righteous, but sinners to repentance.

MARK 2:13-17

13 And he went forth again by the sea side; and all the multitude resorted unto him, and he taught them.

14 And as he passed by, he saw Levi the *son* Alpheus sitting at the receipt of custom, and said unto him, Follow me. And he arose and followed him.

15 And it came to pass, that, as Jesus sat at meat in his house, many publicans and sinners sat also together with Jesus and his disciples; for there were many, and they followed him.

16 And when the scribes and Pharisees saw him eat with publicans and sinners, they said unto his disciples, How is it that he eateth and drinketh with publicans and sinners?

17 When Jesus heard *it,* he saith unto them, They that are whole have no need of the physician, but they that are sick: I came not to call the righteous, but sinners to repentance.

LUKE 5:27-32

27 And after these things he went forth, and saw a publican, named Levi, sitting at the receipt of custom: and he said unto him, Follow me.

28 And he left all, rose up, and followed him.

29 And Levi made him a great feast in his own house: and there was a great company of publicans and of others that sat down with them.

30 But their scribes and Pharisees murmured against his disciples, saying, Why do ye eat and drink with publicans and sinners?

31 And Jesus answering said unto them, They that are whole need not a physician; but they that are sick.

32 I came not to call the righteous, but sinners to repentance.

The Call of Matthew. *Publicans were despised by the Jews because they were tax collectors for Rome, but Jesus chose one to be an apostle. Just two words from the Master—"follow me"—but they changed Matthew's life and destiny.*

99

Jesus Answers His Critics

Mark 2:18-22

Now John's disciples and the Pharisees were observing a fast, and people came to Jesus and said, "Why is it that John's disciples and the disciples of the Pharisees are observing a fast, but your disciples are not?"

"Should the wedding guests fast while the bridegroom is with them?" replied Jesus. "As long as they have the bridegroom with them, they cannot fast. But the time will come when the bridegroom will be taken away from them, and then they will fast in that day.

"No one sews a patch of unshrunk cloth on an old garment; for if he does, the new cloth which covers the hole shrinks from the old cloth, and a worse tear is made. No one puts new wine into old wineskins; for if he does, the wine will burst the skins, and the wine is lost and the skins are ruined. New wine must be put into new skins."

MATTHEW 9:14-17 ✓

14 Then came to him the disciples of John, saying, Why do we and the Pharisees fast oft, but thy disciples fast not?

15 And Jesus said unto them, Can the children of the bridechamber mourn, as long as the bridegroom is with them? but the days will come, when the bridegroom shall be taken from them, and then shall they fast.

And Jesus said unto them, Can the children of the bridechamber mourn, as long as the bridegroom is with them?

16 No man putteth a piece of new cloth unto an old garment; for that which is put in to fill it up taketh from the garment, and the rent is made worse.

17 Neither do men put new wine into old bottles: else the bottles break, and the wine runneth out, and the bottles perish: but they put new wine into new bottles, and both are preserved.

MARK 2:18-22 ✓

18 And the disciples of John and of the Pharisees used to fast: and they come and say unto him, Why do the disciples of John and of the Pharisees fast, but thy disciples fast not?

19 And Jesus said unto them, Can the children of the bridechamber fast, while the bridegroom is with them? as long as they have the bridegroom with them, they cannot fast.

20 But the days will come, when the bridegroom shall be taken away from them, and then shall they fast in those days.

21 No man also seweth a piece of new cloth on an old garment; else the new piece that filled it up taketh away from the old, and the rent is made worse.

22 And no man putteth new wine into old bottles; else the new wine doth burst the bottles, and the wine is spilled, and the bottles will be marred: but new wine must be put into new bottles.

LUKE 5:33-39 ✓

33 And they said unto him, Why do the disciples of John fast often, and make prayers, and likewise *the disciples* of the Pharisees; but thine eat and drink?

34 And he said unto them, Can ye make the children of the bridechamber fast, while the bridegroom is with them?

35 But the days will come, when the bridegroom shall be taken away from them, and then shall they fast in those days.

36 And he spake also a parable unto them; No man putteth a piece of a new garment upon an old; if otherwise, then both the new maketh a rent, and the piece that was *taken* out of the new agreeth not with the old.

37 And no man putteth new wine into old bottles; else the new wine will burst the bottles, and be spilled, and the bottles shall perish.

38 But new wine must be put into new bottles; and both are preserved.

39 No man also having drunk old *wine* straightway desireth new; for he saith, The old is better.

Healing at the Pool of Bethesda

John 5:1-15

After this there was a feast of the Jews, and Jesus went to Jerusalem. Now at Jerusalem, near the sheep gate, there is a pool with five porches around it which, in the Hebrew, is called Bethesda. In these porches lay a multitude of people who were sick, blind, lame, or paralyzed.

Now there was a certain man there who had been ill thirty-eight years. When Jesus saw him lying there and knew that he had been in that condition a long time, he said to him, "Would you like to be healed?"

"Sir," replied the sick man, "I have no one to put me into the pool when the water is disturbed, but while I am on the way, someone else steps in ahead of me."

"Rise, pick up your pallet, and walk," said Jesus.

The man was immediately healed; and he gathered up his pallet and started walking. Now it was the Sabbath day. Therefore the Jews said to the man who had been healed, "It is the Sabbath! It is not lawful for you to carry your pallet."

But he replied, "The man who healed me told me, 'Pick up your pallet and walk.' "

"Who is the man who said to you, 'Pick up your pallet and walk'?" they asked.

But the man who had been healed did not know who it was, for Jesus had withdrawn, as there was a crowd present in the place. After a time, Jesus found the man in the temple and said to him, "Behold, you are well! Sin no more, lest something worse come upon you."

Then the man went and told the Jews that it was Jesus who had healed him.

JOHN 5:1-15

1 After this there was a feast of the Jews; and Jesus went up to Jerusalem.

2 Now there is at Jerusalem by the sheep *market* a pool, which is called in the Hebrew tongue Bethesda, having five porches.

3 In these lay a great multitude of impotent folk, of blind, halt, withered, waiting for the moving of the water.

4 For an angel went down at a certain season into the pool, and troubled the water: whosoever then first after the troubling of the water stepped in was made whole of whatsoever disease he had.

5 And a certain man was there, which had an infirmity thirty and eight years.

6 When Jesus saw him lie, and knew that he had been now a long time *in that case*, he saith unto him, Wilt thou be made whole?

7 The impotent man answered him, Sir, I have no man, when the water is troubled, to put me into the pool: but while I am coming, another steppeth down before me.

8 Jesus saith unto him, Rise, take up thy bed, and walk.

9 And immediately the man was made whole, and took up his bed, and walked: and on the same day was the sabbath.

10 The Jews therefore said unto him that was cured, It is the sabbath day: it is not lawful for thee to carry *thy* bed.

11 He answered them, He that made me whole, the same said unto me, Take up thy bed, and walk.

12 Then asked they him, What man is that which said unto thee, Take up thy bed, and walk?

13 And he that was healed wist not who it was: for Jesus had conveyed himself away, a multitude being in *that* place.

14 Afterward Jesus findeth him in the temple, and said unto him, behold, thou art made whole: sin no more, lest a worse thing come unto thee.

15 The man departed, and told the Jews that it was Jesus, which had made him whole.

Healing at the Pool of Bethesda. *The
word "Bethesda" means "house of mercy."
Jesus made the term meaningful (John 5) by
healing a man who up to that time had
found no one who would show him mercy.*

Sermon at the Pool of Bethesda

John 5:16-47

Therefore the Jews began to persecute Jesus, because he did such things on the Sabbath. But Jesus answered them, "My Father continues working even now, and so do I."

Then the Jews sought all the more to kill him, because he not only broke the Sabbath, but also called God his own Father, making himself equal with God. Then said Jesus,

"I tell you truly, the Son can do nothing of his own accord, but only what he sees the Father doing. Whatever the Father does, the Son does likewise; for the Father loves the Son and shows him everything that he himself does. And he will show him greater works than these, that you may marvel. For as the Father raises the dead and bestows life, so the Son, too, gives life to whom he will. For the Father judges no one, but has committed all judgment to the Son, that all men may pay homage to the Son even as they do to the Father. He who does not honor the Son does not honor the Father who sent him. I tell you truly, he who heeds my word and believes him who sent me has life eternal; he does not face condemnation, but has passed out of death into life.

"I tell you truly, the hour is coming—in fact it is already here—when the dead will hear the voice of the Son of God, and those who hear will live. For just as the Father has life in himself, so has he granted to the Son, too, to have life in himself; and he has given him authority to execute judgment, because he is the Son of Man. Do not wonder at this, for the hour is coming when all who are in the graves will hear his voice and come forth—those who have done good, to the resurrection of life; and those who have done evil, to the resurrection of judgment and doom.

"I can do nothing of my own accord. As I hear, so do I judge; and my judgment is just, because I do not seek my own will, but the will of him who sent me. If I bear witness about myself, my testimony is not valid. But there is another who bears witness to me, and I know that his testimony about me is true.

16 And therefore did the Jews persecute Jesus, and sought to slay him, because he had done these things on the sabbath day.

17 But Jesus answered them, My Father worketh hitherto, and I work.

18 Therefore the Jews sought the more to kill him, because he not only had broken the sabbath, but said also that God was his Father, making himself equal with God.

19 Then answered Jesus and said unto them, Verily, verily, I say unto you, The Son can do nothing of himself, but what he seeth the Father do: for what things soever he doeth, these also doeth the Son likewise.

20 For the Father loveth the Son, and showeth him all things that himself doeth: and he will show him greater works than these, that ye may marvel.

21 For as the Father raiseth up the dead, and quickeneth *them;* even so the Son quickeneth whom he will.

22 For the Father judgeth no man, but hath committed all judgment unto the Son:

23 That all *men* should honor the Son, even as they honor the Father. He that honoreth not the Son honoreth not the Father which hath sent him.

24 Verily, verily, I say unto you, He that heareth my word, and believeth on him that sent me, hath everlasting life, and shall not come into condemnation; but is passed from death unto life.

25 Verily, verily, I say unto you, The hour is coming, and now is, when the dead shall hear the voice of the Son of God: and they that hear shall live.

26 For as the Father hath life in himself; so hath he given to the Son to have life in himself;

27 And hath given him authority to execute judgment also, because he is the Son of man.

28 Marvel not at this: for the hour is coming, in the which all that are in the graves shall hear his voice,

29 And shall come forth; they that have done good, unto the resurrection of life; and they that have done evil, unto the resurrection of damnation.

30 I can of mine own self do nothing: as I hear, I judge: and my judgment is just; because I seek not mine own will, but the will of the Father which hath sent me.

Sermon at the Pool of Bethesda (continued)

"You sent messengers to John, and he testified to the truth. Not that I rely on testimony from man; but I remind you of this that you may be saved. John was a burning, shining lamp, and for a while you rejoiced in his light.

"But I have a greater witness than John's. For the works which the Father gave me to accomplish, the very works which I am doing, bear witness to me that the Father has sent me. And the Father himself, who sent me, has borne witness to me. You have never heard his voice nor seen his form, and neither do you have his word in your hearts, for you do not believe the one whom he sent.

"You search the scriptures diligently, for you think that by so doing you will gain eternal life. And all the while, the scriptures bear witness to me, yet you refuse to come to me that you may have life.

"I am not concerned about whether I receive praise from men. But I know you, that you have no real love for God in your hearts. I have come in my Father's name, and you refuse to receive me; but if another comes in his own name, you will receive him. How can you believe?—you who seek honor one·from another rather than honor from the one who alone is God! Do not suppose that I will accuse you before the Father. You already have an accuser—Moses, on whom you have set your hope. If you really believed Moses, you would believe me, for he wrote of me. But if you do not believe his writings, how can you believe my words?"

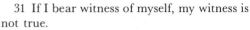

31 If I bear witness of myself, my witness is not true.

32 There is another that beareth witness of me; and I know that the witness which he witnesseth of me is true.

33 Ye sent unto John, and he bare witness unto the truth.

34 But I receive not testimony from man: but these things I say, that ye might be saved.

35 He was a burning and a shining light: and ye were willing for a season to rejoice in his light.

36 But I have greater witness than *that* of John: for the works which the Father hath given me to finish, the same works that I do, bear witness of me, that the Father hath sent me.

37 And the Father himself, which hath sent me, hath borne witness of me. Ye have neither heard his voice at any time, nor seen his shape.

38 And ye have not his word abiding in you: for whom he hath sent, him ye believe not.

39 Search the Scriptures; for in them ye think ye have eternal life: and they are they which testify of me.

40 And ye will not come to me, that ye might have life.

41 I receive not honor from men.

42 But I know you, that ye have not the love of God in you.

43 I am come in my Father's name, and ye receive me not: if another shall come in his own name, him ye will receive.

44 How can ye believe, which receive honor one of another, and seek not the honor that *cometh* from God only?

45 Do not think that I will accuse you to the Father: there is *one* that accuseth you, *even* Moses, in whom ye trust.

46 For had ye believed Moses, ye would have believed me: for he wrote of me.

47 But if ye believe not his writings, how shall ye believe my words?

Eating Grain on the Sabbath

Mark 2:23-28, Matthew 12:5-7

Now it came to pass that, on a Sabbath, Jesus was passing through some grainfields; and as they walked along, his disciples began to pluck heads of grain. And the Pharisees said to Jesus, "Look at that! Why are they doing what is forbidden on the Sabbath by the law?"

But Jesus replied, "Have you never read what David did when he was hungry and had need, he and his companions—how he went into the house of God when Abiathar was High Priest and ate the showbread, which it is unlawful for anyone to eat except the priests, and also gave some to those who were with him? Or have you not read in the law how, on the Sabbath, the priests in the temple profane the Sabbath, but are guiltless? But I say to you, something greater than the temple is here. But if you had understood what this means, 'I desire mercy rather than sacrifice,' you would not have condemned the guiltless. The Sabbath was made for man, and not man for the Sabbath. Therefore the Son of Man is lord also of the Sabbath."

MATTHEW 12:1-8

1 At that time Jesus went on the sabbath day through the corn; and his disciples were ahungered, and began to pluck the ears of corn, and to eat.

2 But when the Pharisees saw *it,* they said unto him, Behold, thy disciples do that which is not lawful to do upon the sabbath day.

3 But he said unto them, Have ye not read what David did, when he was ahungered, and they that were with him;

4 How he entered into the house of God, and did eat the showbread, which was not lawful for him to eat, neither for them which were with him, but only for the priests?

5 Or have ye not read in the law, how that on the sabbath days the priests in the temple profane the sabbath, and are blameless?

6 But I say unto you, That in this place is *one* greater than the temple.

7 But if ye had known what *this* meaneth, I will have mercy, and not sacrifice, ye would not have condemned the guiltless.

8 For the Son of man is Lord even of the sabbath day.

MARK 2:23-28

23 And it came to pass, that he went through the corn fields on the sabbath day; and his disciples began, as they went, to pluck the ears of corn.

24 And the Pharisees said unto him, Behold, why do they on the sabbath day that which is not lawful?

25 And he said unto them, Have ye never read what David did, when he had need, and was ahungered, he, and they that were with him?

26 How he went into the house of God in the days of Abiathar the high priest, and did eat the showbread, which is not lawful to eat but for the priests, and gave also to them which were with him?

27 And he said unto them, The sabbath was made for man, and not man for the sabbath:

28 Therefore the Son of man is Lord also of the sabbath.

LUKE 6:1-5

1 And it came to pass on the second sabbath after the first, that he went through the corn fields; and his disciples plucked the ears of corn, and did eat, rubbing *them* in *their* hands.

2 And certain of the Pharisees said unto them, Why do ye that which is not lawful to do on the sabbath days?

3 And Jesus answering them said, Have ye not read so much as this, what David did, when himself was ahungered, and they which were with him;

4 How he went into the house of God, and did take and eat the showbread, and gave also to them that were with him; which it is not lawful to eat but for the priests alone?

5 And he said unto them, That the Son of man is Lord also of the sabbath.

The Man with the Withered Hand

Matthew 12:9-13

Then Jesus went on from there, and entered their synagogue. Now there was a man there who had a withered hand. And the scribes and Pharisees asked Jesus, "Is it lawful to heal on the Sabbath?" (They were seeking some charge to bring against him.)

"What man among you," said Jesus, "if he has a sheep which falls into a pit on the Sabbath will not take hold of it and lift it out? How much more is a man worth than a sheep! So, then, it is lawful to do good on the Sabbath."

Then Jesus said to the man, "Stretch out your hand."

And the man stretched out his hand, and it was restored and made whole like the other one.

MATTHEW 12:9-13

9 And when he was departed thence, he went into their synagogue:

10 And, behold, there was a man which had *his* hand withered. And they asked him, saying, Is it lawful to heal on the sabbath days? that they might accuse him.

How much then is a man better than a sheep? Wherefore it is lawful to do well on the sabbath days.

11 And he said unto them, What man shall there be among you, that shall have one sheep, and if it fall into a pit on the sabbath day, will he not lay hold on it, and lift *it* out?

12 How much then is a man better than a sheep? Wherefore it is lawful to do well on the sabbath days.

13 Then saith he to the man, Stretch forth thine hand. And he stretched *it* forth; and it was restored whole, like as the other.

MARK 3:1-6

1 And he entered again into the synagogue; and there was a man there which had a withered hand.

2 And they watched him, whether he would heal him on the sabbath day; that they might accuse him.

3 And he saith unto the man which had the withered hand, Stand forth.

4 And he saith unto them, Is it lawful to do good on the sabbath days, or to do evil? to save life, or to kill? But they held their peace.

5 And when he had looked round about on them with anger, being grieved for the hardness of their hearts, he saith unto the man, Stretch forth thine hand. And he stretched *it* out: and his hand was restored whole as the other.

6 And the Pharisees went forth, and straightway took counsel with the Herodians against him, how they might destroy him.

LUKE 6:6-11

6 And it came to pass also on another sabbath, that he entered into the synagogue and taught: and there was a man whose right hand was withered.

7 And the scribes and Pharisees watched him, whether he would heal on the sabbath day; that they might find an accusation against him.

8 But he knew their thoughts, and said to the man which had the withered hand, Rise up, and stand forth in the midst. And he arose and stood forth.

9 Then said Jesus unto them, I will ask you one thing; Is it lawful on the sabbath days to do good, or to do evil? to save life, or to destroy *it*?

10 And looking round about upon them all, he said unto the man, Stretch forth thy hand. And he did so: and his hand was restored whole as the other.

11 And they were filled with madness; and communed one with another what they might do to Jesus.

Jesus Ministers to a Multitude

Matthew 12:14, Mark 3:7-12, Luke 6:17-19

Then the Pharisees went out and took counsel together against Jesus, how they might destroy him.

Then Jesus withdrew with his disciples to the sea. And there followed him a great crowd of people from Galilee, and from Judea and Jerusalem and Idumea, and from beyond the Jordan, and from the region of Tyre and Sidon—a multitude of people came to him, for they had heard what great things he was doing. And he told his disciples to keep a boat ready for him, in case the people should crowd about him too closely. For he had healed many, and all who had diseases thronged about him to touch him.

And evil spirits, when they saw him, fell down before him shouting, "You are the Son of God!" But he charged them not to tell who he was.

And he came down the mountain with them to where there was a level piece of ground. And a great crowd of his disciples and throngs of people from Judea and Jerusalem and the coastlands of Tyre and Sidon came to hear him and to be healed of their diseases. Those who were possessed of evil spirits were delivered, and everyone sought to touch Jesus, for power was going forth from him and healing them all.

MATTHEW 12:14-21

14 Then the Pharisees went out, and held a council against him, how they might destroy him.

15 But when Jesus knew *it,* he withdrew himself from thence: and great multitudes followed him, and he healed them all;

16 And charged them that they should not make him known:

17 That it might be fulfilled which was spoken by Isaiah the prophet, saying,

18 Behold my servant, whom I have chosen; my beloved, in whom my soul is well pleased: I will put my Spirit upon him, and he shall show judgment to the Gentiles.

19 He shall not strive, nor cry; neither shall any man hear his voice in the streets.

20 A bruised reed shall he not break, and smoking flax shall he not quench, till he send forth judgment unto victory.

21 And in his name shall the Gentiles trust.

MARK 3:7-12

7 But Jesus withdrew himself with his disciples to the sea: and a great multitude from Galilee followed him, and from Judea,

8 And from Jerusalem, and from Idumea, and *from* beyond Jordan; and they about Tyre and Sidon, a great multitude, when they had heard what great things he did, came unto him.

9 And he spake to his disciples, that a small ship should wait on him because of the multitude, lest they should throng him.

10 For he had healed many; insomuch that they pressed upon him for to touch him, as many as had plagues.

11 And unclean spirits, when they saw him, fell down before him, and cried, saying, Thou art the Son of God.

12 And he straitly charged them that they should not make him known.

LUKE 6:17-19

17 And he came down with them, and stood in the plain, and the company of his disciples, and a great multitude of people out of all Judea and Jerusalem, and from the seacoast of Tyre and Sidon, which came to hear him, and to be healed of their diseases;

18 And they that were vexed with unclean spirits: and they were healed.

19 And the whole multitude sought to touch him: for there went virtue out of him, and healed *them* all.

Sowing the Seed. *A scene like this must have been common in the first century. Jesus used the illustration to impress on His followers the need to go and reap a spiritual harvest.*

The Plenteous Harvest

MATTHEW 9:35-38

35 And Jesus went about all the cities and villages, teaching in their synagogues, and preaching the gospel of the kingdom, and healing every sickness and every disease among the people.

36 But when he saw the multitudes, he was moved with compassion on them, because they fainted, and were scattered abroad, as sheep having no shepherd.

37 Then saith he unto his disciples, The harvest truly *is* plenteous, but the laborers *are* few;

38 Pray ye therefore the Lord of the harvest, that he will send forth laborers into his harvest.

Jesus Chooses the Twelve Apostles

Luke 6:12-16

Now it came to pass at that time that Jesus retired to a mountain to pray, and continued all night in prayer to God. And when it was day, he called his disciples and chose twelve of them, whom he named apostles: Simon (whom he also named Peter) and Andrew his brother, James and John, Phillip, Bartholomew, Matthew, Thomas, James the son of Alphaeus, Simon (called the Zealot), Judas the son of James, and Judas Iscariot, who became a traitor.

MATTHEW 10:1-4

1 And when he had called unto *him* his twelve disciples, he gave them power *against* unclean spirits, to cast them out, and to heal all manner of sickness and all manner of disease.

2 Now the names of the twelve apostles are these; The first, Simon, who is called Peter, and Andrew his brother; James *the son* of Zebedee, and John his brother;

3 Philip, and Bartholomew; Thomas, and Matthew the publican; James *the son* of Alpheus, and Lebbeus, whose surname was Thaddeus;

4 Simon the Canaanite, and Judas Iscariot, who also betrayed him.

MARK 3:13-19

13 And he goeth up into a mountain, and calleth *unto him* whom he would: and they came unto him.

14 And he ordained twelve, that they should be with him, and that he might send them forth to preach,

15 And to have power to heal sicknesses, and to cast out devils:

16 And Simon he surnamed Peter;

17 And James the *son* of Zebedee, and John the brother of James; and he surnamed them Boanerges, which is, The sons of thunder:

18 And Andrew, and Philip, and Bartholomew, and Matthew, and Thomas, and James the *son* of Alpheus, and Thaddeus, and Simon the Canaanite,

19 And Judas Iscariot, which also betrayed him. And they went into a house.

LUKE 6:12-16

12 And it came to pass in those days, that he went out into a mountain to pray, and continued all night in prayer to God.

13 And when it was day, he called *unto him* his disciples: and of them he chose twelve, whom also he named apostles;

14 Simon, (whom he also named Peter,) and Andrew his brother, James and John, Philip and Bartholomew,

15 Matthew and Thomas, James the *son* of Alpheus, and Simon called Zelotes,

16 And Judas *the brother* of James, and Judas Iscariot, which also was the traitor.

The Apostles Sent to Minister

Mark 6:6b-13, Matthew 10:40-11:1

Then Jesus went about among the villages teaching. And he called to him the twelve and began to send them out two by two, giving them power over evil spirits. And he instructed them to take nothing for their journey except a staff— no bread, no provision bag, no money in their purses; and to wear sandals, but no extra coat. And he said to them,

"In whatever house you receive lodging, stay there until you leave that place. And whatever place will not welcome you or listen to you, when you leave, shake the dust off your feet as a testimony against them.

"He who welcomes you welcomes me, and he who welcomes me welcomes him who sent me. He who welcomes a prophet because he is a prophet will receive a prophet's reward, and he who welcomes a righteous man because he is a righteous man will receive a righteous man's reward. And whoever gives even a cup of cold water to one of the least of these because he is my disciple, I tell you truly, he shall not lose his reward."

And when Jesus had finished instructing his twelve disciples, he departed from there to teach and preach in their towns. And the disciples went out and preached that men should repent. And they cast out many demons and anointed with oil many who were sick, and healed them.

MATTHEW 10:5-11:1	MARK 6:6b-13	LUKE 9:1-6
5 These twelve Jesus sent forth, and commanded them, saying, Go not into the way of the Gentiles, and into *any* city of the Samaritans enter ye not:	And he went round about the villages, teaching.	1 Then he called his twelve disciples together, and gave them power and authority over all devils, and to cure diseases.
6 But go rather to the lost sheep of the house of Israel.	7 And he called *unto him* the twelve, and began to send them forth by two and two; and gave them power over unclean spirits;	2 And he sent them to preach the kingdom of God, and to heal the sick.
7 And as ye go, preach, saying, The kingdom of heaven is at hand.		3 And he said unto them, Take nothing for *your* journey, neither staves, nor scrip, neither bread, neither money; neither have two coats apiece.
8 Heal the sick, cleanse the lepers, raise the dead, cast out devils: freely ye have received, freely give.	8 And commanded them that they should take nothing for *their* journey, save a staff only; no scrip, no bread, no money in *their* purse:	
9 Provide neither gold, nor silver, nor brass in your purses;		4 And whatsoever house ye enter into, there abide, and thence depart.
10 Nor scrip for *your* journey, neither two coats, neither shoes, nor yet staves: for the workman is worthy of his meat.	9 But *be* shod with sandals; and not put on two coats.	5 And whosoever will not receive you, when ye go out of that city, shake off the very dust from your feet for a testimony against them.
11 And into whatsoever city or town ye shall enter, inquire who in it is worthy; and there abide till ye go thence.	10 And he said unto them, In what place soever ye enter into a house, there abide till ye depart from that place.	6 And they departed, and went through the towns, preaching the gospel, and healing everywhere.
12 And when ye come into a house, salute it.		
13 And if the house be worthy, let your peace come upon it: but if it be not worthy, let your peace return to you.	11 And whosoever shall not receive you, nor hear you, when ye depart thence, shake off the dust under your feet for a testimony against them. Verily I say unto you, It shall be more tolerable for Sodom and Gomorrah in the day of judgment, than for that city.	
14 And whosoever shall not receive you, nor hear your words, when ye depart out of that house or city, shake off the dust of your feet.		
15 Verily I say unto you, It shall be more tolerable for the land of Sodom and Gomorrah in the day of judgment, than for that city.		
16 Behold, I send you forth as sheep in the midst of wolves: be ye therefore wise as serpents, and harmless as doves.		

The Apostles Sent to Minister (continued)

17 But beware of men: for they will deliver you up to the councils, and they will scourge you in their synagogues;

18 And ye shall be brought before governors and kings for my sake, for a testimony against them and the Gentiles.

19 But when they deliver you up, take no thought how or what ye shall speak: for it shall be given you in that same hour what ye shall speak.

20 For it is not ye that speak, but the Spirit of your Father which speaketh in you.

21 And the brother shall deliver up the brother to death, and the father the child: and the children shall rise up against *their* parents, and cause them to be put to death.

22 And ye shall be hated of all *men* for my name's sake: but he that endureth to the end shall be saved.

23 But when they persecute you in this city, flee ye into another: for verily I say unto you, Ye shall not have gone over the cities of Israel, till the Son of man be come.

24 The disciple is not above *his* master, nor the servant above his lord.

25 It is enough for the disciple that he be as his master, and the servant as his lord. If they have called the master of the house Beelzebub, how much more *shall they call* them of his household?

26 Fear them not therefore: for there is nothing covered, that shall not be revealed; and hid, that shall not be known.

27 What I tell you in darkness, *that* speak ye in light: and what ye hear in the ear, *that* preach ye upon the housetops.

28 And fear not them which kill the body, but are not able to kill the soul: but rather fear him which is able to destroy both soul and body in hell.

29 Are not two sparrows sold for a farthing? and one of them shall not fall on the ground without your Father.

30 But the very hairs of your head are all numbered.

31 Fear ye not therefore, ye are of more value than many sparrows.

32 Whosoever therefore shall confess me before men, him will I confess also before my Father which is in heaven.

33 But whosoever shall deny me before men, him will I also deny before my Father which is in heaven.

34 Think not that I am come to send peace on earth: I came not to send peace, but a sword.

35 For I am come to set a man at variance against his father, and the daughter against her mother, and the daughter-in-law against her mother-in-law.

36 And a man's foes *shall be* they of his own household.

37 He that loveth father or mother more than me is not worthy of me: and he that loveth son or daughter more than me is not worthy of me.

38 And he that taketh not his cross, and followeth after me, is not worthy of me.

39 He that findeth his life shall lose it: and he that loseth his life for my sake shall find it.

40 He that receiveth you receiveth me; and he that receiveth me receiveth him that sent me.

41 He that receiveth a prophet in the name of a prophet shall receive a prophet's reward; and he that receiveth a righteous man in the name of a righteous man shall receive a righteous man's reward.

42 And whosoever shall give to drink unto one of these little ones a cup of cold *water* only in the name of a disciple, verily I say unto you, he shall in no wise lose his reward.

11:1 And it came to pass, when Jesus had made an end of commanding his twelve disciples, he departed thence to teach and to preach in their cities.

12 And they went out, and preached that men should repent.

13 And they cast out many devils, and anointed with oil many that were sick, and healed *them*.

Sermon on the Mount: The Beatitudes

Matthew 5:1-12

And seeing the multitudes, Jesus went up on the mountain, and when he sat down, his disciples came to him. And he began to teach them, saying:

"Blessed are the humble in spirit, for theirs is the kingdom of heaven.

"Blessed are they that mourn, for they shall be comforted.

"Blessed are the meek, for they shall inherit the earth.

"Blessed are those who hunger and thirst after righteousness, for they shall be satisfied.

"Blessed are the merciful, for they shall obtain mercy.

"Blessed are the pure in heart, for they shall see God.

"Blessed are those who make peace, for they shall be called sons of God.

"Blessed are those who are persecuted for righteousness' sake, for theirs is the kingdom of heaven.

"Blessed are you when men revile you and persecute you and speak all manner of evil against you falsely because you are my disciples. Rejoice and be glad, for great is your reward in heaven, for so did men persecute the prophets who were before you."

MATTHEW 5:1-12

1 And seeing the multitudes, he went up into a mountain: and when he was set, his disciples came unto him:

2 And he opened his mouth, and taught them, saying,

3 Blessed *are* the poor in spirit: for theirs is the kingdom of heaven.

4 Blessed *are* they that mourn: for they shall be comforted.

5 Blessed *are* the meek: for they shall inherit the earth.

6 Blessed *are* they which do hunger and thirst after righteousness: for they shall be filled.

7 Blessed *are* the merciful: for they shall obtain mercy.

8 Blessed *are* the pure in heart: for they shall see God.

9 Blessed *are* the peacemakers: for they shall be called the children of God.

10 Blessed *are* they which are persecuted for righteousness' sake: for theirs is the kingdom of heaven.

11 Blessed are ye, when *men* shall revile you, and persecute *you*, and shall say all manner of evil against you falsely, for my sake.

12 Rejoice, and be exceeding glad: for great *is* your reward in heaven: for so persecuted they the prophets which were before you.

LUKE 6:20-26

20 And he lifted up his eyes on his disciples, and said, Blessed *be ye* poor: for yours is the kingdom of God.

21 Blessed *are ye* that hunger now: for ye shall be filled. Blessed *are ye* that weep now: for ye shall laugh.

22 Blessed are ye, when men shall hate you, and when they shall separate you *from their company*, and shall reproach *you*, and cast out your name as evil, for the Son of man's sake.

23 Rejoice ye in that day, and leap for joy: for, behold, your reward *is* great in heaven: for in the like manner did their fathers unto the prophets.

24 But woe unto you that are rich! for ye have received your consolation.

25 Woe unto you that are full! for ye shall hunger. Woe unto you that laugh now! for ye shall mourn and weep.

26 Woe unto you, when all men shall speak well of you! for so did their fathers to the false prophets.

Church of the Beatitudes. *West of the northern end of the Sea of Galilee is the hill where tradition says Jesus preached the Sermon on the Mount. It is 8-sided, to remind us of the Beatitudes.*

Importance of True Discipleship

Matthew 5:13-20

"You are the salt of the earth; but if salt has lost its taste, how can it be salted? It is then fit only to be thrown out and trampled under foot by men.

"You are the light of the world. A city set on a hill cannot be hid. Nor do men light a lamp and place it under a bushel, but on a lamp stand, and it gives light to all who are in the house. So let your light shine before men, that they may see your good works and give praise to your Father in heaven.

"Do not think that I have come to abolish the law or the prophets; I have come, not to abolish, but to fulfill them. For I tell you truly, till heaven and earth pass away, not one little letter or one little mark will pass from the law until it is all fulfilled. Therefore, whoever disregards one of the least of these commandments and teaches others to do so will be called the least in the kingdom of heaven, but whoever observes them and teaches them will be called great in the kingdom of heaven. For I tell you, unless your righteousness exceeds that of the scribes and Pharisees, you will in no wise enter the kingdom of heaven."

13 Ye are the salt of the earth: but if the salt have lost his savor, wherewith shall it be salted? it is thenceforth good for nothing, but to be cast out, and to be trodden under foot of men.

14 Ye are the light of the world. A city that is set on a hill cannot be hid.

15 Neither do men light a candle, and put it under a bushel, but on a candlestick; and it giveth light unto all that are in the house.

16 Let your light so shine before men, that they may see your good works, and glorify your Father which is in heaven.

17 Think not that I am come to destroy the law, or the prophets: I am not come to destroy, but to fulfil.

18 For verily I say unto you, Till heaven and earth pass, one jot or one tittle shall in no wise pass from the law, till all be fulfilled.

19 Whosoever therefore shall break one of these least commandments, and shall teach men so, he shall be called the least in the kingdom of heaven: but whosoever shall do and teach *them,* the same shall be called great in the kingdom of heaven.

20 For I say unto you, That except your righteousness shall exceed *the righteousness* of the scribes and Pharisees, ye shall in no case enter into the kingdom of heaven.

Righteousness a Matter of the Heart

Matthew 5:21-48

"You have heard that it was said to the people of old, 'You shall not kill; and whoever commits murder shall be liable to judgment.' But I say to you, everyone who is angry with his brother shall be liable to judgment. Whoever shall say to his brother, 'Raca,' shall be answerable to the council, and whoever shall say, 'Moreh,' shall be in danger of hell fire.

"Therefore, if you bring a gift to the altar and there remember that your brother has something

21 Ye have heard that it was said by them of old time, Thou shalt not kill; and whosoever shall kill shall be in danger of the judgment:

22 But I say unto you, that whosoever is angry with his brother without a cause shall be in danger of the judgment: and whosoever shall say to his brother, Raca, shall be in danger of the council: but whosoever shall say, Thou fool, shall be in danger of hell fire.

23 Therefore if thou bring thy gift to the altar, and there rememberest that thy brother hath aught against thee;

24 Leave there thy gift before the altar, and

Righteousness a Matter of the Heart (continued)

against you, leave your gift there at the altar and go your way; first be reconciled to your brother, and then go and offer your gift. Come to agreement with your accuser without delay, lest he hand you over to the judge, and the judge to the jailer, and you be thrown into prison. I tell you truly, you will never get out of there until you pay the last penny.

"You have heard that it was said, 'You shall not commit adultery.' But I say to you, everyone who looks at a woman with lust has already committed adultery with her in his heart. Therefore, if your right eye causes you to sin, pluck it out and throw it away. It is better that one of your members should be lost than that your whole body should be cast into hell. And if your right hand causes you to sin, cut it off and throw it away. It is better that one of your members should be lost than that your whole body should enter into hell.

"It was also said, 'Whoever divorces his wife must give her a certificate of divorce.' But I say to you, everyone who divorces his wife, except on the ground of unfaithfulness, causes her to become an adulteress, and whoever marries the divorced woman commits adultery.

"Again, you have heard that it was said to the people of old, 'You shall not swear falsely, but shall perform your oaths to the Lord.' But I say to you, do not take oaths at all—neither by heaven, for it is God's throne; nor by the earth, for it is his footstool; nor by Jerusalem, for it is the city of the great King. And do not swear by your head, for you cannot make a single hair white or black. But let your word be simply 'yes' or 'no.' Anything more than this is of evil.

"You have heard that it was said, 'An eye for an eye, and a tooth for a tooth.' But I say to you, do not seek to retaliate against an evil man. Rather, if anyone strikes you on the right cheek, turn the other to him also. If anyone wants to sue you for your shirt, give him your coat as well. If anyone compels you to go a mile, go two miles with him. Give to him who asks anything of you, and do not refuse anyone who wishes to borrow from you.

go thy way; first be reconciled to thy brother, and then come and offer thy gift.

25 Agree with thine adversary quickly, while thou art in the way with him; lest at any time the adversary deliver thee to the judge, and the judge deliver thee to the officer, and thou be cast into prison.

26 Verily I say unto thee, Thou shalt by no means come out thence, till thou hast paid the uttermost farthing.

27 Ye have heard that it was said by them of old time, Thou shalt not commit adultery:

28 But I say unto you, That whosoever looketh on a woman to lust after her hath committed adultery with her already in his heart.

29 And if thy right eye offend thee, pluck it out, and cast *it* from thee: for it is profitable for thee that one of thy members should perish, and not *that* thy whole body should be cast into hell.

30 And if thy right hand offend thee, cut it off, and cast *it* from thee: for it is profitable for thee that one of thy members should perish, and not *that* thy whole body should be cast into hell.

31 It hath been said, Whosoever shall put away his wife, let him give her a writing of divorcement:

32 But I say unto you, That whosoever shall put away his wife, saving for the cause of fornication, causeth her to commit adultery: and whosoever shall marry her that is divorced committeth adultery.

33 Again, ye have heard that it hath been said by them of old time, Thou shalt not forswear thyself, but shalt perform unto the Lord thine oaths:

34 But I say unto you, Swear not at all; neither by heaven; for it is God's throne:

35 Nor by the earth; for it is his footstool: neither by Jerusalem; for it is the city of the great King.

36 Neither shalt thou swear by thy head, because thou canst not make one hair white or black.

37 But let your communication be, Yea, yea; Nay, nay: for whatsoever is more than these cometh of evil.

38 Ye have heard that it hath been said, An eye for an eye, and a tooth for a tooth:

39 But I say unto you, That ye resist not evil: but whosoever shall smite thee on thy right cheek, turn to him the other also.

115

"You have heard that it was said, 'You shall love your neighbor and hate your enemy.' But I say to you, love your enemies and pray for those who persecute you, so that you may be sons of your Father who is in heaven; for he causes his sun to rise on both the evil and the good, and sends rain on the righteous and the wicked alike. For if you love only those who love you, why should you expect to be rewarded for that? Even the tax collectors do that much. And if you greet only your friends, are you doing anything remarkable? Even the heathen do that much. But you, however, must strive to be like your Father in heaven."

MATTHEW 5:21-48 ✓

40 And if any man will sue thee at the law, and take away thy coat, let him have *thy* cloak also.

41 And whosoever shall compel thee to go a mile, go with him twain.

42 Give to him that asketh thee, and from him that would borrow of thee turn not thou away.

43 Ye have heard that it hath been said, Thou shalt love thy neighbor, and hate thine enemy.

And whosoever shall compel thee to go a mile, go with him twain.

---

44 But I say unto you, Love your enemies, bless them that curse you, do good to them that hate you, and pray for them which despitefully use you, and persecute you;

45 That ye may be the children of your Father which is in heaven: for he maketh his sun to rise on the evil and on the good, and sendeth rain on the just and on the unjust.

46 For if ye love them which love you, what reward have ye? do not even the publicans the same?

47 And if ye salute your brethren only, what do ye more *than others?* do not even the publicans so?

48 Be ye therefore perfect, even as your Father which is in heaven is perfect.

LUKE 6:27-36 ✓

27 But I say unto you which hear, Love your enemies, do good to them which hate you,

28 Bless them that curse you, and pray for them which despitefully use you.

29 And unto him that smiteth thee on the *one* cheek offer also the other; and him that taketh away thy cloak forbid not *to take thy* coat also.

30 Give to every man that asketh of thee; and of him that taketh away thy goods ask *them* not again.

31 And as ye would that men should do to you, do ye also to them likewise.

32 For if ye love them which love you, what thank have ye? for sinners also love those that love them.

33 And if ye do good to them which do good to you, what thank have ye? for sinners also do even the same.

34 And if ye lend *to them* of whom ye hope to receive, what thank have ye? for sinners also lend to sinners, to receive as much again.

35 But love ye your enemies, and do good, and lend, hoping for nothing again; and your reward shall be great, and ye shall be the children of the Highest: for he is kind unto the unthankful and *to* the evil.

36 Be ye therefore merciful, as your Father also is merciful.

Roman Milestone (right). Roman law of the first century asserted the right of its soldiers to conscript people to carry a load one mile. Jesus asked His disciples to adopt the "second mile" principle.

Importance of Sincerity

Matthew 6:1-18

"Take care that you do not practice your religion publicly merely to be seen by men; for in that case, you will have no reward from your Father in heaven. Therefore, when you give alms, do not sound a trumpet before you, as the hypocrites do in the synagogues and in the streets, in order that they may be admired by men. I tell you truly, they have already received their reward. But you, when you give alms, do not let your left hand know what your right hand is doing, in order that your alms may be secret; and your Father, who sees everything done in secret, will reward you.

"And when you pray, do not be like the hypocrites; for they love to stand and pray in the synagogues and on the street corners, in order that they may be seen by men. I tell you truly, they have already received their reward. But you, when you pray, go into your room and shut the door and pray to your Father in private; and your Father, who sees everything done in secret, will reward you.

"And when you pray, do not repeat empty phrases over and over, as the heathen do; for they think that the longer they speak the more likely they are to be heard. Do not be like them, for your Father knows everything you need before you ask him. After this manner therefore pray:

Our Father in heaven, hallowed be your name.
May your kingdom come, may your will be done on earth, even as it is in heaven.
Give us this day our daily bread.
Forgive us our sins, as we also have forgiven those who have wronged us.
And lead us not into temptation, but deliver us from evil.

"For if you forgive men their trespasses, your heavenly Father will also forgive you; but if you do not forgive men their trespasses, neither will your Father forgive your trespasses.

"And when you fast, do not assume a sad countenance, like the hypocrites; for they disfigure their faces, so that men may be sure

MATTHEW 6:1-18 √

1 Take heed that ye do not your alms before men, to be seen of them: otherwise ye have no reward of your Father which is in heaven.

2 Therefore when thou doest *thine* alms, do not sound a trumpet before thee, as the hypocrites do in the synagogues and in the streets, that they may have glory of men. Verily I say unto you, They have their reward.

3 But when thou doest alms, let not thy left hand know what thy right hand doeth:

4 That thine alms may be in secret: and thy Father which seeth in secret himself shall reward thee openly.

5 And when thou prayest, thou shalt not be as the hypocrites *are:* for they love to pray standing in the synagogues and in the corners of the streets, that they may be seen of men. Verily I say unto you, They have their reward.

6 But thou, when thou prayest, enter into thy closet, and when thou hast shut thy door, pray to thy Father which is in secret; and thy Father which seeth in secret shall reward thee openly.

7 But when ye pray, use not vain repetitions, as the heathen *do:* for they think that they shall be heard for their much speaking.

8 Be not ye therefore like unto them: for your Father knoweth what things ye have need of, before ye ask him.

9 After this manner therefore pray ye: Our Father which art in heaven, Hallowed be thy name.

10 Thy kingdom come. Thy will be done in earth, as *it is* in heaven.

11 Give us this day our daily bread.

12 And forgive us our debts, as we forgive our debtors.

13 And lead us not into temptation, but deliver us from evil: For thine is the kingdom, and the power, and the glory, for ever. Amen.

14 For if ye forgive men their trespasses, your heavenly Father will also forgive you:

15 But if ye forgive not men their trespasses, neither will your Father forgive your trespasses.

16 Moreover when ye fast, be not, as the hypocrites, of a sad countenance: for they disfigure their faces, that they may appear unto men to fast. Verily I say unto you, They have their reward.

17 But thou, when thou fastest, anoint thine head, and wash thy face;

Importance of Sincerity (continued)

to see that they are fasting. I tell you truly, they have already received their reward. But you, when you fast, anoint your head and wash your face, that you may not appear to men to be fasting, but rather only to your Father; and your Father, who sees everything done in secret, will reward you.''

MATTHEW 6:1-18

18 That thou appear not unto men to fast, but unto thy Father which is in secret: and thy Father which seeth in secret shall reward thee openly.

True Devotion Needed

Matthew 6:19-24

''Do not store up treasures for yourselves here on earth, where moths and rust destroy and where thieves break in and steal; but store up for yourselves treasures in heaven, where neither moths nor rust destroy and where thieves do not break in and steal. For where your treasure is, there will your heart be also.

''The eye is the body's lamp. Therefore, if your eye is sound, your whole body will be full of light; but if your eye is defective, your whole body will be full of darkness. In like manner, if the 'light' which is in you is darkness, how great is that darkness!

''No man can serve two masters. For he will hate this one and love the other, or be loyal to this one and despise that one. You cannot serve both God and mammon.

MATTHEW 6:19-24

19 Lay not up for yourselves treasures upon earth, where moth and rust doth corrupt, and where thieves break through and steal:

20 But lay up for yourselves treasures in heaven, where neither moth nor rust doth corrupt, and where thieves do not break through nor steal:

21 For where your treasure is, there will your heart be also.

22 The light of the body is the eye: if therefore thine eye be single, thy whole body shall be full of light.

23 But if thine eye be evil, thy whole body shall be full of darkness. If therefore the light that is in thee be darkness, how great *is* that darkness!

24 No man can serve two masters: for either he will hate the one, and love the other; or else he will hold to the one, and despise the other. Ye cannot serve God and mammon.

Cloister of the Pater Noster Church. Pater Noster means "Our Father," and the church on the Mount of Olives contains the Lord's Prayer in more than 60 different languages. See page 270 for an example.

119

Putting God's Kingdom First

Matthew 6:25-34

"Therefore I say to you, do not be anxious about your life—what you are to eat or to drink, nor about you body—what you are to put on. Is not life more than food, and the body more than clothes? Behold the birds of the air: they neither sow nor reap, nor do they gather into barns; yet your heavenly Father feeds them. Are you not of more value than they? And which of you, by worrying about it, can add another hour to his life? And why be anxious about clothing? Consider the lilies of the field, how they grow: they neither toil nor spin; but I say to you, not even Solomon in all his glory was attired like one of these. But if God so clothes the grass of the field, which is here today and tomorrow is cast into the oven, will he not much more clothe you, O men of little faith?

"Therefore do not worry, saying, 'What shall we eat?' or 'What shall we drink?' or 'What shall we wear?' For your heavenly Father knows that you need all these things; and those are the things the heathen spend all their time anxiously seeking. But seek first the kingdom of God and his righteousness, and all these things will be added to you. Therefore do not worry about tomorrow, for tomorrow will have its own cares. One day's care is enough for the day.''

MATTHEW 6:25-34

25 Therefore I say unto you, Take no thought for your life, what ye shall eat, or what ye shall drink; nor yet for your body, what ye shall put on. Is not the life more than meat, and the body than raiment?

26 Behold the fowls of the air: for they sow not, neither do they reap, nor gather into barns; yet your heavenly Father feedeth them. Are ye not much better than they?

27 Which of you by taking thought can add one cubit unto his stature?

28 And why take ye thought for raiment? Consider the lilies of the field, how they grow; they toil not, neither do they spin:

29 And yet I say unto you, That even Solomon in all his glory was not arrayed like one of these.

30 Wherefore, if God so clothe the grass of the field, which today is, and tomorrow is cast into the oven, *shall he* not much more *clothe* you, O ye of little faith?

31 Therefore take no thought, saying, What shall we eat? or, What shall we drink? or, Wherewithal shall we be clothed?

32 (For after all these things do the Gentiles seek:) for your heavenly Father knoweth that ye have need of all these things.

33 But seek ye first the kingdom of God, and his righteousness; and all these things shall be added unto you.

34 Take therefore no thought for the morrow: for the morrow shall take thought for the things of itself. Sufficient unto the day *is* the evil thereof.

Lilies of the Field. In His Sermon on the Mount Jesus emphasized the need not to be concerned about things like clothing and cited the lilies of the field as examples of the Father's care.

Charity Toward Others

Matthew 7:1-12

"Do not pass judgment on others, lest you be judged yourselves. For with the same judgment you offer of others, you yourselves will be judged, and in the same measure. And why do you stare at the speck in your brother's eye, but disregard the timber-pole in your own eye? How can you say to your brother, 'Let me take the speck out of your eye,' and behold, there is a timber-pole in your own eye? You hypocrite! First take the timber-pole out of your own eye, and then you will see clearly enough to take the speck out of your brother's eye.

"Do not give that which is holy to dogs, nor throw your pearls before pigs, lest they trample them under their feet and turn and attack you.

"Ask, and it will be given you; seek, and you will find; knock, and it will be opened to you. For everyone who asks receives, and he who seeks finds, and to him who knocks it will be opened. What man among you, if his son asks him for a loaf of bread, will give him a stone? And if he asks him for a fish, will he give him a serpent? If you then, being evil, know how to give good gifts to your children, how much more will your Father in heaven give good gifts to those who ask him!

"Therefore, treat others in the same way you wish them to treat you. This is the real meaning of the law and the prophets."

MATTHEW 7:1-12 √

1 Judge not, that ye be not judged.

2 For with what judgment ye judge, ye shall be judged: and with what measure ye mete, it shall be measured to you again.

3 And why beholdest thou the mote that is in thy brother's eye, but considerest not the beam that is in thine own eye?

4 Or how wilt thou say to thy brother, Let me pull out the mote out of thine eye; and, behold, a beam *is* in thine own eye?

5 Thou hypocrite, first cast out the beam out of thine own eye; and then shalt thou see clearly to cast out the mote out of thy brother's eye.

6 Give not that which is holy unto the dogs, neither cast ye your pearls before swine, lest they trample them under their feet, and turn again and rend you.

7 Ask, and it shall be given you; seek, and ye shall find; knock, and it shall be opened unto you:

8 For every one that asketh receiveth; and he that seeketh findeth; and to him that knocketh it shall be opened.

9 Or what man is there of you, whom if his son ask bread, will he give him a stone?

10 Or if he ask a fish, will he give him a serpent?

11 If ye then, being evil, know how to give good gifts unto your children, how much more shall your Father which is in heaven give good things to them that ask him?

12 Therefore all things whatsoever ye would that men should do to you, do ye even so to them: for this is the law and the prophets.

LUKE 6:37-42 √

37 Judge not, and ye shall not be judged: condemn not, and ye shall not be condemned: forgive, and ye shall be forgiven:

38 Give, and it shall be given unto you; good measure, pressed down, and shaken together, and running over, shall men give into your bosom. For with the same measure that ye mete withal it shall be measured to you again.

39 And he spake a parable unto them; Can the blind lead the blind? shall they not both fall into the ditch?

40 The disciple is not above his master: but every one that is perfect shall be as his master.

41 And why beholdest thou the mote that is in thy brother's eye, but perceivest not the beam that is in thine own eye?

42 Either how canst thou say to thy brother, Brother, let me pull out the mote that is in thine eye, when thou thyself beholdest not the beam that is in thine own eye? Thou hypocrite, cast out first the beam out of thine own eye, and then shalt thou see clearly to pull out the mote that is in thy brother's eye.

Solemn Warnings

Matthew 7:13-8:1

"Enter in by the narrow gate; for wide is the gate and broad is the way which leads to destruction, and many there are who enter there. But narrow is the gate and the way which lead to life, and few there are who find it.

"Beware of false prophets, who come to you dressed like sheep but really are ravenous wolves. You will know them by their fruits. Do men gather grapes from thorn bushes, or figs from thistles? Every good tree bears good fruit, but a bad tree bears evil fruit. A good tree cannot bear evil fruit, nor can a bad tree bear good fruit. Every tree which does not produce good fruit is cut down and cast into the fire. Thus, by their fruits you will know them.

"Not everyone who says to me, 'Lord, Lord,' shall enter the kingdom of heaven, but only he who does the will of my Father in heaven. Many will say to me in that day, 'Lord, Lord, did we not preach in your name, and in your name cast out demons, and in your name do many great works?' Then will I declare to them, 'I never knew you; depart from me, you who work evil.'

"Therefore, everyone who hears these words of mine and puts them into practice will be like a wise man who built his house on the rock. The rain fell, and the floods came, and the winds blew and beat against that house; but it did not fall, because it was founded on the rock. And everyone who hears these words of mine and does not put them into practice will be like a foolish man who built his house on the sand. The rain fell, and the floods came, and the winds blew and beat against the house; and it fell, and great was the fall of it."

And when Jesus had finished these sayings, the people were astonished at his teaching, for he taught them as one having authority, and not as the scribes. And when he came down from the mountain, great multitudes followed him.

Site of Pool of Bethesda. *These ruins mark the location where Jesus healed a man who had been ill for 38 years. They are the remains of a Byzantine church built to commemorate the miracle.*

Solemn Warnings (continued)

13 Enter ye in at the strait gate: for wide is the gate, and broad *is* the way, that leadeth to destruction, and many there be which go in thereat:

14 Because strait *is* the gate, and narrow *is* the way, which leadeth unto life, and few there be that find it.

15 Beware of false prophets, which come to you in sheep's clothing, but inwardly they are ravening wolves.

16 Ye shall know them by their fruits. Do men gather grapes of thorns, or figs of thistles?

17 Even so every good tree bringeth forth good fruit; but a corrupt tree bringeth forth evil fruit.

18 A good tree cannot bring forth evil fruit, neither *can* a corrupt tree bring forth good fruit.

19 Every tree that bringeth not forth good fruit is hewn down, and cast into the fire.

20 Wherefore by their fruits ye shall know them.

21 Not every one that saith unto me, Lord, Lord, shall enter into the kingdom of heaven; but he that doeth the will of my Father which is in heaven.

22 Many will say to me in that day, Lord, Lord, have we not prophesied in thy name? and in thy name have cast out devils? and in thy name done many wonderful works?

23 And then will I profess unto them, I never knew you: depart from me, ye that work iniquity.

24 Therefore whosoever heareth these sayings of mine, and doeth them, I will liken him unto a wise man, which built his house upon a rock:

25 And the rain descended, and the floods came, and the winds blew, and beat upon that house; and it fell not: for it was founded upon a rock.

26 And every one that heareth these sayings of mine, and doeth them not, shall be likened unto a foolish man, which built his house upon the sand:

27 And the rain descended, and the floods came, and the winds blew, and beat upon that house; and it fell: and great was the fall of it.

28 And it came to pass, when Jesus had ended these sayings, the people were astonished at his doctrine:

29 For he taught them as *one* having authority, and not as the scribes.

8:1 When he was come down from the mountain, great multitudes followed him.

43 For a good tree bringeth not forth corrupt fruit; neither doth a corrupt tree bring forth good fruit.

44 For every tree is known by his own fruit. For of thorns men do not gather figs, nor of a bramble bush gather they grapes.

45 A good man out of the good treasure of his heart bringeth forth that which is good; and an evil man out of the evil treasure of his heart bringeth forth that which is evil: for of the abundance of the heart his mouth speaketh.

46 And why call ye me, Lord, Lord, and do not the things which I say?

47 Whosoever cometh to me, and heareth my sayings, and doeth them, I will show you to whom he is like:

48 He is like a man which built a house, and digged deep, and laid the foundation on a rock: and when the flood arose, the stream beat vehemently upon that house, and could not shake it; for it was founded upon a rock.

49 But he that heareth, and doeth not, is like a man that without a foundation built a house upon the earth; against which the stream did beat vehemently, and immediately it fell; and the ruin of that house was great.

Rose at Jacob's Well. As the above passages show, Jesus often used plant life to illustrate truth. Many flowers adorn the landscape of Israel, which is becoming known for its lovely roses.

Centurion's Servant Healed. *This man had so much faith in Jesus he believed the Master could heal, even from a distance, just by speaking the word. The Lord responded by performing the miracle and said the centurion had displayed more faith than Jesus' own countrymen.*

Jesus Heals a Centurion's Servant

Matthew 8:5-13

Now as Jesus entered Capernaum, a centurion came to him pleading, "Sir, my servant is lying at home paralyzed and in great distress."

"I will come and heal him," said Jesus.

"Sir," replied the centurion, "I am not worthy to have you come under my roof; but only speak the word, and my servant will be healed. For I, too, am a man under authority, and I have soldiers under me. And I say to this man, 'Go,' and he goes; and to another, 'Come,' and he comes; and to my servant, 'Do this,' and he does it."

When Jesus heard this, he marveled, and said to those who were following him, "I tell you truly, I have not found such great faith in all Israel. I say to you, many will come from the east and the west and sit down around the table with Abraham, Isaac, and Jacob in the kingdom of heaven. But the heirs of the kingdom will be cast into the outer darkness, where there will be weeping and gnashing of teeth."

Then said Jesus to the centurion, "Go your way; it shall be done for you just as you have believed." And the servant was healed that moment.

MATTHEW 8:5-13 ✓

5 And when Jesus was entered into Capernaum, there came unto him a centurion, beseeching him,

6 And saying, Lord, my servant lieth at home sick of the palsy, grievously tormented.

7 And Jesus saith unto him, I will come and heal him.

8 The centurion answered and said, Lord, I am not worthy that thou shouldest come under my roof: but speak the word only, and my servant shall be healed.

9 For I am a man under authority, having soldiers under me: and I say to this *man,* Go, and he goeth; and to another, Come, and he cometh; and to my servant, Do this, and he doeth *it.*

10 When Jesus heard *it,* he marveled, and said to them that followed, Verily I say unto you, I have not found so great faith, no, not in Israel.

11 And I say unto you, That many shall come from the east and west, and shall sit down with Abraham, and Isaac, and Jacob, in the kingdom of heaven:

12 But the children of the kingdom shall be cast out into outer darkness: there shall be weeping and gnashing of teeth.

13 And Jesus said unto the centurion, Go thy way; and as thou hast believed, *so* be it done unto thee. And his servant was healed in the selfsame hour.

LUKE 7:1-10 ✓

1 Now when he had ended all his sayings in the audience of the people, he entered into Capernaum.

2 And a certain centurion's servant, who was dear unto him, was sick, and ready to die.

3 And when he heard of Jesus, he sent unto him the elders of the Jews, beseeching him that he would come and heal his servant.

4 And when they came to Jesus, they besought him instantly, saying, That he was worthy for whom he should do this:

5 For he loveth our nation, and he hath built us a synagogue.

6 Then Jesus went with them. And when he was now not far from the house, the centurion sent friends to him, saying unto him, Lord, trouble not thyself; for I am not worthy that thou shouldest enter under my roof:

7 Wherefore neither thought I myself worthy to come unto thee: but say in a word, and my servant shall be healed.

8 For I also am a man set under authority, having under me soldiers, and I say unto one, Go, and he goeth; and to another, Come, and he cometh; and to my servant, Do this, and he doeth *it.*

9 When Jesus heard these things, he marveled at him, and turned him about, and said unto the people that followed him, I say unto you, I have not found so great faith, no, not in Israel.

10 And they that were sent, returning to the house, found the servant whole that had been sick.

Jesus Raises a Widow's Son

Luke 7:11-17

Now it came to pass that, soon afterward, Jesus went to a town called Nain, and his disciples and a large crowd went with him. And as he drew near to the town gate, behold, a man who had died was being carried out for burial, the only son of his mother, who was a widow; and many people from the town were with her. Now when the Lord saw her, he was moved with pity for her and said to her, "Do not weep."

And he walked up and put his hand on the funeral pallet, and the pallbearers stopped.

"Young man," said Jesus, "I say to you, rise."

And the man who had been dead sat up and began to speak, and Jesus gave him back to his mother. And all the people were filled with reverence and awe, and they began to praise God, saying, "A great prophet has risen among us!" and "God has visited his people!"

And this report concerning Jesus spread through all Judea and all the surrounding country.

11 And it came to pass the day after, that he went into a city called Nain; and many of his disciples went with him, and much people.

12 Now when he came nigh to the gate of the city, behold, there was a dead man carried out, the only son of his mother, and she was a widow: and much people of the city was with her.

13 And when the Lord saw her, he had compassion on her, and said unto her, Weep not.

14 And he came and touched the bier: and they that bare *him* stood still. And he said, Young man, I say unto thee, Arise.

15 And he that was dead sat up, and began to speak. And he delivered him to his mother.

16 And there came a fear on all: and they glorified God, saying, That a great prophet is risen up among us; and, That God hath visited his people.

17 And this rumor of him went forth throughout all Judea, and throughout all the region round about.

Jesus Defends John's Ministry

Luke 7:18-35

And the disciples of John told him of all these things. Then John called two of his disciples to him and sent them to the Lord to ask, "Are you the one who is to come, or are we to look for another?"

And when the men had come to Jesus, they said, "John the Baptist sent us to you to ask, 'Are you the one who is to come, or are we to look for another?'"

And in that same hour, Jesus healed many of diseases and plagues and evil spirits, and gave sight to many who were blind. Then he said to the messengers, "Go and tell John what you have seen and heard—how the blind receive sight, the lame walk, lepers are healed, the deaf hear, the dead are raised, and the poor have good tidings preached to them. And blessed is the man who finds in me no occasion to take offense."

When the messengers of John had departed, Jesus began to speak to the people about John:

"What did you go out to the wilderness to see—a reed shaken by the wind? What did you go out to see—a man dressed in expensive clothes? Behold, those who wear fine clothes and live in luxury are in kings' courts. But what did you go out to see? A prophet? Yes, I tell you—

and more than just a prophet! This is he of whom it is written, 'Behold, I send my messenger before your face, who shall prepare your way before you.'

"I tell you," said Jesus, "among those born of women, there is no one greater than John. Yet he who is least in the kingdom of God is greater than he. And all the people who gave heed to John—even the tax collectors—acknowledged the justice and righteousness of God by submitting to John's baptism. But the Pharisees and the scribes, by refusing John's baptism, rejected God's purpose for them.

"To what shall I compare the men of this generation? What are they like? They are like children sitting in the market place and calling one to another, 'We played the flute for you, but you did not dance; we sang a funeral dirge, but you did not weep.' For John the Baptist came neither eating bread nor drinking wine, and you say, 'He is demon possessed.' And the Son of Man has come eating and drinking, and you say, 'Behold, a glutton and a wine drinker, a friend of tax collectors and sinners!' But wisdom is justified by all her children."

MATTHEW 11:2-19

2 Now when John had heard in the prison the works of Christ, he sent two of his disciples,

3 And said unto him, Art thou he that should come, or do we look for another?

4 Jesus answered and said unto them, Go and show John again those things which ye do hear and see:

5 The blind receive their sight, and the lame walk, the lepers are cleansed, and the deaf hear, the dead are raised up, and the poor have the gospel preached to them.

6 And blessed is *he,* whosoever shall not be offended in me.

7 And as they departed, Jesus began to say unto the multitudes concerning John, What went ye out into the wilderness to see? A reed shaken with the wind?

8 But what went ye out for to see? A man clothed in soft raiment? behold, they that wear soft *clothing* are in kings' houses.

9 But what went ye out for to see? A prophet? yea, I say unto you, and more than a prophet.

10 For this is *he,* of whom it is written, Behold, I send my messenger before thy face, which shall prepare thy way before thee.

11 Verily I say unto you, Among them that are born of women there hath not risen a greater than John the Baptist: notwithstanding, he that is least in the kingdom of heaven is greater than he.

12 And from the days of John the Baptist until now the kingdom of heaven suffereth violence, and the violent take it by force.

LUKE 7:18-35

18 And the disciples of John showed him of all these things.

19 And John calling *unto him* two of his disciples sent *them* to Jesus, saying, Art thou he that should come? or look we for another?

20 When the men were come unto him, they said, John Baptist hath sent us unto thee, saying, Art thou he that should come? or look we for another?

21 And in that same hour he cured many of *their* infirmities and plagues, and of evil spirits; and unto many *that were* blind he gave sight.

22 Then Jesus answering said unto them, Go your way, and tell John what things ye have seen and heard; how that the blind see, the lame walk, the lepers are cleansed, the deaf hear, the dead are raised, to the poor the gospel is preached.

23 And blessed is *he,* whosoever shall not be offended in me.

24 And when the messengers of John were departed, he began to speak unto the people concerning John, What went ye out into the wilderness for to see? A reed shaken with the wind?

25 But what went ye out for to see? A man clothed in soft raiment? Behold, they which are gorgeously appareled, and live delicately, are in kings' courts.

26 But what went ye out for to see? A prophet? Yea, I say unto you, and much more than a prophet.

27 This is *he,* of whom it is written, Behold, I send my messenger before thy face, which shall prepare thy way before thee.

Jesus Defends John's Ministry (continued)

MATTHEW 11:2-19

13 For all the prophets and the law prophesied until John.

14 And if ye will receive *it,* this is Elijah, which was for to come.

15 He that hath ears to hear, let him hear.

16 But whereunto shall I liken this generation? It is like unto children sitting in the markets, and calling unto their fellows,

17 And saying, We have piped unto you, and ye have not danced; we have mourned unto you, and ye have not lamented.

18 For John came neither eating nor drinking, and they say, He hath a devil.

19 The Son of man came eating and drinking, and they say, Behold a man gluttonous, and a winebibber, a friend of publicans and sinners. But wisdom is justified of her children.

Qumran Caves. *The Dead Sea Scrolls, found in 1947, were written before the Christian era by Essenes, a holiness sect living at Qumran. Later they hid them in nearby caves. Some believe John the Baptist was acquainted with these people.*

LUKE 7:18-35

28 For I say unto you, Among those that are born of women there is not a greater prophet than John the Baptist: but he that is least in the kingdom of God is greater than he.

29 And all the people that heard *him,* and the publicans, justified God, being baptized with the baptism of John.

30 But the Pharisees and lawyers rejected the counsel of God against themselves, being not baptized of him.

31 And the Lord said, Whereunto then shall I liken the men of this generation? and to what are they like?

32 They are like unto children sitting in the market place, and calling one to another, and saying, We have piped unto you, and ye have not danced; we have mourned to you, and ye have not wept.

33 For John the Baptist came neither eating bread nor drinking wine; and ye say, He hath a devil.

34 The Son of man is come eating and drinking; and ye say, Behold a gluttonous man, and a winebibber, a friend of publicans and sinners!

35 But wisdom is justified of all her children.

Jesus Welcomes The Weary

Matthew 11:25-30

At that time Jesus said, "Father, Lord of heaven and earth, I praise you for hiding these things from the 'wise' and the 'learned' and revealing them to children. Yes, Father, such was your gracious will."

Then said Jesus, "All things have been put in my charge by my Father; and no one truly knows the Son except the Father, and no one truly knows the Father except the Son and those to whom the Son chooses to reveal him.

"Come to me, all who are weary and burdened, and I will give you rest. Take my yoke upon you and learn from me, for I am gentle and humble in heart. You will find rest for your souls, for my yoke is easy and my burden is light."

MATTHEW 11:25-30 ✓

25 At that time Jesus answered and said, I thank thee, O Father, Lord of heaven and earth, because thou hast hid these things from the wise and prudent, and hast revealed them unto babes.

26 Even so, Father; for so it seemed good in thy sight.

27 All things are delivered unto me of my Father: and no man knoweth the Son, but the Father; neither knoweth any man the Father, save the Son, and *he* to whomsoever the Son will reveal *him*.

28 Come unto me, all *ye* that labor and are heavy laden, and I will give you rest.

29 Take my yoke upon you, and learn of me; for I am meek and lowly in heart: and ye shall find rest unto your souls.

30 For my yoke *is* easy, and my burden is light.

A Widow's Son Raised to Life. It was at Nain, according to Luke 7:11-17, that Jesus met a funeral procession leaving the gate of the city. They were planning to bury the only son of a widow. Jesus brought the young man back to life.

129

Jesus Anointed at Simon's House

Luke 7:36-50

Then one of the Pharisees invited Jesus to have dinner with him, and Jesus entered the Pharisee's house and sat down at the table. And a certain woman in the town—a sinner with a bad reputation, when she learned that Jesus was having dinner in the Pharisee's house, brought an alabaster flask of perfume and came and stood behind him, beside his feet, weeping. And she began to wash his feet with her tears and to wipe them with her hair. And she kissed his feet and anointed them with the perfume.

Now when the Pharisee who had invited Jesus to dinner saw this, he said to himself, "If this fellow were really a prophet, he would know who this woman is who is touching him and what kind of person she is, for she is a notorious sinner."

"Simon," said Jesus, "I have something to say to you."

"Speak, Master," he replied.

"A certain money-lender had two debtors, one of whom owed him five hundred denarii, and the other fifty. And when they were unable to pay, he excused them both from their obligations. Now which of them will love him most?"

"I suppose," answered Simon, "the one whom he excused from the larger debt."

"You are right," replied Jesus. Then he turned toward the woman and said to Simon, "Do you see this woman? I entered your house as a guest, and you gave me no water to wash my feet; but she has washed my feet with her tears and wiped them with her hair. You gave me no kiss; but from the time I came in, she has not ceased to kiss my feet. You did not anoint my head with oil; but she has anointed my feet with perfume. Therefore I say to you, her sins, which are many, are forgiven, for her love is great. But he to whom little is forgiven has little love."

Then Jesus said to the woman, "Your sins are forgiven."

Then those who were sitting at the table with him began to say to themselves, "Who is this fellow who even presumes to forgive sins?"

But Jesus said to the woman, "Your faith has saved you; go in peace."

36 And one of the Pharisees desired him that he would eat with him. And he went into the Pharisee's house, and sat down to meat.

37 And, behold, a woman in the city, which was a sinner, when she knew that *Jesus* sat at meat in the Pharisee's house, brought an alabaster box of ointment,

38 And stood at his feet behind *him* weeping, and began to wash his feet with tears, and did wipe *them* with the hairs of her head, and kissed his feet, and anointed *them* with the ointment.

39 Now when the Pharisee which had bidden him saw *it,* he spake within himself, saying, This man, if he were a prophet, would have known who and what manner of woman *this is* that toucheth him; for she is a sinner.

40 And Jesus answering said unto him, Simon, I have somewhat to say unto thee. And he saith, Master, say on.

41 There was a certain creditor which had two debtors: the one owed five hundred pence, and the other fifty.

42 And when they had nothing to pay, he frankly forgave them both. Tell me therefore, which of them will love him most?

43 Simon answered and said, I suppose that *he,* to whom he forgave most. And he said unto him, Thou hast rightly judged.

44 And he turned to the woman, and said unto Simon, Seest thou this woman? I entered into thine house, thou gavest me no water for my feet: but she hath washed my feet with tears, and wiped *them* with the hairs of her head.

45 Thou gavest me no kiss: but this woman, since the time I came in, hath not ceased to kiss my feet.

46 My head with oil thou didst not anoint: but this woman hath anointed my feet with ointment.

47 Wherefore I say unto thee, Her sins, which are many, are forgiven; for she loved much: but to whom little is forgiven, *the same* loveth little.

48 And he said unto her, Thy sins are forgiven.

49 And they that sat at meat with him began to say within themselves, Who is this that forgiveth sins also?

50 And he said to the woman, Thy faith hath saved thee; go in peace.

Anointing Jesus' feet. *It is a touching story. A woman, who had been a great sinner, came and washed the feet of Jesus with tears of repentance, then wiped them with her hair. By doing so she showed her love for the Master. Jesus responded by forgiving her.*

131

Jesus in Galilee

Luke 8:1-3

Now it came to pass soon afterward that Jesus went about through the towns and villages, preaching the good news of the kingdom of God. And the twelve were with him, as were certain women who had been healed of evil spirits and infirmities: Mary Magdalene, out of whom had been cast seven demons; and Joanna, the wife of Chuza, Herod's steward; and Susanna, and many others, who provided for their needs out of their personal means.

1 And it came to pass afterward, that he went throughout every city and village, preaching and showing the glad tidings of the kingdom of God: and the twelve *were* with him,

2 And certain women, which had been healed of evil spirits and infirmities, Mary called Magdalene, out of whom went seven devils,

3 And Joanna the wife of Chuza Herod's steward, and Susanna, and many others, which ministered unto him of their substance.

The Sin Against the Holy Spirit

Matthew 12:22-37

Then a man who was possessed of a demon, and unable to see or speak, was brought to Jesus; and he healed him, so that he could speak and see. And all the people were amazed, and said, "Is not this the Son of David?"

But when the Pharisees heard them, they said, "It is only by Beelzebub, the prince of demons, that this fellow casts out demons."

Then Jesus, knowing their thoughts, said to them, "Every kingdom divided against itself is brought to ruin, and no city or house divided against itself will continue to stand. And if Satan is casting out Satan, he is divided against himself. How then will his kingdom stand? And if I am casting out demons by Beelzebub, by whom do your sons cast them out? Let them therefore be your judges! But if it is by the Spirit of God that I am casting out demons, then the kingdom of God has appeared among you. How can a person enter a strong man's house and steal his goods unless he first binds the strong man? Only then may he rob his house.

"He who is not with me is against me, and he who does not gather with me scatters abroad. Therefore I say to you, every sin and blasphemy may be forgiven men, but blasphemy against the Spirit cannot be forgiven. And whoever speaks a word against the Son of Man may be forgiven,

22 Then was brought unto him one possessed with a devil, blind, and dumb: and he healed him, insomuch that the blind and dumb both spake and saw.

23 And all the people were amazed, and said, Is not this the Son of David?

24 But when the Pharisees heard *it,* they said, This *fellow* doth not cast out devils, but by Beelzebub the prince of the devils.

25 And Jesus knew their thoughts, and said unto them, Every kingdom divided against itself is brought to desolation; and every city or house divided against itself shall not stand:

26 And if Satan cast out Satan, he is divided against himself; how shall then his kingdom stand?

27 And if I by Beelzebub cast out devils, by whom do your children cast *them* out? therefore they shall be your judges.

28 But if I cast out devils by the Spirit of God, then the kingdom of God is come unto you.

29 Or else, how can one enter into a strong man's house, and spoil his goods, except he first bind the strong man? and then he will spoil his house.

30 He that is not with me is against me; and he that gathereth not with me scattereth abroad.

31 Wherefore I say unto you, All manner of sin and blasphemy shall be forgiven unto men: but the blasphemy *against* the *Holy* Ghost shall not be forgiven unto men.

The Sin Against the Holy Spirit (continued)

but whoever speaks against the Holy Spirit will not be forgiven, either in this age or in the age to come.

"Let the tree be good and its fruit good, or let it be bad and its fruit bad, but the tree will be known by its fruit. You brood of vipers!—how can you speak good things when you yourselves are evil? For out of the abundance of the heart the mouth speaks. A good man brings forth good things out of his storehouse of good, and an evil man brings forth evil things out of his storehouse of evil. But I tell you, men shall give account in the day of judgment for every harmful word they speak; your words will either justify you, or condemn you."

MATTHEW 12:22-37 ✓

32 And whosoever speaketh a word against the Son of man, it shall be forgiven him: but whosoever speaketh against the Holy Ghost, it shall not be forgiven him, neither in this world, neither in the *world* to come.

33 Either make the tree good, and his fruit good; or else make the tree corrupt, and his fruit corrupt: for the tree is known by *his* fruit.

34 O generation of vipers, how can ye, being evil, speak good things? for out of the abundance of the heart the mouth speaketh.

35 A good man out of the good treasure of the heart bringeth forth good things: and an evil man out of the evil treasure bringeth forth evil things.

36 But I say unto you, That every idle word that men shall speak, they shall give account thereof in the day of judgment.

37 For by thy words thou shalt be justified, and by thy words thou shalt be condemned.

MARK 3:20-30 ✓

20 And the multitude cometh together again, so that they could not so much as eat bread.

21 And when his friends heard *of it,* they went out to lay hold on him: for they said, He is beside himself.

22 And the scribes which came down from Jerusalem said, He hath Beelzebub, and by the prince of the devils casteth he out devils.

23 And he called them *unto him,* and said unto them in parables, How can Satan cast out Satan?

24 And if a kingdom be divided against itself, that kingdom cannot stand.

25 And if a house be divided against itself, that house cannot stand.

26 And if Satan rise up against himself, and be divided, he cannot stand, but hath an end.

27 No man can enter into a strong man's house, and spoil his goods, except he will first bind the strong man; and then he will spoil his house.

28 Verily I say unto you, All sins shall be forgiven unto the sons of men, and blasphemies wherewith soever they shall blaspheme:

29 But he that shall blaspheme against the Holy Ghost hath never forgiveness, but is in danger of eternal damnation:

30 Because they said, He hath an unclean spirit.

LUKE 11:14-15, 17-23 ✓

14 And he was casting out a devil, and it was dumb. And it came to pass, when the devil was gone out, the dumb spake; and the people wondered.

15 But some of them said, He casteth out devils through Beelzebub the chief of the devils.

17 But he, knowing their thoughts, said unto them, Every kingdom divided against itself is brought to desolation; and a house *divided* against a house falleth.

18 If Satan also be divided against himself, how shall his kingdom stand? because ye say that I cast out devils through Beelzebub.

19 And if I by Beelzebub cast out devils, by whom do your sons cast *them* out? therefore shall they be your judges.

20 But if I with the finger of God cast out devils, no doubt the kingdom of God is come upon you.

21 When a strong man armed keepeth his palace, his goods are in peace:

22 But when a stronger than he shall come upon him, and overcome him, he taketh from him all his armor wherein he trusted, and divideth his spoils.

23 He that is not with me is against me; and he that gathereth not with me scattereth.

Cave 4, Qumran. *The Qumran writers of the Dead Sea Scrolls hid them in caves of the hills west of the Dead Sea. The discovery took us back 1,000 years nearer the original writings. Cave 4 contained a large number of the scrolls.*

A Wicked Generation Rebuked

Matthew 12:38-45

Then some of the scribes and Pharisees said to Jesus, "Master, we should like to see some sort of sign from you."

"An evil and adulterous generation seeks a sign!" replied Jesus. "But no sign shall be given to it except the sign of the prophet Jonah. For as Jonah was three days and nights in the belly of the whale, so will the Son of Man be three days and nights in the heart of the earth. The men of Nineveh will stand up in the judgment with this generation and condemn it; for they repented at the preaching of Jonah, and behold, one greater than Jonah is here. The Queen of the South will stand up in the judgment with this generation and condemn it; for she came from a faraway part of the earth to hear the wisdom of Solomon, and behold, one greater than Solomon is here."

"When an evil spirit has gone out of a man, it wanders about in the desert places seeking rest, but finds none. Then it says, 'I will return to my house from which I came.' And when it comes, it finds it unoccupied, swept, and newly decorated. Then it goes and gathers together seven other spirits more evil than itself, and they all move in and make their home there. Then the last state of that man is worse than the first. So shall it be with this evil generation."

MATTHEW 12:38-45

38 Then certain of the scribes and of the Pharisees answered, saying, Master, we would see a sign from thee.

39 But he answered and said unto them, An evil and adulterous generation seeketh after a sign; and there shall no sign be given to it, but the sign of the prophet Jonah:

40 For as Jonah was three days and three nights in the whale's belly; so shall the Son of man be three days and three nights in the heart of the earth.

41 The men of Nineveh shall rise in judgment with this generation, and shall condemn it: because they repented at the preaching of Jonah; and, behold, a greater than Jonah *is* here.

42 The queen of the south shall rise up in the judgment with this generation, and shall condemn it: for she came from the uttermost parts of the earth to hear the wisdom of Solomon; and, behold, a greater than Solomon *is* here.

43 When the unclean spirit is gone out of a man, he walketh through dry places, seeking rest, and findeth none.

44 Then he saith, I will return into my house from whence I came out; and when he is come, he findeth *it* empty, swept, and garnished.

45 Then goeth he, and taketh with himself seven other spirits more wicked than himself, and they enter in and dwell there: and the last *state* of that man is worse than the first. Even so shall it be also unto this wicked generation.

LUKE 11:16, 24-26, 29-36

16 And others, tempting *him,* sought of him a sign from heaven.

24 When the unclean spirit is gone out of a man, he walketh through dry places, seeking rest; and finding none, he saith, I will return unto my house whence I came out.

25 And when he cometh, he findeth *it* swept and garnished.

26 Then goeth he, and taketh *to him* seven other spirts more wicked than himself; and they enter in, and dwell there: and the last *state* of that man is worse than the first.

29 And when the people were gathered thick together, he began to say, This is an evil generation: they seek a sign; and there shall no sign be given it, but the sign of Jonah the prophet.

30 For as Jonah was a sign unto the Ninevites, so shall also the Son of man be to this generation.

31 The queen of the south shall rise up in the judgment with the men of this generation, and condemn them: for she came from the utmost parts of the earth to hear the wisdom of Solomon; and, behold, a greater than Solomon *is* here.

32 The men of Nineveh shall rise up in the judgment with this generation, and shall condemn it: for they repented at the preaching of Jonah; and, behold, a greater than Jonah *is* here.

33 No man, when he hath lighted a candle, putteth *it* in a secret place, neither under a bushel, but on a candlestick, that they which come in may see the light.

A Wicked Generation Rebuked (continued)

34 The light of the body is the eye: therefore when thine eye is single, thy whole body also is full of light; but when *thine eye* is evil, thy body also *is* full of darkness.

35 Take heed therefore, that the light which is in thee be not darkness.

36 If thy whole body therefore *be* full of light, having no part dark, the whole shall be full of light, as when the bright shining of a candle doth give thee light.

The True Family of Christ

Matthew 12:46-50, Luke 11:27-28

While Jesus was still speaking to the people, behold, his mother and his brothers were standing at the edge of the crowd, desiring to speak to him. And someone said to him, "Your mother and brothers are standing over yonder, asking to speak to you."

"Who is my mother," said Jesus, "and who are my brothers?"

And extending his hand toward his disciples, he said, "Behold, here are my mother and brothers! For whoever does the will of my Father in heaven is my brother and sister and mother."

And it came to pass, as he said these things, that a woman in the crowd exclaimed to him, "Blessed is the womb that bore you, and the breasts you sucked!"

"Yes," replied Jesus, "but more blessed are those who hear the word of God, and keep it!"

MATTHEW 12:46-50

46 While he yet talked to the people, behold, *his* mother and his brethren stood without, desiring to speak with him.

47 Then one said unto him, Behold, thy mother and thy brethren stand without, desiring to speak with thee.

48 But he answered and said unto him that told him, Who is my mother? and who are my brethren?

49 And he stretched forth his hand toward his disciples, and said, Behold my mother and my brethren!

50 For whosoever shall do the will of my Father which is in heaven, the same is my brother, and sister, and mother.

MARK 3:31-35

31 There came then his brethren and his mother, and, standing without, sent unto him, calling him.

32 And the multitude sat about him, and they said unto him, Behold, thy mother and thy brethren without seek for thee.

33 And he answered them, saying, Who is my mother, or my brethren?

34 And he looked round about on them which sat about him, and said, Behold my mother and my brethren!

35 For whosoever shall do the will of God, the same is my brother, and my sister, and mother.

LUKE 8:19-21, 11:27-28

19 Then came to him *his* mother and his brethren, and could not come at him for the press.

20 And it was told him *by certain* which said, Thy mother and thy brethren stand without, desiring to see thee.

21 And he answered and said unto them, My mother and my brethren are these which hear the word of God, and do it.

27 And it came to pass, as he spake these things, a certain woman of the company lifted up her voice, and said unto him, Blessed *is* the womb that bare thee, and the paps which thou hast sucked.

28 But he said, Yea, rather, blessed *are* they that hear the word of God, and keep it.

Parable of the Sower

Matthew 13:1-9

The same day, Jesus went out and sat down by the sea. But such great crowds gathered about him that he got into a boat and sat down; and the throng of people stood on the shore. And he told them many things in parables, saying,

"Behold, a sower went out to sow. And as he sowed, some seeds fell along the road, and the birds came and ate them up. And some fell on rocky ground where they had little soil. And because they had no deep soil, they quickly sprouted; but when the sun was high, they were scorched, and because they had no root, they withered away. And some fell among thorns, and the thorns grew up and choked them. But some fell on good ground and yielded fruit—some a hundred-fold, some sixty, and some thirty. He who has ears, let him hear."

MATTHEW 13:1-9

1 The same day went Jesus out of the house, and sat by the sea side.

2 And great multitudes were gathered together unto him, so that he went into a ship, and sat; and the whole multitude stood on the shore.

3 And he spake many things unto them in parables, saying, Behold, a sower went forth to sow;

4 And when he sowed, some *seeds* fell by the wayside, and the fowls came and devoured them up:

5 Some fell upon stony places, where they had not much earth: and forthwith they sprung up, because they had no deepness of earth:

6 And when the sun was up, they were scorched; and because they had no root, they withered away.

7 And some fell among thorns; and the thorns sprung up, and choked them:

8 But other fell into good ground, and brought forth fruit, some a hundredfold, some sixtyfold, some thirtyfold.

9 Who hath ears to hear, let him hear.

MARK 4:1-9

1 And he began again to teach by the sea side: and there was gathered unto him a great multitude, so that he entered into a ship, and sat in the sea; and the whole multitude was by the sea on the land.

2 And he taught them many things by parables, and said unto them in his doctrine,

3 Hearken; Behold, there went out a sower to sow:

4 And it came to pass, as he sowed, some fell by the wayside, and the fowls of the air came and devoured it up.

5 And some fell on stony ground, where it had not much earth; and immediately it sprang up, because it had no depth of earth:

6 But when the sun was up, it was scorched; and because it had no root, it withered away.

7 And some fell among thorns, and the thorns grew up, and choked it, and it yielded no fruit.

8 And other fell on good ground, and did yield fruit that sprang up and increased, and brought forth, some thirty, and some sixty, and some a hundred.

9 And he said unto them, He that hath ears to hear, let him hear.

LUKE 8:4-8

4 And when much people were gathered together, and were come to him out of every city, he spake by a parable:

5 A sower went out to sow his seed: and as he sowed, some fell by the wayside; and it was trodden down, and the fowls of the air devoured it.

6 And some fell upon a rock; and as soon as it was sprung up, it withered away, because it lacked moisture.

7 And some fell among thorns; and the thorns sprang up with it, and choked it.

8 And other fell on good ground, and sprang up, and bare fruit a hundredfold. And when he had said these things, he cried, He that hath ears to hear, let him hear.

Sowing the Seed. *When telling His parables
Jesus used scenes and activities which were familiar
to His listeners. Here is shown a man broadcasting
his seed as was customary in the First Century. It is
easy to see why it could fall on various kinds of soil.*

Purpose of the Parables

Matthew 13:36a, 10-17

Then Jesus left the crowds and went to the house, and his disciples came to him and said, "Why do you speak to them in parables?"

"To you it has been given to know the secrets of the kingdom of heaven," replied Jesus, "but to them it has not. For to him who holds it fast, more will be given, and he will have abundance; but whoever does not hold it fast, from him will be taken away even what he has. Therefore, I speak to them in parables because, when they see, they do not really see, and when they hear, they do not really hear, nor do they understand. And in them is fulfilled the prophecy of Isaiah, 'Hearing, you shall hear, but not understand; seeing, you shall see, but not perceive. For this people's heart has become calloused, and their ears are hard of hearing, and they have closed their eyes, lest they should see with their eyes and hear with their ears and understand with their heart, and return, and I should heal them.'

"But blessed are your eyes, for they see; and your ears, for they hear. For I tell you truly, many prophets and righteous men longed to see what you are seeing, but did not live to see it; and to hear what you are hearing, but did not hear it."

MATTHEW 13:36a, 10-17

36 Then Jesus sent the multitude away, and went into the house:

10 And the disciples came, and said unto him, Why speakest thou unto them in parables?

11 He answered and said unto them, Because it is given unto you to know the mysteries of the kingdom of heaven, but to them it is not given.

12 For whosoever hath, to him shall be given, and he shall have more abundance: but whosoever hath not, from him shall be taken away even that he hath.

13 Therefore speak I to them in parables: because they seeing see not; and hearing they hear not, neither do they understand.

14 And in them is fulfilled the prophecy of Isaiah, which saith, By hearing ye shall hear, and shall not understand; and seeing ye shall see, and shall not perceive:

15 For this people's heart is waxed gross, and *their* ears are dull of hearing, and their eyes they have closed; lest at any time they should see with *their* eyes, and hear with *their* ears, and should understand with *their* heart, and should be converted, and I should heal them.

16 But blessed *are* your eyes, for they see: and your ears, for they hear.

17 For verily I say unto you, That many prophets and righteous *men* have desired to see *those things* which ye see, and have not seen *them;* and to hear *those things* which ye hear, and have not heard *them.*

MARK 4:10-12

10 And when he was alone, they that were about him with the twelve asked of him the parable.

11 And he said unto them, Unto you it is given to know the mystery of the kingdom of God: but unto them that are without, all *these* things are done in parables:

12 That seeing they may see, and not perceive; and hearing they may hear, and not understand; lest at any time they should be converted, and *their* sins should be forgiven them.

LUKE 8:9-10

9 And his disciples asked him, saying, What might this parable be?

10 And he said, Unto you it is given to know the mysteries of the kingdom of God: but to others in parables; that seeing they might not see, and hearing they might not understand.

The Sower

Matthew 13:18, Luke 8:11-15

"Hear, then, the parable of the sower. This is the meaning of the parable: The seed is the word of God. Those along the road are those who hear, but then the devil comes and takes away the word from their hearts, lest they should believe and be saved. Those on the rock are those who, when they hear the word, receive it with joy, but they have no root. For a while, they believe; but when a time of testing comes along, they fall away. And that which fell among the thorns are those who hear, but as they go along, they are choked by the cares and riches and pleasures of life, and they bring no fruit to maturity. But that on the good ground are those who, having heard the word, hold it fast in a good and honest heart and bring forth fruit with patience."

MATTHEW 13:18-23 ✓

18 Hear ye therefore the parable of the sower.

19 When any one heareth the word of the kingdom, and understandeth *it* not, then cometh the wicked one, and catcheth away that which was sown in his heart. This is he which received seed by the wayside.

20 But he that received the seed into stony places, the same is he that heareth the word, and anon with joy receiveth it;

21 Yet hath he not root in himself, but dureth for a while: for when tribulation or persecution ariseth because of the word, by and by he is offended.

22 He also that received seed among the thorns is he that heareth the word; and the care of this world, and the deceitfulness of riches, choke the word, and he becometh unfruitful.

23 But he that received seed into the good ground is he that heareth the word, and understandeth *it;* which also beareth fruit, and bringeth forth, some a hundredfold, some sixty, some thirty.

MARK 4:13-20 ✓

13 And he said unto them, Know ye not this parable? and how then will ye know all parables?

14 The sower soweth the word.

15 And these are they by the wayside, where the word is sown; but when they have heard, Satan cometh immediately, and taketh away the word that was sown in their hearts.

16 And these are they likewise which are sown on stony ground; who, when they have heard the word, immediately receive it with gladness;

17 And have no root in themselves, and so endure but for a time: afterward, when affliction or persecution ariseth for the word's sake, immediately they are offended.

18 And these are they which are sown among thorns; such as hear the word,

19 And the cares of this world, and the deceitfulness of riches, and the lusts of other things entering in, choke the word, and it becometh unfruitful.

20 And these are they which are sown on good ground; such as hear the word, and receive *it,* and bring forth fruit, some thirtyfold, some sixty, and some a hundred.

LUKE 8:11-15 ✓

11 Now the parable is this: The seed is the word of God.

12 Those by the wayside are they that hear; then cometh the devil, and taketh away the word out of their hearts, lest they should believe and be saved.

13 They on the rock *are they*, which, when they hear, receive the word with joy; and these have no root, which for a while believe, and in time of temptation fall away.

...that on the good ground are they, which...having heard the word, keep it.

14 And that which fell among thorns are they, which, when they have heard, go forth, and are choked with cares and riches and pleasures of *this* life, and bring no fruit to perfection.

15 But that on the good ground are they, which in an honest and good heart, having heard the word, keep *it*, and bring forth fruit with patience.

Wheat Ready for Harvest. *In His
parable chapter, Matthew 13, Jesus began
by telling how to have a good harvest.
The good soil, a responsive heart, will
produce great results.*

141

Jesus Warns His Hearers

Mark 4:21-25

Then said Jesus, "Is a lamp fetched to be placed under a bushel or under a bed, and not on a lamp stand? There is nothing hidden that will not be revealed, nor anything secret that will not be brought to light. If any man has ears to hear, let him hear.

"Take heed how you hear. The measure you give will be the measure you receive. For more will be given to him who holds fast what he receives, but even what he has will be taken from him who does not hold it fast."

MARK 4:21-25

21 And he said unto them, Is a candle brought to be put under a bushel, or under a bed? and not to be set on a candlestick?

22 For there is nothing hid, which shall not be manifested; neither was any thing kept secret, but that it should come abroad.

23 If any man have ears to hear, let him hear.

24 And he said unto them, Take heed what ye hear. With what measure ye mete, it shall be measured to you; and unto you that hear shall more be given.

25 For he that hath, to him shall be given; and he that hath not, from him shall be taken even that which he hath.

LUKE 8:16-18

16 No man, when he hath lighted a candle, covereth it with a vessel, or putteth *it* under a bed; but setteth *it* on a candlestick, that they which enter in may see the light.

17 For nothing is secret, that shall not be made manifest; neither *any thing* hid, that shall not be known and come abroad.

18 Take heed therefore how ye hear: for whosoever hath, to him shall be given; and whosoever hath not, from him shall be taken even that which he seemeth to have.

Cave 4, Qumran (interior). The Dead Sea Scrolls were found in many caves, but this cave contained the largest supply. It was one of archaeology's greatest discoveries.

How the Harvest Comes

Mark 4:26-29

"The kingdom of God," said Jesus, "is like a man scattering seed on the ground, and then while he sleeps by night and rises each day, the seed sprouts and grows—how, he does not know. The earth produces fruit of itself: first the blade, then the head, then the full grain in the head. But when the grain is ripe, he immediately puts in the sickle, because the harvest has come."

MARK 4:26-29

26 And he said, So is the kingdom of God, as if a man should cast seed into the ground;

27 And should sleep, and rise night and day, and the seed should spring and grow up, he knoweth not how.

28 For the earth bringeth forth fruit of herself; first the blade, then the ear, after that the full corn in the ear.

29 But when the fruit is brought forth, immediately he putteth in the sickle, because the harvest is come.

The Tares

Matthew 13:24-30

Jesus put another parable before them, saying, "The kingdom of heaven is like a man who sowed good seed in his field, but while his men were asleep, his enemy came and sowed darnel among the wheat, and went his way. When the crop sprouted and began heading out, then the darnel showed up.

"Then the servants of the landowner came to him and said, 'Sir, did you not sow good seed in your field? Where did the darnel come from?'

" 'An enemy has done this,' he replied.

"Then the servants said to him, 'Do you want us to go and gather out the tares?'

"But he said, 'No, lest in gathering out the tares, you root out the wheat along with them. Let them both grow together until the harvest, and at harvest time, I will say to the reapers, 'Gather the tares first and bind them into bundles to burn; but gather the wheat into my barn.' "

MATTHEW 13:24-30

24 Another parable put he forth unto them, saying, The kingdom of heaven is likened unto a man which sowed good seed in his field:

25 But while men slept, his enemy came and sowed tares among the wheat, and went his way.

26 But when the blade was sprung up, and brought forth fruit, then appeared the tares also.

27 So the servants of the householder came and said unto him, Sir, didst not thou sow good seed in thy field? from whence then hath it tares?

28 He said unto them, An enemy hath done this. The servants said unto him, Wilt thou then that we go and gather them up?

29 But he said, Nay; lest while ye gather up the tares, ye root up also the wheat with them.

30 Let both grow together until the harvest: and in the time of harvest I will say to the reapers, Gather ye together first the tares, and bind them in bundles to burn them: but gather the wheat into my barn.

Mustard Seed, Leaven

Matthew 13:31-35

Jesus put another parable before them, saying, "The kingdom of heaven is like a grain of mustard seed which a man took and sowed in his field, which indeed is the smallest of all seeds, but when it is grown, it is the largest of herbs and becomes a tree, so that the birds of the air come and build nests in its branches."

And he told them another parable: "The kingdom of heaven is like leaven which a woman took and hid in three measures of meal, till all of it was leavened."

All these things Jesus spoke to the crowds in parables. Indeed, he said nothing to them except in a parable, in fulfillment of the word of the prophet,

I will open my mouth in parables;
I will utter things hidden since the foundation
   of the world.

MATTHEW 13:31-35

31 Another parable put he forth unto them, saying, The kingdom of heaven is like to a grain of mustard seed, which a man took, and sowed in his field:

32 Which indeed is the least of all seeds: but when it is grown, it is the greatest among herbs, and becometh a tree, so that the birds of the air come and lodge in the branches thereof.

33 Another parable spake he unto them; The kingdom of heaven is like unto leaven, which a woman took, and hid in three measures of meal, till the whole was leavened.

34 All these things spake Jesus unto the multitude in parables; and without a parable spake he not unto them:

35 That it might be fulfilled which was spoken by the prophet, saying, I will open my mouth in parables; I will utter things which have been kept secret from the foundation of the world.

MARK 4:30-34

30 And he said, Whereunto shall we liken the kingdom of God? or with what comparison shall we compare it?

31 *It is* like a grain of mustard seed, which, when it is sown in the earth, is less than all the seeds that be in the earth:

32 But when it is sown, it groweth up, and becometh greater than all herbs, and shooteth out great branches; so that the fowls of the air may lodge under the shadow of it.

33 And with many such parables spake he the word unto them, as they were able to hear *it*.

34 But without a parable spake he not unto them: and when they were alone, he expounded all things to his disciples.

Agricultural Products of Israel. People throng to the flea market at Beer-Sheba to buy the many items offered for sale. Here is shown the great variety offered.

Cedar of Lebanon.
*Few of these are found
away from the original grove
in the mountains of
Lebanon. This one is at the
foot of Mount Herzl,
named after Theodore Herzl,
the founder of Zionism.*

The Tares Explained

Matthew 13:36b-43

Then the disciples said to Jesus, "Explain to us the parable of the tares in the field."

"He who sows the good seed is the Son of Man," replied Jesus, "and the field is the world. The good seed are the sons of the kingdom, but the tares are the sons of the evil one, and the enemy who sowed them is the devil. The harvest is the end of the age, and the reapers are angels. Just as the tares are gathered and burned in the fire, so will it be at the end of the age. The Son of Man will send forth his angels, and they will gather out of his kingdom all offenders and those who practice wickedness, and will cast them into the furnace of fire, where there will be weeping and gnashing of teeth. Then the righteous will shine forth as the sun in the kingdom of their Father. He who has ears, let him hear."

36b and his disciples came unto him, saying, Declare unto us the parable of the tares of the field.

37 He answered and said unto them, He that soweth the good seed is the Son of man;

38 The field is the world; the good seed are the children of the kingdom; but the tares are the children of the wicked one;

39 The enemy that sowed them is the devil; the harvest is the end of the world; and the reapers are the angels.

40 As therefore the tares are gathered and burned in the fire; so shall it be in the end of this world.

Then shall the righteous shine forth as the sun in the kingdom of their Father. Who hath ears to hear, let him hear.

41 The Son of man shall send forth his angels, and they shall gather out of his kingdom all things that offend, and them which do iniquity;

42 And shall cast them into a furnace of fire: there shall be wailing and gnashing of teeth.

43 Then shall the righteous shine forth as the sun in the kingdom of their Father. Who hath ears to hear, let him hear.

The Hidden Treasure, the Costly Pearl

Matthew 13:44-46

"The kingdom of heaven," said Jesus, "is like treasure hidden in a field which a man finds and hides; and in his joy over it, he goes and sells all he has and buys that field.

"Again, the kingdom of heaven is like a merchant seeking exquisite pearls. Finding one very precious pearl, he went and sold all he had and bought it."

44 Again, the kingdom of heaven is like unto treasure hid in a field; the which when a man hath found, he hideth, and for joy thereof goeth and selleth all that he hath, and buyeth that field.

45 Again, the kingdom of heaven is like unto a merchantman, seeking goodly pearls:

46 Who, when he had found one pearl of great price, went and sold all that he had, and bought it.

Good Fish and Bad

Matthew 13:47-53

"Again," said Jesus, "the kingdom of heaven is like a net which was cast into the sea, gathering all sorts of fish. When it was full, the men drew it ashore and sat down and sorted out the good fish into tubs, but the worthless ones they threw away. So will it be at the end of the age. The angels will go forth and separate the wicked from the righteous and cast them into the furnace of fire, where there will be weeping and gnashing of teeth. Have you understood all these things?"

"Yes," they replied.

"Therefore," said Jesus, "every scribe who has become a disciple of the kingdom of heaven is like a householder who brings forth out of his storehouse new treasures, as well as old."

And when Jesus had finished these parables, he departed from there.

MATTHEW 13:47-53

47 Again, the kingdom of heaven is like unto a net, that was cast into the sea, and gathered of every kind:

48 Which, when it was full, they drew to shore, and sat down, and gathered the good into vessels, but cast the bad away.

49 So shall it be at the end of the world: the angels shall come forth, and sever the wicked from among the just,

50 And shall cast them into the furnace of fire: there shall be wailing and gnashing of teeth.

51 Jesus saith unto them, Have ye understood all these things? They say unto him, Yea, Lord.

52 Then said he unto them, Therefore every scribe *which* is instructed unto the kingdom of heaven, is like unto a man *that* is a householder, which bringeth forth out of his treasure *things* new and old.

53 And it came to pass, *that* when Jesus had finished these parables, he departed thence.

Catch of Fish. *Fish are a favorite food of the Near East. One such meal features "St. Peter's Fish," caught in the Sea of Galilee, reminding us how Peter got tax money from the mouth of a fish.*

Jesus Calms the Storm

Luke 8:22-25

Now it came to pass on a certain day that Jesus got into a boat with his disciples and said to them, "Let us go over to the other side of the lake."

So they set out, and as they sailed, Jesus fell asleep. And a windstorm swept down on the lake, and they were fillng with water and were in danger. And the disciples came and woke Jesus, exclaiming, "Master, Master, we are perishing!"

Then Jesus rose and rebuked the wind and the raging waves, and they ceased, and there was a calm. And he said to them, "Where is your faith?"

And they were afraid, and marveled, saying one to another, "Who is this man? He commands even the winds and the sea, and they obey him!"

MATTHEW 8:23-27

23 And when he was entered into a ship, his disciples followed him.

24 And, behold, there arose a great tempest in the sea, insomuch that the ship was covered with the waves: but he was asleep.

25 And his disciples came to *him,* and awoke him, saying, Lord, save us: we perish.

...the men marveled, saying, What manner of man is this, that even the winds and the sea obey him!

---

26 And he saith unto them, Why are ye fearful, O ye of little faith? Then he arose, and rebuked the winds and the sea; and there was a great calm.

27 But the men marveled, saying, What manner of man is this, that even the winds and the sea obey him!

MARK 4:35-41

35 And the same day, when the even was come, he saith unto them, Let us pass over unto the other side.

36 And when they had sent away the multitude, they took him even as he was in the ship. And there were also with him other little ships.

37 And there arose a great storm of wind, and the waves beat into the ship, so that it was now full.

38 And he was in the hinder part of the ship, asleep on a pillow: and they awake him, and say unto him, Master, carest thou not that we perish?

39 And he arose, and rebuked the wind, and said unto the sea, Peace, be still. And the wind ceased, and there was a great calm.

40 And he said unto them, Why are ye so fearful? how is it that ye have no faith?

41 And they feared exceedingly, and said one to another, What manner of man is this, that even the wind and the sea obey him?

LUKE 8:22-25

22 Now it came to pass on a certain day, that he went into a ship with his disciples: and he said unto them, Let us go over unto the other side of the lake. And they launched forth.

23 But as they sailed, he fell asleep: and there came down a storm of wind on the lake; and they were filled *with water,* and were in jeopardy.

24 And they came to him, and awoke him, saying, Master, Master, we perish. Then he arose, and rebuked the wind and the raging of the water: and they ceased, and there was a calm.

25 And he said unto them, Where is your faith? And they being afraid wondered, saying one to another, What manner of man is this! for he commandeth even the winds and water, and they obey him.

Jesus Stills the Storm. *Usually calm, this lake can suddenly become rough. It must have done so on the occasion when Jesus and His disciples were making their way to the eastern shore of the Sea of Galilee. Jesus spoke peace to the troubled waters.*

149

Jesus Delivers a Demoniac

Luke 8:26-39

And they arrived at the country of the Gerasenes, which is across the lake from Galilee. And as Jesus stepped ashore, a man from the town met him who was demon possessed and who, for a long time, had not worn clothes nor lived in a house, but stayed out in the tombs. When he saw Jesus, he cried out and fell down before him, shouting, "What have you to do with me, Jesus, Son of the Most High God? I beg you, do not torment me!"

For Jesus was already commanding the evil spirit to come out of the man. Many times it had overpowered him, and even though he was bound with chains and shackles and kept under guard, he snapped the bonds and fled out into the wilderness, driven by the demon.

"What is your name?" asked Jesus.

"Legion," he replied, for many demons had entered into him. And they begged Jesus not to command them to depart into the Abyss.

Now there was a large herd of pigs feeding on the hillside, and the demons begged Jesus to allow them to enter into the pigs; and he gave them permission. Then the demons went out of the man and entered into the pigs, and the herd rushed down the steep bank into the lake and were drowned.

Now when the herdsmen saw what had happened, they ran and told the news in the town and countryside, and the people went out to see what had happened. And they came to Jesus and found the man from whom the demons had departed, sitting at Jesus' feet, clothed, and in his right mind; and they were afraid. And those who had seen it told them how the man had been healed. Then all the people of the country of the Gerasenes begged Jesus to depart from them, for they were filled with fear.

Then Jesus got into the boat and turned back. And the man from whom the demons had departed begged Jesus to let him go with him, but Jesus sent him away, saying, "Go back home and tell what great things God has done for you."

And he went his way, proclaiming throughout the whole town what great things Jesus had done for him.

MATT. 8:28-34	MARK 5:1-20	LUKE 8:26-39
28 And when he was come to the other side into the country of the Gergesenes, there met him two possessed with devils, coming out of the tombs, exceeding fierce, so that no man might pass by that way. 29 And, behold, they cried out, saying, What have we to do with thee, Jesus, thou Son of God? art thou come hither to torment us before the time? 30 And there was	1 And they came over unto the other side of the sea, into the country of the Gadarenes. 2 And when he was come out of the ship, immediately there met him out of the tombs a man with an unclean spirit, 3 Who had *his* dwelling among the tombs; and no man could bind him, no, not with chains: 4 Because that he had been often bound with fetters and chains, and the chains had been plucked asunder by him, and the fetters broken in pieces: neither could any *man* tame him. 5 And always, night and day, he was in the mountains, and in the tombs, crying, and cutting himself with stones. 6 But when he saw Jesus afar off, he ran and worshipped him, 7 And cried with a loud voice, and said, What have I to do with thee, Jesus,	26 And they arrived at the country of the Gadarenes, which is over against Galilee. 27 And when he went forth to land, there met him out of the city a certain man, which had devils long time, and ware no clothes, neither abode in *any* house, but in the tombs. 28 When he saw Jesus, he cried out, and fell down before him, and with a loud voice said, What have I to do with thee, Jesus, *thou* Son of God most high? I beseech thee, torment me not. 29 (For he had commanded the unclean spirit to come out of the man. For oftentimes it had caught him: and he was kept bound with chains and in fetters; and he brake the bands, and was driven of the devil into the wilderness.) 30 And Jesus asked him, saying, What is thy name? And he said, Legion:

Jesus Delivers a Demoniac (continued)

a good way off from them a herd of many swine feeding.

31 So the devils besought him, saying, If thou cast us out, suffer us to go away into the herd of swine.

32 And he said unto them, Go. And when they were come out, they went into the herd of swine: and, behold, the whole herd of swine ran violently down a steep place into the sea, and perished in the waters.

33 And they that kept them fled, and went their ways into the city, and told every thing, and what was befallen to the possessed of the devils.

34 And, behold, the whole city came out to meet Jesus: and when they saw him, they besought *him* that he would depart out of their coasts.

thou Son of the most high God? I adjure thee by God, that thou torment me not.

8 For he said unto him, Come out of the man, *thou* unclean spirit.

9 And he asked him, What *is* thy name? And he answered, saying, My name *is* Legion: for we are many.

10 And he besought him much that he would not send them away out of the country.

11 Now there was there nigh unto the mountains a great herd of swine feeding.

12 And all the devils besought him, saying, Send us into the swine, that we may enter into them.

13 And forthwith Jesus gave them leave. And the unclean spirits went out, and entered into the swine; and the herd ran violently down a steep place into the sea, (they were about two thousand,) and were choked in the sea.

14 And they that fed the swine fled, and told *it* in the city, and in the country. And they went out to see what it was that was done.

15 And they come to Jesus, and see him that was possessed with the devil, and had the legion, sitting, and clothed, and in his right mind; and they were afraid.

16 And they that saw *it* told them how it befell to him that was possessed with the devil, and *also* concerning the swine.

17 And they began to pray him to depart out of their coasts.

18 And when he was come into the ship, he that had been possessed with the devil prayed him that he might be with him.

19 Howbeit Jesus suffered him not, but saith unto him, Go home to thy friends, and tell them how great things the Lord hath done for thee, and hath had compassion on thee.

20 And he departed, and began to publish in Decapolis how great things Jesus had done for him: and all *men* did marvel.

because many devils were entered into him.

31 And they besought him that he would not command them to go out into the deep.

32 And there was there a herd of many swine feeding on the mountain: and they besought him that he would suffer them to enter into them. And he suffered them.

33 Then went the devils out of the man, and entered into the swine: and the herd ran violently down a steep place into the lake, and were choked.

34 When they that fed *them* saw what was done, they fled, and went and told *it* in the city and in the country.

35 Then they went out to see what was done; and came to Jesus, and found the man, out of whom the devils were departed, sitting at the feet of Jesus, clothed, and in his right mind: and they were afraid.

36 They also which saw *it* told them by what means he that was possessed of the devils was healed.

37 Then the whole multitude of the country of the Gadarenes round about besought him to depart from them; for they were taken with great fear: and he went up into the ship, and returned back again.

38 Now the man, out of whom the devils were departed, besought him that he might be with him: but Jesus sent him away, saying,

39 Return to thine own house, and show how great things God hath done unto thee. And he went his way, and published throughout the whole city how great things Jesus had done unto him.

Jesus Brings Healing and Life

Mark 5:21-43

Now when Jesus had crossed again by boat to the other side, many people gathered about him on the shore. And there came one of the rulers of the synagogue, a man named Jairus; and when he saw Jesus, he fell down at his feet and earnestly implored him, saying, "My little daughter is at the point of death. I beg of you, come and lay your hands on her, that she may be healed and live."

Then Jesus went with him, and many people followed him, thronging about him. Now there was a woman who for twelve years had had a hemorrhage and had suffered much at the hands of many physicians, having spent everything she had, and continually growing worse instead of better. Having heard about Jesus, she came up behind him in the crowd and touched his cloak. For she said to herself, "If only I can touch even his cloak, I shall be healed."

At once the hemorrhage was stopped, and she felt in her body that she was healed of her affliction. And Jesus, knowing in himself that power had gone forth from him, immediately turned around in the crowd and said, "Who touched my clothes?"

"You see the multitude crowding around you," said his disciples, "and yet you ask, 'Who touched me?'"

But Jesus continued to look around to see who had touched him. Then the woman, knowing what had happened to her, came with fear and trembling and fell down before him and told him the whole story.

"Daughter," said Jesus, "your faith has made you well. Go in peace, and be healed of your affliction."

While Jesus was still speaking, messengers came from the home of the ruler of the synagogue and said, "Your daughter is dead. Why bother the Master any longer?"

But Jesus, disregarding their words, said to the ruler of the synagogue, "Do not fear, only believe."

Then Jesus allowed no one to accompany him except Peter, James, and John, the brother of James. And they came to the ruler's house, where Jesus found a great commotion—people weeping and wailing loudly. Jesus entered and said to them, "Why are you weeping and carrying on this way? The child is not dead, but asleep."

Then they laughed and jeered at Jesus. But he ordered them all out; and taking the child's father and mother and those who were with him, he went in where the child was. And he took her by the hand and said, "Little girl, I say to you, rise."

Immediately the girl got up and began walking about (she was twelve years old), and they were astonished. Then Jesus charged them that no one should know what had occurred, and told them to give her something to eat.

MATT. 9:18-26	MARK 5:21-43	LUKE 8:40-56
18 While he spake these things unto them, behold, there came a certain ruler, and worshipped him, saying, My daughter is even now dead: but come and lay thy hand upon her, and she shall live. 19 And Jesus arose, and followed	21 And when Jesus was passed over again by ship unto the other side, much people gathered unto him; and he was nigh unto the sea. 22 And, behold, there cometh one of the rulers of the synagogue, Jairus by name; and when he saw him, he fell at his feet, 23 And besought him greatly, saying, My little daughter lieth at the point of death: *I pray thee,* come and lay thy hands on her, that she may be healed; and she shall live.	40 And it came to pass, that, when Jesus was returned, the people *gladly* received him: for they were all waiting for him. 41 And, behold, there came a man named Jairus, and he was a ruler of the synagogue; and he fell down at Jesus' feet, and besought him that he would come into his house: 42 For he had one only daughter, about twelve years of age, and she lay a dying. But as he went the people thronged him.

Jesus Brings Healing and Life (continued)

him, and *so did* his disciples.

20 And, behold, a woman, which was diseased with an issue of blood twelve years, came behind *him,* and touched the hem of his garment:

21 For she said within herself, If I may but touch his garment, I shall be whole.

22 But Jesus turned him about, and when he saw her, he said, Daughter, be of good comfort; thy faith hath made thee whole. And the woman was made whole from that hour.

23 And when Jesus came into the ruler's house, and saw the minstrels and the people making a noise,

24 He said unto them, Give place: for the maid is not dead, but sleepeth. And they laughed him to scorn.

25 But when the people were put forth, he went in, and took her by the hand, and the maid arose.

26 And the fame hereof went abroad into all that land.

24 And *Jesus* went with him. And much people followed him, and thronged him.

25 And a certain woman, which had an issue of blood twelve years,

26 And had suffered many things of many physicians, and had spent all that she had, and was nothing bettered, but rather grew worse,

27 When she had heard of Jesus, came in the press behind, and touched his garment.

28 For she said, If I may touch but his clothes, I shall be whole.

29 And straightway the fountain of her blood was dried up; and she felt in *her* body that she was healed of that plague.

30 And Jesus, immediately knowing in himself that virtue had gone out of him, turned him about in the press, and said, Who touched my clothes?

31 And his disciples said unto him, Thou seest the multitude thronging thee, and sayest thou, Who touched me?

32 And he looked round about to see her that had done this thing.

33 But the woman fearing and trembling, knowing what was done in her, came and fell down before him, and told him all the truth.

34 And he said unto her, Daughter, thy faith hath made thee whole; go in peace, and be whole of thy plague.

35 While he yet spake, there came from the ruler of the synagogue's *house certain* which said, Thy daughter is dead; why troublest thou the Master any further?

36 As soon as Jesus heard the word that was spoken, he saith unto the ruler of the synagogue, Be not afraid, only believe.

37 And he suffered no man to follow him, save Peter, and James, and John the brother of James.

38 And he cometh to the house of the ruler of the synagogue, and seeth the tumult, and them that wept and wailed greatly.

39 And when he was come in, he saith unto them, Why make ye this ado, and

43 And a woman having an issue of blood twelve years, which had spent all her living upon physicians, neither could be healed of any,

44 Came behind *him,* and touched the border of his garment: and immediately her issue of blood stanched.

45 And Jesus said, Who touched me? When all denied, Peter and they that were with him said, Master, the multitude throng thee and press *thee,* and sayest thou, Who touched me?

And he said unto her, Daughter, be of good comfort: thy faith hath made thee whole; go in peace.

---

46 And Jesus said, Somebody hath touched me: for I perceive that virtue is gone out of me.

47 And when the woman saw that she was not hid, she came trembling, and falling down before him, she declared unto him before all the people for what cause she had touched him, and how she was healed immediately.

48 And he said unto her, Daughter, be of good comfort: thy faith hath made thee whole; go in peace.

49 While he yet spake, there cometh one from the ruler of the synagogue's *house,* saying to him, Thy daughter is dead; trouble not the Master.

50 But when Jesus heard *it,* he answered him, saying, Fear not: believe only, and she shall be made whole.

Jesus Brings Healing and Life (continued)

	MARK 5:21-43	LUKE 8:40-56
	weep? the damsel is not dead, but sleepeth.	51 And when he came into the house, he suffered no man to go in, save Peter, and James, and John, and the father and the mother of the maiden.
	40 And they laughed him to scorn. But when he had put them all out, he taketh the father and the mother of the damsel, and them that were with him, and entereth in where the damsel was lying.	52 And all wept, and bewailed her: but he said, Weep not; she is not dead, but sleepeth.
	41 And he took the damsel by the hand, and said unto her, Talitha cumi; which is, being interpreted, Damsel, (I say unto thee,) arise.	53 And they laughed him to scorn, knowing that she was dead.
	42 And straightway the damsel arose, and walked; for she was *of the age* of twelve years. And they were astonished with a great astonishment.	54 And he put them all out, and took her by the hand, and called, saying, Maid, arise.
	43 And he charged them straitly that no man should know it; and commanded that something should be given her to eat.	55 And her spirit came again, and she arose straightway: and he commanded to give her meat.
		56 And her parents were astonished: but he charged them that they should tell no man what was done.

Jesus Heals the Blind and Deaf

Matthew 9:27-34

Now as Jesus passed on his way from there, two blind men followed him, crying, "Have mercy on us, Son of David!"

And when Jesus had entered the house, they came to him, and Jesus said, "Do you believe that I am able to do this?"

"Yes, Lord," they answered.

Then Jesus touched their eyes, saying, "Let it be done for you according to your faith."

And their eyes were opened. Then Jesus charged them, "See that you do not let anyone know of this." But they went out and told the whole countryside about him.

Now as Jesus and his disciples were leaving, a man dumb and demon possessed was brought to him. And after the demon had been cast out, the man began to talk. And the people marveled, saying, "Never has anything like this been seen in Israel!"

But the Pharisees said, "It is by the prince of the demons that he casts out demons."

27 And when Jesus departed thence, two blind men followed him, crying, and saying, *Thou* Son of David, have mercy on us.

28 And when he was come into the house, the blind men came to him: and Jesus saith unto them, Believe ye that I am able to do this? They said unto him, Yea, Lord.

29 Then touched he their eyes, saying, According to your faith be it unto you.

30 And their eyes were opened; and Jesus straitly charged them, saying, See *that* no man know *it.*

31 But they, when they were departed, spread abroad his fame in all that country.

32 As they went out, behold, they brought to him a dumb man possessed with a devil.

33 And when the devil was cast out, the dumb spake: and the multitudes marveled, saying, It was never so seen in Israel.

34 But the Pharisees said, He casteth out devils through the prince of the devils.

Waterfront at Capernaum. *Much happened at this location. Jesus had to teach from a boat because of the great throngs. Matthew was called from his business nearby to become an apostle.*

Jesus Rejected Again in Nazareth

Mark 6:1-6a

Then Jesus went away from there and came to his own country, and his disciples followed him. And when the Sabbath came, he began to teach in the synagogue; and when they heard him, many were astonished and said,

"Where does this fellow get all this? What about this wisdom that has been given to him, and the mighty works which are wrought by his hands? Isn't this the carpenter—the son of Mary and the brother of James, Joses, Judas, and Simon? And don't his sisters live here with us?"

And they took offense at him. Then Jesus said to them, "A prophet is not without honor, except in his own country, and among his kinsmen, and in his own house."

And he could do no mighty work there, except that he laid his hands on a few sick folk and healed them. And he marveled at their unbelief.

MATTHEW 13:54-58

54 And when he was come into his own country, he taught them in their synagogue, insomuch that they were astonished, and said, Whence hath this *man* this wisdom, and *these* mighty works?

55 Is not this the carpenter's son? is not his mother called Mary? and his brethren, James, and Joses, and Simon, and Judas?

56 And his sisters, are they not all with us? Whence then hath this *man* all these things?

57 And they were offended in him. But Jesus said unto them, A prophet is not without honor, save in his own country, and in his own house.

58 And he did not many mighty works there because of their unbelief.

MARK 6:1-6a

1 And he went out from thence, and came into his own country; and his disciples follow him.

2 And when the sabbath day was come, he began to teach in the synagogue: and many hearing *him* were astonished, saying, From whence hath this *man* these things? and what wisdom *is* this which is given unto him, that even such mighty works are wrought by his hands?

3 Is not this the carpenter, the son of Mary, the brother of James, and Joses, and of Judas, and Simon? and are not his sisters here with us? And they were offended at him.

4 But Jesus said unto them, A prophet is not without honor, but in his own country, and among his own kin, and in his own house.

5 And he could there do no mighty work, save that he laid his hands upon a few sick folk, and healed *them*.

6 And he marveled because of their unbelief.

Hill of Precipitation.
It is sad that Jesus was not accepted by the people of His own town, Nazareth. On one occasion they tried to cast Him from a cliff; tradition says this one.

Death of John the Baptist

Mark 6:14-29

Now King Herod began to hear of Jesus, for his name had become widely known. Some were saying, "John the Baptist has risen from the dead, and that is why such powers are working in him."

"It is Elijah," some said; and others were saying, "It is a prophet, like one of the prophets of old."

But Herod, when he heard of him, said, "John, whom I beheaded, has been raised to life."

For Herod had sent and arrested John and bound him in prison because of Herodias, his brother Philip's wife. For Herod had married her, and John told him, "It is not lawful for you to have your brother's wife."

Herodias hated John for this, and wanted to kill him. But she could not do so; for Herod feared John, knowing him to be a righteous and holy man, and kept him in safe custody. Whenever he listened to John, he was deeply disturbed; yet he liked to hear him.

But an opportune time came when Herod, on his birthday, gave a banquet for his courtiers and officers and the leading men of Galilee. For when Herodias' daughter came in and danced, she delighted Herod and his guests, and the king said to the girl,

"Ask me anything you wish, and I will give it to you. Whatever you ask me," he vowed to her, "I will give you—even half my kingdom!"

Then she went out and said to her mother, "What shall I ask?"

"The head of John the Baptist!" she replied.

And she hurried back to the king and said, "I want you to give me the head of John the Baptist on a platter, at once!"

The king was extremely sorry, but because of his vow and out of regard for his guests, he was unwilling to refuse her. And he immediately sent a guard and ordered him to bring John's head. And he went and beheaded him in the prison and brought his head on a platter and gave it to the girl, and she gave it to her mother. And when John's disciples heard of it, they came and took away his body and laid it in a tomb.

MATTHEW 14:1-12

1 At that time Herod the tetrarch heard of the fame of Jesus,

2 And said unto his servants, This is John the Baptist; he is risen from the dead; and therefore mighty works do show forth themselves in him.

3 For Herod had laid hold on John, and bound him, and put *him* in prison for Herodias' sake, his brother Philip's wife.

4 For John said unto him, It is not lawful for thee to have her.

5 And when he would have put him to death, he feared the multitude, because they counted him as a prophet.

6 But when Herod's birthday was kept, the daughter of Herodias danced before them, and pleased Herod.

7 Whereupon he promised with an oath to give her whatsoever she would ask.

MARK 6:14-29

14 And king Herod heard *of him;* (for his name was spread abroad;) and he said, That John the Baptist was risen from the dead, and therefore mighty works do show forth themselves in him.

15 Others said, That it is Elijah. And others said, That it is a prophet, or as one of the prophets.

16 But when Herod heard *thereof,* he said, It is John, whom I beheaded: he is risen from the dead.

17 For Herod himself had sent forth and laid hold upon John, and bound him in prison for Herodias' sake, his brother Philip's wife; for he had married her.

18 For John had said unto Herod, It is not lawful for thee to have thy brother's wife.

19 Therefore Herodias had a quarrel against him, and would have killed him; but she could not:

LUKE 9:7-9

7 Now Herod the tetrarch heard of all that was done by him: and he was perplexed, because that it was said of some, that John was risen from the dead;

8 And of some, that Elijah had appeared; and of others, that one of the old prophets was risen again.

9 And Herod said, John have I beheaded; but who is this, of whom I hear such things? And he desired to see him.

Death of John the Baptist (continued)

8 And she, being before instructed of her mother, said, Give me here John Baptist's head in a charger.

9 And the king was sorry: nevertheless for the oath's sake, and them which sat with him at meat, he commanded *it* to be given *her.*

10 And he sent, and beheaded John in the prison.

11 And his head was brought in a charger, and given to the damsel: and she brought *it* to her mother.

12 And his disciples came, and took up the body, and buried it, and went and told Jesus.

20 For Herod feared John, knowing that he was a just man and a holy, and observed him; and when he heard him, he did many things, and heard him gladly.

21 And when a convenient day was come, that Herod on his birthday made a supper to his lords, high captains, and chief *estates* of Galilee;

22 And when the daughter of the said Herodias came in, and danced, and pleased Herod and them that sat with him, the king said unto the damsel, Ask of me whatsoever thou wilt, and I will give *it* thee.

23 And he sware unto her, Whatsoever thou shalt ask of me, I will give *it* thee, unto the half of my kingdom.

24 And she went forth, and said unto her mother, What shall I ask? And she said, The head of John the Baptist.

25 And she came in straightway with haste unto the king, and asked, saying, I will that thou give me by and by in a charger the head of John the Baptist.

26 And the king was exceeding sorry; *yet* for his oath's sake, and for their sakes which sat with him, he would not reject her.

27 And immediately the king sent an executioner, and commanded his head to be brought: and he went and beheaded him in the prison,

28 And brought his head in a charger, and gave it to the damsel; and the damsel gave it to her mother.

29 And when his disciples heard *of it,* they came and took up his corpse, and laid it in a tomb.

Jesus Feeds the Five Thousand

Mark 6:30-37, John 6:8-15

Then the apostles returned to Jesus and told him all the things they had done and taught. And Jesus said to them,

"Come away to some quiet place where you can be alone and rest a while."

For there were many people coming and going, and they had no leisure time even to eat. So they left by boat for a quiet place where they could be alone. But many saw them going and recognized them, and ran on foot from all the towns and got there ahead of them. When Jesus came ashore, he found a great crowd waiting. And he was moved with compassion for them, because they were like sheep without a shepherd. And he began to teach them many things. Now when the day was nearly gone, his disciples came to him and said,

"This is a remote place, and the hour is late. Send the people away, that they may go into the country and villages round about and buy themselves something to eat."

"You give them something to eat," replied Jesus.

"Shall we go and buy two hundred denarii worth of bread and give it to them to eat?" they asked.

One of his disciples, Andrew, Simon Peter's brother, said to Jesus, "There is a little boy here who has five barley loaves and two small fish, but what is that for so many people?"

"Have the people sit down," said Jesus.

Now the ground there was covered with grass, so the men sat down, about five thousand in number. Then Jesus took the loaves, and when he had given thanks, he passed them out to all who were sitting there; and also the fish, as much as they wanted. And when they had eaten their fill, he said to his disciples, "Gather up the pieces that are left over, that nothing may be wasted."

So they gathered them up and filled twelve baskets with pieces of the five barley loaves left by those who had eaten. Now when the people saw the miracle that Jesus performed, they began to say, "Without doubt, this is the prophet who is to come into the world!"

MATTHEW 14:13-21	MARK 6:30-44	LUKE 9:10-17	JOHN 6:1-15
13 When Jesus heard *of it,* he departed thence by ship into a desert place apart: and when the people had heard *thereof,* they followed him on foot out of the cities.	30 And the apostles gathered themselves together unto Jesus, and told him all things, both what they had done, and what they had taught.	10 And the apostles, when they were returned, told him all that they had done. And he took them, and went aside privately into a desert place belonging to the city called Bethsaida.	1 After these things Jesus went over the sea of Galilee, which is *the sea* of Tiberias.
14 And Jesus went forth, and saw a great multitude, and was moved with compassion toward them, and he healed their sick.	31 And he said unto them, Come ye yourselves apart into a desert place, and rest a while: for there were many coming and going, and they had no leisure so much as to eat.	11 And the people, when they knew *it,* followed him: and he received them, and spake unto them of the kingdom of God, and healed them that had need of healing.	2 And a great multitude followed him, because they saw his miracles which he did on them that were diseased.
15 And when it was evening, his disciples came to him, saying, This is a desert place, and the time is now past; send the multitude away, that they may go into the villages, and buy themselves victuals.	32 And they departed into a desert place by ship privately.	12 And when the day began to wear away, then came the twelve, and said unto him, Send the multitude away, that they may go into the towns and country round about, and lodge, and get	3 And Jesus went up into a mountain, and there he sat with his disciples.
16 But Jesus said unto	33 And the people saw them departing, and many knew him, and ran afoot thither out of all cities, and outwent them, and came together unto him.		4 And the passover, a feast of the Jews, was nigh.
			5 When Jesus then lifted up *his* eyes, and saw a great company come unto him, he saith unto Philip, Whence shall we buy bread, that these may eat?

Feeding the 5,000 Site. *There are two schools of thought concerning the correct location. Some favor Bethsaida on the northeastern shore of the Sea of Galilee; others, Tabgha on the northwestern shore.*

160

Jesus Feeds the Five Thousand (continued)

MATT. 14:13-21

them, They need not depart; give ye them to eat.

17 And they say unto him, We have here but five loaves, and two fishes.

18 He said, Bring them hither to me.

19 And he commanded the multitude to sit down on the grass, and took the five loaves, and the two fishes, and looking up to heaven, he blessed, and brake, and gave the loaves to *his* disciples, and the disciples to the multitude.

20 And they did all eat, and were filled: and they took up of the fragments that remained twelve baskets full.

21 And they that had eaten were about five thousand men, beside women and children.

MARK 6:30-44

34 And Jesus, when he came out, saw much people, and was moved with compassion toward them, because they were as sheep not having a shepherd: and he began to teach them many things.

35 And when the day was now far spent, his disciples came unto him, and said, This is a desert place, and now the time *is* far passed:

36 Send them away, that they may go into the country round about, and into the villages, and buy themselves bread: for they have nothing to eat.

37 He answered and said unto them, Give ye them to eat. And they say unto him, Shall we go and buy two hundred pennyworth of bread, and give them to eat?

38 He saith unto them, How many loaves have ye? go and see. And when they knew, they say, Five, and two fishes.

39 And he commanded them to make all sit down by companies upon the green grass.

40 And they sat down in ranks, by hundreds, and by fifties.

41 And when he had taken the five loaves and the two fishes, he looked up to heaven, and blessed, and brake the loaves, and gave *them* to his disciples to set before them; and the two fishes divided he among them all.

LUKE 9:10-17

victuals: for we are here in a desert place.

13 But he said unto them, Give ye them to eat. And they said, We have no more but five loaves and two fishes; except we should go and buy meat for all this people.

14 For they were about five thousand men. And he said to his disciples, Make them sit down by fifties in a company.

JOHN 6:1-15

6 And this he said to prove him: for he himself knew what he would do.

7 Philip answered him, Two hundred pennyworth of bread is not sufficient for them, that every one of them may take a little.

8 One of his disciples, Andrew, Simon Peter's brother, saith unto him,

9 There is a lad here, which hath five barley loaves, and two small fishes: but what are they among so many?

Loaves and Fishes.
This is the only miracle told in all four Gospels. The bread used on this occasion was probably flat, round pita bread still used extensively in the Middle East.

Jesus Feeds the Five Thousand (continued)

MARK 6:30-44

42 And they did all eat, and were filled.

43 And they took up twelve baskets full of the fragments, and of the fishes.

44 And they that did eat of the loaves were about five thousand men.

LUKE 9:10-17

15 And they did so, and made them all sit down.

16 Then he took the five loaves and the two fishes, and looking up to heaven, he blessed them, and brake, and gave to the disciples to set before the multitude.

17 And they did eat, and were all filled: and there was taken up of fragments that remained to them twelve baskets.

JOHN 6:1-15

10 And Jesus said, Make the men sit down. Now there was much grass in the place. So the men sat down, in number about five thousand.

11 And Jesus took the loaves; and when he had given thanks, he distributed to the disciples, and the disciples to them that were set down; and likewise of the fishes as much as they would.

12 When they were filled, he said unto his disciples, Gather up the fragments that remain, that nothing be lost.

13 Therefore they gathered *them* together, and filled twelve baskets with the fragments of the five barley loaves, which remained over and above unto them that had eaten.

14 Then those men, when they had seen the miracle that Jesus did, said, This is of a truth that Prophet that should come into the world.

15 When Jesus therefore perceived that they would come and take him by force, to make him a king, he departed again into a mountain himself alone.

Bread and Fishes Mosaic. *At Tabgha, on the western side of the Sea of Galilee, is a church dating back to the early centuries. It contains a mosaic floor commemorating the miracle.*

Jesus Walks on the Water

Matthew 14:22-33

Then Jesus told the disciples to get into the boat and go before him to the other side while he sent away the crowds. And when he had sent the people away, he went up into the hills by himself to pray; and when evening came, he was there alone. But the boat was now many furlongs from land, and tossed by the waves, for the wind was against them.

And in the fourth watch of the night Jesus went to them, walking on the sea. But when the disciples saw him walking on the sea, they were terrified and said, "It is a ghost!" And they cried out for fear.

But Jesus immediately called to them and said, "Be of good courage; it is I, do not be afraid."

"Lord, if it is you," said Peter, "tell me to come to you on the water!"

"Come," said Jesus.

Then Peter got out of the boat and walked on the water to go to Jesus. But when he saw the wind he was frightened, and beginning to sink, he cried, "Lord, save me!"

Jesus immediately reached out his hand and caught him, saying, "O man of little faith! Why did you doubt?"

And when they climbed into the boat, the wind ceased. Then those in the boat fell down before him and worshipped him, saҰng, "Truly, you are the Son of God!"

MATTHEW 14:22-33

22 And straightway Jesus constrained his disciples to get into a ship, and to go before him unto the other side, while he sent the multitudes away.

23 And when he had sent the multitudes away, he went up into a mountain apart to pray: and when the evening was come, he was there alone.

24 But the ship was now in the midst of the sea, tossed with waves: for the wind was contrary.

25 And in the fourth watch of the night Jesus went unto them, walking on the sea.

26 And when the disciples saw him walking on the sea, they were troubled, saying, It is a spirit; and they cried out for fear.

27 But straightway Jesus spake unto them, saying, Be of good cheer; it is I; be not afraid.

28 And Peter answered him and said, Lord, if it be thou, bid me come unto thee on the water.

MARK 6:45-52

45 And straightway he constrained his disciples to get into the ship, and to go to the other side before unto Bethsaida, while he sent away the people.

46 And when he had sent them away, he departed into a mountain to pray.

And he saw them toiling in rowing; for the wind was contrary unto them.

---

47 And when even was come, the ship was in the midst of the sea, and he alone on the land.

48 And he saw them toiling in rowing; for the wind was contrary unto them: and about the fourth watch of the night he cometh unto them, walking upon the sea, and would have passed by them.

JOHN 6:16-21

16 And when even was *now* come, his disciples went down unto the sea,

17 And entered into a ship, and went over the sea toward Capernaum. And it was now dark, and Jesus was not come to them.

18 And the sea arose by reason of a great wind that blew.

19 So when they had rowed about five and twenty or thirty furlongs, they see Jesus walking on the sea, and drawing nigh unto the ship: and they were afraid.

20 But he saith unto them, It is I; be not afraid.

21 Then they willingly received him into the ship: and immediately the ship was at the land whither they went.

Jesus Walks on the Water (continued)

29 And he said, Come. And when Peter was come down out of the ship, he walked on the water, to go to Jesus.

30 But when he saw the wind boisterous, he was afraid; and beginning to sink, he cried, saying, Lord, save me.

31 And immediately Jesus stretched forth *his* hand, and caught him, and said unto him, O thou of little faith, wherefore didst thou doubt?

32 And when they were come into the ship, the wind ceased.

33 Then they that were in the ship came and worshipped him, saying, Of a truth thou art the Son of God.

49 But when they saw him walking upon the sea, they supposed it had been a spirit, and cried out:

50 For they all saw him, and were troubled. And immediately he talked with them, and saith unto them, Be of good cheer: it is I; be not afraid.

51 And he went up unto them into the ship; and the wind ceased: and they were sore amazed in themselves beyond measure, and wondered.

52 For they considered not *the miracle* of the loaves; for their heart was hardened.

Healed by a Touch

Matthew 14:34-36

And when they had crossed over the sea, they came to land at Gennesaret. When the men of that place recognized him, they sent word to all the surrounding countryside and brought to him all who were sick and begged him that they might simply touch the fringe of his cloak. And as many as touched it were completely cured.

34 And when they were gone over, they came into the land of Gennesaret.

35 And when the men of that place had knowledge of him, they sent out into all that country round about, and brought unto him all that were diseased;

36 And besought him that they might only touch the hem of his garment: and as many as touched were made perfectly whole.

53 And when they had passed over, they came into the land of Gennesaret, and drew to the shore.

54 And when they were come out of the ship, straightway they knew him,

55 And ran through that whole region round about, and began to carry about in beds those that were sick, where they heard he was.

56 And whithersoever he entered, into villages, or cities, or country, they laid the sick in the streets, and besought him that they might touch if it were but the border of his garment: and as many as touched him were made whole.

The Sea of Galilee. *This body of water is not large, not more than 14 by 9 miles at its greatest extremities, but what a story it could tell. Jesus calmed its storm and walked on its waters.*

Sermon on the Bread of Life

John 6:22-71

The next day, people were still lingering on the other side of the lake. They had seen that there had been only one boat there, and that Jesus had not got into the boat with his disciples, but his disciples had gone away alone. However, boats from Tiberias landed near the place where they ate the bread, after the Lord had given thanks. So when the people saw that neither Jesus nor his disciples were there, they got into the boats and went to Capernaum, seeking Jesus. When they found him on the other side of the lake, they said to him, ''Rabbi, when did you come here?''

''I tell you truly,'' replied Jesus, ''you seek me, not because you saw miracles, but because you ate of the loaves and were satisfied. Do not labor merely for food that perishes, but for the food that endures to life eternal—the food which the Son of Man will give you; for he is the one on whom the Father, even God, has set his seal of approval.''

''What must we do if we are to do the works of God?'' they asked.

''The true work and service of God,'' replied Jesus, ''is this: that you believe in him whom he has sent.''

''What will you do as a sign, that we may see and believe in you?'' they said. ''What work will you perform? Our fathers ate manna in the wilderness; as it is written, 'He gave them bread from heaven to eat.' ''

''I tell you truly,'' said Jesus, ''it was not Moses who gave you the bread from heaven; it is my Father who is giving you the true bread from heaven, for the bread of God is that bread which comes down from heaven and gives life to the world.''

''Lord, evermore give us this bread!'' they said.

''I am the bread of life,'' said Jesus. ''He who comes to me shall not hunger, and he who trusts in me shall never thirst. But I told you that you have seen, but do not believe. All that the Father gives me will come to me, and I will not refuse anyone who comes to me. For I have come down from heaven, not to do my own will, but to do the will of him who sent me. And this is the will of him who sent me, that I should lose nothing of all that he has given me, but should raise it up at the last day. For this is my Father's will, that every one who beholds the Son and trusts in him shall have eternal life, and I will raise him up at the last day.''

Then the Jews began to find fault with Jesus because he said, ''I am the bread which came down from heaven.'' And they said, ''Isn't this Jesus, the son of Joseph, whose father and mother we know? How can he say, 'I have come down from heaven'?''

''Stop finding fault with me among yourselves,'' said Jesus. ''No one can come to me unless the Father who sent me draws him, and I will raise him up at the last day. It is written in the prophets, 'And they shall all be taught of God.' Every one who has listened and learned from the Father comes to me. Not that anyone has seen the Father; only he who has come from God has seen the Father. I tell you truly, he who believes in him has life eternal.

''I am the bread of life. Your fathers ate manna in the wilderness, and died. This is the bread that comes down from heaven, that men may eat of it and not die. I am the living bread which came down from heaven; if anyone eats of this bread, he will live for ever. And the bread I will give for the life of the world is my flesh.''

Then the Jews began to argue among themselves, saying, ''How can this man give us his flesh to eat?''

Jesus therefore said to them, ''I tell you truly, unless you eat the flesh of the Son of Man and drink his blood, you do not have life in you. He who eats my flesh and drinks my blood lives in me, and I in him. As the living Father sent me, and I live by the Father, so he who feeds on me shall live by me. This is the bread which came down out of heaven—not such as the fathers ate, and died; he who feeds on this bread will live for ever.''

Sermon on the Bread of Life (continued)

These things Jesus said in the synagogue, as he taught in Capernaum. And when they heard it, many of his disciples said, "This is an offensive and intolerable doctrine! Who can accept it?"

But Jesus, knowing that many of his disciples were finding fault with his teaching, said to them, "Does this offend you? Then what if you were to see the Son of Man ascending to where he was before? It is the spirit that gives life; the flesh is of no profit. The words I have spoken to you are spirit and life, but there are some of you who do not believe."

For Jesus knew all along those who did not believe, and who would betray him. And he said, "That is why I told you that no one can come to me unless it be granted to him by the Father."

From that time, many of his disciples turned back and walked no more with him. Then said Jesus to the twelve, "Will you also go away?"

"Lord," replied Peter, "to whom shall we go? You alone have the words of eternal life. And as for us, we believe and are sure that you are the Holy One of God."

"Did not I myself choose you as the Twelve?" said Jesus. "Yet even of you, one is a devil."

He was speaking of Judas, the son of Simon Iscariot. For he, one of the Twelve, was even then thinking of betraying him.

JOHN 6:22-71

22 The day following, when the people, which stood on the other side of the sea, saw that there was none other boat there, save that one whereinto his disciples were entered, and that Jesus went not with his disciples into the boat, but *that* his disciples were gone away alone;

23 (Howbeit there came other boats from Tiberias nigh unto the place where they did eat bread, after that the Lord had given thanks:)

24 When the people therefore saw that Jesus was not there, neither his disciples, they also took shipping, and came to Capernaum, seeking for Jesus.

25 And when they had found him on the other side of the sea, they said unto him, Rabbi, when camest thou hither?

26 Jesus answered them and said, Verily, verily, I say unto you, Ye seek me, not because ye saw the miracles, but because ye did eat of the loaves, and were filled.

27 Labor not for the meat which perisheth, but for that meat which endureth unto everlasting life, which the Son of man shall give unto you: for him hath God the Father sealed.

28 Then said they unto him, What shall we do, that we might work the works of God?

29 Jesus answered and said unto them, This is the work of God, that ye believe on him whom he hath sent.

30 They said therefore unto him, What sign showest thou then, that we may see, and believe thee? what dost thou work?

31 Our fathers did eat manna in the desert; as it is written, He gave them bread from heaven to eat.

32 Then Jesus said unto them, Verily, verily, I say unto you, Moses gave you not that bread from heaven; but my Father giveth you the true bread from heaven.

33 For the bread of God is he which cometh down from heaven, and giveth life unto the world.

34 Then said they unto him, Lord, evermore give us this bread.

35 And Jesus said unto them, I am the bread of life: he that cometh to me shall never hunger; and he that believeth on me shall never thirst.

36 But I said unto you, That ye also have seen me, and believe not.

Capernaum Synagogue. *Jesus spent much time in this city and often taught in the synagogue. The ruins date back to the Second Century and probably mark the location of the one where Jesus preached the sermon on the Bread of Life.*

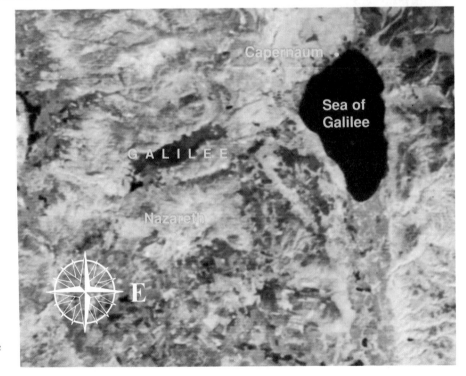

Capernaum, on the north-west shore of the Sea of Galilee, was an important trade center on the caravan route between Mesopotamia and Egypt.

Sermon on the Bread of Life (continued)

37 All that the Father giveth me shall come to me; and him that cometh to me I will in no wise cast out.

38 For I came down from heaven, not to do mine own will, but the will of him that sent me.

39 And this is the Father's will which hath sent me, that of all which he hath given me I should lose nothing, but should raise it up again at the last day.

40 And this is the will of him that sent me, that every one which seeth the Son, and believeth on him, may have everlasting life: and I will raise him up at the last day.

41 The Jews then murmured at him, because he said, I am the bread which came down from heaven.

42 And they said, Is not this Jesus, the son of Joseph, whose father and mother we know? how is it then that he saith, I came down from heaven?

43 Jesus therefore answered and said unto them, Murmur not among yourselves.

44 No man can come to me, except the Father which hath sent me draw him: and I will raise him up at the last day.

45 It is written in the prophets, And they shall be all taught of God. Every man therefore that hath heard, and hath learned of the Father, cometh unto me.

46 Not that any man hath seen the Father, save he which is of God, he hath seen the Father.

47 Verily, verily, I say unto you, He that believeth on me hath everlasting life.

48 I am that bread of life.

49 Your fathers did eat manna in the wilderness, and are dead.

50 This is the bread which cometh down from heaven, that a man may eat thereof, and not die.

51 I am the living bread which came down from heaven: if any man eat of this bread, he shall live for ever: and the bread that I will give is my flesh, which I will give for the life of the world.

52 The Jews therefore strove among themselves, saying, How can this man give us *his* flesh to eat?

53 Then Jesus said unto them, Verily, verily, I say unto you, Except ye eat the flesh of the Son of man, and drink his blood, ye have no life in you.

54 Whoso eateth my flesh, and drinketh my blood, hath eternal life; and I will raise him up at the last day.

55 For my flesh is meat indeed, and my blood is drink indeed.

56 He that eateth my flesh, and drinketh my blood, dwelleth in me, and I in him.

57 As the living Father hath sent me, and I live by the Father; so he that eateth me, even he shall live by me.

58 This is that bread which came down from heaven: not as your fathers did eat manna, and are dead: he that eateth of this bread shall live for ever.

59 These things said he in the synagogue, as he taught in Capernaum.

60 Many therefore of his disciples, when they had heard *this*, said, This is a hard saying; who can hear it?

> *It is the Spirit that quickeneth; the flesh profiteth nothing: the words that I speak unto you, they are spirit, and they are life.*

61 When Jesus knew in himself that his disciples murmured at it, he said unto them, Doth this offend you?

62 *What* and if ye shall see the Son of man ascend up where he was before?

63 It is the Spirit that quickeneth; the flesh profiteth nothing: the words that I speak unto you, *they* are spirit, and *they* are life.

64 But there are some of you that believe not. For Jesus knew from the beginning who they were that believed not, and who should betray him.

65 And he said, Therefore said I unto you, that no man can come unto me, except it were given unto him of my Father.

66 From that *time* many of his disciples went back, and walked no more with him.

67 Then said Jesus unto the twelve, Will ye also go away?

68 Then Simon Peter answered him, Lord, to whom shall we go? thou hast the words of eternal life.

69 And we believe and are sure that thou art that Christ, the Son of the living God.

70 Jesus answered them, Have not I chosen you twelve, and one of you is a devil?

71 He spake of Judas Iscariot *the son* of Simon: for he it was that should betray him, being one of the twelve.

Jesus Condemns Hypocrisy

Mark 7:1-16, Matthew 15:12-20

Now the Pharisees and some of the scribes who had come from Jerusalem came together to Jesus. For they had noticed that some of his disciples ate their food with "defiled" (that is, unwashed) hands.

For the Pharisees and all of the Jews do not eat unless they first wash their hands, carefully observing the tradition of the elders. And when they come from the market, they do not eat unless they first bathe. And there are many other traditions which they carefully observed, such as the washing of cups and pitchers and bronze vessels.

And the Pharisees and scribes asked Jesus, "Why do your disciples not follow the tradition of the elders, but eat with defiled hands?"

Jesus replied, "Isaiah rightly prophesied of you hypocrites, as it is written, 'This people honors me with their lips, but their heart is far away from me. In vain do they worship me, teaching as doctrines the precepts of men.' Casting aside the commandment of God, you hold fast the tradition of men!

"You have a wonderful way of setting aside the commandment of God in order to observe your tradition! For Moses said, 'Honor your father and your mather,' and, 'Whoever speaks evil of father or mother, let him be put to death.' But you say, 'If a man says to his father or mother, "Everything of mine which might have been used for your assistance is Corban" ' — then you excuse him from doing anything more

for his father or mother, thus making the word of God void by your tradition which you have handed down. And you do many such things."

Then Jesus called the multitude to him again and said,

"Hear me now, all of you, and understand this. There is nothing outside a man which can defile him by entering into him. But the things which come out of the man are the things which defile him."

Then the disciples came to Jesus and said, "Do you know that the Pharisees were offended when they heard what you said?"

But Jesus answered, "Every plant which my heavenly Father has not planted will be pulled— root and all. Let them alone. They are blind guides, and if a blind man leads a blind man, both will fall into a ditch."

Then Peter said to Jesus, "Explain the parable to us."

"Are you, too, still without understanding?" asked Jesus. "Do you not understand that everything that enters the mouth goes into the stomach and is expelled as waste? But the things that come forth out of the mouth come from the heart, and these things defile a man. For out of the heart come evil thoughts, murders, adulteries, fornications, thefts, perjuries, blasphemies—these are the things that defile a man. But to eat with unwashed hands does not defile a man."

MATTHEW 15:1-20

1 Then came to Jesus scribes and Pharisees, which were of Jerusalem, saying,

2 Why do thy disciples transgress the tradition of the elders? for they wash not their hands when they eat bread.

3 But he answered and said unto them, Why do ye also transgress the commandment of God by your tradition?

4 For God commanded, saying, Honor thy father and mother: and, He that curseth father or mother, let him die the death.

5 But ye say, Whosoever shall say to *his* father or *his* mother, *It is* a gift, by whatsoever thou mightest

MARK 7:1-23

1 Then came together unto him the Pharisees, and certain of the scribes, which came from Jerusalem.

2 And when they saw some of his disciples eat bread with defiled, that is to say, with unwashen hands, they found fault.

3 For the Pharisees, and all the Jews, except they wash *their* hands oft, eat not, holding the tradition of the elders.

4 And *when they come* from the market, except they wash, they eat not. And many other things there be, which they have received to hold, *as* the washing of cups, and pots, brazen vessels, and of tables.

5 Then the Pharisees and scribes asked him, Why

Jesus Condemns Hypocrisy (continued)

be profited by me;

6 And honor not his father or his mother, *he shall be free.* Thus have ye made the commandment of God of none effect by your tradition.

7 *Ye* hypocrites, well did Esaias prophesy of you, saying,

8 This people draweth nigh unto me with their mouth, and honoreth me with *their* lips; but their heart is far from me.

9 But in vain they do worship me, teaching *for* doctrines the commandments of men.

10 And he called the multitude, and said unto them, Hear, and understand:

11 Not that which goeth into the mouth defileth a man; but that which cometh out of the mouth, this defileth a man.

12 Then came his disciples, and said unto him, Knowest thou that the Pharisees were offended, after they heard this saying?

This people draweth nigh unto me with their mouth, and honoreth me with their lips; but their heart is far from me.

---

13 But he answered and said, Every plant, which my heavenly Father hath not planted, shall be rooted up.

14 Let them alone: they be blind leaders of the blind. And if the blind lead the blind, both shall fall into the ditch.

15 Then answered Peter and said unto him, Declare unto us this parable.

16 And Jesus said, Are ye also yet without understanding?

17 Do not ye yet understand, that whatsoever entereth in at the mouth goeth into the belly, and is cast out into the draught?

18 But those things which proceed out of the mouth come forth from the heart; and they defile the man.

19 For out of the heart proceed evil thoughts, murders, adulteries, fornications, thefts, false witness, blasphemies:

20 These are *the things* which defile a man: but to eat with unwashen hands defileth not a man.

walk not thy disciples according to the tradition of the elders, but eat bread with unwashen hands?

6 He answered and said unto them, Well hath Isaiah prophesied of you hypocrites, as it is written, This people honoreth me with *their* lips, but their heart is far from me.

7 Howbeit in vain do they worship me, teaching *for* doctrines the commandments of men.

8 For laying aside the commandment of God, ye hold the tradition of men, *as* the washing of pots and cups: and many other such like things ye do.

9 And he said unto them, Full well ye reject the commandment of God, that ye may keep your own tradition.

10 For Moses said, Honor thy father and thy mother; and, Whoso curseth father or mother, let him die the death:

11 But ye say, If a man shall say to his father or mother, *It is* Corban, that is to say, a gift, by whatsoever thou mightest be profited by me; *he shall be free.*

12 And ye suffer him no more to do aught for his father or his mother;

13 Making the word of God of none effect through your tradition, which ye have delivered: and many such like things do ye.

14 And when he had called all the people *unto him,* he said unto them, Hearken unto me every one *of you,* and understand:

15 There is nothing from without a man, that entering into him can defile him: but the things which come out of him, those are they that defile the man.

16 If any man have ears to hear, let him hear.

17 And when he was entered into the house from the people, his disciples asked him concerning the parable.

18 And he saith unto them, Are ye so without understanding also? Do ye not perceive, that whatsoever thing from without entereth into the man, *it* cannot defile him;

19 Because it entereth not into his heart, but into the belly, and goeth out into the draught, purging all meats?

20 And he said, That which cometh out of the man, that defileth the man.

21 For from within, out of the heart of men proceed evil thoughts, adulteries, fornications, murders,

22 Thefts, covetousness, wickedness, deceit, lasciviousness, an evil eye, blasphemy, pride, foolishness:

23 All these evil things come from within, and defile the man.

Jesus Ministers to Gentiles

Matthew 15:21-31, Mark 7:31-37

Then Jesus left Capernaum and withdrew into the country of Tyre and Sidon. And a Canaanite woman of that region came to him, crying, "Have mercy on me, O Lord, Son of David! My daughter is completely demon possessed."

But Jesus made no reply. And his disciples came to him and implored him, saying, "Send her away, for she keeps following us and crying out."

But Jesus replied, "I was sent only to the lost sheep of the house of Israel."

Then the woman came and fell at his feet, saying, "Lord, help me!"

But he replied, "It is not right to take the children's bread and throw it to the little dogs."

"That is true, Lord," she said, "yet the little dogs eat the crumbs that fall from their master's table."

"O woman, great is your faith!" replied Jesus. "It shall be as you wish."

And from that hour, her daughter was healed.

And journeying on from the region of Tyre, Jesus passed through Sidon into the region of Decapolis, near the Sea of Galilee. And they brought him a man who was deaf and had an impediment in his speech, and begged him to lay his hand on him. And when he had taken him aside from the crowd, Jesus spat and touched the man's tongue with his saliva and put his fingers in the man's ears. Then, looking up to heaven, he sighed, and said to him, "Be opened!" And his ears were opened and his tongue was loosed, and he began to talk plainly.

Then Jesus charged them not to tell anyone; but the more he admonished them, the more they told it. And they were greatly astonished, and said, "He has done everything well—he even makes the deaf hear and the dumb speak!"

And great crowds came to him, bringing with them the lame, the maimed, the blind, the dumb, and many others. And they laid them at his feet, and he healed them. Then the crowd was amazed when they saw the dumb speaking, the maimed whole, the lame walking, and the blind seeing; and they praised the God of Israel.

MATTHEW 15:21-31

21 Then Jesus went thence, and departed into the coasts of Tyre and Sidon.

22 And, behold, a woman of Canaan came out of the same coasts, and cried unto him, saying, Have mercy on me, O Lord, *thou* Son of David; my daughter is grievously vexed with a devil.

23 But he answered her not a word. And his disciples came and besought him, saying, Send her away; for she crieth after us.

24 But he answered and said, I am not sent but unto the lost sheep of the house of Israel.

25 Then came she and worshipped him, saying, Lord, help me.

26 But he answered and said, It is not meet to take the children's bread, and to cast *it* to dogs.

MARK 7:24-37

24 And from thence he arose, and went into the borders of Tyre and Sidon, and entered into a house, and would have no man know *it:* but he could not be hid.

25 For a *certain* woman, whose young daughter had an unclean spirit, heard of him, and came and fell at his feet:

26 The woman was a Greek, a Syrophoenician by nation; and she besought him that he would cast forth the devil out of her daughter.

27 But Jesus said unto her, Let the children first be filled: for it is not meet to take the children's bread, and to cast *it* unto the dogs.

28 And she answered and said unto him, Yes, Lord: yet the dogs under the table eat of the children's crumbs.

Castle at Sidon. *This structure traces its origin to the Crusaders. It was near this city that Jesus ministered to a Gentile woman saying, "Great is thy faith," and healing her demon-possessed daughter.*

Jesus Ministers to Gentiles (continued)

27 And she said, Truth, Lord: yet the dogs eat of the crumbs which fall from their masters' table.

28 Then Jesus answered and said unto her, O woman, great *is* thy faith: be it unto thee even as thou wilt. And her daughter was made whole from that very hour.

29 And Jesus departed from thence, and came nigh unto the sea of Galilee; and went up into a mountain, and sat down there.

30 And great multitudes came unto him, having with them *those that were* lame, blind, dumb, maimed, and many others, and cast them down at Jesus' feet; and he healed them:

31 Insomuch that the multitude wondered, when they saw the dumb to speak, the maimed to be whole, the lame to walk, and the blind to see: and they glorified the God of Israel.

29 And he said unto her, For this saying go thy way; the devil is gone out of thy daughter.

30 And when she was come to her house, she found the devil gone out, and her daughter laid upon the bed.

31 And again, departing from the coasts of Tyre and Sidon, he came unto the sea of Galilee, through the midst of the coasts of Decapolis.

32 And they bring unto him one that was deaf, and had an impediment in his speech; and they beseech him to put his hand upon him.

33 And he took him aside from the multitude, and put his fingers into his ears, and he spit, and touched his tongue;

34 And looking up to heaven, he sighed, and saith unto him, Ephphatha, that is, Be opened.

35 And straightway his ears were opened, and the string of his tongue was loosed, and he spake plain.

36 And he charged them that they should tell no man: but the more he charged them, so much the more a great deal they published *it;*

37 And were beyond measure astonished, saying, He hath done all things well: he maketh both the deaf to hear, and the dumb to speak.

Jesus Feeds a Multitude

Matthew 15:32-39

Then Jesus called his disciples to him and said, "I have compassion on the multitude, for they have been with me three days now, and have nothing to eat. I will not send them away hungry, lest they faint on the way."

"Where can we get enough bread in this wilderness to feed such a crowd?" said the disciples.

"How many loaves have you?" asked Jesus.

"Seven," they replied, "and a few small fish."

Then Jesus commanded the crowd to sit down on the ground, and took the seven loaves and the fish and gave thanks. And he broke them and gave them to the disciples, and the disciples gave them to the people. And they all ate and were satisfied; and they gathered up seven baskets full of the broken pieces that were left. Those who ate numbered four thousand men, besides women and children. Then Jesus sent the crowds away, and got into the boat and went to the region of Magdala.

Jesus Feeds a Multitude (continued)

MATTHEW 15:32-39

32 Then Jesus called his disciples *unto him,* and said, I have compassion on the multitude, because they continue with me now three days, and have nothing to eat: and I will not send them away fasting, lest they faint in the way.

33 And his disciples say unto him, Whence should we have so much bread in the wilderness, as to fill so great a multitude?

34 And Jesus saith unto them, How many loaves have ye? And they said, Seven, and a few little fishes.

35 And he commanded the multitude to sit down on the ground.

36 And he took the seven loaves and the fishes, and gave thanks, and brake *them,* and gave to his disciples, and the disciples to the multitude.

37 And they did all eat, and were filled: and they took up of the broken *meat* that was left seven baskets full.

38 And they that did eat were four thousand men, beside women and children.

39 And he sent away the multitude, and took ship, and came into the coasts of Magdala.

MARK 8:1-10

1 In those days the multitude being very great, and having nothing to eat, Jesus called his disciples *unto him,* and saith unto them,

2 I have compassion on the multitude, because they have now been with me three days, and have nothing to eat:

3 And if I send them away fasting to their own houses, they will faint by the way: for divers of them came from far.

4 And his disciples answered him, From whence can a man satisfy these *men* with bread here in the wilderness?

5 And he asked them, How many loaves have ye? And they said, Seven.

6 And he commanded the people to sit down on the ground: and he took the seven loaves, and gave thanks, and brake, and gave to his disciples to set before *them;* and they did set *them* before the people.

7 And they had a few small fishes: and he blessed, and commanded to set them also before *them.*

8 So they did eat, and were filled: and they took up of the broken *meat* that was left seven baskets.

9 And they that had eaten were about four thousand: and he sent them away.

10 And straightway he entered into a ship with his disciples, and came into the parts of Dalmanutha.

Sign Seeking and Wrong Doctrine

Matthew 16:1-12

And the Pharisees and Sadducees came to Jesus and, to test him, they asked him to show them a sign from heaven. But he replied,

"When it is evening, you say, 'There will be fair weather, for the sky is red.' And in the morning, 'There will be a storm today, for the sky is red and threatening.' You know how to interpret the face of the sky, but you cannot interpret the signs of the times. A wicked and faithless generation is demanding a sign, but no sign shall be given to it except the sign of Jonah."

Then Jesus left the Pharisees and Sadducees and departed. And when the disciples reached the other side of the lake, they had forgotten to bring bread. Then Jesus said to them,

"Take heed and beware the leaven of the Pharisees and Sadducees."

Then they began to reason among themselves, saying, "It is because we brought no bread."

But Jesus, aware of their reasoning, said, "O you of little faith! Why are you discussing among yourselves the fact that you brought no bread? Do you not understand yet, nor remember the five loaves for the five thousand, and how many baskets you gathered up? Do you not remember the seven loaves for the four thousand, and how many baskets you gathered up? How is it that you do not understand that I was not talking to you about bread when I told you to beware the leaven of the Pharisees and Sadducees?"

Then they understood that he had not told them to beware leaven in bread, but to beware the teaching of the Pharisees and Sadducees.

175

Sign Seeking and Wrong Doctrine (continued)

MATTHEW 16:1-12

1 The Pharisees also with the Sadducees came, and tempting desired him that he would show them a sign from heaven.

2 He answered and said unto them, When it is evening, ye say, *It will be* fair weather: for the sky is red.

3 And in the morning, *It will be* foul weather to-day: for the sky is red and lowering. O *ye* hypocrites, ye can discern the face of the sky; but can ye not *discern* the signs of the times?

4 A wicked and adulterous generation seeketh after a sign; and there shall no sign be given unto it, but the sign of the prophet Jonas. And he left them, and departed.

5 And when his disciples were come to the other side, they had forgotten to take bread.

6 Then Jesus said unto them, Take heed and beware of the leaven of the Pharisees and of the Sadducees.

7 And they reasoned among themselves, saying, *It is* because we have taken no bread.

8 *Which* when Jesus perceived, he said unto them, O ye of little faith, why reason ye among yourselves, because ye have brought no bread?

9 Do ye not yet understand, neither remember the five loaves of the five thousand, and how many baskets ye took up?

10 Neither the seven loaves of the four thousand, and how many baskets ye took up?

11 How is it that ye do not understand that I spake *it* not to you concerning bread, that ye should beware of the leaven of the Pharisees and of the Sadducees?

12 Then understood they how that he bade *them* not beware of the leaven of bread, but of the doctrine of the Pharisees and of the Sadducees.

MARK 8:11-21

11 And the Pharisees came forth, and began to question with him, seeking of him a sign from heaven, tempting him.

12 And he sighed deeply in his spirit, and saith, Why doth this generation seek after a sign? verily I say unto you, There shall no sign be given unto this generation.

13 And he left them, and entering into the ship again departed to the other side.

14 Now *the disciples* had forgotten to take bread, neither had they in the ship with them more than one loaf.

15 And he charged them, saying, Take heed, beware of the leaven of the Pharisees, and *of* the leaven of Herod.

16 And they reasoned among themselves, saying, *It is* because we have no bread.

17 And when Jesus knew *it*, he saith unto them, Why reason ye, because ye have no bread? perceive ye not yet, neither understand? have ye your heart yet hardened?

18 Having eyes, see ye not? and having ears, hear ye not? and do ye not remember?

19 When I brake the five loaves among five thousand, how many baskets full of fragments took ye up? They say unto him, Twelve.

20 And when the seven among four thousand, how many baskets full of fragments took ye up? And they said, Seven.

21 And he said unto them, How is it that ye do not understand?

Mount Hermon. Over 9,200 feet high, and adorned with snow most of the year, this mountain looked down on Caesarea-Philippi at its base, as Peter triumphantly proclaimed Jesus to be the Son of God.

Blind Man Healed at Bethsaida

Mark 8:22-26

And they came to Bethsaida, and some people brought a blind man to Jesus and begged him to touch him. And Jesus took the blind man by the hand and led him out of the village. When he had spit on his eyes and laid his hands on him, he asked, "Can you see anything?"

And he looked up and said, "I can see the people—they look like trees walking about."

Then Jesus laid his hands on his eyes again, and the man stared intently, and was restored and saw everything clearly. Then Jesus sent him away to his home, saying, "Be sure you don't go into the village."

MARK 8:22-26

22 And he cometh to Bethsaida; and they bring a blind man unto him, and besought him to touch him.

23 And he took the blind man by the hand, and led him out of the town; and when he had spit on his eyes, and put his hands upon him, he asked him if he saw aught.

24 And he looked up, and said, I see men as trees, walking.

25 After that he put *his* hands again upon his eyes, and made him look up; and he was restored, and saw every man clearly.

26 And he sent him away to his house, saying, Neither go into the town, nor tell *it* to any in the town.

Peter Affirms Jesus' Deity

Matthew 16:13-20

Now when Jesus came into the region of Caesarea Philippi, he began to question his disciples, saying, "Who are men saying that I, the Son of Man, am?"

"Some say you are John the Baptist," they said, "others Elijah, and others Jeremiah or one of the prophets."

"But you—who do you say I am?" asked Jesus.

"You are the Messiah, the Son of the living God!" answered Simon Peter.

"Blessed are you, Simon, son of Jonah," replied Jesus, "for flesh and blood has not revealed this to you, but my Father in heaven. And I say to you, you are Peter; and on this rock I will build my church, and the powers of death shall not prevail against it. I will give you the keys of the kingdom of heaven, and whatever you bind on earth will be bound in heaven, and whatever you loose on earth will be loosed in heaven."

Then Jesus charged the disciples to tell no one that he was the Messiah.

MATTHEW 16:13-20

13 When Jesus came into the coasts of Caesarea Philippi, he asked his disciples, saying, Whom do men say that I, the Son of man, am?

14 And they said, Some *say that thou art* John the Baptist; some, Elijah; and others, Jeremiah, or one of the prophets.

15 He saith unto them, But whom say ye that I am?

16 And Simon Peter answered and said, Thou art the Christ, the Son of the living God.

MARK 8:27-30

27 And Jesus went out, and his disciples, into the towns of Caesarea Philippi: and by the way he asked his disciples, saying unto them, Whom do men say that I am?

28 And they answered, John the Baptist: but some *say,* Elijah; and others, One of the prophets.

LUKE 9:18-21

18 And it came to pass, as he was alone praying, his disciples were with him; and he asked them, saying, Whom say the people that I am?

19 They answering said, John the Baptist; but some *say,* Elijah; and others *say,* that one of the old prophets is risen again.

Peter Affirms Jesus' Deity (continued)

MATTHEW 16:13-20

17 And Jesus answered and said unto him, Blessed art thou, Simon Bar-jona: for flesh and blood hath not revealed *it* unto thee, but my Father which is in heaven.

18 And I say also unto thee, That thou art Peter, and upon this rock I will build my church; and the gates of hell shall not prevail against it.

19 And I will give unto thee the keys of the kingdom of heaven: and whatsoever thou shalt bind on earth shall be bound in heaven; and whatsoever thou shalt loose on earth shall be loosed in heaven.

20 Then charged he his disciples that they should tell no man that he was Jesus the Christ.

MARK 8:27-30

29 And he saith unto them, But whom say ye that I am? And Peter answereth and saith unto him, Thou art the Christ.

30 And he charged them that they should tell no man of him.

LUKE 9:18-21

20 He said unto them, But whom say ye that I am? Peter answering said, The Christ of God.

21 And he straitly charged them, and commanded *them* to tell no man that thing;

Peter Declares Jesus' Deity. It was near Caesarea-Philippi that Jesus asked His disciples who people thought Him to be. After they replied He asked their personal view. Then it was that Peter forthrightly stated, "Thou art the Christ, the Son of the living God."

Jesus Foretells His Death and Resurrection

Matthew 16:21-28, Luke 9:26-27

From that time Jesus began to show his disciples that he must go to Jerusalem and suffer many things at the hands of the elders and chief priests and scribes, and be killed, and on the third day be raised. Then Peter took him aside and began to rebuke him, saying, "God have mercy on you, Lord! This must never happen to you."

But Jesus turned away from Peter and said, "Get behind me, Satan! You are a hindrance and a snare to me, for you are not thinking of things from God's viewpoint, but from men's."

Then said Jesus to his disciples, "If any man will come after me, let him deny himself and take up his cross and follow me. Whoever chooses to save his life for himself will lose it, and whoever loses his life for my sake will find it. For what will it profit a man if he should gain the whole world, but forfeit his soul? What could a man give to buy back his soul? For whoever is ashamed of me and my words, of him will the Son of Man be ashamed when he comes in his glory—all the glory of the Father and the holy angels!

"But I tell you truly," said Jesus, "there are some standing here who will not taste death before they see the kingdom of God."

MATTHEW 16:21-28

21 From that time forth began Jesus to show unto his disciples, how that he must go unto Jerusalem, and suffer many things of the elders and chief priests and scribes, and be killed, and be raised again the third day.
22 Then Peter took him, and began to rebuke him, saying, Be it far from thee, Lord: this shall not be unto thee.
23 But he turned, and said unto Peter, Get thee behind me, Satan: thou art an offense unto me: for thou savorest not the things that be of God, but those that be of men.
24 Then said Jesus unto his disciples, If any *man* will come after me, let him deny himself, and take up his cross, and follow me.
25 For whosoever will save his life shall lose it: and whosoever will lose his life for my sake shall find it.
26 For what is a man profited, if he shall gain the whole world, and lose his own soul? or what shall a man give in exchange for his soul?

MARK 8:31-9:1

31 And he began to teach them, that the Son of man must suffer many things, and be rejected of the elders, and *of* the chief priests, and scribes, and be killed, and after three days rise again.
32 And he spake that saying openly. And Peter took him, and began to rebuke him.
33 But when he had turned about and looked on his disciples, he rebuked Peter, saying, Get thee behind me, Satan: for thou savorest not the things that be of God, but the things that be of men.
34 And when he had called the people *unto him* with his disciples also, he said unto them, Whosoever will come after me, let him deny himself, and take up his cross, and follow me.
35 For whosoever will save his life shall lose it; but whosoever shall lose his life for my sake and the gospel's, the same shall save it.
36 For what shall it profit a man, if he shall gain the whole world, and lose his own soul?

LUKE 9:22-27

22 Saying, The Son of man must suffer many things, and be rejected of the elders and chief priests and scribes, and be slain, and be raised the third day.
23 And he said to *them* all, If any *man* will come after me, let him deny himself, and take up his cross daily, and follow me.
24 For whosoever will save his life shall lose it: but whosoever will lose his life for my sake, the same shall save it.
25 For what is a man advantaged, if he gain the whole world, and lose himself, or be cast away?
26 For whosoever shall be ashamed of me and of my words, of him shall the Son of man be ashamed, when he shall come in his own glory, and *in his* Father's, and of the holy angels.
27 But I tell you of a truth, there be some standing here, which shall not taste of death, till they see the kingdom of God.

Jesus Foretells His Death and Resurrection (continued)

27 For the Son of man shall come in the glory of his Father with his angels; and then he shall reward every man according to his works.

28 Verily I say unto you, There be some standing here, which shall not taste of death, till they see the Son of man coming in his kingdom.

37 Or what shall a man give in exchange for his soul?

38 Whosoever therefore shall be ashamed of me and of my words, in this adulterous and sinful generation, of him also shall the Son of man be ashamed, when he cometh in the glory of his Father with the holy angels.

9:1 And he said unto them, Verily I say unto you, That there be some of them that stand here, which shall not taste of death, till they have seen the kingdom of God come with power.

Mount Tabor. *This small mountain, about 1,800 feet high and located less than 10 miles southeast of Nazareth, was the site of numerous battles in Old Testament times. Some scholars consider it to be the location of the Transfiguration.*

The Transfiguration

Luke 9:28-31, Mark 9:5-6, Matthew 17:5-13

Now about eight days after saying these things, Jesus took Peter and John and James and went up on the mountain to pray. And as he was praying, the appearance of his countenance was changed, and his clothes became dazzling white. And behold, two men—Moses and Elijah—appeared in glory and talked with him concerning his death which he was to accomplish at Jerusalem.

Then Peter exclaimed to Jesus, ''Rabbi, it is a good thing we are here! Let us make three booths—one for you, and one for Moses, and one for Elijah.'' For he did not know what to say, for they were much afraid.

While he was still speaking, behold, a bright cloud overshadowed them, and a voice out of the cloud said, ''This is my beloved Son, in whom I am well pleased. Listen to him and heed what he says!''

And when the disciples heard it, they fell on their faces and were filled with fear. But Jesus came and touched them, saying, ''Rise, and do not be afraid.'' And when they looked up, they saw no one but Jesus only.

And as they were coming down the mountain, Jesus commanded them, ''Do not tell anyone what you have seen until the Son of Man has been raised from the dead.''

Then the disciples asked him, ''Why, then, do the scribes say that Elijah must first come?''

''Elijah will indeed come and restore all things,'' replied Jesus. ''But I say to you, Elijah has already come; and they did not know him, but treated him just as they pleased. Thus the Son of Man, too, will suffer at their hands.''

Then the disciples understood that he was speaking about John the Baptist.

MATTHEW 17:1-13

1 And after six days Jesus taketh Peter, James, and John his brother, and bringeth them up into a high mountain apart,

2 And was transfigured before them: and his face did shine as the sun, and his raiment was white as the light.

3 And, behold, there appeared unto them Moses and Elijah talking with him.

4 Then answered Peter, and said unto Jesus, Lord, it is good for us to be here: if thou wilt, let us make here three tabernacles; one for thee, and one for Moses, and one for Elijah.

5 While he yet spake, behold, a bright cloud overshadowed them: and behold a voice out of the cloud, which said, This is my beloved Son, in whom I am well pleased; hear ye him.

6 And when the disciples heard *it,* they fell on their face, and were sore afraid.

MARK 9:2-13

2 And after six days Jesus taketh *with him* Peter, and James, and John, and leadeth them up into a high mountain apart by themselves: and he was transfigured before them.

3 And his raiment became shining, exceeding white as snow; so as no fuller on earth can white them.

4 And there appeared unto them Elijah with Moses: and they were talking with Jesus.

5 And Peter answered and said to Jesus, Master, it is good for us to be here: and let us make three tabernacles; one for thee, and one for Moses, and one for Elijah.

6 For he wist not what to say; for they were sore afraid.

7 And there was a cloud that overshadowed them: and a voice came out of the cloud, saying, This is my beloved Son: hear him.

LUKE 9:28-36

28 And it came to pass about an eight days after these sayings, he took Peter and John and James, and went up into a mountain to pray.

29 And as he prayed, the fashion of his countenance was altered, and his raiment *was* white *and* glistering.

30 And, behold, there talked with him two men, which were Moses and Elijah:

31 Who appeared in glory, and spake of his decease which he should accomplish at Jerusalem.

32 But Peter and they that were with him were heavy with sleep: and when they were awake, they saw his glory, and the two men that stood with him.

The Transfiguration. *Here Peter, James, and John*
witnessed a special revelation of the Son of God. Moses,
who represented the Law, and Elijah, who represented
the Prophets, met with the One whose death and resur-
rection ushered in the New Testament gospel era.

The Transfiguration (continued)

MATTHEW 17:1-13

7 And Jesus came and touched them, and said, Arise, and be not afraid.

8 And when they had lifted up their eyes, they saw no man, save Jesus only.

9 And as they came down from the mountain, Jesus charged them, saying, Tell the vision to no man, until the Son of man be risen again from the dead.

10 And his disciples asked him, saying, Why then say the scribes that Elijah must first come?

11 And Jesus answered and said unto them, Elijah truly shall first come, and restore all things.

12 But I say unto you, That Elijah is come already, and they knew him not, but have done unto him whatsoever they listed. Likewise shall also the Son of man suffer of them.

13 Then the disciples understood that he spake unto them of John the Baptist.

MARK 9:2-13

8 And suddenly, when they had looked round about, they saw no man any more, save Jesus only with themselves.

9 And as they came down from the mountain, he charged them that they should tell no man what things they had seen, till the Son of man were risen from the dead.

10 And they kept that saying with themselves, questioning one with another what the rising from the dead should mean.

11 And they asked him, saying, Why say the scribes that Elijah must first come?

12 And he answered and told them, Elijah verily cometh first, and restoreth all things; and how it is written of the Son of man, that he must suffer many things, and be set at nought.

13 But I say unto you, That Elijah is indeed come, and they have done unto him whatsoever they listed, as it is written of him.

LUKE 9:28-36

33 And it came to pass, as they departed from him, Peter said unto Jesus, Master, it is good for us to be here: and let us make three tabernacles; one for thee, and one for Moses, and one for Elijah: not knowing what he said.

34 While he thus spake, there came a cloud, and overshadowed them: and they feared as they entered into the cloud.

35 And there came a voice out of the cloud, saying, This is my beloved Son: hear him.

36 And when the voice was past, Jesus was found alone. And they kept it close, and told no man in those days any of those things which they had seen.

Mosaic of the Transfiguration. The church at the top of Mount Tabor, at the eastern end of the Jezreel Valley, portrays Jesus, Moses and Elijah, and Peter, James and John who witnessed the event.

Jesus Heals an Afflicted Boy

Matthew 17:14-17, 19-21, Mark 9:20-29

And as they returned to the crowd, a man came to Jesus and knelt before him, saying, "Lord, have mercy on my son, for he is an epileptic and in dreadful condition. He often falls into the fire, and often into the water. I brought him to your disciples, but they were unable to heal him."

"O faithless and perverse generation!" cried Jesus, "how long must I be with you? How long must I bear with you? Bring him here to me."

And they brought him to Jesus, and when he saw him, the spirit immediately threw the boy into convulsions, and he fell to the ground and rolled about, foaming at the mouth.

"How long has he had this?" Jesus asked the father.

"From childhood," he replied. "Many times it has thrown him into the fire or into the water to destroy him. But if you can do anything, have mercy on us and help us."

" 'If you can do anything!' " exclaimed Jesus. "All things are possible to him who believes!"

"I do believe—please help me to believe!" cried the child's father.

When Jesus saw that a crowd was quickly gathering, he rebuked the unclean spirit, saying, "You dumb and deaf spirit, I command you, come out of him and do not enter him again!"

And when he had screamed loudly, with violent convulsions, the spirit came out; and the boy appeared to be dead, so that most of the people said, "He is dead." But Jesus took him by the hand and lifted him up, and he rose to his feet.

And when Jesus had entered the house, his disciples asked him privately, "Why were we unable to cast it out?"

"Because of your little faith," replied Jesus. "I tell you truly, if you have faith as a grain of mustard seed, you can say to this mountain, 'Move from here to yonder place,' and it will move. Nothing will be impossible to you. But nothing can drive this kind out except prayer."

MATTHEW 17:14-21	MARK 9:14-29	LUKE 9:37-43a
14 And when they were come to the multitude, there came to him a *certain* man, kneeling down to him, and saying,	14 And when he came to *his* disciples, he saw a great multitude about them, and the scribes questioning with them.	37 And it came to pass, that on the next day, when they were come down from the hill, much people met him.
15 Lord, have mercy on my son; for he is lunatic, and sore vexed: for ofttimes he falleth into the fire, and oft into the water.	15 And straightway all the people, when they beheld him, were greatly amazed, and running to *him* saluted him.	38 And, behold, a man of the company cried out, saying, Master, I beseech thee, look upon my son; for he is mine only child.
(16) And I brought him to thy disciples, and they could not cure him.	16 And he asked the scribes, What question ye with them?	39 And, lo, a spirit taketh him, and he suddenly crieth out; and it teareth him that he foameth again, and bruising him, hardly departeth from him.
17 Then Jesus answered and said, O faithless and perverse generation, how long shall I be with you? how long shall I suffer you? bring him hither to me.	17 And one of the multitude answered and said, Master, I have brought unto thee my son, which hath a dumb spirit;	(40) And I besought thy disciples to cast him out; and they could not.
18 And Jesus rebuked the devil; and he departed out	18 And wheresoever he taketh him, he teareth him; and he foameth, and gnasheth with his teeth, and pineth away: and I spake to thy disciples that they should cast him out; and they could not.	41 And Jesus answering said, O faithless and
	19 He answereth him, and saith, O faithless generation, how long shall I be with you? how long shall I suffer you? bring him unto me.	
	20 And they brought him unto him: and when he saw him, straightway the spirit tare	

Jesus Heals an Afflicted Boy (continued)

of him: and the child was cured from that very hour.

19 Then came the disciples to Jesus apart, and said, Why could not we cast him out?

20 And Jesus said unto them, Because of your unbelief: for verily I say unto you, If ye have faith as a grain of mustard seed, ye shall say unto this mountain, Remove hence to yonder place; and it shall remove: and nothing shall be impossible unto you.

21 Howbeit this kind goeth not out but by prayer and fasting.

him; and he fell on the ground, and wallowed foaming.

21 And he asked his father, How long is it ago since this came unto him? And he said, Of a child.

22 And ofttimes it hath cast him into the fire, and into the waters, to destroy him: but if thou canst do any thing, have compassion on us, and help us.

23 Jesus said unto him, If thou canst believe, all things *are* possible to him that believeth.

24 And straightway the father of the child cried out, and said with tears, Lord, I believe; help thou mine unbelief.

25 When Jesus saw that the people came running together, he rebuked the foul spirit, saying unto him, *Thou* dumb and deaf spirit, I charge thee, come out of him, and enter no more into him.

26 And *the spirit* cried, and rent him sore, and came out of him: and he was as one dead; insomuch that many said, He is dead.

27 But Jesus took him by the hand, and lifted him up; and he arose.

28 And when he was come into the house, his disciples asked him privately, Why could not we cast him out?

29 And he said unto them, This kind can come forth by nothing, but by prayer and fasting.

perverse generation, how long shall I be with you, and suffer you? Bring thy son hither.

42 And as he was yet a coming, the devil threw him down, and tare *him*. And Jesus rebuked the unclean spirit, and healed the child, and delivered him again to his father.

43 And they were all amazed at the mighty power of God.

Harvest Scene. *After grain has been harvested, it is crushed, either by flailing or by the trampling of oxen's hooves. Then it is tossed in the air, the chaff blown away and the grain falling to the ground.*

Jesus Again Foretells His Death

Mark 9:30-32

And they went on from there and passed through Galilee. But Jesus did not want anyone to know of his presence, for he was teaching his disciples. And he said to them, "The Son of Man will be delivered into the hands of men, and they will kill him; and after he is killed, he will rise again after three days."

But they did not understand the saying, and feared to ask him about it.

MATTHEW 17:22-23

22 And while they abode in Galilee, Jesus said unto them, The Son of man shall be betrayed into the hands of men:

23 And they shall kill him, and the third day he shall be raised again. And they were exceeding sorry.

MARK 9:30-32

30 And they departed thence, and passed through Galilee; and he would not that any man should know *it*.

31 For he taught his disciples, and said unto them, The Son of man is delivered into the hands of men, and they shall kill him; and after that he is killed, he shall rise the third day.

32 But they understood not that saying, and were afraid to ask him.

LUKE 9:43b-45

43b But while they wondered every one at all things which Jesus did, he said unto his disciples,

44 Let these sayings sink down into your ears: for the Son of man shall be delivered into the hands of men.

45 But they understood not this saying, and it was hid from them, that they perceived it not: and they feared to ask him of that saying.

Jesus Pays the Temple Tax

Matthew 17:24-27

When they arrived at Capernaum, those who collected the half-shekel came to Peter and said, "Doesn't your teacher pay the half-shekel?"

"Yes, indeed," replied Peter.

And when Peter came into the house, Jesus spoke first, saying "What do you think, Simon? From whom do the kings of the earth collect toll or tribute—from their sons, or from others?"

"From others," replied Peter.

"Then the sons are free," said Jesus. "However, lest we offend them, go to the sea and cast a hook and take the first fish that comes up. When you open its mouth, you will find a shekel. Take that and give it to them for me, and for you."

MATTHEW 17:24-27

24 And when they were come to Capernaum, they that received tribute *money* came to Peter, and said, Doth not your master pay tribute?

25 He saith, Yes. And when he was come into the house, Jesus prevented him, saying, What thinkest thou, Simon? of whom do the kings of the earth take custom or tribute? of their own children, or of strangers?

26 Peter saith unto him, Of strangers. Jesus saith unto him, Then are the children free.

27 Notwithstanding, lest we should offend them, go thou to the sea, and cast a hook, and take up the fish that first cometh up; and when thou hast opened his mouth, thou shalt find a piece of money: that take, and give unto them for me and thee.

Ministry of Reconciliation

Matthew 18:1-35

At that time the disciples came to Jesus, asking, "Who is the greatest in the kingdom of heaven?"

Then Jesus called a little child to him and set him in the midst of them and said, "I tell you truly, unless you are completely changed in attitude and become as little children, you will not even enter the kingdom of heaven. Therefore, whoever humbles himself as this little child, he is 'the greatest' in the kingdom of heaven.

"Whoever receives one such little child in my name receives me," said Jesus, "but whoever causes one of these little ones who believe in me to sin, it would be better for him to have a great millstone hung about his neck and to be drowned in the depths of the sea.

"Woe to the world because of the temptations to sin! It is inevitable that temptations will come, but woe to the man by whom the temptation comes! Therefore, if your hand or your foot causes you to sin, cut it off and cast it from you. It is better for you to enter into life maimed or crippled than, having two hands or two feet, to be cast into the eternal fire. And if your eye causes you to sin, pluck it out and cast it from you. It is better for you to enter into life with one eye than, having two eyes, to be cast into hell fire.

"See that you do not regard one of these little ones as unimportant; for I tell you that in heaven their angels do always behold the face of my Father in heaven. What do you think? If a man has a hundred sheep, and one of them has gone astray, will he not leave the ninety-nine on the mountains and go seek the one that went astray? And if he finds it, I tell you truly, he rejoices over it more than over the ninety-nine that did not go astray. Even so, it is not the will of my Father in heaven that one of these little ones should perish."

"If your brother wrongs you," said Jesus, "go and tell him his fault privately. If he will listen to you, you have gained your brother. But if he will not listen, take one or two others with you, that every word may be confirmed by the testimony of two or three witnesses. If he refuses to listen to them, tell it to the church. If he refuses to listen to the church, let him be regarded as a pagan and a tax collector. I tell you truly, whatever you bind on earth will be bound in heaven, and whatever you loose on earth will be loosed in heaven.

"Again I say to you that if two of you shall agree on earth concerning anything they ask, it will be done for them by my Father in heaven. For where two or three are gathered together in my name, there am I in the midst of them."

Then Peter came to Jesus and said, "Lord, how often shall my brother sin against me, and I forgive him? Until seven times?"

"I say to you, not seven times," replied Jesus, "but seventy times seven. For the kingdom of heaven is like a king who decided to settle accounts with his servants. When he began the settlement, one was brought to him who owed him ten thousand talents. And as he was unable to pay, his lord ordered him to be sold, and his wife and children and everything he had, and payment to be made. Then the servant fell down before him and cried, 'Have patience with me, and I will pay you everything.' Then the lord of that servant was moved with pity, and he released him and forgave him the debt.

"But when that same servant went out, he found one of his fellow servants who owed him a hundred denarii. And he seized him by the throat and began to choke him, saying, 'Pay me what you owe!' Then his fellow servant fell down and began to beg him, saying, 'Have patience with me, and I will pay you.' But he refused, and had him arrested and thrown into prison till he should pay the debt.

"When his fellow servants saw what had happened, they were greatly distressed and went and told their lord all that had taken place. Then his lord called him to appear before him, and said, 'You wicked servant! Because you implored me, I forgave you all that debt. Should you not have had mercy on your fellow servant, even as I had mercy on you?' And his lord was angry and delivered him to the tormentors, till he should pay all his debt.

"And that is exactly what my heavenly Father will do to you, if you do not each forgive his brother with all your heart."

Ministry of Reconciliation (continued)

1 At the same time came the disciples unto Jesus, saying, Who is the greatest in the kingdom of heaven?

2 And Jesus called a little child unto him, and set him in the midst of them,

3 And said, Verily I say unto you, Except ye be converted, and become as little children, ye shall not enter into the kingdom of heaven.

4 Whosoever therefore shall humble himself as this little child, the same is greatest in the kingdom of heaven.

5 And whoso shall receive one such little child in my name receiveth me.

6 But whoso shall offend one of these little ones which believe in me, it were better for him that a millstone were hanged about his neck and *that* he were drowned in the depth of the sea.

7 Woe unto the world because of offenses! for it must needs be that offenses come; but woe to that man by whom the offense cometh!

8 Wherefore if thy hand or thy foot offend thee, cut them off, and cast *them* from thee: it is better for thee to enter into life halt or maimed, rather than having two hands or two feet to be cast into everlasting fire.

9 And if thine eye offend thee, pluck it out, and cast *it* from thee: it is better for thee to enter into life with one eye, rather than having two eyes to be cast into hell fire.

10 Take heed that ye despise not one of these little ones; for I say unto you, That in heaven their angels do always behold the face of my Father which is in heaven.

11 For the Son of man is come to save that which was lost.

12 How think ye? if a man have a hundred sheep, and one of them be gone astray, doth he not leave the ninety and nine, and goeth into the mountains, and seeketh that which is gone astray?

13 And if so be that he find it, verily I say unto you, he rejoiceth more of that *sheep,* than of the ninety and nine which went not astray.

14 Even so it is not the will of your Father which is in heaven, that one of these little ones should perish.

15 Moreover if thy brother shall trespass against thee, go and tell him his fault between thee and him alone: if he shall hear thee, thou hast gained thy brother.

33 And he came to Capernaum: and being in the house he asked them, What was it that ye disputed among yourselves by the way?

34 But they held their peace: for by the way they had disputed among themselves, who *should be* the greatest.

35 And he sat down, and called the twelve, and saith unto them, If any man desire to be first, *the same* shall be last of all, and servant of all.

36 And he took a child, and set him in the midst of them: and when he had taken him in his arms, he said unto them,

37 Whosoever shall receive one of such children in my name, receiveth me; and whosoever shall receive me, receiveth not me, but him that sent me.

38 And John answered him, saying, Master, we saw one casting out devils in thy name, and he followeth not us; and we forbade him, because he followeth not us.

39 But Jesus said, Forbid him not: for there is no man which shall do a miracle in my name, that can lightly speak evil of me.

40 For he that is not against us is on our part.

41 For whosoever shall give you a cup of water to drink in my name, because ye belong to Christ, verily I say unto you, he shall not lose his reward.

42 And whosoever shall offend one of *these* little ones that believe in me, it is bet-

46 Then there arose a reasoning among them, which of them should be greatest.

47 And Jesus, perceiving the thought of their heart, took a child, and set him by him,

48 And said unto them, Whosoever shall receive this child in my name receiveth me; and whosoever shall receive me, receiveth him that sent me: for he that is least among you all, the same shall be great.

49 And John answered and said, Master, we saw one casting out devils in thy name; and we forbade him, because he followeth not with us.

50 And Jesus said unto him, Forbid *him* not: for he that is not against us is for us.

Ministry of Reconciliation (continued)

MATTHEW 18:1-35

16 But if he will not hear *thee,* *then* take with thee one or two more, that in the mouth of two or three witnesses every word may be established.

17 And if he shall neglect to hear them, tell *it* unto the church: but if he neglect to hear the church, let him be unto thee as a heathen man and a publican.

18 Verily I say unto you, Whatsoever ye shall bind on earth shall be bound in heaven; and whatsoever ye shall loose on earth shall be loosed in heaven.

19 Again I say unto you, That if two of you shall agree on earth as touching any thing that they shall ask, it shall be done for them of my Father which is in heaven.

20 For where two or three are gathered together in my name, there am I in the midst of them.

21 Then came Peter to him, and said, Lord, how oft shall my brother sin against me, and I forgive him? till seven times?

22 Jesus saith unto him, I say not unto thee, Until seven times: but, Until seventy times seven.

23 Therefore is the kingdom of heaven likened unto a certain king, which would take account of his servants.

24 And when he had begun to reckon, one was brought unto him, which owed him ten thousand talents.

25 But forasmuch as he had not to pay, his lord commanded him to be sold, and his wife, and children, and all that he had, and payment to be made.

26 The servant therefore fell down, and worshipped him, saying, Lord, have patience with me, and I will pay thee all.

27 Then the Lord of that servant was moved with compassion, and loosed him, and forgave him the debt.

28 But the same servant went out, and found one of his fellow servants, which owed him a hundred pence: and he laid hands on him, and took *him* by the throat, saying, Pay me that thou owest.

29 And his fellow servant fell down at his feet, and besought him, saying, Have patience with me, and I will pay thee all.

30 And he would not: but went and cast him into prison, till he should pay the debt.

31 So when his fellow servants saw what was

MARK 9:33-50

ter for him that a millstone were hanged about his neck, and he were cast into the sea.

43 And if thy hand offend thee, cut it off: it is better for thee to enter into life maimed, than having two hands to go into hell, into the fire that never shall be quenched:

44 Where their worm dieth not, and the fire is not quenched.

45 And if thy foot offend thee, cut it off: it is better for thee to enter halt into life, than having two feet to be cast into hell, into the fire that never shall be quenched:

46 Where their worm dieth not, and the fire is not quenched.

47 And if thine eye offend thee, pluck it out: it is better for thee to enter into the kingdom of God with one eye, than having two eyes to be cast into hell fire:

48 Where their worm dieth not, and the fire is not quenched.

49 For every one shall be salted with fire, and every sacrifice shall be salted with salt.

50 Salt *is* good: but if the salt have lost his saltness, wherewith will ye season it? Have salt in yourselves, and have peace one with another.

LUKE 9:46-50

Ministry of Reconciliation (continued)

done, they were very sorry, and came and told unto their lord all that was done.

32 Then his lord, after that he had called him, said unto him, O thou wicked servant, I forgave thee all that debt, because thou desiredst me:

33 Shouldest not thou also have had compassion on thy fellow servant, even as I had pity on thee?

34 And his lord was wroth, and delivered him to the tormentors, till he should pay all that was due unto him.

35 So likewise shall my heavenly Father do also unto you, if ye from your hearts forgive not every one his brother their trespasses.

Jesus Leaves Galilee

Luke 9:51-56

And it came to pass, when the days were drawing near that he should be received up, Jesus steadfastly set his face to go to Jerusalem. And he sent messengers before him, who went into a village of the Samaritans to make ready for him. But the Samaritans refused to receive him, because he was on his way to Jerusalem. And when the disciples James and John saw this, they said, "Lord, do you want us to call fire down from heaven to consume them?"

But he turned and rebuked them, and they went on to another village.

51 And it came to pass, when the time was come that he should be received up, he stead-fastly set his face to go to Jerusalem,

52 And sent messengers before his face: and they went, and entered into a village of the Samaritans, to make ready for him.

53 And they did not receive him, because his face was as though he would go to Jerusalem.

54 And when his disciples James and John saw *this,* they said, Lord, wilt thou that we command fire to come down from heaven, and consume them, even as Elijah did?

55 But he turned, and rebuked them, and said, Ye know not what manner of spirit ye are of.

56 For the Son of man is not come to destroy men's lives, but to save *them.* And they went to another village.

Cost of Discipleship

Luke 9:57-62

Now as they were journeying along the road, a certain man said to Jesus, "I intend to follow you wherever you go."

"The foxes have dens and the birds of the air have nests," replied Jesus, "but the Son of Man has no place to lay his head."

To another man, Jesus said, "Follow me."

"Lord," he replied, "let me first go and bury my father."

"Leave the dead to bury their dead," said Jesus, "but you go and proclaim the kingdom of God."

"Lord, I will follow you," said another, "but first, let me close my affairs at home."

But Jesus said, "No one who puts his hand to the plow and then looks back to the things behind is fit for the service of the kingdom of God."

MATTHEW 8:18-22

18 Now when Jesus saw great multitudes about him, he gave commandment to depart unto the other side.

19 And a certain scribe came, and said unto him, Master, I will follow thee whithersoever thou goest.

20 And Jesus saith unto him, The foxes have holes, and the birds of the air *have* nests; but the Son of man hath not where to lay *his* head.

21 And another of his disciples said unto him, Lord, suffer me first to go and bury my father.

22 But Jesus said unto him, Follow me; and let the dead bury their dead.

LUKE 9:57-62

57 And it came to pass, that, as they went in the way, a certain *man* said unto him, Lord, I will follow thee whithersoever thou goest.

58 And Jesus said unto him, Foxes have holes, and birds of the air *have* nests; but the Son of man hath not where to lay *his* head.

59 And he said unto another, Follow me. But he said, Lord, suffer me first to go and bury my father.

60 Jesus said unto him, Let the dead bury their dead: but go thou and preach the kingdom of God.

61 And another also said, Lord, I will follow thee; but let me first go bid them farewell, which are at home at my house.

62 And Jesus said unto him, No man, having put his hand to the plow, and looking back, is fit for the kingdom of God.

Jesus at the Feast of Tabernacles

John 7:2-9, 11-52

Now a feast of the Jews, the Feast of Tabernacles, was at hand. Jesus' brothers therefore said to him, "Why don't you leave here and go to Judea, so your disciples there may see the works that you are doing? For nobody does anything in secret if he wants to be known publicly. If you are doing these things, show yourself to the world." For his own brothers did not believe in him.

"My time has not yet come," replied Jesus, "but your time is always present. The world cannot hate you, but it hates me, because I bear witness of it that its works are evil. You go on to the feast. I will not go up to the feast as yet, for my time has not yet come."

Having said these things, he remained in Galilee.

Now the Jews were looking for Jesus at the feast, and people kept asking, "Where is he?" And there were many quiet discussions about him among the people. Some said, "He is a good man." But others said, "No, he is leading the people astray." However, no one spoke of him openly, for fear of the Jewish authorities.

But about the middle of the festival, Jesus went up to the temple and began to teach. And the

Jews marveled, saying, "How does this man know the scriptures, never having gone to school?"

"My teaching is not mine," replied Jesus, "but his who sent me. If any man wants to do God's will, he shall know whether my teaching is from God, or whether I am speaking only on my own authority. A man who speaks on his own authority is seeking his own glory, but one who seeks the glory of the one who sent him is sincere, and there is nothing false in him.

"Did not Moses give you the law?" said Jesus. "And yet, not one of you is keeping the law. Why, then, are you seeking to kill me?"

"You must be demon possessed! Who is seeking to kill you?" answered the crowd.

"I performed a single work," replied Jesus, "a work at which you all marvel. Moses commanded circumcision (not that it is from Moses, but from the fathers) and you will circumcise a man on the Sabbath. If a man receives circumcision on the Sabbath, so that the law of Moses may not be broken, why be angry with me because I made a man's entire body well on the Sabbath? Do not judge merely according to appearances, but be honest and fair in your judgments."

Then some of the people of Jerusalem said, "Isn't this the man they are seeking to kill? Look! He is speaking openly, and yet they are not saying anything to him! Have the rulers found out that this is really the Messiah? But we know where this man is from, and when the Messiah comes, no one will know where he is from."

Jesus therefore exclaimed, as he taught in the temple, "You know me, and where I am from. But I have not come of my own accord. He who sent me is true, and you do not know him. I know him, because I came from him, and he sent me."

Then the authorities sought to arrest him; but no one laid a hand on him, because his hour had not yet come. But many of the people believed on him, and said, "When the Messiah comes, will he do more miracles than this man has done?"

The Pharisees overheard the people saying these things about him, and they and the chief priests sent officers to arrest him. Jesus therefore said,

"I will be with you only a little while longer, and then I will go to him who sent me. You will seek me and not find me, and where I am, you cannot come."

The Jews then said among themselves, "Where does this fellow intend to go, that we shall not find him? Does he intend to go to the Jews scattered among the Gentiles, and to teach the Gentiles? What can be the meaning of his statement, 'You will seek me and not find me, and where I am, you cannot come'?"

Now on the last day, the great day of the feast, Jesus stood and cried, "If any man thirst, let him come to me and drink. He who trusts in me, as the scripture said, out of his inmost being shall flow rivers of living water."

(Now this he said concerning the Spirit, whom those who believed in him were to receive; for the Spirit had not yet been given, because Jesus had not yet been glorified.)

When they heard these words, some of the people said, "This is truly the Prophet!"

"This is the Messiah!" said others.

But some said, "Is the Messiah, then, to come from Galilee? Hasn't the scripture said that the Messiah will come from the line of David, and from Bethlehem, the village where David lived?"

So the people were divided over him. Some wanted to seize him, but no one laid hands on him. Then the officers returned to the chief priests and Pharisees.

"Why didn't you bring him?" asked the priests and Pharisees.

"No man ever spoke like that man!" answered the officers.

"Have you, too, been led astray?" replied the Pharisees. "Have any of the authorities or any of the Pharisees believed in him? But this rabble, who do not know the law, are accursed!"

Nicodemus, who earlier came to Jesus, and who was one of them, said to them, "Does our law judge a man without giving him a hearing first and finding out what he is doing?"

"Are you, too, from Galilee?" they replied. "Search for yourself; you will find that no prophet comes from Galilee!"

Jesus at the Feast of Tabernacles (continued)

1 After these things Jesus walked in Galilee: for he would not walk in Jewry, because the Jews sought to kill him.

2 Now the Jews' feast of tabernacles was at hand.

3 His brethren therefore said unto him, Depart hence, and go into Judea, that thy disciples also may see the works that thou doest.

4 For *there is* no man *that* doeth any thing in secret, and he himself seeketh to be known openly. If thou do these things, show thyself to the world.

5 For neither did his brethren believe in him.

6 Then Jesus said unto them, My time is not yet come: but your time is always ready.

7 The world cannot hate you; but me it hateth, because I testify of it, that the works thereof are evil.

8 Go ye up unto this feast: I go not up yet unto this feast; for my time is not yet full come.

9 When he had said these words unto them, he abode *still* in Galilee.

10 But when his brethren were gone up, then went he also up unto the feast, not openly, but as it were in secret.

11 Then the Jews sought him at the feast, and said, Where is he?

12 And there was much murmuring among the people concerning him: for some said, He is a good man: others said, Nay; but he deceiveth the people.

13 Howbeit no man spake openly of him for fear of the Jews.

14 Now about the midst of the feast Jesus went up into the temple, and taught.

15 And the Jews marveled, saying, How knoweth this man letters, having never learned?

16 Jesus answered them, and said, My doctrine is not mine, but his that sent me.

17 If any man will do his will, he shall know of the doctrine, whether it be of God, or *whether* I speak of myself.

18 He that speaketh of himself seeketh his own glory: but he that seeketh his glory that sent him, the same is true, and no unrighteousness is in him.

19 Did not Moses give you the law, and *yet* none of you keepeth the law? Why go ye about to kill me?

20 The people answered and said, Thou hast a devil: who goeth about to kill thee?

21 Jesus answered and said unto them, I have done one work, and ye all marvel.

22 Moses therefore gave unto you circumcision; (not because it is of Moses, but of the fathers;) and ye on the sabbath day circumcise a man.

23 If a man on the sabbath day receive circumcision, that the law of Moses should not be broken; are

ye angry at me, because I have made a man every whit whole on the sabbath day?

24 Judge not according to the appearance, but judge righteous judgment.

25 Then said some of them of Jerusalem, Is not this he, whom they seek to kill?

26 But, lo, he speaketh boldly, and they say nothing unto him. Do the rulers know indeed that this is the very Christ?

27 Howbeit we know this man whence he is: but when Christ cometh, no man knoweth whence he is.

28 Then cried Jesus in the temple as he taught, saying, Ye both know me, and ye know whence I am: and I am not come of myself, but he that sent me is true, whom ye know not.

29 But I know him; for I am from him, and he hath sent me.

30 Then they sought to take him: but no man laid hands on him, because his hour was not yet come.

31 And many of the people believed on him, and said, When Christ cometh, will he do more miracles than these which this *man* hath done?

32 The Pharisees heard that the people murmured such things concerning him; and the Pharisees and the chief priests sent officers to take him.

33 Then said Jesus unto them, Yet a little while am I with you, and *then* I go unto him that sent me.

34 Ye shall seek me, and shall not find *me*: and where I am, *thither* ye cannot come.

35 Then said the Jews among themselves, Whither will he go, that we shall not find him? will he go unto the dispersed among the Gentiles, and teach the Gentiles?

36 What *manner of* saying is this that he said, Ye shall seek me, and shall not find *me:* and where I am, *thither* ye cannot come?

37 In the last day, that great *day* of the feast, Jesus stood and cried, saying, If any man thirst, let him come unto me, and drink.

38 He that believeth on me, as the Scripture hath said, out of his belly shall flow rivers of living water.

39 (But this spake he of the Spirit, which they that believe on him should receive: for the Holy Ghost was not yet *given;* because that Jesus was not yet glorified.)

40 Many of the people therefore, when they heard this saying, said, Of a truth this is the Prophet.

41 Others said, This is the Christ. But some said, Shall Christ come out of Galilee?

42 Hath not the Scripture said, That Christ cometh of the seed of David, and out of the town of Bethlehem, where David was?

The Light of the World. *That is how Jesus described himself as He taught in the Temple area. This beautiful chandelier illustrates the truth that Jesus is the One who can light our way through life.*

194

Jesus at the Feast of Tabernacles (continued)

43 So there was a division among the people because of him.

44 And some of them would have taken him; but no man laid hands on him.

45 Then came the officers to the chief priests and Pharisees; and they said unto them, Why have ye not brought him?

46 The officers answered, Never man spake like this man.

47 Then answered them the Pharisees, Are ye also deceived?

48 Have any of the rulers or of the Pharisees believed on him?

49 But this people who knoweth not the law are cursed.

50 Nicodemus saith unto them, (he that came to Jesus by night, being one of them,)

51 Doth our law judge *any* man, before it hear him, and know what he doeth?

52 They answered and said unto him, Art thou also of Galilee? Search, and look: for out of Galilee ariseth no prophet.

53 And every man went unto his own house.

Jesus Declares His Deity

John 8:12-59

Then Jesus spoke to them again, saying, "I am the light of the world. He who follows me will not walk in darkness, but will have the light of life."

"You are bearing witness to yourself," said the Pharisees. "Your testimony is not valid."

"Even though I am bearing witness to myself, my testimony is true," replied Jesus, "for I know where I have come from, and where I am going. But you do not know where I am from or where I am going. You are judging me according to appearances; I am not judging at all. And yet if I am declaring a verdict, my verdict is true, for I do not stand alone: the Father who sent me is with me. It is written in your law that the testimony of two men is true: I am bearing witness to myself, and the Father who sent me is bearing witness to me."

"Where is your father?" they asked.

"You know neither me nor my Father," replied Jesus. "If you knew me, you would know my Father also."

These things said Jesus in the treasury, as he taught in the temple. But no one arrested him, for his hour had not yet come.

Again, Jesus said to them, "I am going away, and you will seek me, but you will die in your sins. Where I am going, you cannot come."

Then said the Jews, "Is he going to kill himself? Is that why he said, 'Where I am going, you cannot come'?"

"You are from below," said Jesus, "but I am from above. You are of this world, but I am not of this world. That is why I told you that you will die in your sins. For unless you believe that I am he, you will die in your sins."

"Just who are you, anyway?" they asked.

"I am just what I am telling you," replied Jesus. "There is much I could say about you— much I could condemn. But he who sent me is true, and I am declaring to the world what I have heard from him."

They did not understand that he was speaking to them of the Father. Then said Jesus,

"When you have lifted up the Son of Man, then you will know that I am he, and that I do nothing on my own authority, but I am saying these things only as my Father has taught me. And he who sent me is with me. He has not left me alone, for I always do the things that are pleasing to him."

As he said these things, many believed in him. Then said Jesus to the Jews who believed in him, "If you continue in my teaching, you are truly my disciples. And you will know the truth, and the truth will make you free."

"We are Abraham's descendants, and have never been in bondage to anyone," they replied. "Why do you say, 'You will be made free'?"

"I tell you truly, everyone who lives in sin is

a slave of sin," replied Jesus. "Now a slave does not continue in the household forever, but a son does. Therefore, if the Son sets you free, you will be free indeed. I know that you are descendants of Abraham; yet you are seeking to kill me, because my word is unacceptable to you. I am declaring to you what I have learned from my Father, and you are doing what you have learned from your father."

"Abraham is our father!" they replied.

"If you were really children of Abraham, " said Jesus, "you would do the things Abraham did. But instead, you are seeking to kill me—a man who has told you the truth which I heard from God. This is not the kind of things Abraham did. You are doing the works of your real father."

"We were not born of fornication," they replied. "We have one Father—God!"

"If God were your Father," said Jesus, "you would love me, for I came forth from God. I have not come of my own accord, but the Father sent me. Why is it that you do not understand what I say? It is because you do not want to listen to my word. You are of your father the devil, and you wish only to practice the lusts of your father. He was a murderer from the beginning, and did not continue in the truth, for the truth is not in him. When he lies, he is speaking true to form, for he is a liar and the father of lies. And because I speak the truth, you do not believe me. Who of you can prove me guilty of sin? But if I am speaking the truth, why do you not believe me?

He who is of God will listen to the words of God; but you will not listen, because you are not of God."

"Are we not right in saying that you are a Samaritan, and demon possessed?" replied the Jews.

"I am not demon possessed," answered Jesus. "I am honoring my Father, and you are dishonoring me. But I am not seeking glory for myself; there is One who seeks my glory, and who judges. I tell you truly, if anyone keeps my word, he will never see death."

"Now we *know* you are demon possessed!" said the Jews. "Abraham died, and so did the prophets. But you say, 'If anyone keeps my word, he will never taste death.' Are you greater than our father Abraham? He died, and so did the prophets. Just who do you claim to be?"

"If I honor myself," said Jesus, "my honor is worthless. It is my Father who honors me, whom you say is your God; but you have not known him. But I know him, and if I should say that I do not know him, I should be a liar like you. But I know him, and keep his word. Your father Abraham rejoiced to see my day; he saw it, and was glad."

"You are not yet fifty years old," said the Jews, "and have you seen Abraham?"

"I tell you truly," said Jesus, "before Abraham was, I am."

Then they picked up stones to hurl at him. But Jesus vanished in the crowd and went his way out of the temple.

JOHN 8:12-59

12 Then spake Jesus again unto them, saying, I am the light of the world: he that followeth me shall not walk in darkness, but shall have the light of life.

13 The Pharisees therefore said unto him, Thou bearest record of thyself; thy record is not true.

14 Jesus answered and said unto them, Though I bear record of myself, *yet* my record is true: for I know whence I came, and whither I go; but ye cannot tell whence I come, and whither I go.

15 Ye judge after the flesh; I judge no man.

16 And yet if I judge, my judgment is true: for I am not alone, but I and the Father that sent me.

17 It is also written in your law, that the testimony of two men is true.

18 I am one that bear witness of myself, and the Father that sent me beareth witness of me.

19 Then said they unto him, Where is thy Father? Jesus answered, Ye neither know me, nor my Father: if ye had known me, ye should have known my Father also.

20 These words spake Jesus in the treasury, as he taught in the temple: and no man laid hands on him; for his hour was not yet come.

21 Then said Jesus again unto them, I go my way, and ye shall seek me, and shall die in your sins: whither I go, ye cannot come.

22 Then said the Jews, Will he kill himself? because he saith, Whither I go, ye cannot come.

A Traveling Family. *The donkey has been called "the jeep of the Middle East." Here it provides transportation for members of a family in their journey.*

Jesus Declares His Deity (continued)

23 And he said unto them, Ye are from beneath; I am from above: ye are of this world; I am not of this world.

24 I said therefore unto you, that ye shall die in your sins: for if ye believe not that I am *he*, ye shall die in your sins.

25 Then said they unto him, Who art thou? And Jesus saith unto them, Even *the same* that I said unto you from the beginning.

26 I have many things to say and to judge of you: but he that sent me is true; and I speak to the world those things which I have heard of him.

27 They understood not that he spake to them of the Father.

28 Then said Jesus unto them, When ye have lifted up the Son of man, then shall ye know that I am *he*, and *that* I do nothing of myself; but as my Father that taught me, I speak these things.

29 And he that sent me is with me: the Father hath not left me alone; for I do always those things that please him.

30 As he spake these words, many believed on him.

31 Then said Jesus to those Jews which believed on him, If ye continue in my word, *then* are ye my disciples indeed;

32 And ye shall know the truth, and the truth shall make you free.

33 They answered him, We be Abraham's seed, and were never in bondage to any man: how sayest thou, Ye shall be made free?

34 Jesus answered them, Verily, verily, I say unto you, Whosoever committeth sin is the servant of sin.

35 And the servant abideth not in the house for ever: *but* the Son abideth ever.

36 If the Son therefore shall make you free, ye shall be free indeed.

37 I know that ye are Abraham's seed; but ye seek to kill me, because my word hath no place in you.

38 I speak that which I have seen with my Father: and ye do that which ye have seen with your father.

39 They answered and said unto him, Abraham is our father. Jesus saith unto them, If ye were Abraham's children, ye would do the works of Abraham.

40 But now ye seek to kill me, a man that hath told you the truth, which I have heard of God: this did not Abraham.

41 Ye do the deeds of your father. Then said they to him, We be not born of fornication; we have one Father, *even* God.

42 Jesus said unto them, If God were your Father, ye would love me: for I proceeded forth and came from God; neither came I of myself, but he sent me.

43 Why do ye not understand my speech? *even* because ye cannot hear my word.

44 Ye are of *your* father the devil, and the lusts of your father ye will do: he was a murderer from the beginning, and abode not in the truth, because there is no truth in him. When he speaketh a lie, he speaketh of his own: for he is a liar, and the father of it.

45 And because I tell *you* the truth, ye believe me not.

46 Which of you convinceth me of sin? And if I say the truth, why do ye not believe me?

47 He that is of God heareth God's words: ye therefore hear *them* not, because ye are not of God.

48 Then answered the Jews, and said unto him, Say we not well that thou art a Samaritan, and hast a devil?

49 Jesus answered, I have not a devil; but I honor my Father, and ye do dishonor me.

50 And I seek not mine own glory: there is one that seeketh and judgeth.

51 Verily, verily, I say unto you, If a man keep my saying, he shall never see death.

52 Then said the Jews unto him, Now we know that thou hast a devil. Abraham is dead, and the prophets; and thou sayest, If a man keep my saying, he shall never taste of death.

53 Art thou greater than our father Abraham, which is dead? and the prophets are dead: whom makest thou thyself?

54 Jesus answered, If I honor myself, my honor is nothing: it is my Father that honoreth me; of whom ye say, that he is your God:

55 Yet ye have not known him; but I know him: and if I should say, I know him not, I shall be a liar like unto you: but I know him, and keep his saying.

56 Your father Abraham rejoiced to see my day: and he saw *it*, and was glad.

57 Then said the Jews unto him, Thou art not yet fifty years old, and hast thou seen Abraham?

58 Jesus said unto them, Verily, verily, I say unto you, Before Abraham was, I am.

59 Then took they up stones to cast at him: but Jesus hid himself, and went out of the temple, going through the midst of them, and so passed by.

Jesus Heals the Man Born Blind

John 9:1-41

As Jesus passed by, he saw a man who had been blind from birth. And his disciples asked him, "Master, who sinned—this man, or his parents—that he was born blind?"

"It was not because this man sinned, or his parents," answered Jesus, "but in order that the works of God might be manifested in him. We must do the works of him who sent me, while it is still day; the night is coming, when no one can work. As long as I am in the world, I am the light of the world."

After saying these things, Jesus spat on the ground and made clay of the spittle. And he anointed the eyes of the blind man with clay, and said, "Go and wash in the pool of Siloam" (which means "sent").

So the man went and washed, and came back seeing. Then his neighbors and those who had observed him as a beggar said, "Isn't this the man who used to sit by the wayside and beg?"

"Yes, he is the man," said some.

"No, he only looks like him," said others.

Then the man himself said, "I'm the man!"

"How were your eyes opened?" they asked.

"The man called Jesus made clay and anointed my eyes and said, 'Go to Siloam and wash,' " he replied, "so I went and washed, and received sight!"

"Where is this fellow?" they asked.

"I don't know," he replied.

Then they took the man who had been blind to the Pharisees. Now it was a Sabbath day when Jesus made clay and opened his eyes. The Pharisees therefore asked him again how he had received his sight.

"He put clay on my eyes, and I washed, and now I can see," he said.

Then some of the Pharisees said, "This man is not from God, for he does not keep the Sabbath."

"But how can a man who is a sinner do such miracles?" said others.

And they were divided in their opinion. Then they spoke to the blind man again: "What do *you* say about him? It was your eyes that he opened!"

"He is surely a prophet!" replied the man.

But the Jews doubted that the man actually had been blind and had received his sight until they called his parents and asked them, "Is this your son, who you say was born blind? How is it that he is now able to see?"

"We know that this is our son, and that he was born blind," answered his parents, "but we don't know how it is that he now can see, nor do we know who opened his eyes. Ask him; he is of age, and he will speak for himself."

This the parents said because they feared the Jews, for the Jews had agreed that if anyone should acknowledge Jesus to be the Messiah, he should be put out of the synagogue. That is why his parents said, "He is of age; ask him."

So for the second time, they summoned the man who had been blind and said to him, "Give God the praise! We know that this man is a sinner."

"Whether he is a sinner or not, I don't know," replied the man, "but I can tell you one thing for sure: I used to be blind, but now I can see!"

"What did he do to you? How did he open your eyes?" they asked.

"I have already told you, but you wouldn't listen," he replied. "Why do you want to hear it again? Do you, too, want to become his disciples?"

At this, they turned on him in a rage, shouting, "*You* are his disciple! We are disciples of Moses! We know that God spoke to Moses, but as for this fellow, we don't even know where he came from."

"Now isn't this an amazing thing!" replied the man. "You don't know where he came from, and yet he opened my eyes! We know that God does not hearken to sinners, but to those who truly fear him and do his will. From the beginning of the world it has never been heard that anyone opened the eyes of a man born blind. If this man were not from God, he could do nothing."

"You were altogether born in sins!" they shouted, "and are *you* presuming to teach *us*?" And they threw him out.

Jesus heard that they had cast him out. And

The Pool of Siloam. *It is situated south of the Temple area and is the terminus of Hezekiah's Tunnel. Here the man born blind went at Jesus' command, washed and received his sight.*

when he had found him, he said, "Do you believe in the Son of God?"

"Who is he, sir?" asked the man. "Tell me, that I may believe in him."

"You have seen him," said Jesus, "and it is he who is speaking to you."

"Lord, I believe!" he said. And he knelt before him in worship.

Then said Jesus, "I have come into this world bringing judgment, that the blind may see, and that those who see may become blind."

Some of the Pharisees standing near Jesus, hearing his words, said, "And are *we* blind?"

"If you were blind," said Jesus, "you would not be guilty; but since you insist 'We see,' your guilt remains."

JOHN 9:1-41

1 And as *Jesus* passed by, he saw a man which was blind from *his* birth.

2 And his disciples asked him, saying, Master, who did sin, this man, or his parents, that he was born blind?

3 Jesus answered, Neither hath this man sinned, nor his parents: but that the works of God should be made manifest in him.

4 I must work the works of him that sent me, while it is day: the night cometh, when no man can work.

5 As long as I am in the world, I am the light of the world.

6 When he had thus spoken, he spat on the ground, and made clay of the spittle, and he anointed the eyes of the blind man with the clay.

7 And said unto him, Go, wash in the pool of Siloam, (which is by interpretation, Sent.) He went his way therefore, and washed, and came seeing.

8 The neighbors therefore, and they which before had seen him that he was blind, said, Is not this he that sat and begged?

9 Some said, This is he: others *said*, He is like him: *but* he said, I am *he*.

10 Therefore said they unto him, How were thine eyes opened?

11 He answered and said, A man that is called Jesus made clay, and anointed mine eyes, and said unto me, Go to the pool of Siloam, and wash: and I went and washed, and I received sight.

12 Then said they unto him, Where is he? He said, I know not.

13 They brought to the Pharisees him that aforetime was blind.

14 And it was the sabbath day when Jesus made the clay, and opened his eyes.

15 Then again the Pharisees also asked him how he had received his sight. He said unto them, He put clay upon mine eyes, and I washed, and do see.

16 Therefore said some of the Pharisees, This man is not of God, because he keepeth not the sabbath day. Others said, How can a man that is a sinner do such miracles? And there was a division among them.

17 They say unto the blind man again, What sayest thou of him, that he hath opened thine eyes? He said, He is a prophet.

18 But the Jews did not believe concerning him, that he had been blind, and received his sight, until they called the parents of him that had received his sight.

19 And they asked them, saying, Is this your son, who ye say was born blind? how then doth he now see?

...one thing I know, that, whereas I was blind, now I see.

20 His parents answered them and said, We know that this is our son, and that he was born blind:

21 But by what means he now seeth, we know not; or who hath opened his eyes, we know not: he is of age; ask him: he shall speak for himself.

22 These *words* spake his parents, because they feared the Jews: for the Jews had agreed already, that if any man did confess that he was Christ, he should be put out of the synagogue.

23 Therefore said his parents, He is of age; ask him.

24 Then again called they the man that was blind, and said unto him, Give God the praise: we know that this man is a sinner.

25 He answered and said, Whether he be a sinner *or no*, I know not: one thing I know, that, whereas I was blind, now I see.

26 Then said they to him again, What did he to thee? how opened he thine eyes?

Jesus Heals the Man Born Blind (continued)

27 He answered them, I have told you already, and ye did not hear: wherefore would ye hear *it* again? will ye also be his disciples?

28 Then they reviled him, and said, Thou art his disciple; but we are Moses' disciples.

29 We know that God spake unto Moses: *as for* this *fellow*, we know not from whence he is.

30 The man answered and said unto them, Why herein is a marvelous thing, that ye know not from whence he is, and *yet* he hath opened mine eyes.

31 Now we know that God heareth not sinners: but if any man be a worshipper of God, and doeth his will, him he heareth.

32 Since the world began was it not heard that any man opened the eyes of one that was born blind.

33 If this man were not of God, he could do nothing.

34 They answered and said unto him, Thou wast altogether born in sins, and dost thou teach us? And they cast him out.

35 Jesus heard that they had cast him out; and when he had found him, he said unto him, Dost thou believe on the Son of God?

36 He answered and said, Who is he, Lord, that I might believe on him?

37 And Jesus said unto him, Thou hast both seen him, and it is he that talketh with thee.

38 And he said, Lord, I believe. And he worshipped him.

39 And Jesus said, For judgment I am come into this world, that they which see not might see; and that they which see might be made blind.

40 And *some* of the Pharisees which were with him heard these words, and said unto him, Are we blind also?

41 Jesus said unto them, If ye were blind, ye should have no sin: but now ye say, We see; therefore your sin remaineth.

Jesus, the Good Shepherd

John 10:1-21

Then said Jesus, "I tell you truly, he who does not enter the sheepfold by the door, but climbs in by some other way, is a thief and a robber, but he who enters in through the door is the shepherd of the sheep. To him the doorkeeper opens, and the sheep hearken to his voice. He calls his own sheep by name, and leads them out. And when he has brought all his sheep out of the fold, he leads the way before them, and the sheep follow him, because they know his voice. They will not follow a stranger, but will run away from him, for they do not know the voice of strangers."

Jesus told them this parable, but they did not understand the meaning of what he said. Therefore, Jesus spoke to them again:

"I tell you truly, I am the door for the sheep. All who came before me were thieves and robbers, but the sheep did not hearken to them. I am the door: if anyone enters the fold through me, he will be safe, and will go in and out and find pasture. The thief comes only to steal and to kill and destroy, but I came that men may have life, and that they may have it abundantly. I am the good shepherd: the good shepherd gives his life for his sheep. He who is only a hireling rather than a shepherd, who does not really own the sheep, sees the wolf coming and leaves the sheep and runs away, and the wolf catches them and scatters the flock. He runs away because he is only a hireling and does not really care about the sheep.

"I am the good shepherd, and I know those who are mine, and they know me, just as the Father knows me and I know the Father. I will give my life for the sheep. And I have other sheep, which are not of this fold. I must lead them also, and they will hearken to my voice, and there will be one flock and one shepherd.

"This is why the Father loves me: because I lay down my life, that I may take it up again. No one takes it from me, but I lay it down of my own choice. I have authority to lay it down, and I have authority to take it up again. This is the commandment I received from my Father."

Jesus, the Good Shepherd (continued)

Again, there was a division of opinion among the Jews because of these words. Many said, "He has a demon and is mad. Why listen to him?"

"These are not the words of a man who is demon possessed," said others. "Can a demon open the eyes of the blind?"

JOHN 10:1-21

1 Verily, verily, I say unto you, He that entereth not by the door into the sheepfold, but climbeth up some other way, the same is a thief and a robber.

2 But he that entereth in by the door is the shepherd of the sheep.

3 To him the porter openeth; and the sheep hear his voice: and he calleth his own sheep by name, and leadeth them out.

4 And when he putteth forth his own sheep, he goeth before them, and the sheep follow him: for they know his voice.

5 And a stranger will they not follow, but will flee from him; for they know not the voice of strangers.

6 This parable spake Jesus unto them; but they understood not what things they were which he spake unto them.

Flock of Sheep. *"The Lord is my shepherd" is an expression believers delight in using to express their relationship to God. Jesus used the same illustration to reveal His care.*

Jesus, the Good Shepherd (continued)

7 Then said Jesus unto them again, Verily, verily, I say unto you, I am the door of the sheep.

8 All that ever came before me are thieves and robbers: but the sheep did not hear them.

9 I am the door: by me if any man enter in, he shall be saved, and shall go in and out, and find pasture.

10 The thief cometh not, but for to steal, and to kill, and to destroy: I am come that they might have life, and that they might have *it* more abundantly.

11 I am the good shepherd: the good shepherd giveth his life for the sheep.

12 But he that is a hireling, and not the shepherd, whose own the sheep are not, seeth the wolf coming, and leaveth the sheep, and fleeth; and the wolf catcheth them, and scattereth the sheep.

13 The hireling fleeth, because he is a hireling, and careth not for the sheep.

14 I am the good shepherd, and know my *sheep*, and am known of mine.

15 As the Father knoweth me, even so know I the Father: and I lay down my life for the sheep.

16 And other sheep I have, which are not of this fold: them also I must bring, and they shall hear my voice; and there shall be one fold, *and* one shepherd.

17 Therefore doth my Father love me, because I lay down my life, that I might take it again.

18 No man taketh it from me, but I lay it down of myself. I have power to lay it down, and I have power to take it again. This commandment have I received of my Father.

19 There was a division therefore again among the Jews for these sayings.

20 And many of them said, He hath a devil, and is mad; why hear ye him?

21 Others said, These are not the words of him that hath a devil. Can a devil open the eyes of the blind?

Shepherds and Sheep. *In the Middle East shepherds do not drive their sheep as in Western lands. They lead them, know them by name, protect and guide them—the same as our Good Shepherd does.*

Mission of the Seventy

Luke 10:1-12, 16-20, Matthew 11:21-24

Now after these things, the Lord chose seventy others and sent them on before him, two by two, into every town and district where he himself was about to come. And he said to them,

"The harvest truly is abundant, but the reapers are few. Pray therefore the Lord of the harvest to send out reapers into his harvest. Go your way. Behold, I am sending you forth as lambs among wolves. Do not carry a purse, or a bag for provisions, or an extra pair of sandals, and do not stop to exchange greetings with anyone along the way. Into whatever house you enter, first say, 'Peace be to this house.' And if a son of peace is there, your peace shall rest upon him; and if not, it shall return to you. Stay in the same house, eating and drinking whatever they provide, for the laborer is worthy of his wages. Do not move from house to house.

"Whatever town you enter where the people receive you, eat whatever is set before you, heal the sick, and say to the people, 'The kingdom of God has come near you.' But whatever town you enter where the people do not receive you, go out into the streets and say, 'Even the dust of your town which clings to our feet, we wipe off as a protest against you. Nevertheless, be sure of this: the kingdom of God has come near you.' I say to you, it will be better for Sodom in the day of judgment than for that town.

"Alas for you, Chorazin! Alas for you, Bethsaida! For if the mighty works done in you had been done in Tyre and Sidon, they would have repented long ago in sackcloth and ashes. But I say to you, it will be more tolerable for Tyre and Sidon in the day of judgment than for you! And you, Capernaum, are you to be exalted to heaven? You shall be brought down to hell! For if the mighty works which have been done in you had been done in Sodom, it would have remained to this day. But I say to you, it will be more tolerable for the land of Sodom in the day of judgment than for you!"

Then said Jesus to the seventy, "He who listens to you listens to me, and he who rejects you rejects me, and he who rejects me rejects the Father who sent me."

And the seventy returned with joy, saying, "Lord, even the demons are subject to us in your name!"

Then said Jesus, "I saw Satan fall like lightning from heaven. Behold, I have given you authority to tread on serpents and scorpions and over all the power of the enemy, and nothing can harm you in any way. Nevertheless, do not rejoice that the spirits are subject to you; but instead, rejoice that your names are written in heaven."

MATTHEW 11:20-24

20 Then began he to upbraid the cities wherein most of his mighty works were done, because they repented not:

21 Woe unto thee, Chorazin! woe unto thee, Bethsaida! for if the mighty works, which were done in you, had been done in Tyre and Sidon, they would have repented long ago in sackcloth and ashes.

22 But I say unto you, It shall be more tolerable for Tyre and Sidon at the day of judgment, than for you.

23 And thou, Capernaum, which art exalted unto heaven, shalt be brought down to hell: for if the mighty works, which have been done in thee, had been done in Sodom, it would have remained until this day.

24 But I say unto you, That it shall be more tolerable for the land of Sodom in the day of judgment, than for thee.

LUKE 10:1-24

1 After these things the Lord appointed other seventy also, and sent them two and two before his face into every city and place, whither he himself would come.

2 Therefore said he unto them, The harvest truly *is* great, but the laborers *are* few: pray ye therefore the Lord of the harvest, that he would send forth laborers into his harvest.

3 Go your ways: behold, I send you forth as lambs among wolves.

4 Carry neither purse, nor scrip, nor shoes: and salute no man by the way.

5 And into whatsoever house ye enter, first say, Peace *be* to this house.

6 And if the son of peace be there, your peace shall rest upon it: if not, it shall turn to you again.

Mission of the Seventy (continued)

7 And in the same house remain, eating and drinking such things as they give: for the laborer is worthy of his hire. Go not from house to house.

8 And into whatsoever city ye enter, and they receive you, eat such things as are set before you:

9 And heal the sick that are therein, and say unto them, The kingdom of God is come nigh unto you.

10 But into whatsoever city ye enter, and they receive you not, go your ways out into the streets of the same, and say,

11 Even the very dust of your city, which cleaveth on us, we do wipe off against you: notwithstanding, be ye sure of this, that the kingdom of God is come nigh unto you.

12 But I say unto you, that it shall be more tolerable in that day for Sodom, than for that city.

13 Woe unto thee, Chorazin! woe unto thee, Bethsaida! for if the mighty works had been done in Tyre and Sidon, which have been done in you, they had a great while ago repented, sitting in sackcloth and ashes.

14 But it shall be more tolerable for Tyre and Sidon at the judgment, than for you.

15 And thou, Capernaum, which art exalted to heaven, shalt be thrust down to hell.

16 He that heareth you heareth me; and he that despiseth you despiseth me; and he that despiseth me despiseth him that sent me.

17 And the seventy returned again with joy, saying, Lord, even the devils are subject unto us through thy name.

18 And he said unto them, I beheld Satan as lightning fall from heaven.

19 Behold, I give unto you power to tread on serpents and scorpions, and over all the power of the enemy; and nothing shall by any means hurt you.

20 Notwithstanding, in this rejoice not, that the spirits are subject unto you; but rather rejoice, because your names are written in heaven.

21 In that hour Jesus rejoiced in spirit, and said, I thank thee, O Father, Lord of heaven and earth, that thou hast hid these things from the wise and prudent, and hast revealed them unto babes: even so, Father; for so it seemed good in thy sight.

22 All things are delivered to me of my Father: and no man knoweth who the Son is, but the Father; and who the Father is, but the Son, and *he* to whom the Son will reveal *him*.

23 And he turned him unto *his* disciples, and said privately, Blessed *are* the eyes which see the things that ye see:

24 For I tell you, that many prophets and kings have desired to see those things which ye see, and have not seen *them;* and to hear those things which ye hear, and have not heard *them.*

Parable of the Good Samaritan

Luke 10:25-37

And a certain lawyer stood up to put Jesus to a test. And he said, "Master, what must I do to inherit eternal life?"

"What is written in the law?" asked Jesus, "how does it read to you?"

"You shall love the Lord your God with all your heart, with all your soul, with all your strength, and with all your mind," he replied, "and your neighbor as yourself."

"You have answered correctly," said Jesus. "This do, and you will live."

"But who is my neighbor?" he asked, wanting to justify himself. In reply, Jesus said,

25 And, behold, a certain lawyer stood up, and tempted him, saying, Master, what shall I do to inherit eternal life?

26 He said unto him, What is written in the law? how readest thou?

27 And he answering said, Thou shalt love the Lord thy God with all thy heart, and with all thy soul, and with all thy strength, and with all thy mind; and thy neighbor as thyself.

28 And he said unto him, Thou hast answered right: this do, and thou shalt live.

29 But he, willing to justify himself, said unto Jesus, And who is my neighbor?

30 And Jesus answering said, A certain *man* went down from Jerusalem to Jericho, and fell among thieves, which stripped him of his raiment, and wounded *him,* and departed, leav-

The Good Samaritan Inn. *Though Jesus told the story as a parable, it could have been based on a true incident. It is located on the Jerusalem to Jericho road, about half way between the two cities.*

Parable of the Good Samaritan (continued)

"A certain man was going down from Jerusalem to Jericho. And he fell among thieves who stripped him of his clothing and beat him and departed, leaving him half dead. Now it happened that a certain priest was going down that road, but when he saw the man, he passed by on the other side. In like manner a Levite, too, when he came to the place and saw him, passed by on the other side.

"But a certain Samaritan, as he journeyed, came to where he was. And when he saw him, he had compassion on him and went to him and bound up his wounds, pouring in oil and wine, and set him on his own beast and brought him to an inn and took care of him. And the next day, when he departed, he took out two denarii and gave them to the innkeeper and said, 'Take care of him, and whatever more you spend, when I come back I will repay you.' Which of these three do you think was a neighbor to the man who fell among the thieves?"

"The man who showed mercy to him," replied the lawyer.

"Go and do likewise," said Jesus.

LUKE 10:25-37

ing *him* half dead.

31 And by chance there came down a certain priest that way; and when he saw him, he passed by on the other side.

32 And likewise a Levite, when he was at the place, came and looked *on him,* and passed by on the other side.

33 But a certain Samaritan, as he journeyed, came where he was; and when he saw him, he had compassion *on him,*

34 And went to *him,* and bound up his wounds, pouring in oil and wine, and set him on his own beast, and brought him to an inn, and took care of him.

35 And on the morrow when he departed, he took out two pence, and gave *them* to the host, and said unto him, Take care of him: and whatsoever thou spendest more, when I come again, I will repay thee.

36 Which now of these three, thinkest thou, was neighbor unto him that fell among the thieves?

37 And he said, He that showed mercy on him. Then said Jesus unto him, Go, and do thou likewise.

Jesus Visits Mary and Martha

Luke 10:38-42

Now as they went on their way, Jesus entered a village, and a woman named Martha received him into her house. And she had a sister named Mary, who sat down at the Lord's feet and was listening to his teaching. But Martha was distracted about much serving, and she came to Jesus and said, "Lord, don't you care that my sister has left me to serve alone? Tell her to help me."

"Martha, Martha," replied Jesus, "you are troubled and concerned about so many things. There is really need for only one. Mary has chosen what is best, and it shall not be taken away from her."

LUKE 10:38-42

38 Now it came to pass, as they went, that he entered into a certain village: and a certain woman named Martha received him into her house.

39 And she had a sister called Mary, which also sat at Jesus' feet, and heard his word.

40 But Martha was cumbered about much serving, and came to him, and said, Lord, dost thou not care that my sister hath left me to serve alone? bid her therefore that she help me.

41 And Jesus answered and said unto her, Martha, Martha, thou art careful and troubled about many things:

42 But one thing is needful; and Mary hath chosen that good part, which shall not be taken away from her.

Praying at the Wailing Wall. *Herod the Great had the wall placed there when he enlarged the Temple of Jesus' day. Through the centuries devout Jews have prayed here, weeping over the lost glories of the nation and praying for the coming of the Messiah.*

Jesus Teaches About Prayer

Luke 11:1-13

Now it came to pass that, as Jesus was praying in a certain place, when he had finished, one of his disciples said to him, "Lord, teach us to pray, as John taught his disciples."

"When you pray," said Jesus, "say,
Father, hallowed be your name.
May your kingdom come.
Give us each day our necessary bread.
And forgive us our sins,
for we forgive everyone who has wronged us.
And lead us not into temptation."

"Suppose," said Jesus, "one of you goes to a friend at midnight and says to him, 'Friend, lend me three loaves, for a friend of mine has come to me on a journey, and I have nothing to set before him.' The friend will answer from within, 'Don't bother me. The door is already locked for the night, and my children and I are in bed. I can't get up and give you anything.' I tell you, though he will not get up and give him anything just because he is his friend, yet because of his persistence he will rise and give him whatever he needs.

"I say to you therefore, ask, and it will be given to you; seek, and you will find; knock, and it will be opened to you. For everyone who asks receives, and he who seeks finds, and to him who knocks it will be opened.

"What father among you, if his son asks for a fish, will give him a serpent instead of a fish? Or if he asks for an egg, will you give him a scorpion? If you therefore, being evil, know how to give good gifts to your children, how much more will the heavenly Father give the Holy Spirit to those who ask him.''

1 And it came to pass, that, as he was praying in a certain place, when he ceased, one of his disciples said unto him, Lord, teach us to pray, as John also taught his disciples.

2 And he said unto them, When ye pray, say, Our Father which art in heaven, Hallowed be thy name. Thy kingdom come. They will be done, as in heaven, so in earth.

3 Give us day by day our daily bread.

4 And forgive us our sins; for we also forgive every one that is indebted to us. And lead us not into temptation; but deliver us from evil.

5 And he said unto them, Which of you shall have a friend, and shall go unto him at midnight, and say unto him, Friend, lend me three loaves;

...Ask, and it shall be given you; seek, and ye shall find; knock, and it shall be opened unto you.

---

6 For a friend of mine in his journey is come to me, and I have nothing to set before him?

7 And he from within shall answer and say, Trouble me not: the door is now shut, and my children are with me in bed; I cannot rise and give thee.

8 I say unto you, Though he will not rise and give him, because he is his friend, yet because of his importunity he will rise and give him as many as he needeth.

9 And I say unto you, Ask, and it shall be given you; seek, and ye shall find; knock, and it shall be opened unto you.

10 For every one that asketh receiveth; and he that seeketh findeth; and to him that knocketh it shall be *opened*.

11 If a son shall ask bread of any of you that is a father, will he give him a stone? or if *he* ask a fish, will he for a fish give him a serpent?

12 Or if he shall ask an egg, will he offer him a scorpion?

13 If ye then, being evil, know how to give good gifts unto your children; how much more shall *your* heavenly Father give the Holy Spirit to them that ask him?

Jesus Denounces Hypocrisy

Luke 11:37-54

When Jesus had finished speaking, a Pharisee invited him to dine with him. And he went in and sat down at table. The Pharisee noticed with astonishment that he did not wash before the meal. But the Lord said to him,

"You Pharisees clean the outside of the cup and the dish, but inside you are full of greed and wickedness. You fools! Did not the God who made the outside make the inside too? But give alms of those things which are within, and behold, all things will be clean for you.

"But woe to you Pharisees! for you tithe mint and rue and every herb, and disregard justice and the love of God. These things ought you to have done, without neglecting the others. Woe to you Pharisees! for you love the chief seat in the synagogues and salutations in the market places. Woe to you! for you are like unseen graves, over which men walk without knowing it."

Then one of the lawyers said to Jesus, "Master, in saying these things you are insulting us also."

"Woe to you doctors of the law, too!" said Jesus, "for you load men with burdens hard to bear, and you yourselves will not so much as touch those burdens with one of your fingers. Woe to you! for you build tombs for the prophets whom your fathers murdered. Thus you testify that you approve of the deeds of your fathers, for they killed them, and you build memorials. Therefore the wisdom of God has said, 'I will send them prophets and apostles, some of whom they will kill and some of whom they will persecute,' that the blood of all the prophets shed from the foundation of the world, from the blood of Abel to the blood of Zechariah who died between the altar and the sanctuary, may be required of this generation. Yes, I tell you, it shall be required of this generation!

"Woe to you lawyers! for you have taken away the key of knowledge. You did not enter the kingdom yourselves, and you hindered those who were trying to enter.

And as Jesus left the house, the scribes and Pharisees began to harass him and to try to provoke him to speak of many things, watching craftily for an opportunity to trap him in something he might say.

Megiddo Altar. At the site of this famous city, which has been destroyed and rebuilt more than 20 times, archaeologists discovered the remains of a Canaanite altar. The Battle of Armageddon ("hill of Megiddo") will take place nearby.

Garden of Gethsemane.
The word means "olive press" and was a place where Jesus often retired to pray. As olives are crushed to provide the oil, Jesus was crushed so His blessings could flow to us.

LUKE 11:37-54

37 And as he spake, a certain Pharisee besought him to dine with him: and he went in, and sat down to meat.

38 And when the Pharisee saw *it,* he marveled that he had not first washed before dinner.

39 And the Lord said unto him, Now do ye Pharisees make clean the outside of the cup and the platter; but your inward part is full of ravening and wickedness.

40 *Ye* fools, did not he, that made that which is without, make that which is within also?

41 But rather give alms of such things as ye have; and, behold, all things are clean unto you.

42 But woe unto you, Pharisees! for ye tithe mint and rue and all manner of herbs, and pass over judgment and the love of God: these ought ye to have done, and not to leave the other undone.

43 Woe unto you, Pharisees! for ye love the uppermost seats in the synagogues, and greetings in the markets.

44 Woe unto you, scribes and Pharisees, hypocrites! for ye are as graves which appear not, and the men that walk over *them* are not aware *of them.*

45 Then answered one of the lawyers, and said unto him, Master, thus saying thou reproachest us also.

46 And he said, Woe unto you also, *ye* lawyers! for ye lade men with burdens grievous to be borne, and ye yourselves touch not the burdens with one of your fingers.

47 Woe unto you! for ye build the sepulchres of the prophets, and your fathers killed them.

48 Truly ye bear witness that ye allow the deeds of your fathers: for they indeed killed them, and ye build their sepulchres.

49 Therefore also said the wisdom of God, I will send them prophets and apostles, and *some* of them they shall slay and persecute:

50 That the blood of all the prophets, which was shed from the foundation of the world, may be required of this generation;

51 From the blood of Abel unto the blood of Zechariah, which perished between the altar and the temple: verily I say unto you, It shall be required of this generation.

52 Woe unto you, lawyers! for ye have taken away the key of knowledge: ye entered not in yourselves, and them that were entering in ye hindered.

53 And as he said these things unto them, the scribes and the Pharisees began to urge *him* vehemently, and to provoke him to speak of many things:

54 Laying wait for him, and seeking to catch something out of his mouth, that they might accuse him.

Great Teachings of the Master

Luke 12:1-9, 13-21, 49-53

While these things were taking place, a large crowd gathered—so large that people were jostling one another. Then Jesus began to speak, first to his disciples:

"Beware the leaven of the Pharisees, which is hypocrisy. There is nothing covered up that will not be revealed, nor anything hidden that will not be known. Whatever you have said in the dark will be heard in the light, and whatever you have whispered in private chambers will be shouted from the housetops.

"I tell you—my friends, do not fear those who kill the body, and after that, can do nothing more. I will tell you whom to fear: fear him who, after he has killed, has the power to cast you into hell! Yes, I tell you, fear him!

"Are not five sparrows sold for two pennies? And yet, not one of them is forgotten before God. Even the hairs of your head are all numbered. Fear not, for you are worth more than many sparrows! And I tell you, everyone who acknowledges me before men, the Son of Man will acknowledge before the angels of God; but he who disowns me before men will be disowned before the angels of God."

Then someone in the crowd said to Jesus, "Master, tell my brother to divide his inheritance with me."

"Man, who appointed me a judge or arbitrator over you?" replied Jesus. Then he said to the people, "Take heed, and beware of all covetousness, for a man's life does not consist of the abundance of the things he possesses."

And he told them a parable, saying,

"The land of a certain rich man yielded an abundant harvest. So he said to himself, 'What shall I do? I don't have room enough to store my harvest!' Then he said, 'This will I do: I will tear down my barns and build larger ones, and there I will store all my grain and goods. And I will say to my soul, "Soul, you have plenty of good things laid up for many years. Take it easy—eat, drink, and enjoy yourself!" ' But God said to him, 'You fool! This night your soul is required of you, and whose will all these things be which you have prepared?' So it is with the man who stores up treasure for himself and is not rich in the things of God."

"I have come to bring fire to the earth," said Jesus, "and how I wish it were already ablaze! There is a baptism with which I must be baptized, and with what urgency am I driven onward until it is accomplished! Do you think I have come to bring peace on the earth? I tell you, no! I have come to bring division. From now on, five in one house will be divided, three against two, and two against three. They will be divided—father against son, and son against father; mother against daughter, and daughter against mother; mother-in-law against daughter-in-law, and daughter-in-law against mother-in-law."

LUKE 12:1-59

1 In the mean time, when there were gathered together an innumerable multitude of people, insomuch that they trode one upon another, he began to say unto his disciples first of all, Beware ye of the leaven of the Pharisees, which is hypocrisy.

2 For there is nothing covered, that shall not be revealed; neither hid, that shall not be known.

3 Therefore, whatsoever ye have spoken in darkness shall be heard in the light; and that which ye have spoken in the ear in closets shall be proclaimed upon the housetops.

4 And I say unto you my friends, Be not afraid of them that kill the body, and after that have no more that they can do.

5 But I will forewarn you whom ye shall fear: Fear him, which after he hath killed hath power to cast into hell; yea, I say unto you, Fear him.

6 Are not five sparrows sold for two farthings, and not one of them is forgotten before God?

7 But even the very hairs of your head are all numbered. Fear not therefore: ye are of more value than many sparrows.

8 Also I say unto you, Whosoever shall confess me before men, him shall the Son of man also confess before the angels of God:

Great Teachings of the Master (continued)

9 But he that denieth me before men shall be denied before the angels of God.

10 And whosoever shall speak a word against the Son of man, it shall be forgiven him: but unto him that blasphemeth against the Holy Ghost it shall not be forgiven.

11 And when they bring you unto the synagogues, and *unto* magistrates, and powers, take ye no thought how or what thing ye shall answer, or what ye shall say:

12 For the Holy Ghost shall teach you in the same hour what ye ought to say.

13 And one of the company said unto him, Master, speak to my brother, that he divide the inheritance with me.

14 And he said unto him, Man, who made me a judge or a divider over you?

15 And he said unto them, Take heed, and beware of covetousness: for a man's life consisteth not in the abundance of the things which he possesseth.

16 And he spake a parable unto them, saying, The ground of a certain rich man brought forth plentifully:

17 And he thought within himself, saying, What shall I do, because I have no room where to bestow my fruits?

18 And he said, This will I do: I will pull down my barns, and build greater; and there will I bestow all my fruits and my goods.

19 And I will say to my soul, Soul, thou hast much goods laid up for many years; take thine ease, eat, drink, *and* be merry.

20 But God said unto him, *Thou* fool, this night thy soul shall be required of thee: then whose shall those things be, which thou hast provided?

21 So *is* he that layeth up treasure for himself, and is not rich toward God.

22 And he said unto his disciples, Therefore I say unto you, Take no thought for your life, what ye shall eat; neither for the body, what ye shall put on.

23 The life is more than meat, and the body *is more* than raiment.

24 Consider the ravens: for they neither sow nor reap; which neither have storehouse nor barn; and God feedeth them: how much more are ye better than the fowls?

25 And which of you with taking thought can add to his stature one cubit?

26 If ye then be not able to do that thing which is least, why take ye thought for the rest?

27 Consider the lilies how they grow: they toil not, they spin not; and yet I say unto you, that Solomon in all his glory was not arrayed like one of these.

28 If then God so clothe the grass, which is today in the field, and tomorrow is cast into the oven; how much more *will he clothe* you, O ye of little faith?

29 And seek not ye what ye shall eat, or what ye shall drink, neither be ye of doubtful mind.

30 For all these things do the nations of the world seek after: and your Father knoweth that ye have need of these things.

31 But rather seek ye the kingdom of God; and all these things shall be added unto you.

32 Fear not, little flock; for it is your Father's good pleasure to give you the kingdom.

...seek not ye what ye shall eat, or what ye shall drink, neither be ye of doubtful mind.

33 Sell that ye have, and give alms; provide yourselves bags which wax not old, a treasure in the heavens that faileth not, where no thief approacheth, neither moth corrupteth.

34 For where your treasure is, there will your heart be also.

35 Let your loins be girded about, and *your* lights burning;

36 And ye yourselves like unto men that wait for their lord, when he will return from the wedding; that, when he cometh and knocketh, they may open unto him immediately.

37 Blessed *are* those servants, whom the lord when he cometh shall find watching: verily I say unto you, that he shall gird himself, and make them to sit down to meat, and will come forth and serve them.

38 And if he shall come in the second watch, or come in the third watch, and find *them* so, blessed are those servants.

39 And this know, that if the goodman of the house had known what hour the thief would come, he would have watched, and not have suffered his house to be broken through.

Great Teachings of the Master (continued)

40 Be ye therefore ready also: for the Son of man cometh at an hour when ye think not.

41 Then Peter said unto him, Lord, speakest thou this parable unto us, or even to all?

42 And the Lord said, Who then is that faithful and wise steward, whom *his* lord shall make ruler over his household, to give *them their* portion of meat in due season?

43 Blessed *is* that servant, whom his lord when he cometh shall find so doing.

44 Of a truth I say unto you, that he will make him ruler over all that he hath.

45 But and if that servant say in his heart, My lord delayeth his coming; and shall begin to beat the menservants and maidens, and to eat and drink, and to be drunken;

46 The lord of that servant will come in a day when he looketh not for *him,* and at an hour when he is not aware, and will cut him in sunder, and will appoint him his portion with the unbelievers.

47 And that servant, which knew his lord's will, and prepared not *himself,* neither did according to his will, shall be beaten with many *stripes.*

48 But he that knew not, and did commit things worthy of stripes, shall be beaten with few *stripes.* For unto whomsoever much is given, of him shall be much required; and to whom men have committed much, of him they will ask the more.

49 I am come to send fire on the earth; and what will I, if it be already kindled?

50 But I have a baptism to be baptized with; and how am I straitened till it be accomplished!

51 Suppose ye that I am come to give peace on earth? I tell you, Nay; but rather division:

52 For from henceforth there shall be five in one house divided, three against two, and two against three.

53 The father shall be divided against the son, and the son against the father; the mother against the daughter, and the daughter against the mother; the mother-in-law against her daughter-in-law, and the daughter-in-law against her mother-in-law.

54 And he said also to the people, When ye see a cloud rise out of the west, straightway ye say, There cometh a shower; and so it is.

55 And when *ye see* the south wind blow, ye say, There will be heat; and it cometh to pass.

56 *Ye* hypocrites, ye can discern the face of the sky and of the earth; but how is it that ye do not discern this time?

57 Yea, and why even of yourselves judge ye not what is right?

58 When thou goest with thine adversary to the magistrate, *as thou art* in the way, give diligence that thou mayest be delivered from him; lest he hale thee to the judge, and the judge deliver thee to the officer, and the officer cast thee into prison.

59 I tell thee, thou shalt not depart thence, till thou hast paid the very last mite.

Sunset. *In His sermon (above) Jesus accused His listeners of being able to discern weather by observing "the face of the sky," but not being spiritually perceptive.*

215

Jesus' Warning to Repent

Fig Leaves and Fruit.
An unusual feature of fig trees is that the fruit appears before the leaves do. Jesus once cursed a fig tree because it had leaves but no fruit.

Luke 13:1-9

There were some present at that time who told Jesus of the Galileans whose blood Pilate had mingled with their sacrifices.

"Do you suppose that those Galileans suffered these things because they were worse sinners than all the other Galileans?" asked Jesus. "I tell you, no. And unless you repent, you will all likewise perish. And what about those eighteen people on whom the tower in Siloam fell, killing them all? Do you suppose that they were worse offenders than all the other people who lived in Jerusalem? I tell you, no. And unless you repent, you will all likewise perish."

Then he told this parable:

"A certain man had a fig tree in his vineyard, and he came seeking fruit on it, but found none. So he said to his caretaker, 'Behold, for three years I have come seeking fruit on this fig tree, and I find no fruit. Chop it down! Why should it waste the ground?' But the caretaker replied, 'Sir, leave it one more year till I can dig around it and apply some manure. Then if it bears fruit after that, well and good; and if not, you can chop it down.' "

LUKE 13:1-9

1 There were present at that season some that told him of the Galileans, whose blood Pilate had mingled with their sacrifices.

2 And Jesus answering said unto them, Suppose ye that these Galileans were sinners above all the Galileans, because they suffered such things?

3 I tell you, Nay: but, except ye repent, ye shall all likewise perish.

4 Or those eighteen, upon whom the tower in Siloam fell, and slew them, think ye that they were sinners above all men that dwelt in Jerusalem?

5 I tell you, Nay: but, except ye repent, ye shall all likewise perish.

6 He spake also this parable; A certain *man* had a fig tree planted in his vineyard; and he came and sought fruit thereon, and found none.

7 Then said he unto the dresser of his vineyard, Behold, these three years I come seeking fruit on this fig tree, and find none: cut it down; why cumbereth it the ground?

8 And he answering said unto him, Lord, let it alone this year also, till I shall dig about it, and dung *it:*

9 And if it bear fruit, *well:* and if not, *then* after that thou shalt cut it down.

Jesus Heals on the Sabbath

Luke 13:10-21

Jesus was teaching in one of the synagogues on the Sabbath day, and there was a woman present who for eighteen years had suffered an infirmity. She was bent over and unable to stand erect. When Jesus saw her, he called her and said, "Woman, you are freed from your infirmity."

And he laid his hands on her, and immediately she was made straight. And she began to praise God. But the ruler of the synagogue, indignant because Jesus had healed on the Sabbath day, said to the people,

"There are six days in which men can work. Therefore, come on those days and be healed, but not on the Sabbath day."

Then the Lord answered him, saying,

"You hypocrites! Does not every one of you untie his ox or his ass from the manger on the Sabbath and lead it away to drink? And should not this woman, a daughter of Abraham whom Satan has bound for eighteen years, be released from this bond on the Sabbath day?"

And when he had said these things, all his adversaries were put to shame, and all the people began to rejoice at all the wonderful things he was doing.

Then said Jesus, "What is the kingdom of God like? To what shall I compare it? It is like a grain of mustard seed which a man took and dropped in his garden; and it grew and became a tree, and the birds of the air nested in its branches."

And again he said, "To what shall I compare the kingdom of God? It is like leaven which a woman took and hid in three measures of meal, till all was leavened."

10 And he was teaching in one of the synagogues on the sabbath.

11 And, behold, there was a woman which had a spirit of infirmity eighteen years, and was bowed together, and could in no wise lift up *herself.*

12 And when Jesus saw her, he called *her to him,* and said unto her, Woman, thou art loosed from thine infirmity.

13 And he laid *his* hands on her: and immediately she was made straight, and glorified God.

14 And the ruler of the synagogue answered with indignation, because that Jesus had healed on the sabbath day, and said unto the people, There are six days in which men ought to work: in them therefore come and be healed, and not on the sabbath day.

15 The Lord then answered him, and said, *Thou* hypocrite, doth not each one of you on the sabbath loose his ox or *his* ass from the stall, and lead *him* away to watering?

16 And ought not this woman, being a daughter of Abraham, whom Satan hath bound, lo, these eighteen years, be loosed from this bond on the sabbath day?

17 And when he had said these things, all his adversaries were ashamed: and all the people rejoiced for all the glorious things that were done by him.

...immediately she was made straight, and glorified God.

18 Then said he, Unto what is the kingdom of God like? and whereunto shall I resemble it?

19 It is like a grain of mustard seed, which a man took, and cast into his garden; and it grew, and waxed a great tree, and the fowls of the air lodged in the branches of it.

20 And again he said, Whereunto shall I liken the kingdom of God?

21 It is like leaven, which a woman took and hid in three measures of meal, till the whole was leavened.

Jesus Teaches as He Travels

Luke 13:22-33

And Jesus went on his way through the towns and villages, teaching, and journeying toward Jerusalem. And someone said to him, "Lord, will only a few be saved?"

And Jesus said to them,

"Strive earnestly to enter in through the narrow door. For I tell you, many will seek to enter and will not be able, once the master of the house has got up and locked the door. You may be left standing outside and knocking at the door, crying, 'Lord, open the door for us!' But he will answer you, 'I don't know you, or where you are from.' Then you will begin to say, 'We ate and drank in your presence, and you taught in our streets.' But he will say, 'I tell you, I don't know where you are from. Depart from me, all you evil doers!'

"There will be weeping and gnashing of teeth when you see Abraham and Isaac and Jacob and all the prophets in the kingdom of God, and you yourselves excluded. And people will come from the east and the west, and from the north and the south, and will sit down in the kingdom of God. And behold, some are now last who will be first, and some are now first who will be last."

At that same hour, certain Pharisees came to Jesus and said, "You must leave this place and be on your way, for Herod intends to kill you."

But Jesus replied, "Go and tell that fox, 'Behold, today and tomorrow I will cast out demons and perform healings, and the third day I will finish.' Nevertheless, I must journey onward today, tomorrow, and the day following, for it would never do for a prophet to be killed anywhere but at Jerusalem!"

22 And he went through the cities and villages, teaching, and journeying toward Jerusalem.

23 Then said one unto him, Lord, are there few that be saved? And he said unto them,

24 Strive to enter in at the strait gate: for many, I say unto you, will seek to enter in, and shall not be able.

...behold, there are last which shall be first; and there are first which shall be last.

25 When once the master of the house is risen up, and hath shut to the door, and ye begin to stand without, and to knock at the door, saying, Lord, Lord, open unto us; and he shall answer and say unto you, I know you not whence ye are:

26 Then shall ye begin to say, We have eaten and drunk in thy presence, and thou hast taught in our streets.

27 But he shall say, I tell you, I know you not whence ye are; depart from me, all *ye* workers of iniquity.

28 There shall be weeping and gnashing of teeth, when ye shall see Abraham, and Isaac, and Jacob, and all the prophets, in the kingdom of God, and you *yourselves* thrust out.

29 And they shall come from the east, and *from* the west, and from the north, and *from* the south, and shall sit down in the kingdom of God.

30 And, behold, there are last which shall be first; and there are first which shall be last.

31 The same day there came certain of the Pharisees, saying unto him, Get thee out, and depart hence; for Herod will kill thee.

32 And he said unto them, Go ye, and tell that fox, Behold, I cast out devils, and I do cures today and tomorrow, and the third *day* I shall be perfected.

33 Nevertheless I must walk today, and tomorrow, and the *day* following: for it cannot be that a prophet perish out of Jerusalem.

Wayside Teaching. *For most of His travels Jesus walked, accompanied by His disciples. He must often have shared truths with them, using as illustrations familiar objects they observed while on their journey. What marvelous Bible studies these must have been!*

Jesus Tells Some Pointed Parables

Luke 14:1-24

And it came to pass that Jesus went on a Sabbath day to dine at the home of a leading Pharisee. And they kept watching Jesus closely, for before him was a man who had dropsy.

And Jesus spoke to the lawyers and Pharisees, saying, "Is it lawful to heal on the Sabbath day, or not?"

But they were silent. Then Jesus laid his hand on the man and healed him, and sent him on his way. And he said to the lawyers and Pharisees,

"Which of you, having an ass or an ox that has fallen into a well, will not pull him out at once on a Sabbath day?"

And they had nothing to say in reply.

Then Jesus told a parable to those who were invited to the dinner, when he noticed how they chose the places of honor:

"When you are invited by someone to a wedding feast, do not sit down in the place of honor, lest a more distinguished person than you may have been invited, and the man who invited you both will come and say to you, 'Give your place to this man,' and with embarrassment, you will have to take the lowest place. Instead, when you are invited, go and sit down in the lowest place, so that when your host comes in he may say to you, 'Friend, come take a better seat,' and you will be honored before those who are seated at the table with you. For everyone who exalts himself will be humbled, and he who humbles himself will be exalted."

Then he said to the man who had invited him,

"When you give a dinner or a banquet, do not invite your friends or brothers or relatives or wealthy neighbors, lest they invite you in return and you be repaid. Instead, when you entertain, invite the poor, the maimed, the lame, and the blind. Then you will be blessed, for they have nothing with which to repay you. You will be repaid at the resurrection of the just."

Now when one of those who sat at table with him heard these things, he said to Jesus, "Blessed is he who shall eat bread in the kingdom of God!"

But Jesus said to him,

"A certain man gave a banquet and invited many people. And at the time for the banquet, he sent his servant to say to those who had been invited, 'Come, for everything is now ready.' But they all alike began to offer excuses. The first one said to him, 'I have bought a field, and I must go and see it. I beg of you, please excuse me.' 'I have bought five yoke of oxen,' said another, 'and I am on my way to try them out. I beg of you, please excuse me.' And another said, 'I have just married a wife, and therefore I cannot come.' So the servant came and reported these things to his master. Then the master of the house was angry and said to his servant, 'Go out quickly into the streets and lanes of the city and gather in the poor, the maimed, the blind, and the lame.' And the servant said, 'Sir, it has been done as you commanded, but there is still room.' Then the master said to his servant, 'Go out into the highways and the bypaths and persuade people to come in, that my house may be filled. For I tell you, none of those men who were invited shall taste of my banquet.'"

LUKE 14:1-24

1 And it came to pass, as he went into the house of one of the chief Pharisees to eat bread on the sabbath day, that they watched him.

2 And, behold, there was a certain man before him which had the dropsy.

3 And Jesus answering spake unto the lawyers and Pharisees, saying, Is it lawful to heal on the sabbath day?

4 And they held their peace. And he took *him,* and healed him, and let him go;

5 And answered them, saying, Which of you shall have an ass or an ox fallen into a pit, and will not straightway pull him out on the sabbath day?

6 And they could not answer him again to these things.

7 And he put forth a parable to those which were

Jesus Tells Some Pointed Parables (continued)

bidden, when he marked how they chose out the chief rooms; saying unto them,

8 When thou art bidden of any *man* to a wedding, sit not down in the highest room; lest a more honorable man than thou be bidden of him;

9 And he that bade thee and him come and say to thee, Give this man place; and thou begin with shame to take the lowest room.

10 But when thou art bidden, go and sit down in the lowest room; that when he that bade thee cometh, he may say unto thee, Friend, go up higher: then shalt thou have worship in the presence of them that sit at meat with thee.

11 For whosoever exalteth himself shall be abased; and he that humbleth himself shall be exalted.

12 Then said he also to him that bade him, When thou makest a dinner or a supper, call not thy friends, nor thy brethren, neither thy kinsmen, nor *thy* rich neighbors; lest they also bid thee again, and a recompense be made thee.

13 But when thou makest a feast, call the poor, the maimed, the lame, the blind:

14 And thou shalt be blessed; for they cannot recompense thee: for thou shalt be recompensed at the resurrection of the just.

15 And when one of them that sat at meat with him heard these things, he said unto him, Blessed *is* he that shall eat bread in the kingdom of God.

16 Then said he unto him, A certain man made a great supper, and bade many:

17 And sent his servant at supper time to say to them that were bidden, Come; for all things are now ready.

18 And they all with one *consent* began to make excuse. The first said unto him, I have bought a piece of ground, and I must needs go and see it: I pray thee have me excused.

19 And another said, I have bought five yoke of oxen, and I go to prove them: I pray thee have me excused.

20 And another said, I have married a wife, and therefore I cannot come.

21 So that servant came, and showed his lord these things. Then the master of the house being angry said to his servant, Go out quickly into the streets and lanes of the city, and bring in hither the poor, and the maimed, and the halt, and the blind.

22 And the servant said, Lord, it is done as thou hast commanded, and yet there is room.

23 And the lord said unto the servant, Go out into the highways and hedges, and compel *them* to come in, that my house may be filled.

24 For I say unto you, That none of those men which were bidden shall taste of my supper.

Pinnacle of the Temple. In Jesus' time on earth there was a 150-foot tower at the southeast corner of the Temple area seen here. From it priests would watch for the rising of the sun and then announce the time for the morning sacrifice.

The Cost of True Discipleship

Luke 14:25-35

Now great crowds were following along after Jesus, and he turned and said to them,

"If anyone comes to me and does not hate his father and mother and wife and children and brothers and sisters—yes, and his own life too, he cannot be my disciple. Whoever does not follow after me bearing a cross of his own cannot be my disciple.

"Which of you, intending to build a tower, does not sit down first and count the cost to see whether he has enough to complete it? Otherwise, when he has laid a foundation and is unable to complete the tower, all who see it begin to scoff at him, saying, 'This man began to build, but wasn't able to finish the job!'

"Or what king, going to war against another king, will not first sit down and consider whether he is able, with ten thousand men, to meet him who comes against him with twenty thousand? And if not, while the other is still afar off, he sends an envoy and asks terms of peace. Just so, every one of you who does not surrender all that he possesses cannot be my disciple.

"Salt is good, but if salt has lost its taste, what can restore it? There is nothing to do but throw it away as useless, for it is no good for the ground or for the manure pile. He who has ears to hear, let him hear."

LUKE 14:25-35

25 And there went great multitudes with him: and he turned, and said unto them,

26 If any *man* come to me, and hate not his father, and mother, and wife, and children, and brethren, and sisters, yea, and his own life also, he cannot be my disciple.

27 And whosoever doth not bear his cross, and come after me, cannot be my disciple.

28 For which of you, intending to build a tower, sitteth not down first, and counteth the cost, whether he have *sufficient* to finish *it?*

29 Lest haply, after he hath laid the foundation, and is not able to finish *it,* all that behold *it* begin to mock him,

30 Saying, This man began to build, and was not able to finish.

31 Or what king, going to make war against another king, sitteth not down first, and consulteth whether he be able with ten thousand to meet him that cometh against him with twenty thousand?

32 Or else, while the other is yet a great way off, he sendeth an ambassage, and desireth conditions of peace.

33 So likewise, whosoever he be of you that forsaketh not all that he hath, he cannot be my disciple.

34 Salt *is* good: but if the salt have lost his savor, wherewith shall it be seasoned?

35 It is neither fit for the land, nor yet for the dunghill; *but* men cast it out. He that hath ears to hear, let him hear.

Tower in a Vineyard. *Jesus was undoubtedly talking of a much larger tower, when He spoke of counting the cost, but towers were often put in vineyards for living and protection during the harvest.*

Jesus Meets the Jews' Challenge

John 10:22-42

Then occurred the Feast of Dedication at Jerusalem. It was winter, and Jesus was walking in the temple, in Solomon's porch. Then the Jews surrounded him and said, "How long do you intend to keep us in suspense? If you are really the Messiah, tell us plainly."

"I told you," replied Jesus, "but you do not believe. The works that I do in my Father's name, they bear witness to me. But you do not believe, because you are not my sheep. My sheep listen to my voice, and I know them. They follow me, and I give them eternal life and they will never perish, and no one can snatch them out of my hand. My Father who gave them to me is stronger than all, and no one can snatch them out of my Father's hand. The Father and I are one."

Once again the Jews picked up stones to stone him to death.

"I have shown you many good works from the Father," said Jesus. "For which of those works are you going to stone me?"

"We are not stoning you for a good work," replied the Jews, "but for blasphemy, because you—a man—claim to be God."

"Is it not written in your law, 'I said, you are gods'?" answered Jesus. "If he called them gods to whom the word of God came (and the scripture cannot be broken), how is it that you say to him whom the Father consecrated and sent into the world, 'You are blaspheming,' because I said, 'I am the Son of God'? If I am not doing the works of my Father, do not believe me. But if I am doing his works, even though you do not believe in me for my own sake, believe the testimony of the works, that you may come to know and understand that the Father is in me, and I am in the Father."

Then they tried again to arrest him, but he escaped from their hands. And he went away again across the Jordan to the place where John had first baptized, and there he remained. And many came to him, and said, "John showed us no miracle, but all that he said about this man was true."

And many believed in him there.

22 And it was at Jerusalem the feast of the dedication, and it was winter.

23 And Jesus walked in the temple in Solomon's porch.

24 Then came the Jews round about him, and said unto him, How long dost thou make us to doubt? If thou be the Christ, tell us plainly.

25 Jesus answered them, I told you, and ye believed not: the works that I do in my Father's name, they bear witness of me.

26 But ye believe not, because ye are not of my sheep, as I said unto you.

27 My sheep hear my voice, and I know them, and they follow me:

28 And I give unto them eternal life; and they shall never perish, neither shall any *man* pluck them out of my hand.

29 My Father, which gave *them* me, is greater than all; and no *man* is able to pluck *them* out of my Father's hand.

30 I and *my* Father are one.

31 Then the Jews took up stones again to stone him.

32 Jesus answered them, Many good works have I showed you from my Father; for which of those works do ye stone me?

33 The Jews answered him, saying, For a good work we stone thee not; but for blasphemy; and because that thou, being a man, makest thyself God.

34 Jesus answered them, Is it not written in your law, I said, Ye are gods?

35 If he called them gods, unto whom the word of God came, and the Scripture cannot be broken;

36 Say ye of him, whom the Father hath sanctified, and sent into the world, Thou blasphemest; because I said, I am the Son of God?

37 If I do not the works of my Father, believe me not.

38 But if I do, though ye believe not me, believe the works; that ye may know, and believe, that the Father *is* in me, and I in him.

39 Therefore they sought again to take him; but he escaped out of their hand,

40 And went away again beyond Jordan into the place where John at first baptized; and there he abode.

Jesus Meets the Jews' Challenge (continued)

41 And many resorted unto him, and said, John did no miracle: but all things that John spake of this man were true.

42 And many believed on him there.

1 And it came to pass, *that* when Jesus had finished these sayings, he departed from Galilee, and came into the coasts of Judea beyond Jordan;

2 And great multitudes followed him; and he healed them there.

1 And he arose from thence, and cometh into the coasts of Judea by the farther side of Jordan: and the people resort unto him again; and, as he was wont, he taught them again.

Shrine of the Book. *It was erected in the 1960's to house the treasured Dead Sea Scrolls. The top is shaped like the lid of the jars containing the first scrolls; inside it appears to be a cave.*

Lost: A Sheep, Silver, a Son

Luke 15:1-32

Now all the tax collectors and sinners were coming to Jesus to hear him. And the Pharisees and scribes complained, saying, "This man welcomes sinners and even eats with them."

Then Jesus told them a parable, saying,

"What man of you, if he has a hundred sheep and loses one of them, does not leave the ninety-nine in the pasture and go search for the one that is lost until he finds it? And when he has found it, he lays it on his shoulders, rejoicing. And when he comes home, he calls his friends and neighbors together and says, 'Rejoice with me, for I have found my sheep which was lost!' Just so, I tell you, there is more joy in heaven over one sinner who repents than over ninety-nine righteous people who have no need to repent.

"Or what woman, if she has ten silver coins and loses one, does not light a lamp and sweep the house and search carefully until she finds it? And when she has found it, she calls her friends and neighbors together and says, 'Rejoice with me, for I have found the coin which I had lost!' Just so, I tell you, there is joy in the presence of the angels of God over one sinner who repents."

Then he said,

"A certain man had two sons, and the younger of them said to his father, 'Father, give me the share of property that falls to me.' And he divided his estate between them. Not long afterward, the younger son gathered together all that he had and took his journey into a far country, and there he squandered his money in riotous living. And when he had spent all, there arose a great famine in that country, and he began to be in want. And he went and hired out to one of the citizens of that country, who sent him into his fields to feed swine. And he would gladly have eaten the pods that the swine ate, and no one gave him anything. Then he came to his senses and said, 'How many hired servants of my father have bread enough and to spare, and here I am—dying of hunger! I will rise and go to my father, and I will say to him, "Father, I have sinned against heaven, and against you.

1 Then drew near unto him all the publicans and sinners for to hear him.

2 And the Pharisees and scribes murmured, saying, This man receiveth sinners, and eateth with them.

3 And he spake this parable unto them, saying,

4 What man of you, having a hundred sheep, if he lose one of them, doth not leave the ninety and nine in the wilderness, and go after that which is lost, until he find it?

5 And when he hath found *it,* he layeth *it* on his shoulders, rejoicing.

6 And when he cometh home, he calleth together *his* friends and neighbors, saying unto them, Rejoice with me; for I have found my sheep which was lost.

7 I say unto you, that likewise joy shall be in heaven over one sinner that repenteth, more than over ninety and nine just persons, which need no repentance.

8 Either what woman having ten pieces of silver, if she lose one piece, doth not light a candle, and sweep the house, and seek diligently till she find *it?*

9 And when she hath found *it,* she calleth *her* friends and *her* neighbors together, saying, Rejoice with me; for I have found the piece which I had lost.

10 Likewise, I say unto you, there is joy in the presence of the angels of God over one sinner that repenteth.

11 And he said, A certain man had two sons:

12 And the younger of them said to *his* father, Father, give me the portion of goods that falleth *to me.* And he divided unto them *his* living.

13 And not many days after the younger son gathered all together, and took his journey into a far country, and there wasted his substance with riotous living.

14 And when he had spent all, there arose a mighty famine in that land; and he began to be in want.

15 And he went and joined himself to a citizen of that country; and he sent him into his fields to feed swine.

16 And he would fain have filled his belly with the husks that the swine did eat: and no man gave unto him.

17 And when he came to himself, he said, How many hired servants of my father's have bread enough and to spare, and I perish with hunger!

225

Lost: A Sheep, Silver, a Son (continued)

I am no longer worthy to be called your son. Let me be as one of your hired servants.'' '

"And he rose and went to his father. But while he was still a long way off, his father saw him and had compassion, and ran and threw his arms around him and kissed him. But the son said, 'Father, I have sinned against heaven, and against you. I am no longer worthy to be called your son.' But the father called to his servants, 'Hurry and bring the best robe and put it on him, and put a ring on his finger and shoes on his feet. And go get the fatted calf and kill it, and let us eat and be merry. For this my son was dead, and is alive again! He was lost, and is found!' And they began to be merry.

"Now the elder son was in the field, and as he came near the house, he heard music and dancing. And he called one of the servants and asked what these things meant. 'Your brother has come,' said the servant, 'and your father has killed the fatted calf, because he has received him safe and sound.'

"But the elder son was angry and refused to go inside the house. So his father came out and pleaded with him. But he answered his father, 'Lo, these many years I have served you and never disobeyed your instructions, and you never gave me even so much as a kid, so I could celebrate with my friends. But when this your son came back, who squandered your money on harlots, for him you killed the fatted calf!' 'Son,' replied the father, 'you are always with me, and all I have is yours. But it was right to be merry and rejoice, because this your brother was dead, and is alive. He was lost, and is found.' ''

LUKE 15:1-32

18 I will arise and go to my father, and will say unto him, Father, I have sinned against heaven, and before thee,

19 And am no more worthy to be called thy son: make me as one of thy hired servants.

20 And he arose, and came to his father. But when he was yet a great way off, his father saw him, and had compassion, and ran, and fell on his neck, and kissed him.

21 And the son said unto him, Father, I have sinned against heaven, and in thy sight, and am no more worthy to be called thy son.

22 But the father said to his servants, Bring forth the best robe, and put *it* on him; and put a ring on his hand, and shoes on *his* feet:

23 And bring hither the fatted calf, and kill *it;* and let us eat, and be merry:

24 For this my son was dead, and is alive again; he was lost, and is found. And they began to be merry.

25 Now his elder son was in the field: and as he came and drew nigh to the house, he heard music and dancing.

26 And he called one of the servants, and asked what these things meant.

27 And he said unto him, Thy brother is come; and thy father hath killed the fatted calf, because he hath received him safe and sound.

28 And he was angry, and would not go in: therefore came his father out, and entreated him.

29 And he answering said to *his* father, Lo, these many years do I serve thee, neither transgressed I at any time thy commandment; and yet thou never gavest me a kid, that I might make merry with my friends:

30 But as soon as this thy son was come, which hath devoured thy living with harlots, thou hast killed for him the fatted calf.

31 And he said unto him, Son, thou art ever with me, and all that I have is thine.

32 It was meet that we should make merry, and be glad: for this thy brother was dead, and is alive again; and was lost, and is found.

The Proper Use of Wealth

Luke 16:1-15

Then Jesus said to his disciples,

"There was a certain rich man who had a steward who, according to reports that came to him, was squandering his goods. And he called him in and said to him, 'What is this I hear about you? Turn in an account of your management, for you can no longer be steward.' Then the steward said to himself, 'My master is taking away my job as steward, and what shall I do? I am not able to dig, and I am ashamed to beg. I know what I'll do, so that when I have been dismissed as steward, people will welcome me into their homes.'

"And calling each of his master's debtors, he said to the first one, 'How much do you owe my master?' 'A hundred measures of oil,' he replied. Then the steward told him, 'Take your bill and sit down quickly and change it to fifty.' Then he said to another, 'And you—how much do you owe?' 'A hundred measures of wheat,' he replied. 'Take your bill and write eighty,' said the steward.

"And the master praised the dishonest steward for acting so shrewdly. For the sons of this world are wiser in their dealings with their own kind of men than the sons of light. And I say to you, make friends for yourselves through your use of

1 And he said also unto his disciples, There was a certain rich man, which had a steward; and the same was accused unto him that he had wasted his goods.

2 And he called him, and said unto him, How is it that I hear this of thee? give an account of thy stewardship; for thou mayest be no longer steward.

3 Then the steward said within himself, What shall I do? for my lord taketh away from me the stewardship: I cannot dig; to beg I am ashamed.

4 I am resolved what to do, that, when I am put out of the stewardship, they may receive me into their houses.

5 So he called every one of his lord's debtors *unto him,* and said unto the first, How much owest thou unto my lord?

6 And he said, A hundred measures of oil. And he said unto him, Take thy bill, and sit down quickly, and write fifty.

7 Then said he to another, And how much owest thou? And he said, A hundred measures of wheat. And he said unto him, Take thy bill, and write fourscore.

8 And the lord commended the unjust steward, because he had done wisely: for the children of this world are in their generation wiser than the children of light.

9 And I say unto you, Make to yourselves

Heavily-loaded Donkey. This small animal is used for many purposes, including travel (Jesus rode one into Jerusalem), but will also carry unbelievably heavy loads.

227

The Proper Use of Wealth (continued)

earthly possessions, so that when its usefulness is past, your friends may welcome you into the everlasting dwellings.

"He who is faithful in little things is faithful also in much, and he who is unjust in little things is unjust also in much. Therefore, if you have not been faithful in your use of earthly treasure, who will entrust to you the true riches? And if you have not been faithful in your use of what really belongs to another, who will give you anything for your own? No servant can serve two masters: either he will hate this one and love that one, or else he will be devoted to this one and despise that one. You cannot serve both God and mammon."

Now the Pharisees, who were lovers of money, heard these things and scoffed at Jesus. But he said to them, "You are the ones who want to impress men with your righteousness, but God knows your hearts. Many who are highly esteemed by men are an abomination in the sight of God."

friends of the mammon of unrighteousness; that, when ye fail, they may receive you into everlasting habitations.

10 He that is faithful in that which is least is faithful also in much: and he that is unjust in the least is unjust also in much.

11 If therefore ye have not been faithful in the unrighteous mammon, who will commit to your trust the true *riches?*

12 And if ye have not been faithful in that which is another man's, who shall give you that which is your own?

13 No servant can serve two masters: for either he will hate the one, and love the other; or else he will hold to the one, and despise the other. Ye cannot serve God and mammon.

14 And the Pharisees also, who were covetous, heard all these things: and they derided him.

15 And he said unto them, Ye are they which justify yourselves before men; but God knoweth your hearts: for that which is highly esteemed among men is abomination in the sight of God.

16 The law and the prophets *were* until John: since that time the kingdom of God is preached, and every man presseth into it.

17 And it is easier for heaven and earth to pass, than one tittle of the law to fail.

Mary and Martha.
Jesus often visited the home in Bethany where Lazarus and his sisters, Mary and Martha, lived. On one occasion Martha busied herself preparing a meal for the Master, but Jesus said that Mary, who sat at His feet and listened to Him, had made the better choice.

The Rich Man and Lazarus

Luke 16:19-31

"There was a certain rich man," said Jesus, "who always dressed in the finest clothing and lived luxuriously every day. And there was a certain beggar named Lazarus who had been laid at his gate, covered with sores. He longed to be fed with the scraps from the rich man's table, and the dogs used to come and lick his sores. And it came to pass that the beggar died and was carried by the angels to Abraham's bosom. The rich man also died, and was buried. And in hell he lifted up his eyes, being in torment, and saw Abraham afar off, and Lazarus with him. And he cried, 'Father Abraham, have mercy on me and send Lazarus, that he may dip the tip of his finger in water and cool my tongue, for I am in anguish in this flame!'' But Abraham replied, 'Son, remember that in your lifetime you received your good things, and Lazarus received bad things. But now he is comforted here, and you are in anguish. And besides all this, between us and you a great chasm has been placed, so that any who would pass from here to you cannot do so, nor can anyone cross from there to us.'

" 'Then I beg of you, Father,' replied the rich man, 'send Lazarus to my father's house, for I have five brothers. Send him to warn them, lest they also come to this place of torment.' But Abraham said, 'They have Moses and the prophets; let them listen to them.' 'No, Father Abraham,' he said, 'but if someone goes to them from the dead, they will repent.' But Abraham replied, 'If they do not listen to Moses and the prophets, they will not be persuaded even if someone should rise from the dead.' ''

LUKE 16:19-31

19 There was a certain rich man, which was clothed in purple and fine linen, and fared sumptuously every day:

20 And there was a certain beggar named Lazarus, which was laid at his gate, full of sores,

21 And desiring to be fed with the crumbs which fell from the rich man's table: moreover the dogs came and licked his sores.

22 And it came to pass, that the beggar died, and was carried by the angels into Abraham's bosom: the rich man also died, and was buried;

...They have Moses and the prophets; let them hear them.

23 And in hell he lifted up his eyes, being in torments, and seeth Abraham afar off, and Lazarus in his bosom.

24 And he cried and said, Father Abraham, have mercy on me, and send Lazarus, that he may dip the tip of his finger in water, and cool my tongue; for I am tormented in this flame.

25 But Abraham said, Son, remember that thou in thy lifetime receivedst thy good things, and likewise Lazarus evil things: but now he is comforted, and thou art tormented.

26 And beside all this, between us and you there is a great gulf fixed: so that they which would pass from hence to you cannot; neither can they pass to us, that *would come* from thence.

27 Then he said, I pray thee therefore, father, that thou wouldest send him to my father's house:

28 For I have five brethren; that he may testify unto them, lest they also come into this place of torment.

29 Abraham saith unto him, They have Moses and the prophets; let them hear them.

30 And he said, Nay, father Abraham: but if one went unto them from the dead, they will repent.

31 And he said unto him, If they hear not Moses and the prophets, neither will they be persuaded, though one rose from the dead.

Forgiveness, Faith and Duty

1 Then said he unto the disciples, It is impossible but that offenses will come: but woe *unto him*, through whom they come!

2 It were better for him that a millstone were hanged about his neck, and he cast into the sea, than that he should offend one of these little ones.

3 Take heed to yourselves: If thy brother trespass against thee, rebuke him; and if he repent, forgive him.

4 And if he trespass against thee seven times in a day, and seven times in a day turn again to thee, saying, I repent; thou shalt forgive him.

5 And the apostles said unto the Lord, Increase our faith.

6 And the Lord said, If ye had faith as a grain of mustard seed, ye might say unto this sycamine tree, Be thou plucked up by the root, and be thou planted in the sea; and it should obey you.

7 But which of you, having a servant plowing or feeding cattle, will say unto him by and by, when he is come from the field, Go and sit down to meat?

8 And will not rather say unto him, Make ready wherewith I may sup, and gird thyself, and serve me, till I have eaten and drunken; and afterward thou shalt eat and drink?

9 Doth he thank that servant because he did the things that were commanded him? I trow not.

10 So likewise ye, when ye shall have done all those things which are commanded you, say, We are unprofitable servants: we have done that which was our duty to do.

Sunrise, Mount of Olives. *The Mount of Olives is not a single peak but a 2700-foot-high ridge running north and southeast of Jerusalem. It affords a marvelous panorama of the city.*

Jesus Restores a Friend to Life

John 11:1-54

Now a certain man was sick, Lazarus of Bethany, the village of Mary and her sister Martha. (It was the Mary who anointed the Lord with perfume and wiped his feet with her hair, whose brother Lazarus was sick.) So the sisters sent word to Jesus, saying, "Lord, your dear friend is sick."

When Jesus heard that Lazarus was sick, he said, "This sickness is not to end in death, but in the glory of God, that the Son of God may be glorified through it." Therefore, though he loved Martha and her sister and Lazarus, when he heard that Lazarus was sick, Jesus remained where he was for two more days. Then, after two days, he said to the disciples, "Let us go into Judea again."

"Rabbi," said the disciples, "only a little while ago the Jews were wanting to stone you; are you going back there again?"

"Are there not twelve hours in the day?" replied Jesus. "If a man walks in the day, he does not stumble, because he can see by the daylight. But if a man walks in the night, he stumbles, because he has no light."

Having said these things, Jesus then said, "Our friend Lazarus has fallen asleep, but I go to awake him."

"Lord, if he has fallen asleep," said the disciples, "he is going to get well."

Now Jesus had spoken of his death, but they thought he was speaking of taking rest in sleep. Then Jesus plainly said, "Lararus is dead; and for your sakes, I am glad I was not there, that you may learn to believe. But let us go to him."

Then Thomas, called the Twin, said to his fellow disciples, "Let us go, too, that we may die with him."

When Jesus arrived, he found that Lazarus had already been in the tomb four days. Now Bethany was near Jerusalem, about fifteen furlongs out, and many of the Jews had come to Martha and Mary to console them concerning their brother. When Martha heard that Jesus was coming, she went to meet him, but Mary remained in the house.

JOHN 11:1-54

1 Now a certain *man* was sick, *named* Lazarus, of Bethany, the town of Mary and her sister Martha.

✓ 2 (It was *that* Mary which anointed the Lord with ointment, and wiped his feet with her hair, whose brother Lazarus was sick.)

3 Therefore his sisters sent unto him, saying, Lord, behold, he whom thou lovest is sick.

4 When Jesus heard *that*, he said, This sickness is not unto death, but for the glory of God, that the Son of God might be glorified thereby.

5 Now Jesus loved Martha, and her sister, and Lazarus.

6 When he had heard therefore that he was sick, he abode two days still in the same place where he was.

7 Then after that saith he to *his* disciples, Let us go into Judea again.

8 *His* disciples say unto him, Master, the Jews of late sought to stone thee; and goest thou thither again?

9 Jesus answered, Are there not twelve hours in the day? If any man walk in the day, he stumbleth not, because he seeth the light of this world.

10 But if a man walk in the night, he stumbleth, because there is no light in him.

11 These things said he: and after that he saith unto them, Our friend Lazarus sleepeth; but I go, that I may awake him out of sleep.

12 Then said his disciples, Lord, if he sleep, he shall do well.

13 Howbeit Jesus spake of his death: but they thought that he had spoken of taking of rest in sleep.

14 Then said Jesus unto them plainly, Lazarus is dead.

15 And I am glad for your sakes that I was not there, to the intent ye may believe; nevertheless let us go unto him.

16 Then said Thomas, which is called Didymus, unto his fellow disciples, Let us also go, that we may die with him.

17 Then when Jesus came, he found that he had *lain* in the grave four days already.

18 Now Bethany was nigh unto Jerusalem, about fifteen furlongs off:

19 And many of the Jews came to Martha and Mary, to comfort them concerning their brother.

Tomb of Lazarus and Mosaic. *The traditional tomb has more than 30 steps leading below. A mosaic in the nearby church depicts the moment when Lazarus, restored to life, appeared at the tomb's entrance.*

Jesus Restores a Friend to Life (continued)

"Lord," said Martha to Jesus, "if only you had been here, my brother would not have died. And even now, I know that whatever you ask of God, God will give you."

"Your brother will rise again," said Jesus.

"I know that he will rise again in the resurrection at the last day," replied Martha.

"I am the resurrection and the life," said Jesus. "He who believes in me, though he die, yet shall he live; and whoever lives and believes in me shall never die. Do you believe this?"

"Yes, Lord," she replied, "I believe that you are the Messiah, the Son of God, who was to come into the world."

Then Martha went and called her sister privately, saying, "The Master has come, and is calling for you."

When Mary heard this, she rose at once and went to Jesus. Now Jesus had not yet come into the village, but was still where Martha had met him. Then the Jews who were with Mary in the house, consoling her, when they saw that she got up hurriedly and went out, followed her, thinking that she was going to the tomb to weep there.

When Mary arrived where Jesus was and saw him, she fell at his feet and said, "Lord, if only you had been here, my brother would not have died."

When Jesus saw her weeping, and saw the Jews weeping who followed her, he was distressed and deeply touched.

"Where have you laid him?" he asked.

"Come and see, Lord," they replied.

Jesus quietly wept.

"See how he loved him!" said the Jews.

But some said, "This man who opened the eyes of the blind—wasn't he able to keep this man from dying?"

Then Jesus, deeply moved again, came to the tomb. Now it was a cave, and a stone was lying against the opening.

"Take away the stone," said Jesus.

"Lord," protested Martha, "by this time there will be a stench, for he has been dead four days."

JOHN 11:1-54

20 Then Martha, as soon as she heard that Jesus was coming, went and met him: but Mary sat *still* in the house.

21 Then said Martha unto Jesus, Lord, if thou hadst been here, my brother had not died.

22 But I know, that even now, whatsoever thou wilt ask of God, God will give *it* thee.

23 Jesus saith unto her, Thy brother shall rise again.

24 Martha saith unto him, I know that he shall rise again in the resurrection at the last day.

25 Jesus said unto her, I am the resurrection, and the life: he that believeth in me, though he were dead, yet shall he live:

26 And whosoever liveth and believeth in me shall never die. Believest thou this?

27 She saith unto him, Yea, Lord: I believe that thou art the Christ, the Son of God, which should come into the world.

28 And when she had so said, she went her way, and called Mary her sister secretly, saying, The Master is come, and calleth for thee.

29 As soon as she heard *that*, she arose quickly, and came unto him.

30 Now Jesus was not yet come into the town, but was in that place where Martha met him.

31 The Jews then which were with her in the house, and comforted her, when they saw Mary, that she rose up hastily and went out, followed her, saying, She goeth unto the grave to weep there.

32 Then when Mary was come where Jesus was, and saw him, she fell down at his feet, saying unto him, Lord, if thou hadst been here, my brother had not died.

33 When Jesus therefore saw her weeping, and the Jews also weeping which came with her, he groaned in the spirit, and was troubled.

34 And said, Where have ye laid him? They say unto him, Lord, come and see.

35 Jesus wept.

36 Then said the Jews, Behold how he loved him!

37 And some of them said, Could not this man, which opened the eyes of the blind, have caused that even this man should not have died?

38 Jesus therefore again groaning in himself cometh to the grave. It was a cave, and a stone lay upon it.

Jesus Restores a Friend to Life (continued)

"Did I not tell you that if you believed," said Jesus, "you would see the glory of God?"

Then they took away the stone, and Jesus lifted up his eyes and said, "Father, I thank you that you have heard me. I know that you always hear me, but I have said this for the sake of the people standing by, that they may believe that you sent me."

When he had said these things, Jesus shouted, "Lazarus, come out!"

And he who had been dead came out, bound hand and foot with winding cloths, and with a napkin bound about his face.

"Untie him, and let him go," said Jesus.

Then many of the Jews who had come with Mary, when they saw what Jesus did, believed in him. But some went to the Pharisees and told them what Jesus had done. Then the chief priests and the Pharisees called the Council together and said, "What are we to do? For this man is performing many miracles. If we let him go on doing these things, all the people will believe in him, and then the Romans will come and destroy both our temple and our nation."

But one of them, Caiaphas, who was High Priest that year, said, "You know nothing at all, nor do you understand that it is expedient for you that one man should die for the people, rather than that the whole nation perish."

(Now he did not say this of his own accord, but being High Priest that year, he prophesied that Jesus should die for the nation, and not only for the nation, but also that he might gather together all the children of God scattered abroad.)

So from that day on, they plotted how they might kill him. Jesus therefore no longer walked openly in Judea, but retired to the countryside near the wilderness, to a town called Ephraim, and there remained with his disciples.

39 Jesus said, Take ye away the stone. Martha, the sister of him that was dead, saith unto him, Lord, by this time he stinketh: for he hath been *dead* four days.

40 Jesus saith unto her, Said I not unto thee, that, if thou wouldest believe, thou shouldest see the glory of God?

41 Then they took away the stone *from the place* where the dead was laid. And Jesus lifted up *his* eyes, and said, Father, I thank thee that thou hast heard me.

42 And I knew that thou hearest me always: but because of the people which stand by I said *it*, that they may believe that thou hast sent me.

43 And when he thus had spoken, he cried with a loud voice, Lazarus, come forth.

44 And he that was dead came forth, bound hand and foot with graveclothes; and his face was bound about with a napkin. Jesus saith unto them, Loose him, and let him go.

45 Then many of the Jews which came to Mary, and had seen the things which Jesus did, believed on him.

46 But some of them went their ways to the Pharisees, and told them what things Jesus had done.

47 Then gathered the chief priests and the Pharisees a council, and said, What do we? for this man doeth many miracles.

48 If we let him thus alone, all *men* will believe on him; and the Romans shall come and take away both our place and nation.

49 And one of them, *named* Caiaphas, being the high priest that same year, said unto them, Ye know nothing at all,

50 Nor consider that it is expedient for us, that one man should die for the people, and that the whole nation perish not.

51 And this spake he not of himself: but being high priest that year, he prophesied that Jesus should die for that nation;

52 And not for that nation only, but that also he should gather together in one the children of God that were scattered abroad.

53 Then from that day forth they took counsel together for to put him to death.

54 Jesus therefore walked no more openly among the Jews; but went thence into a country near to the wilderness, into a city called Ephraim, and there continued with his disciples.

Healing of Ten Lepers

Luke 17:11-19

Now it came to pass that on his way to Jerusalem, Jesus passed through the border of Samaria and Galilee. And as he entered a certain village, he was met by ten lepers who stood at a distance and shouted, "Jesus, Master, have mercy on us!"

When Jesus saw them, he said, "Go show yourselves to the priests."

And it came to pass that as they went, they were cleansed. Then one of them, when he saw that he was healed, turned back and praised God with a loud voice and fell on his face before Jesus and thanked him. Now he was a Samaritan.

Then said Jesus, "Were there not ten who were cleansed? Where are the nine? Are none to be found returning to praise God except this foreigner?"

And he said to the man, "Rise, and go your way. Your faith has made you whole."

11 And it came to pass, as he went to Jerusalem, that he passed through the midst of Samaria and Galilee.

12 And as he entered into a certain village, there met him ten men that were lepers, which stood afar off:

13 And they lifted up *their* voices, and said, Jesus, Master, have mercy on us.

14 And when he saw *them,* he said unto them, Go show yourselves unto the priests. And it came to pass, that, as they went, they were cleansed.

15 And one of them, when he saw that he was healed, turned back, and with a loud voice glorified God,

16 And fell down on *his* face at his feet, giving him thanks: and he was a Samaritan.

17 And Jesus answering said, Were there not ten cleansed? but where *are* the nine?

18 There are not found that returned to give glory to God, save this stranger.

19 And he said unto him, Arise, go thy way: thy faith hath made thee whole.

Jesus' Coming Requires Preparedness

Luke 17:20-37

Now Jesus was asked by some Pharisees when the kingdom of God would come, and he said, "The kingdom of God is not coming with great public display, neither will people say, 'Look, here it is!' or 'Look, there it is!' For behold, the kingdom of God is in your midst."

Then Jesus said to the disciples, "The time will come when you will long to see one of the days of the Son of Man, but will not see it. And they will say to you, 'Look, he is there!' or 'Look, he is here!' Do not go out to see, do not follow them. For as the lightning flashes across the sky from one end to the other, so shall the Son of Man be in his day. But first he must suffer many things and be rejected by this generation. As it was in the days of Noah, so shall it be in

20 And when he was demanded of the Pharisees, when the kingdom of God should come, he answered them and said, The kingdom of God cometh not with observation:

21 Neither shall they say, Lo here! or, lo there! for, behold, the kingdom of God is within you.

22 And he said unto the disciples, The days will come, when ye shall desire to see one of the days of the Son of man, and ye shall not see *it.*

23 And they shall say to you, See here; or, see there: go not after *them,* nor follow *them.*

24 For as the lightning, that lighteneth out of the one *part* under heaven, shineth unto the other *part* under heaven; so shall also the Son of man be in his day.

25 But first must he suffer many things, and be rejected of this generation.

Damascus Gate. *The major entrance to the Old City, it received its title because the road leading north begins there. The original gate is to the left and lower down.*

Jesus' Coming Requires Preparedness (continued)

the days of the Son of Man. They were eating, they were drinking, they were marrying and being married, until the day Noah entered the ark, and then the flood came and destroyed them all. And as it was in the days of Lot—they were eating and drinking, they were buying and selling, they were planting and building, but on the day Lot departed from Sodom, it rained fire and brimstone from heaven and destroyed them all—so shall it be in the day when the Son of Man is revealed.

"In that day, let not the man who is on the housetop come down to carry away his possessions in the house, and let not the man who is out in the field return for the things he left behind. Remember Lot's wife. Whoever seeks to keep his life for himself will lose it, but whoever surrenders his life will preserve it. I tell you, in that night there will be two men in one bed; one will be taken, and the other left. Two women will be grinding together; one will be taken, and the other left."

"Where will all this take place, Lord?" they asked.

"Wherever the body is, there the vultures will be gathered together," replied Jesus.

LUKE 17:20-37

26 And as it was in the days of Noah, so shall it be also in the days of the Son of man.

27 They did eat, they drank, they married wives, they were given in marriage, until the day that Noah entered into the ark, and the flood came, and destroyed them all.

28 Likewise also as it was in the days of Lot; they did eat, they drank, they bought, they sold, they planted, they builded;

29 But the same day that Lot went out of Sodom it rained fire and brimstone from heaven, and destroyed *them* all.

30 Even thus shall it be in the day when the Son of man is revealed.

31 In that day, he which shall be upon the housetop, and his stuff in the house, let him not come down to take it away: and he that is in the field, let him likewise not return back.

32 Remember Lot's wife.

33 Whosoever shall seek to save his life shall lose it; and whosoever shall lose his life shall preserve it.

34 I tell you, in that night there shall be two *men* in one bed; the one shall be taken, and the other shall be left.

35 Two *women* shall be grinding together; the one shall be taken, and the other left.

36 Two *men* shall be in the field; the one shall be taken, and the other left.

37 And they answered and said unto him, Where, Lord? And he said unto them, Wheresoever the body *is,* thither will the eagles be gathered together.

The Right Kind of Praying

Luke 18:1-14

Then Jesus told them a parable to teach them that they ought always to pray and not to lose heart.

"In a certain city," he said, "there was a judge who neither feared God nor regarded men. And there was a widow in that city who kept coming to him and saying, 'Please see that I

LUKE 18:1-14

1 And he spake a parable unto them *to this end,* that men ought always to pray, and not to faint;

2 Saying, There was in a city a judge, which feared not God, neither regarded man:

3 And there was a widow in that city; and she came unto him, saying, Avenge me of mine adversary.

The Right Kind of Praying (continued)

receive justice against my adversary.' For a long while, he refused. But later he said to himself, 'Though I neither fear God nor regard men, yet because this widow is annoying me, I will secure justice for her, lest she wear me out by her continual coming.' "

Then the Lord said, "Listen to what the unrighteous judge said. And will not God secure justice for his elect who cry to him day and night, toward whom he is so patient? I tell you, he will secure justice for them speedily. But when the Son of Man comes, will he find such persistent faith on the earth?"

Jesus also told this parable to some who were very sure that they themselves were righteous and who looked with disdain on everyone else:

"Two men went up to the temple to pray, one a Pharisee, and the other a tax collector. The Pharisee stood erect in a conspicuous place and began to pray, 'God, I thank you that I am not like other men—greedy, deceitful, adulterers—or like this tax collector here. I fast twice a week, and I give tithes of all my income!'

"But the tax collector, standing to one side, would not even look up toward heaven, but kept striking his breast and saying, 'God, have mercy on me, a sinner!' I tell you, this man went home justified before God, rather than the other. For everyone who exalts himself shall be humbled, and he who humbles himself shall be exalted."

LUKE 18:1-14

4 And he would not for a while: but afterward he said within himself, Though I fear not God, nor regard man;

5 Yet because this widow troubleth me, I will avenge her, lest by her continual coming she weary me.

6 And the Lord said, Hear what the unjust judge saith.

7 And shall not God avenge his own elect, which cry day and night unto him, though he bear long with them?

8 I tell you that he will avenge them speedily. Nevertheless, when the Son of man cometh, shall he find faith on the earth?

9 And he spake this parable unto certain which trusted in themselves that they were righteous, and despised others:

10 Two men went up into the temple to pray; the one a Pharisee, and the other a publican.

11 The Pharisee stood and prayed thus with himself, God, I thank thee, that I am not as other men *are,* extortioners, unjust, adulterers, or even as this publican.

12 I fast twice in the week, I give tithes of all that I possess.

13 And the publican, standing afar off, would not lift up so much as *his* eyes unto heaven, but smote upon his breast, saying, God be merciful to me a sinner.

14 I tell you, this man went down to his house justified *rather* than the other: for every one that exalteth himself shall be abased; and he that humbleth himself shall be exalted.

Jesus Questioned About Divorce

Matthew 19:3-12

There came to Jesus some Pharisees, to test him.

"Is it lawful," they asked, "for a man to divorce his wife for just any cause whatever?"

"Have you not read," answered Jesus, "that he who made them in the beginning made them male and female, and said, 'For this cause a man shall leave his father and mother and be joined

Jesus Questioned About Divorce (continued)

to his wife, and the two shall become one flesh'? Thus they are no longer two, but one flesh. Therefore, what God has joined together, let not man separate.''

''Then why did Moses command us to give a wife a certificate of divorce and dismiss her?'' they replied.

''Because of your hardness of heart, Moses permitted you to divorce your wives,'' said Jesus, ''but from the beginning it was not so. And I tell you, whoever divorces his wife for any cause other than her unfaithfulness, and marries another, commits adultery.''

Then the disciples said to Jesus, ''If that is a man's situation with respect to a wife, it is best not to marry.''

''Not everyone can accept this teaching,'' replied Jesus, ''but only those to whom it has been granted. For while some are incapable of marriage from birth, and some are made incapable by men, there are some who have chosen to forego marriage for the sake of the kingdom of heaven. Whoever is able to accept this, let him accept it.''

MATTHEW 19:3-12

3 The Pharisees also came unto him, tempting him, and saying unto him, Is it lawful for a man to put away his wife for every cause?

4 And he answered and said unto them, Have ye not read, that he which made *them* at the beginning made them male and female,

5 And said, For this cause shall a man leave father and mother, and shall cleave to his wife: and they twain shall be one flesh?

6 Wherefore they are no more twain, but one flesh. What therefore God hath joined together, let not man put asunder.

7 They say unto him, Why did Moses then command to give a writing of divorcement, and to put her away?

8 He saith unto them, Moses because of the hardness of your hearts suffered you to put away your wives: but from the beginning it was not so.

9 And I say unto you, Whosoever shall put away his wife, except *it be* for fornication, and shall marry another, committeth adultery: and whoso marrieth her which is put away doth commit adultery.

10 His disciples say unto him, If the case of the man be so with *his* wife, it is not good to marry.

11 But he said unto them, All *men* cannot receive this saying, save *they* to whom it is given.

12 For there are some eunuchs, which were so born from *their* mother's womb: and there are some eunuchs, which were made eunuchs of men: and there be eunuchs, which have made themselves eunuchs for the kingdom of heaven's sake. He that is able to receive *it,* let him receive *it.*

MARK 10:2-12

2 And the Pharisees came to him, and asked him, Is it lawful for a man to put away *his* wife? tempting him.

3 And he answered and said unto them, What did Moses command you?

4 And they said, Moses suffered to write a bill of divorcement, and to put *her* away.

5 And Jesus answered and said unto them, For the hardness of your heart he wrote you this precept.

6 But from the beginning of the creation God made them male and female.

7 For this cause shall a man leave his father and mother, and cleave to his wife;

8 And they twain shall be one flesh: so then they are no more twain, but one flesh.

9 What therefore God hath joined together, let not man put asunder.

10 And in the house his disciples asked him again of the same *matter.*

11 And he saith unto them, Whosoever shall put away his wife, and marry another, committeth adultery against her.

12 And if a woman shall put away her husband, and be married to another, she committeth adultery.

LUKE 16:18

18 Whosoever putteth away his wife, and marrieth another, committeth adultery: and whosoever marrieth her that is put away from *her* husband committeth adultery.

Jesus Blesses the Children

Mark 10:13-16

Some were bringing little children to Jesus, that he might lay his hands on them. But the disciples were forbidding them, and when Jesus noticed this, he was indignant and said, "Let the little children come to me. Do not hinder them, for the kingdom of God belongs to such as these. I tell you truly, whoever does not receive the kingdom of God like a little child shall not enter it."

And he took the children in his arms and blessed them, laying his hands upon them.

MATTHEW 19:13-15	MARK 10:13-16	LUKE 18:15-17
13 Then were there brought unto him little children, that he should put *his* hands on them, and pray: and the disciples rebuked them.	13 And they brought young children to him, that he should touch them; and *his* disciples rebuked those that brought *them.*	15 And they brought unto him also infants, that he would touch them: but when *his* disciples saw *it,* they rebuked them.
14 But Jesus said, Suffer little children, and forbid them not, to come unto me; for of such is the kingdom of heaven.	14 But when Jesus saw *it,* he was much displeased, and said unto them, Suffer the little children to come unto me, and forbid them not; for of such is the kingdom of God.	16 But Jesus called them *unto him,* and said, Suffer little children to come unto me, and forbid them not: for of such is the kingdom of God.
15 And he laid *his* hands on them, and departed thence.	15 Verily I say unto you, Whosoever shall not receive the kingdom of God as a little child, he shall not enter therein.	17 Verily I say unto you, Whosoever shall not receive the kingdom of God as a little child shall in no wise enter therein.
	16 And he took them up in his arms, put *his* hands upon them, and blessed them.	

The Pathway of Mercy

Luke 18:18-30

A certain councilman asked Jesus, "Good Master, what shall I do to inherit eternal life?"

"Why do you call me good?" replied Jesus. "No one is truly good except God alone. You know the commandments: 'Do not commit adultery; do not kill; do not steal; do not bear false witness; honor your father and mother.'"

"All these have I observed from my youth," he replied.

When Jesus heard this, he said to him, "You still lack one thing. Sell everything you have and give the money to the poor, that you may have treasure in heaven, and come follow me."

But when the man heard this, he was sad, for he was very rich. Then Jesus, looking at him, said, "How difficult it is for those who have riches to enter the kingdom of God! It is easier for a camel to pass through the eye of a needle than for a rich man to enter the kingdom of God."

Then those who heard these words exclaimed, "Who, then, can be saved?"

"Things impossible for men are possible for God," replied Jesus.

Then said Peter, "Lo, we have left everything we had and followed you."

"I tell you truly," said Jesus, "there is no man who has left house, or wife, or brothers, parents, or children for the sake of the kingdom of God who will not receive far more in this present time, and in the world to come, eternal life."

Jesus and the Children. *What was Jesus like? We know that He related well to all classes of society. It is especially interesting that the children were drawn to Him. Those whom children love are a special kind of people. The disciples tried to send them away, but Jesus had time for them.*

241

The Pathway of Mercy (continued)

16 And, behold, one came and said unto him, Good Master, what good thing shall I do, that I may have eternal life?

17 And he said unto him, Why callest thou me good? *there* is none good but one, *that is,* God: but if thou wilt enter into life, keep the commandments.

18 He saith unto him, Which? Jesus said, Thou shalt do no murder, Thou shalt not commit adultery, Thou shalt not steal, Thou shalt not bear false witness,

19 Honor thy father and *thy* mother: and, Thou shalt love thy neighbor as thyself.

20 The young man saith unto him, All these things have I kept from my youth up: what lack I yet?

21 Jesus said unto him, If thou wilt be perfect, go *and* sell that thou hast, and give to the poor, and thou shalt have treasure in heaven: and come *and* follow me.

22 But when the young man heard that saying, he went away sorrowful: for he had great possessions.

23 Then said Jesus unto his disciples, Verily I say unto you, That a rich man shall hardly enter into the kingdom of heaven.

24 And again I say unto you, It is easier for a camel to go through the eye of a needle, than for a rich man to enter into the kingdom of God.

25 When his disciples heard *it,* they were exceedingly amazed, saying, Who then can be saved?

26 But Jesus beheld *them,* and said unto them, With men this is impossible; but with God all things are possible.

27 Then answered Peter and said unto him, Behold, we have forsaken all, and followed thee; what shall we have therefore?

17 And when he was gone forth into the way, there came one running, and kneeled to him, and asked him, Good Master, what shall I do that I may inherit eternal life?

18 And Jesus said unto him, Why callest thou me good? *there is* none good but one, *that is,* God.

19 Thou knowest the commandments, Do not commit adultery, Do not kill, Do not steal, Do not bear false witness, Defraud not, Honor thy father and mother.

20 And he answered and said unto him, Master, all these have I observed from my youth.

21 Then Jesus beholding him loved him, and said unto him, One thing thou lackest: go thy way, sell whatsoever thou hast, and give to the poor, and thou shalt have treasure in heaven: and come, take up the cross, and follow me.

22 And he was sad at that saying, and went away grieved: for he had great possessions.

23 And Jesus looked round about, and saith unto his disciples, How hardly shall they that have riches enter into the kingdom of God!

24 And the disciples were astonished at his words. But Jesus answereth again, and saith unto them, Children, how hard is it for them that trust in riches to enter into the kingdom of God!

25 It is easier for a camel to go through the eye of a needle, than for a rich man to enter into the kingdom of God.

26 And they were astonished out of measure, saying among themselves, Who then can be saved?

27 And Jesus looking upon them saith, With men *it is* impossible, but not with God: for with God all things are possible.

28 Then Peter began to say unto him, Lo, we have left all, and have followed thee.

18 And a certain ruler asked him, saying, Good Master, what shall I do to inherit eternal life?

19 And Jesus said unto him, Why callest thou me good? none *is* good, save one, *that is,* God.

Verily I say unto you, Whosoever shall not receive the kingdom of God as a little child shall in no wise enter therein.

20 Thou knowest the commandments, Do not commit adultery, Do not kill, Do not steal, Do not bear false witness, Honor thy father and thy mother.

21 And he said, All these have I kept from my youth up.

22 Now when Jesus heard these things, he said unto him, Yet lackest thou one thing: sell all that thou hast, and distribute unto the poor, and thou shalt have treasure in heaven: and come, follow me.

23 And when he heard this, he was very sorrowful: for he was very rich.

24 And when Jesus saw that he was very sorrowful, he said, How hardly shall they that have riches enter into the kingdom of God!

25 For it is easier for a camel to go through a needle's eye, than for a rich man to enter into the kingdom of God.

The Pathway of Mercy (continued)

28 And Jesus said unto them, Verily I say unto you, That ye which have followed me, in the regeneration when the Son of man shall sit in the throne of his glory, ye also shall sit upon twelve thrones, judging the twelve tribes of Israel.

29 And every one that hath forsaken houses, or brethren, or sisters, or father, or mother, or wife, or children, or lands, for my name's sake, shall receive a hundredfold, and shall inherit everlasting life.

30 But many *that are* first shall be last; and the last *shall be* first.

29 And Jesus answered and said, Verily I say unto you, There is no man that hath left house, or brethren, or sisters, or father, or mother, or wife, or children, or lands, for my sake, and the gospel's,

30 But he shall receive a hundredfold now in this time, houses, and brethren, and sisters, and mothers, and children, and lands, with persecutions; and in the world to come eternal life.

31 But many *that are* first shall be last; and the last first.

26 And they that heard *it* said, Who then can be saved?

27 And he said, The things which are impossible with men are possible with God.

28 Then Peter said, Lo, we have left all, and followed thee.

29 And he said unto them, Verily I say unto you, There is no man that hath left house, or parents, or brethren, or wife, or children, for the kingdom of God's sake,

30 Who shall not receive manifold more in this present time, and in the world to come life everlasting.

Rewards of Discipleship

Matthew 20:1-16

"For the kingdom of heaven," said Jesus, "is like a landowner who went out at daybreak to hire laborers for his vineyard. And having agreed with them on a wage of one denarius for the day, he sent them into his vineyard. And he went out about nine o'clock and saw other laborers standing idle in the market place and said to them, 'You go to the vineyard too, and I will pay you whatever is right.' And so they went. And he went out again about noon and about three o'clock and hired others. And about five o'clock he went out and found others standing around and said to them, 'Why have you been standing here idle all day?' 'Because no one has hired us,' they replied. 'You go to the vineyard too,' he said.

"And when evening came, the owner of the vineyard said to his steward, 'Call the laborers and pay them their wages, beginning with the last ones and proceeding to the first ones.' And when those hired about five o'clock came, they each received a denarius. And when those came who were hired first, they thought they would

1 For the kingdom of heaven is like unto a man *that is* a householder, which went out early in the morning to hire laborers into his vineyard.

2 And when he had agreed with the laborers for a penny a day, he sent them into his vineyard.

3 And he went out about the third hour, and saw others standing idle in the market place,

4 And said unto them; Go ye also into the vineyard, and whatsoever is right I will give you. And they went their way.

5 Again he went out about the sixth and ninth hour, and did likewise.

6 And about the eleventh hour he went out, and found others standing idle, and saith unto them, Why stand ye here all the day idle?

7 They say unto him, Because no man hath hired us. He saith unto them, Go ye also into the vineyard; and whatsoever is right, *that* shall ye receive.

8 So when even was come, the lord of the vineyard saith unto his steward, Call the laborers, and give them *their* hire, beginning from the last unto the first.

9 And when they came that *were hired* about the eleventh hour, they received every man a penny.

243

Rewards of Discipleship (continued)

receive more; but they, too, each received a denarius. And when they had received their pay, they began to complain against the landowner, saying, 'These last have worked only one hour, and you have paid them the same as us who have borne the burden of the day and the scorching heat.'

"But the landowner replied to one of them, 'Friend, I am not doing you any injustice. Did you not agree with me on a wage of one denarius? Take your pay, and go. I choose to give this last fellow the same amount I am giving you. Is it not lawful for me to do whatever I please with what belongs to me? Why be offended because I am generous?'

"So the last will be first, and the first last."

MATTHEW 20:1-16

10 But when the first came, they supposed that they should have received more; and they likewise received every man a penny.

11 And when they had received *it,* they murmured against the goodman of the house.

12 Saying, These last have wrought *but* one hour, and thou hast made them equal unto us, which have borne the burden and heat of the day.

13 But he answered one of them, and said, Friend, I do thee no wrong: didst not thou agree with me for a penny?

14 Take *that* thine *is,* and go thy way: I will give unto this last, even as unto thee.

15 Is it not lawful for me to do what I will with mine own? Is thine eye evil, because I am good?

16 So the last shall be first, and the first last: for many be called, but few chosen.

Death and Resurrection

Luke 18:31-34

Then Jesus took the twelve aside and said to them,

"Behold, we are going up to Jerusalem, and all the things written by the prophets concerning the Son of Man will be accomplished. For he will be handed over to the Gentiles, and will be mocked and insulted and spit upon. And after they have scourged him, they will kill him; but on the third day, he will rise again."

But they did not understand any of these things. They were perplexed by his words and did not know what he meant.

MATTHEW 20:17-19

17 And Jesus going up to Jerusalem took the twelve disciples apart in the way, and said unto them,

18 Behold, we go up to Jerusalem; and the Son of man shall be betrayed unto the chief priests and unto the scribes, and they shall condemn him to death,

19 And shall deliver him to the Gentiles to mock, and to scourge, and to crucify *him:* and the third day he shall rise again.

MARK 10:32-34

32 And they were in the way going up to Jerusalem; and Jesus went before them: and they were amazed; and as they followed, they were afraid. And he took again the twelve, and began to tell them what things should happen unto him,

33 *Saying,* Behold, we go up to Jerusalem; and the Son of man shall be delivered unto the chief priests, and unto the scribes; and they shall condemn him to death, and shall deliver him to the Gentiles:

LUKE 18:31-34

31 Then he took *unto him* the twelve, and said unto them, Behold, we go up to Jerusalem, and all things that are written by the prophets concerning the Son of man shall be accomplished.

32 For he shall be delivered unto the Gentiles, and shall be mocked, and spitefully entreated, and spitted on:

33 And they shall scourge *him,* and put him to death; and the third day he shall rise again.

34 And they understood none

A Vineyard. *In telling the story about workers in a vineyard Jesus was using an illustration very well understood by His hearers. Vineyards abound throughout the Holy Land.*

Death and Resurrection (continued)

MARK 10:32-34

34 And they shall mock him, and shall scourge him, and shall spit upon him, and shall kill him; and the third day he shall rise again.

LUKE 18:31-34

of these things: and this saying was hid from them, neither knew they the things which were spoken.

An Ambitious Request

Matthew 20:20-28

Then the mother of the sons of Zebedee came to Jesus with her sons and knelt before him to ask a favor.

"What do you wish?" asked Jesus.

"Please say that these my two sons may sit, one at your right hand and one at your left, in your kingdom," she replied.

But Jesus answered, "You do not know what you are asking. Can you drink the cup that I am about to drink?"

"We can," they replied.

"You will indeed drink my cup," said Jesus, "but to sit at my right hand and at my left is not mine to grant; it is for those for whom it has been prepared by my Father."

Now when the ten heard about their request, they were indignant toward the two brothers. But Jesus called them to him and said,

"You know that the rulers of the Gentiles lord it over them, and their great men wield authority over them. It is not to be that way among you. Whoever would become great among you must be your servant, and whoever would have first place among you must be your slave, even as the Son of Man did not come to be served, but to serve, and to give his life a ransom for many."

MATTHEW 20:20-28

20 Then came to him the mother of Zebedee's children with her sons, worshipping *him*, and desiring a certain thing of him.

21 And he said unto her, What wilt thou? She saith unto him, Grant that these my two sons may sit, the one on thy right hand, and the other on the left, in thy kingdom.

22 But Jesus answered and said, Ye know not what ye ask. Are ye able to drink of the cup that I shall drink of, and to be baptized with the baptism that I am baptized with? They say unto him, We are able.

23 And he saith unto them, Ye shall drink indeed of my cup, and be baptized with the baptism that I am baptized with: but to sit on my right hand, and on my left, is not mine to give, but *it shall be given to them* for whom it is prepared of my Father.

24 And when the ten heard *it*, they were moved with indignation against the two brethren.

25 But Jesus called them *unto him*, and said, Ye know that the princes of the Gentiles exercise

MARK 10:35-45

35 And James and John, the sons of Zebedee, come unto him, saying, Master, we would that thou shouldest do for us whatsoever we shall desire.

36 And he said unto them, What would ye that I should do for you?

37 They said unto him, Grant unto us that we may sit, one on thy right hand, and the other on thy left hand, in thy glory.

38 But Jesus said unto them, Ye know not what ye ask: can ye drink of the cup that I drink of? and be baptized with the baptism that I am baptized with?

39 And they said unto him, We can. And Jesus said unto them, Ye shall indeed drink of the cup that I drink of; and with the baptism that I am baptized withal shall ye be baptized:

40 But to sit on my right hand and on my left hand is not mine to give; but *it shall be given to them* for whom it is prepared.

41 And when the ten heard *it*, they began to be much displeased with James and John.

42 But Jesus called them *to him*, and saith unto

246

Statue of Jerome. *From A.D. 385 to 420 he lived in Bethlehem, devoting himself to the translation of the Scriptures, the Vulgate Version. He kept a skull before him to remind himself of the brevity of time.*

An Ambitious Request (continued)

dominion over them, and they that are great exercise authority upon them.

26 But it shall be not so among you: but whosoever will be great among you, let him be your minister;

27 And whosoever will be chief among you, let him be your servant:

28 Even as the Son of man came not to be ministered unto, but to minister, and to give his life a ransom for many.

them, Ye know that they which are accounted to rule over the Gentiles exercise lordship over them; and their great ones exercise authority upon them.

43 But so shall it not be among you: but whosoever will be great among you, shall be your minister:

44 And whosoever of you will be the chiefest, shall be servant of all.

45 For even the Son of man came not to be ministered unto, but to minister, and to give his life a ransom for many.

A Blind Man Healed

Luke 18:35-43

And it came to pass as Jesus drew near to Jericho, a certain blind man was sitting by the roadside begging. Hearing a crowd passing by, he asked what was going on.

"Jesus of Nazareth is passing by," they told him.

"Jesus, Son of David, have mercy on me!" cried the blind man.

Then those in front of him told him to be quiet, but he shouted all the more, "Son of David, have mercy on me!"

Jesus stopped and ordered the man to be brought to him, and when he came near, Jesus asked, "What do you want me to do for you?"

"Lord, let me recover my sight!" he replied.

"Your sight is restored," said Jesus, "your faith has healed you."

And immediately the man regained his sight, and he began to follow Jesus, praising God. And when they had seen this, all the people gave praise to God.

29 And as they departed from Jericho, a great multitude followed him.

30 And, behold, two blind men sitting by the wayside, when they heard that Jesus passed by, cried out, saying, Have mercy on us, O Lord, *thou* Son of David.

31 And the multitude rebuked them, because they should hold their peace: but they cried the more, saying, Have mercy on us, O Lord, *thou* Son of David.

32 And Jesus stood still, and called them, and said, What will ye that I shall do unto you?

33 They say unto him, Lord, that our eyes may be opened.

46 And they came to Jericho: and as he went out of Jericho with his disciples and a great number of people, blind Bartimeus, the son of Timeus, sat by the highway side begging.

47 And when he heard that it was Jesus of Nazareth, he began to cry out, and say, Jesus, *thou* Son of David, have mercy on me.

48 And many charged him that he should hold his peace: but he cried the more a great deal, *Thou* Son of David, have mercy on me.

49 And Jesus stood still, and commanded him to be called. And they call the blind man, saying unto him, Be of good comfort,

35 And it came to pass, that as he was come nigh unto Jericho, a certain blind man sat by the wayside begging:

36 And hearing the multitude pass by, he asked what it meant.

37 And they told him, that Jesus of Nazareth passeth by.

38 And he cried, saying, Jesus, *thou* Son of David, have mercy on me.

39 And they which went before rebuked him, that he should hold his peace: but he cried so much the more, *Thou* Son of David, have mercy on me.

40 And Jesus stood, and commanded him to be brought unto

A Blind Man Healed (continued)

34 So Jesus had compassion *on them,* and touched their eyes: and immediately their eyes received sight, and they followed him.

The Dead Sea. *The remarkable body of water is the lowest spot on earth, nearly 1300 feet below sea level. Because of its 27% mineral content, no fish can live in it. Its minerals are valuable.*

rise; he calleth thee.

50 And he, casting away his garment, rose, and came to Jesus.

51 And Jesus answered and said unto him, What wilt thou that I should do unto thee? The blind man said unto him, Lord, that I might receive my sight.

52 And Jesus said unto him, Go thy way; thy faith hath made thee whole. And immediately he received his sight, and followed Jesus in the way.

him: and when he was come near, he asked him,

41 Saying, What wilt thou that I shall do unto thee? And he said, Lord, that I may receive my sight.

42 And Jesus said unto him, Receive thy sight: thy faith hath saved thee.

43 And immediately he received his sight, and followed him, glorifying God: and all the people, when they saw *it,* gave praise unto God.

Sycamore Tree. *The story of how Zac-chaeus overcame his height handicap always strikes a responsive chord in our hearts. The low-lying branches made it easy for him to get a "front row" view.*

250

Zacchaeus Becomes a Follower

Luke 19:1-10

Jesus entered Jericho and was passing through, and a man named Zacchaeus—chief tax collector, and wealthy—was trying to get a good look at him, but could not do so because of the crowd, for he was a man of short stature. And he ran on ahead and climbed up into a sycamore tree so that he might see Jesus, for he was to pass that way. When Jesus came to the place, he looked up and said,

"Zacchaeus, hurry and come down, for I must stay at your house today."

Then Zacchaeus came down at once and welcomed Jesus joyfully.

But when the people saw what happened, they all grumbled, saying, "Now he has gone to be the guest of a man who is a sinner!"

Then Zacchaeus stood before the Lord and said, "Behold, Lord, I am going to give half of my possessions to the poor, and if I have taken anything from anyone unjustly, I will return it fourfold."

"Salvation has come to this house today," said Jesus, "for this man, too, is a son of Abraham. For the Son of Man came to seek and to save the lost."

LUKE 19:1-10

1 And *Jesus* entered and passed through Jericho.

2 And, behold, *there was* a man named Zaccheus, which was the chief among the publicans, and he was rich.

3 And he sought to see Jesus who he was; and could not for the press, because he was little of stature.

4 And he ran before, and climbed up into a sycamore tree to see him; for he was to pass that *way.*

5 And when Jesus came to the place, he looked up, and saw him, and said unto him, Zaccheus, make haste, and come down; for to-day I must abide at thy house.

6 And he made haste, and came down, and received him joyfully.

7 And when they saw *it,* they all murmured, saying, That he was gone to be guest with a man that is a sinner.

8 And Zaccheus stood, and said unto the Lord; Behold, Lord, the half of my goods I give to the poor; and if I have taken any thing from any man by false accusation, I restore *him* fourfold.

9 And Jesus said unto him, This day is salvation come to this house, forasmuch as he also is a son of Abraham.

10 For the Son of man is come to seek and to save that which was lost.

Jericho is about 20 miles distant from Jerusalem, but because of the steep ascent, it would have taken two days to make the journey.

Parable of the Pounds

Luke 19:11-28

And as they were listening to these things, Jesus told a parable, because he was nearing Jerusalem and they supposed that the kingdom of God was to appear immediately. He said therefore,

"A certain nobleman went into a far country to receive for himself a kingdom and to return. And he called ten of his servants and gave them each a mina and said to them, 'Use this money to trade with until I come back.'

"But the nobleman's citizens hated him, and after he left, they sent a delegation to say, 'We do not want this man to be our king.'

"And when he had received his kingdom, he returned and called for the servants to whom he had given the money, so that he might know what they had gained by trading. And the first one came and said, 'Lord, your mina has made ten minas.' And the king said to him, 'Well done, good servant! Because you have been faithful in a little matter, you shall have authority over ten cities.' And the second servant came and said, 'Lord, your mina has made five minas.' And the king said to him, 'You shall be over five cities.' Then another servant came and said, 'Lord, here is your mina; I have kept it laid away in a handkerchief. For I was afraid of you, because you are a hard man; you take up what you did not lay down, and reap what you did not sow.'

" 'You wicked servant,' said the king, 'I will judge you by your own words. You say that I am a hard man, taking up what I did not lay down and reaping what I did not sow. Then why did you not put my money in the bank, so that I could have withdrawn it with interest when I came?' Then the king said to those standing nearby, 'Take the mina from him and give it to him who has ten minas.'

" 'But Lord,' they said, 'he has ten minas already!'

" 'I say to you,' replied the king, 'to everyone who acquires, more will be given; but even what he has will be taken away from him who does not acquire. And as for these enemies of mine who did not want me to be their king, bring them here and slay them before me.' "

And having said these things, he journeyed onward toward Jerusalem.

LUKE 19:11-28

11 And as they heard these things, he added and spake a parable, because he was nigh to Jerusalem, and because they thought that the kingdom of God should immediately appear.

12 He said therefore, A certain nobleman went into a far country to receive for himself a kingdom, and to return.

13 And he called his ten servants, and delivered them ten pounds, and said unto them, Occupy till I come.

14 But his citizens hated him, and sent a message after him, saying, We will not have this *man* to reign over us.

15 And it came to pass, that when he was returned, having received the kingdom, then he commanded these servants to be called unto him, to whom he had given the money, that he might know how much every man had gained by trading.

16 Then came the first, saying, Lord, thy pound hath gained ten pounds.

17 And he said unto him, Well, thou good servant: because thou hast been faithful in a very little, have thou authority over ten cities.

18 And the second came, saying, Lord, thy pound hath gained five pounds.

19 And he said likewise to him, Be thou also over five cities.

20 And another came, saying, Lord, behold, *here is* thy pound, which I have kept laid up in a napkin:

21 For I feared thee, because thou art an austere man: thou takest up that thou layedst not down, and reapest that thou didst not sow.

22 And he saith unto him, Out of thine own mouth will I judge thee, *thou* wicked servant. Thou knewest that I was an austere man, taking up that I laid not down, and reaping that I did not sow:

Parable of the Pounds (continued)

23 Wherefore then gavest not thou my money into the bank, that at my coming I might have required mine own with usury?

24 And he said unto them that stood by, Take from him the pound, and give *it* to him that hath ten pounds.

25 (And they said unto him, Lord, he hath ten pounds.)

26 For I say unto you, That unto every one which hath shall be given; and from him that hath not, even that he hath shall be taken away from him.

27 But those mine enemies, which would not that I should reign over them, bring hither, and slay *them* before me.

28 And when he had thus spoken, he went before, ascending up to Jerusalem.

Anticipation of Jesus' Arrival

John 11:55-57

Now the Passover of the Jews was near, and many went up from the country to Jerusalem to purify themselves before the Passover. And they kept watching for Jesus and saying one to another as they stood around in the temple, ''What do you think? Will he dare to come to the feast?''

Now the chief priests and the Pharisees had given orders that if any man knew where Jesus was, he should tell them, so that they might arrest him.

JOHN 11:55-57

55 And the Jews' passover was nigh at hand: and many went out of the country up to Jerusalem before the passover, to purify themselves.

56 Then sought they for Jesus, and spake among themselves, as they stood in the temple, What think ye, that he will not come to the feast?

57 Now both the chief priests and the Pharisees had given a commandment, that, if any man knew where he were, he should show *it*, that they might take him.

View of Jerusalem. This present-day photo helps in understanding how Jerusalem appeared to Jesus shortly after He left Bethany behind and came within sight of the Holy City.

Anointing of Jesus

John 12:1-11

Now six days before the Passover, Jesus came to Bethany where Lazarus was, whom he raised from the dead, and they prepared a supper for him there. Martha served, and Lazarus was one of those who reclined at the table with Jesus. And Mary took a pound of perfume of pure spikenard, very costly, and anointed the feet of Jesus and wiped his feet with her hair, and the house was filled with the fragrance of the perfume.

But one of the disciples, Judas Iscariot (who was planning to betray Jesus), said, "Why wasn't this perfume sold for three hundred denarii and the money given to the poor?"

(This he said, not because he cared about the poor, but because he was a thief and, having charge of the purse, was in the habit of taking money from it.)

But Jesus said, "Let her alone, let her do this in preparation for my burial. For you have the poor with you always, but you will not always have me."

Now when the Jews learned that Jesus was there, they came in great numbers, not only because of Jesus, but also to see Lazarus whom he had raised from the dead. The chief priests therefore agreed among themselves to put Lazarus to death too, for because of him, many of the Jews were turning away from them and believing in Jesus.

MATTHEW 26:6-13	MARK 14:3-9	JOHN 12:1-11
6 Now when Jesus was in Bethany, in the house of Simon the leper,	3 And being in Bethany, in the house of Simon the leper, as he sat at meat, there came a woman having an alabaster box of ointment of spikenard very precious; and she brake the box, and poured *it* on his head.	1 Then Jesus six days before the passover came to Bethany, where Lazarus was which had been dead, whom he raised from the dead.
7 There came unto him a woman having an alabaster box of very precious ointment, and poured it on his head, as he sat at meat.		2 There they made him a supper; and Martha served: but Lazarus was one of them that sat at the table with him.
		3 Then took Mary a pound of ointment of spikenard, very costly, and anointed the feet of Jesus, and wiped his feet with her hair: and the

Jordan River at Its Source. The only major river of Israel, and not very large, begins its southward journey, about 1,700 feet above sea level, fed by the melting snows of Mount Hermon.

As Jesus left Jericho and the Jordan Valley behind, He would climb the steep Jericho Road, come to Bethany, two miles away from Jerusalem, and perhaps stop there for lodging.

Anointing of Jesus (continued)

MATTHEW 26:6-13

8 But when his disciples saw *it,* they had indignation, saying, To what purpose *is* this waste?

9 For this ointment might have been sold for much, and given to the poor.

10 When Jesus understood *it,* he said unto them, Why trouble ye the woman? for she hath wrought a good work upon me.

11 For ye have the poor always with you; but me ye have not always.

12 For in that she hath poured this ointment on my body, she did *it* for my burial.

13 Verily I say unto you, Wheresoever this gospel shall be preached in the whole world, *there* shall also this, that this woman hath done, be told for a memorial of her.

MARK 14:3-9

4 And there were some that had indignation within themselves, and said, Why was this waste of the ointment made?

5 For it might have been sold for more than three hundred pence, and have been given to the poor. And they murmured against her.

6 And Jesus said, Let her alone; why trouble ye her? she hath wrought a good work on me.

7 For ye have the poor with you always, and whensoever ye will ye may do them good: but me ye have not always.

8 She hath done what she could: she is come aforehand to anoint my body to the burying.

9 Verily I say unto you, Wheresoever this gospel shall be preached throughout the whole world, *this* also that she hath done shall be spoken of for a memorial of her.

JOHN 12:2-11

house was filled with the odor of the ointment.

4 Then saith one of his disciples, Judas Iscariot, Simon's *son,* which should betray him,

5 Why was not this ointment sold for three hundred pence, and given to the poor?

6 This he said, not that he cared for the poor; but because he was a thief, and had the bag, and bare what was put therein.

7 Then said Jesus, Let her alone: against the day of my burying hath she kept this.

8 For the poor always ye have with you; but me ye have not always.

9 Much people of the Jews therefore knew that he was there: and they came not for Jesus' sake only, but that they might see Lazarus also, whom he had raised from the dead.

10 But the chief priests consulted that they might put Lazarus also to death;

11 Because that by reason of him many of the Jews went away, and believed on Jesus.

Masada. *A mountain fortress, a short distance west of lower part of Dead Sea. After the A.D. 70 destruction of Jerusalem, Jews held out until A.D. 73, then committed mass suicide rather than surrender.*

Jesus Acclaimed by the Crowds

Matthew 21:1-11, Luke 19:29-44, John 12:19, Mark 11:11

Now when they drew near to Jerusalem and came to Bethphage and the Mount of Olives, Jesus sent two disciples, saying, "Go into the village just ahead, and you will immediately find an ass tied, and a colt with her. Untie them and bring them to me. If anyone says anything to you, just say, 'The Lord has need of them,' and he will send them at once."

Now all this happened in fulfillment of the word of the prophet,

Tell the daughter of Zion,

Behold, your king is coming to you—

meek, and riding upon an ass,

and upon a colt, the foal of an ass.

Then the disciples went and did as Jesus had instructed them, and brought the ass and the colt and spread their cloaks on them, and Jesus sat on them. And a great crowd spread their cloaks on the road, and others cut branches from the trees and spread them on the road. And marching along in front of Jesus and following along behind him, the crowds shouted, "Hosanna to the Son of David! Blessed is he who comes in the name of the Lord! Hosanna in the highest!"

Then some of the Pharisees in the crowd said to Jesus, "Master, rebuke your disciples!"

"I say to you," replied Jesus, "if these were to hold their peace, the very stones themselves would shout."

Then the Pharisees said among themselves, "You see? There is nothing you can do. Look! the whole world is running after him."

Now when Jesus drew near and beheld the city, he began to weep over it, saying, "If only you knew, today, the things on which peace depends! But now they are hidden from your sight. For the days are coming when your enemies will cast a rampart about you and surround you on every side. And they will dash you and your children to the ground, and will not leave in you one stone upon another, because you did not recognize the time of your visitation."

And when he entered Jerusalem, the whole city was stirred, saying, "Who is this?"

"This is the prophet Jesus, from Nazareth of Galilee," the crowds replied.

And Jesus entered the temple. And when he had observed everything, he went out to Bethany with the twelve, for it was already late in the day.

The Triumphal Entry. It was a time of cheers and tears. According to John, a great reason for the joyous welcome was the raising of Lazarus. However, Jesus wept over Jerusalem because He knew His own people would reject Him, and that some years later the city would be completely destroyed.

257

Jesus Acclaimed by the Crowds (continued)

MATTHEW 21:1-11

1 And when they drew nigh unto Jerusalem, and were come to Bethphage, unto the mount of Olives, then sent Jesus two disciples,

2 Saying unto them, Go into the village over against you, and straightway ye shall find an ass tied, and a colt with her: loose *them,* and bring *them* unto me.

3 And if any *man* say aught unto you, ye shall say, The Lord hath need of them; and straightway he will send them.

4 All this was done, that it might be fulfilled which was spoken by the prophet, saying,

5 Tell ye the daughter of Zion, Behold, thy King cometh unto thee, meek, and sitting upon an ass, and a colt the foal of an ass.

6 And the disciples went, and did as Jesus commanded them,

7 And brought the ass, and the colt, and put on them their clothes, and they set *him* thereon.

8 And a very great multitude spread their garments in the way; others cut down branches from the trees, and strewed *them* in the way.

9 And the multitudes that went before, and that followed, cried, saying, Hosanna to the Son of David: Blessed *is* he that cometh in the name of the Lord; Hosanna in the highest.

10 And when he was come into Jerusalem, all the city was moved, saying, Who is this?

11 And the multitude said, This is Jesus the prophet of Nazareth of Galilee.

MARK 11:1-11

1 And when they came nigh to Jerusalem, unto Bethphage and Bethany, at the mount of Olives, he sendeth forth two of his disciples,

2 And saith unto them, Go your way into the village over against you: and as soon as ye be entered into it, ye shall find a colt tied, whereon never man sat; loose him, and bring *him.*

3 And if any man say unto you, Why do ye this? say ye that the Lord hath need of him; and straightway he will send him hither.

4 And they went their way, and found the colt tied by the door without in a place where two ways met; and they loose him.

5 And certain of them that stood there said unto them, What do ye, loosing the colt?

6 And they said unto them even as Jesus had commanded: and they let them go.

7 And they brought the colt to Jesus, and cast their garments on him; and he sat upon him.

8 And many spread their garments in the way; and others cut down branches off the trees, and strewed *them* in the way.

9 And they that went before, and they that followed, cried, saying, Hosanna; Blessed *is* he that cometh in the name of the Lord:

10 Blessed *be* the kingdom of our father David, that cometh in the name of the Lord: Hosanna in the highest.

11 And Jesus entered into Jerusalem, and into the temple: and when he had looked round about upon all things, and now the eventide was come, he went out unto Bethany with the twelve.

Jesus Acclaimed by the Crowds (continued)

29 And it came to pass, when he was come nigh to Bethphage and Bethany, at the mount called *the mount* of Olives, he sent two of his disciples,

30 Saying, Go ye into the village over against *you;* in the which at your entering ye shall find a colt tied, whereon yet never man sat: loose him, and bring *him hither.*

31 And if any man ask you, Why do ye loose *him?* thus shall ye say unto him, Because the Lord hath need of him.

32 And they that were sent went their way, and found even as he had said unto them.

33 And as they were loosing the colt, the owners thereof said unto them, Why loose ye the colt?

34 And they said, The Lord hath need of him.

35 And they brought him to Jesus: and they cast their garments upon the colt, and they set Jesus thereon.

36 And as he went, they spread their clothes in the way.

37 And when he was come nigh, even now at the descent of the mount of Olives, the whole multitude of the disciples began to rejoice and praise God with a loud voice for all the mighty works that they had seen;

38 Saying, Blessed *be* the King that cometh in the name of the Lord: peace in heaven, and glory in the highest.

39 And some of the Pharisees from among the multitude said unto him, Master, rebuke thy disciples.

40 And he answered and said unto them, I tell you that, if these should hold their peace, the stones would immediately cry out.

41 And when he was come near, he beheld the city, and wept over it,

42 Saying, If thou hadst known, even thou, at least in this thy day, the things *which belong* unto thy peace! but now they are hid from thine eyes.

43 For the days shall come upon thee, that thine enemies shall cast a trench about thee, and compass thee round, and keep thee in on every side,

44 And shall lay thee even with the ground, and thy children within thee; and they shall not leave in thee one stone upon another; because thou knewest not the time of thy visitation.

12 On the next day much people that were come to the feast, when they heard that Jesus was coming to Jerusalem,

13 Took branches of palm trees, and went forth to meet him, and cried. Hosanna: Blessed *is* the King of Israel that cometh in the name of the Lord.

14 And Jesus, when he had found a young ass, sat thereon; as it is written,

15 Fear not, daughter of Sion: behold, thy King cometh, sitting on an ass's colt.

16 These things understood not his disciples at the first: but when Jesus was glorified, then remembered they that these things were written of him, and *that* they had done these things unto him.

17 The people therefore that was with him when he called Lazarus out of his grave, and raised him from the dead bare record.

18 For this cause the people also met him, for that they heard that he had done this miracle.

19 The Pharisees therefore said among themselves, Perceive ye how ye prevail nothing? behold, the world is gone after him.

In His Triumphal Entry Jesus came over the Mount of Olives, crossed the narrow Kidron Valley, and entered the city through the Eastern Gate. Directly ahead of Him then was the "Beautiful Gate" of the temple.

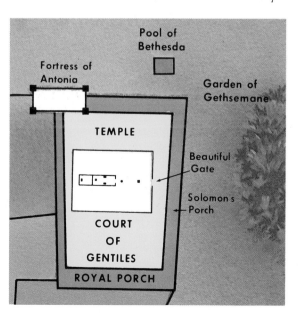

Golden Gate. *Sometimes called the Eastern Gate. The scene of the Triumphal Entry, riding over the palm leaf-covered road.*

Cursing the Fig Tree

Mark 11:12-14

On the following day, when they came from Bethany, Jesus was hungry, and seeing in the distance a fig tree already in leaf, he went to see if he could find any fruit on it. But when he came to it, he found nothing but leaves, for it was not the season for figs. And he said to it, "May no one ever eat fruit of you again." And his disciples heard it.

MATTHEW 21:18-19 √

18 Now in the morning, as he returned into the city, he hungered.

19 And when he saw a fig tree in the way, he came to it, and found nothing thereon, but leaves only, and said unto it, Let no fruit grow on thee henceforward for ever. And presently the fig tree withered away.

MARK 11:12-14 √

12 And on the morrow, when they were come from Bethany, he was hungry:

13 And seeing a fig tree afar off having leaves, he came, if haply he might find any thing thereon: and when he came to it, he found nothing but leaves; for the time of figs was not *yet*.

14 And Jesus answered and said unto it, No man eat fruit of thee hereafter for ever. And his disciples heard *it*.

The Temple Cleansed Again

Matthew 21:12-17

And Jesus entered the temple and drove out all who sold and bought in the temple, and overturned the tables of the money-changers and the benches of those who sold doves. And he said to them, "It is written, 'My house shall be called a house of prayer,' but you have made it a den of robbers!"

And the blind and the lame came to him in the temple, and he healed them. But when the chief priests and the scribes saw the wonderful things he was doing and heard the children shouting in the temple, "Hosanna to the Son of David!" they were filled with indignation and said to him, "Do you hear what they are saying?"

"Yes!" replied Jesus. "Have you never read, 'Out of the mouth of babes and sucklings you have brought forth perfect praise'?"

And Jesus left them, and went out from the city to Bethany and lodged there.

MATTHEW 21:12-17 √

12 And Jesus went into the temple of God, and cast out all them that sold and bought in the temple, and overthrew the tables of the money changers, and the seats of them that sold doves,

13 And said unto them, It is written, My house shall be called the house of prayer; but ye have

MARK 11:15-19 √

15 And they come to Jerusalem: and Jesus went into the temple, and began to cast out them that sold and bought in the temple, and overthrew the tables of the money changers, and the seats of them that sold doves;

16 And would not suffer that any man should carry *any* vessel through the temple.

LUKE 19:45-48 √

45 And he went into the temple, and began to cast out them that sold therein, and them that bought;

46 Saying unto them, It is written, My house is the house of prayer; but ye have made it a den of thieves.

47 And he taught daily in the temple. But the chief priests and

The Temple Cleansed Again (continued)

made it a den of thieves.

14 And the blind and the lame came to him in the temple; and he healed them.

15 And when the chief priests and scribes saw the wonderful things that he did, and the children crying in the temple, and saying, Hosanna to the Son of David; they were sore displeased,

16 And said unto him, Hearest thou what these say? And Jesus saith unto them, Yea; have ye never read, Out of the mouth of babes and sucklings thou hast perfected praise?

17 And he left them, and went out of the city into Bethany; and he lodged there.

17 And he taught, saying unto them, Is it not written, My house shall be called of all nations the house of prayer? but ye have made it a den of thieves.

18 And the scribes and chief priests heard *it,* and sought how they might destroy him: for they feared him, because all the people was astonished at his doctrine.

19 And when even was come, he went out of the city.

the scribes and the chief of the people sought to destroy him,

48 And could not find what they might do: for all the people were very attentive to hear him.

Jesus and the Money Changers.
Jesus was incensed because the temple, which was to be a place to worship God, had become a mere marketplace. His description of it as a "den of thieves" implies there was also much dishonesty.

The Fig Tree Found Withered

Valley of Jezreel. The stage for the climactic battle of Armageddon, it lives up to the meaning of its name, "fat valley." Its rich soil produces up to four crops a year.

Mark 11:20-26

Now as they passed by in the morning, they found the fig tree dried up from the roots. And Peter, remembering, said to Jesus, "Rabbi, look! The fig tree which you cursed has withered away."

Then Jesus, answering, said to them, "Have faith in God. I tell you truly, whoever says to this mountain, 'Be lifted up and cast into the sea!' and does not doubt in his heart, but has faith to believe that what he says will come to pass, it shall be done for him. Therefore I say to you, whatever you ask in prayer, believe that you have received it, and it will be yours. And whenever you stand praying, if you have anything against anyone, forgive him, that your Father in heaven may also forgive you your trespasses."

MATTHEW 21:20-22 ✓

20 And when the disciples saw *it,* they marveled, saying, How soon is the fig tree withered away!

21 Jesus answered and said unto them, Verily I say unto you, If ye have faith, and doubt not, ye shall not only do this *which is done* to the fig tree, but also if ye shall say unto this mountain, Be thou removed, and be thou cast into the sea; it shall be done.

22 And all things, whatsoever ye shall ask in prayer, believing, ye shall receive.

MARK 11:20-26 ✓

20 And in the morning, as they passed by, they saw the fig tree dried up from the roots.

21 And Peter calling to remembrance saith unto him, Master, behold, the fig tree which thou cursedst is withered away.

22 And Jesus answering saith unto them, Have faith in God.

23 For verily I say unto you, That whosoever shall say unto this mountain, Be thou removed, and be thou cast into the sea; and shall not doubt in his heart, but shall believe that those things which he saith shall come to pass; he shall have whatsoever he saith.

24 Therefore I say unto you, What things soever ye desire, when ye pray, believe that ye receive *them,* and ye shall have *them.*

25 And when ye stand praying, forgive, if ye have aught against any; that your Father also which is in heaven may forgive you your trespasses.

26 But if ye do not forgive, neither will your Father which is in heaven forgive your trespasses.

Jesus' Authority Questioned

Matthew 21:23-27

Now when Jesus had entered the temple, the chief priests and the elders of the people came to him as he was teaching and said, "By what authority are you doing these things, and who gave you that authority?"

"I will also ask you one question," replied Jesus, "and if you answer me, then I will tell you by what authority I do these things. John's baptism—was it from heaven, or merely of human origin?"

Then they began to reason among themselves, saying, "If we say, 'From heaven,' he will say to us, 'Then why did you not believe him?' But if we say, 'It was merely of human origin,' we will be in trouble with the people, for they all regard John as a prophet."

So they answered Jesus, "We do not know."

"Then I will not tell you by what authority I do these things," replied Jesus.

MATTHEW 21:23-27

23 And when he was come into the temple, the chief priests and the elders of the people came unto him as he was teaching, and said, By what authority doest thou these things? and who gave thee this authority?

24 And Jesus answered and said unto them, I also will ask you one thing, which if ye tell me, I in like wise will tell you by what authority I do these things.

25 The baptism of John, whence was it? from heaven, or of men? And they reasoned with themselves, saying, If we shall say, From heaven; he will say unto us, Why did ye not then believe him?

26 But if we shall say, Of men; we fear the people; for all hold John as a prophet.

27 And they answered Jesus, and said, We cannot tell. And he said unto them, Neither tell I you by what authority I do these things.

MARK 11:27-33

27 And they come again to Jerusalem: and as he was walking in the temple, there come to him the chief priests, and the scribes, and the elders,

28 And say unto him, By what authority doest thou these things? and who gave thee this authority to do these things?

29 And Jesus answered and said unto them, I will also ask of you one question, and answer me, and I will tell you by what authority I do these things.

30 The baptism of John, was it from heaven, or of men? answer me.

31 And they reasoned with themselves, saying, If we shall say, From heaven; he will say, Why then did ye not believe him?

32 But if we shall say, Of men; they feared the people: for all *men* counted John, that he was a prophet indeed.

33 And they answered and said unto Jesus, We cannot tell. And Jesus answering saith unto them, Neither do I tell you by what authority I do these things.

LUKE 20:1-8

1 And it came to pass, *that* on one of those days, as he taught the people in the temple, and preached the gospel, the chief priests and the scribes came upon *him* with the elders,

2 And spake unto him, saying, Tell us, by what authority doest thou these things? or who is he that gave thee this authority?

3 And he answered and said unto them, I will also ask you one thing; and answer me:

4 The baptism of John, was it from heaven, or of men?

5 And they reasoned with themselves, saying, If we shall say, From heaven; he will say, Why then believed ye him not?

6 But and if we say, Of men; all the people will stone us: for they be persuaded that John was a prophet.

7 And they answered, that they could not tell whence *it was.*

8 And Jesus said unto them, Neither tell I you by what authority I do these things.

Menorah and Knesset.
The candlestick (left) and the Knesset (below) represent the highest authority in Israel, the Mosaic Law and the political heart of Israel, where its Parliament meets.

265

Fate of Those Who Oppose Christ

Matthew 21:28-22:14

"But what do you think about this? A man had two sons, and he went to the first one and said, 'Son, go work in the vineyard today.' And the son answered, 'I will, sir,' But he failed to go. And he went to the second son and said the same thing, and the son answered, 'I will not.' But afterward, he repented and went. Which of the two did the will of the father?"

"The second one," they replied.

"I tell you truly," said Jesus, "the tax collectors and harlots enter the kingdom of God ahead of you. For John came to you preaching righteousness, and you did not believe him, but the tax collectors and harlots did. And even after seeing that, you did not repent and believe him."

"Listen to another parable," said Jesus. "There was a landowner who planted a vineyard, built a fence around it, dug a wine press in it, and built a tower. Then he let it out to tenants and went away to another country. And when the harvest season drew near, he sent his servants to the tenants to collect his share of the crop. But the tenants seized his servants and beat one, killed another, and stoned another. Then the landowner sent some other servants, more than the first time, but the tenants treated them the same way. Finally, the landowner sent his son, saying, 'They will respect my son.' But when the tenants saw the son, they said to themselves, 'This is the heir! Come, let us kill him and take over his inheritance.' And they seized him and cast him out of the vineyard and killed him. Now when the owner of the vineyard comes, what will he do to those tenants?"

"He will put those scoundrels to death without mercy," they replied, "and will rent out the vineyard to other tenants who will give him his share of the crop every season."

Jesus said to them, "Have you never read in the scriptures, 'The stone which the builders rejected has become the chief cornerstone; this was the Lord's doing, and it is marvelous in our eyes'? Therefore I say to you, the kingdom of God will be taken from you and be given to a people who will produce the fruits of it. And whoever falls on this stone will be broken, and on whomever it falls, it will grind him to powder."

Now when the chief priests and the Pharisees heard his parables, they recognized that he was referring to them. And they wanted to arrest him, but they were afraid of the people, because they regarded him as a prophet.

Then Jesus spoke to them again in a parable, saying,

"The kingdom of heaven is like a king who gave a wedding feast for his son. He sent his servants to summon those who had been invited to the wedding feast, but they refused to come. Again, he sent out other servants, saying, 'Tell those who have been invited, "Behold, I have prepared my feast; my oxen and the fat cattle have been killed, and everything is ready. Come on to the wedding feast!"' But they made light of the invitation and went their ways—one to his farm, and another to his business; and the rest of them seized the king's servants and shamefully mistreated them, and killed them.

"Then the king was angry, and he sent his troops and killed those murderers and burned their city. Then he said to his servants, 'The wedding feast is ready, but those who were invited were not worthy. Go out therefore into the highways and invite everyone you find to come to the wedding feast.' Then those servants went out into the highways and gathered together everyone they could find, both bad and good, and the wedding feast was supplied with guests.

"But when the king came in to see the guests, he saw a man among them who was not dressed in a wedding garment. And he said to him, 'Friend, how did you get in here without a wedding garment?' And the man had nothing to say. Then the king said to the servants, 'Bind his hands and feet and cast him into the darkness outside. That is the place for weeping and gnashing of teeth.'

"For many are called, but few are chosen."

Fate of Those Who Oppose Christ (continued)

28 But what think ye? A *certain* man had two sons; and he came to the first, and said, Son, go work today in my vineyard.

29 He answered and said, I will not; but afterward he repented, and went.

30 And he came to the second, and said likewise. And he answered and said, I *go, sir;* and went not.

31 Whether of them twain did the will of *his* father? They say unto him, The first. Jesus saith unto them, Verily I say unto you, That the publicans and the harlots go into the kingdom of God before you.

32 For John came unto you in the way of righteousness, and ye believed him not; but the publicans and the harlots believed him: and ye, when ye had seen *it,* repented not afterward, that ye might believe him.

33 Hear another parable: There was a certain householder, which planted a vineyard, and hedged it round about, and digged a winepress in it, and built a tower, and let it out to husbandmen, and went into a far country:

34 And when the time of the fruit drew near, he sent his servants to the husbandmen, that they might receive the fruits of it.

35 And the husbandmen took his servants, and beat one, and killed another, and stoned another.

36 Again, he sent other servants more than the first: and they did unto them likewise.

37 But last of all he sent unto them his son, saying, They will reverence my son.

38 But when the husbandmen saw the son, they said among themselves, This is the heir; come, let us kill him, and let us seize on his inheritance.

39 And they caught him, and cast *him* out of the vineyard, and slew *him.*

40 When the lord therefore of the vineyard cometh, what will he do unto those husbandmen?

41 They say unto him, He will miserably destroy those wicked men, and will let out *his* vineyard unto other husbandmen, which shall render him the fruits in their seasons.

42 Jesus saith unto them, Did ye never read in the Scriptures, The stone which the builders rejected, the same is become the head of the corner: this is the Lord's doing, and it is marvelous in our eyes?

1 And he began to speak unto them by parables. A *certain* man planted a vineyard, and set a hedge about *it,* and digged *a place for* the winevat, and built a tower, and let it out to husbandmen, and went into a far country.

2 And at the season he sent to the husbandmen a servant, that he might receive from the husbandmen of the fruit of the vineyard.

3 And they caught *him,* and beat him, and sent *him* away empty.

4 And again he sent unto them another servant; and at him they cast stones, and wounded *him* in the head, and sent *him* away shamefully handled.

5 And again he sent another; and him they killed, and many others; beating some, and killing some.

6 Having yet therefore one son, his well-beloved, he sent him also last unto them, saying, They will reverence my son.

7 But those husbandmen said among themselves, This is the heir; come, let us kill him, and the inheritance shall be ours.

8 And they took him, and killed *him,* and cast *him* out of the vineyard.

9 What shall therefore the lord of the vineyard do? he will come and destroy the husbandmen, and will give the vineyard unto others.

10 And have ye not read this Scripture; The stone which the builders rejected is become the head of the corner:

9 Then began he to speak to the people this parable; A certain man planted a vineyard, and let it forth to husbandmen, and went into a far country for a long time.

10 And at the season he sent a servant to the husbandmen, that they should give him of the fruit of the vineyard: but the husbandmen beat him, and sent *him* away empty.

11 And again he sent another servant: and they beat him also, and entreated *him* shamefully, and sent *him* away empty.

12 And again he sent a third: and they wounded him also, and cast *him* out.

13 Then said the lord of the vineyard, What shall I do? I will send my beloved son: it may be they will reverence *him* when they see him.

14 But when the husbandmen saw him, they reasoned among themselves, saying, This is the heir: come, let us kill him, that the inheritance may be ours.

15 So they cast him out of the vineyard, and killed *him.* What therefore shall the lord of the vineyard do unto them?

16 He shall come and destroy these husbandmen, and shall give the vineyard to others. And when they heard *it,* they said, God forbid.

17 And he beheld them, and said, What is this then that is written, The stone which the builders rejected, the same is become the head of the corner?

Fate of Those Who Oppose Christ (continued)

43 Therefore say I unto you, The kingdom of God shall be taken from you, and given to a nation bringing forth the fruits thereof.

44 And whosoever shall fall on this stone shall be broken: but on whomsoever it shall fall, it will grind him to powder.

45 And when the chief priests and Pharisees had heard his parables, they perceived that he spake of them.

46 But when they sought to lay hands on him, they feared the multitude, because they took him for a prophet.

22:1 And Jesus answered and spake unto them again by parables, and said,

2 The kingdom of heaven is like unto a certain king, which made a marriage for his son,

3 And sent forth his servants to call them that were bidden to the wedding: and they would not come.

4 Again, he sent forth other servants, saying, Tell them which are bidden, Behold, I have prepared my dinner: my oxen and *my* fatlings *are* killed, and all things *are* ready: come unto the marriage.

5 But they made light of *it,* and went their ways, one to his farm, another to his merchandise:

6 And the remnant took his servants, and entreated *them* spitefully, and slew *them.*

7 But when the king heard *thereof,* he was wroth: and he sent forth his armies, and destroyed those murderers, and burned up their city.

8 Then saith he to his servants, The wedding is ready, but they which were bidden were not worthy.

9 Go ye therefore into the highways, and as many as ye shall find, bid to the marriage.

10 So those servants went out into the highways, and gathered together all as many as they found, both bad and good: and the wedding was furnished with guests.

11 And when the king came in to see the guests, he saw there a man which had not on a wedding garment:

12 And he saith unto him, Friend, how camest thou in hither not having a wedding garment? And he was speechless.

13 Then said the king to the servants, Bind him hand and foot, and take him away, and cast *him* into outer darkness; there shall be weeping and gnashing of teeth.

14 For many are called, but few *are* chosen.

11 This was the Lord's doing, and it is marvelous in our eyes?

12 And they sought to lay hold on him, but feared the people; for they knew that he had spoken the parable against them: and they left him, and went their way.

18 Whosoever shall fall upon that stone shall be broken; but on whomsoever it shall fall, it will grind him to powder.

19 And the chief priests and the scribes the same hour sought to lay hands on him; and they feared the people: for they perceived that he had spoken this parable against them.

The Parthenon. Highest expression of Grecian architecture. It was surprising that Greeks (see next page) from the highest culture of that time would endeavor to meet the humble prophet of Nazareth.

The Widow's Mites

Mark 12:41-44

And Jesus sat down opposite the temple treasury and watched the people as they dropped money into the treasury. Many who were rich were dropping in large sums. And a poor widow came and dropped in two mites, which make a penny. And Jesus called his disciples to him and said,

"I tell you truly, this poor widow has given more than all the others who dropped offerings into the treasury. For they all gave out of their abundance, but out of her poverty she has dropped in all she had—everything she had to live on."

41 And Jesus sat over against the treasury, and beheld how the people cast money into the treasury: and many that were rich cast in much.

42 And there came a certain poor widow, and she threw in two mites, which make a farthing.

43 And he called *unto him* his disciples, and saith unto them, Verily I say unto you, That this poor widow hath cast more in, than all they which have cast into the treasury:

44 For all *they* did cast in of their abundance; but she of her want did cast in all that she had, *even* all her living.

1 And he looked up, and saw the rich men casting their gifts into the treasury.

2 And he saw also a certain poor widow casting in thither two mites.

3 And he said, Of a truth I say unto you, that this poor widow hath cast in more than they all:

4 For all these have of their abundance cast in unto the offerings of God: but she of her penury hath cast in all the living that she had.

The Purpose of Jesus' Death

John 12:20-50

Now among those who went up to worship at the feast were some Greeks. And they came to Philip, who was from Bethsaida in Galilee, and said, "Sir, we want to see Jesus."

Philip went and told Andrew, and they both went to tell Jesus.

"The hour has come for the Son of Man to be glorified," said Jesus. "I tell you truly, unless a grain of wheat falls into the ground and dies, it remains alone; but if it dies, it bears much fruit. He who loves his own life loses it, but he who counts his life of no selfish importance in this world will keep it for everlasting life. If any man will serve me, he must follow me; and where

20 And there were certain Greeks among them that came up to worship at the feast:

21 The same came therefore to Philip, which was of Bethsaida of Galilee, and desired him, saying, Sir, we would see Jesus.

22 Philip cometh and telleth Andrew: and again Andrew and Philip tell Jesus.

23 And Jesus answered them, saying, The hour is come, that the Son of man should be glorified.

24 Verily, verily, I say unto you, Except a corn of wheat fall into the ground and die, it abideth alone: but if it die, it bringeth forth much fruit.

25 He that loveth his life shall lose it; and

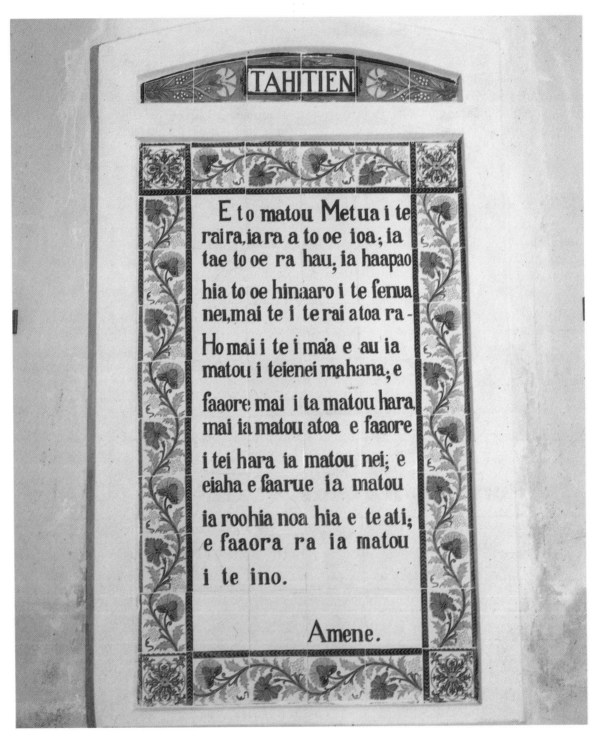

Prayer from Pater Noster Church.

*One of the more than 60 different translations
of the Lord's Prayer found in the Pater
Noster ("Our Father") church on the Mount
of Olives.*

The Purpose of Jesus' Death (continued)

I am, there will my servant be also. If any man will serve me, the Father will honor him.

"Now is my soul troubled, and what shall I say—'Father, save me from this hour'? No, for it was for this purpose that I have come to this hour. Father, glorify your name!"

Then there came a voice from heaven, "I have already glorified it, and I will glorify it again."

The crowd of bystanders, hearing this, said it thundered. Others said, "An angel has spoken to him!"

"This voice came not for my sake, but for yours," said Jesus. "Now is the judgment of this world, now shall the prince of this world be cast out; and I, when I am lifted up from the earth, will draw all men to myself."

(This he said to show the kind of death he was about to die.)

"We have heard out of the scriptures that the Messiah will live forever," answered the people. "What do you mean when you say 'the Son of Man must be lifted up'? Who is this 'Son of Man'?"

"Only a little while longer will the light be with you," said Jesus. "Walk while you have the light, lest the darkness overtake you. He who walks in darkness does not know where he is going. Believe in the light while you still have the light, that you may become sons of light."

Then said Jesus, "He who believes in me believes not only in me, but in him who sent me, and he who recognizes me recognizes him. I have come into the world as light, that whoever believes in me may not live in darkness. If anyone hears my words and does not obey them, I do not judge him, for I did not come to judge the world, but to save it. Nevertheless, he who rejects me and refuses to accept my words has one that judges him: the very word I have spoken will judge him at the last day. For I have not spoken on my own authority, but the Father who sent me has himself commanded me what to say and to teach, and I know that his commandment is eternal life. All that I say, therefore, I speak as the Father has told me."

Having said these things, Jesus departed and

he that hateth his life in this world shall keep it unto life eternal.

26 If any man serve me, let him follow me; and where I am, there shall also my servant be: if any man serve me, him will *my* Father honor.

27 Now is my soul troubled; and what shall I say? Father, save me from this hour: but for this cause came I unto this hour.

28 Father, glorify thy name. Then came there a voice from heaven, *saying*, I have both glorified *it*, and will glorify *it* again.

29 The people therefore that stood by, and heard *it*, said that it thundered: others said, An angel spake to him.

30 Jesus answered and said, This voice came not because of me, but for your sakes.

31 Now is the judgment of this world: now shall the prince of this world be cast out.

32 And I, if I be lifted up from the earth, will draw all *men* unto me.

33 This he said, signifying what death he should die.

34 The people answered him, We have heard out of the law that Christ abideth for ever: and how sayest thou, The Son of man must be lifted up? who is this Son of man?

35 Then Jesus said unto them, Yet a little while is the light with you. Walk while ye have the light, lest darkness come upon you: for he that walketh in darkness knoweth not whither he goeth.

36 While ye have light, believe in the light, that ye may be the children of light. These things spake Jesus, and departed, and did hide himself from them.

37 But though he had done so many miracles before them, yet they believed not on him:

38 That the saying of Isaiah the prophet might be fulfilled, which he spake, Lord, who hath believed our report? and to whom hath the arm of the Lord been revealed?

39 Therefore they could not believe, because that Isaiah said again,

40 He hath blinded their eyes, and hardened their heart; that they should not see with *their* eyes, nor understand with *their* heart, and be converted, and I should heal them.

41 These things said Isaiah, when he saw his glory, and spake of him.

42 Nevertheless among the chief rulers also

271

The Purpose of Jesus' Death (continued)

hid himself from them. And though he had done many miracles in their presence, they did not believe in him, so that the word of the prophet Isaiah was fulfilled,

Lord, who has believed our testimony?

To whom has the Servant of the Lord been revealed?

Therefore they could not believe, for Isaiah also said,

He has blinded their eyes and hardened their heart,

lest they should see with their eyes and understand in their heart and turn,

that I should heal them.

These things said Isaiah, because he saw his glory and spoke of him.

Nevertheless, many even of the authorities themselves believed in him, but for fear of the Pharisees, they did not confess it, lest they should be put out of the synagogue; for they loved the praise of men more than the approval of God.

many believed on him; but because of the Pharisees they did not confess *him*, lest they should be put out of the synagogue:

43 For they loved the praise of men more than the praise of God.

44 Jesus cried and said, He that believeth on me, believeth not on me, but on him that sent me.

45 And he that seeth me seeth him that sent me.

46 I am come a light into the world, that whosoever believeth on me should not abide in darkness.

47 And if any man hear my words, and believe not, I judge him not: for I came not to judge the world, but to save the world.

48 He that rejecteth me, and receiveth not my words, hath one that judgeth him: the word that I have spoken, the same shall judge him in the last day.

49 For I have not spoken of myself; but the Father which sent me, he gave me a commandment, what I should say, and what I should speak.

50 And I know that his commandment is life everlasting: whatsoever I speak therefore, even as the Father said unto me, so I speak.

Steps from Mount Zion. One of the few places it is actually possible to walk where Jesus walked. The Master went down this ancient pathway on His way to Gethsemane.

Jesus and the Woman Taken in Adultery

John 8:2-11

And early in the morning, Jesus came to the temple again and all the people came to him, and he sat down and began to teach them. And the scribes and Pharisees brought in a woman who had been taken in adultery and, placing her in the midst, said to Jesus,

"Master, this woman was caught in adultery, in the very act. Now Moses commanded us in the law that such should be stoned. But what do you say?"

This they said to test him, that they might have something of which to accuse him. But Jesus bent down and, with his finger, began to write on the ground. And as they continued to question him, he stood up and said to them, "Let the man among you who has never sinned cast the first stone."

And again, Jesus bent down and began to write on the ground. And having heard his words, they were convicted by their own consciences and, one by one, they went away, beginning with the eldest and continuing to the last man. Jesus was left alone, and the woman standing there in the midst.

Then Jesus stood up and, seeing no one but the woman, said to her, "Woman, where are your accusers? Has no one condemned you?"

"No one, Lord," she answered.

"Neither do I condemn you," said Jesus. "Go your way, and sin no more."

1 Jesus went unto the mount of Olives.

2 And early in the morning he came again into the temple, and all the people came unto him; and he sat down, and taught them.

3 And the scribes and Pharisees brought unto him a woman taken in adultery; and when they had set her in the midst,

So when they continued asking him, he lifted up himself, and said unto them, He that is without sin among you, let him first cast a stone at her.

4 They say unto him, Master, this woman was taken in adultery, in the very act.

5 Now Moses in the law commanded us, that such should be stoned: but what sayest thou?

6 This they said, tempting him, that they might have to accuse him. But Jesus stooped down, and with *his* finger wrote on the ground, *as though he heard them not.*

7 So when they continued asking him, he lifted up himself, and said unto them, He that is without sin among you, let him first cast a stone at her.

8 And again he stooped down, and wrote on the ground.

9 And they which heard *it*, being convicted by *their own* conscience, went out one by one, beginning at the eldest, *even* unto the last: and Jesus was left alone, and the woman standing in the midst.

10 When Jesus had lifted up himself, and saw none but the woman, he said unto her, Woman, where are those thine accusers? hath no man condemned thee?

11 She said, No man, Lord. And Jesus said unto her, Neither do I condemn thee: go, and sin no more.

Attacks by Religious Leaders

Matthew 22:15-33

Then the Pharisees went off and discussed among themselves how they might trap Jesus in his talk. And they sent some of their disciples to him, with some of the Herodians, saying,

"Master, we know that you are honest and that you teach the way of God in truth, regardless of any man, for you are not influenced by the opinions and positions of men. Tell us therefore what you think. Is it lawful to pay taxes to Caesar, or not?"

But Jesus, aware of their evil intention, said, "Why do you test me, you hypocrites! Show me a tax coin." And they brought him a denarius.

"Whose likeness and inscription are these?" asked Jesus.

"Caesar's," they replied.

"Then give to Caesar the things that are Caesar's, and to God the things that are God's," said Jesus.

When they heard his words, they were astounded. And they left him and went their way.

The same day, some of the Sadducees (who say there is no resurrection) came to Jesus and asked him a question, saying,

"Master, Moses said, 'If a man dies, leaving no children, his brother shall marry his widow and raise up children for his brother.' Now there were seven brothers among us. The first married and died, and having no children, left his wife to his brother. And so did the second, and the third, and all of them, including the seventh. Last of all, the woman died. Now in the resurrection, whose wife of the seven will she be? For all of them had her."

"You are in error," replied Jesus, "for you are ignorant of both the scriptures and the power of God. In the resurrection, people neither marry nor are given in marriage, but are like the angels in heaven. And concerning the resurrection of the dead, have you not read what was spoken to you by God himself? 'I am the God of Abraham, the God of Isaac, and the God of Jacob.' He is not the God of the dead, but of the living."

Now when the people heard these things, they were astonished at his teaching.

MATTHEW 22:15-33

15 Then went the Pharisees, and took counsel how they might entangle him in *his* talk.

16 And they sent out unto him their disciples with the Herodians, saying, Master, we know that thou art true, and teachest the way of God in truth, neither carest thou for any *man:* for thou regardest not the person of men.

17 Tell us therefore, What thinkest thou? Is it lawful to give tribute unto Caesar, or not?

18 But Jesus perceived their wickedness, and said, Why tempt ye me, *ye* hypocrites?

19 Show me the tribute money. And they brought unto him a penny.

20 And he saith unto them, Whose *is* this image and superscription?

21 They say unto him, Caesar's. Then saith he unto

MARK 12:13-27

13 And they send unto him certain of the Pharisees and of the Herodians, to catch him in *his* words.

14 And when they were come, they say unto him, Master, we know that thou art true, and carest for no man; for thou regardest not the person of men, but teachest the way of God in truth: Is it lawful to give tribute to Caesar, or not?

15 Shall we give, or shall we not give? But he, knowing their hypocrisy, said unto them, Why tempt ye me? bring me a penny, that I may see *it.*

16 And they brought *it.* And he saith unto them, Whose *is* this image and superscription? And they said unto him, Caesar's.

17 And Jesus answering said unto them, Render to Caesar the things that are Caesar's, and to

LUKE 20:20-40

20 And they watched *him,* and sent forth spies, which should feign themselves just men, that they might take hold of his words, that so they might deliver him unto the power and authority of the governor.

21 And they asked him, saying, Master, we know that thou sayest and teachest rightly, neither acceptest thou the person *of any,* but teachest the way of God truly:

22 Is it lawful for us to give tribute unto Caesar, or no?

23 But he perceived their craftiness, and said unto them, Why tempt ye me?

24 Show me a penny. Whose image and superscription hath it? They answered and said, Caesar's.

25 And he said unto them, Render therefore unto Caesar the things which be Caesar's, and

Attacks by Religious Leaders (continued)

them, Render therefore unto Caesar the things which are Caesar's; and unto God the things that are God's.

22 When they had heard *these words,* they marveled, and left him, and went their way.

23 The same day came to him the Sadducees, which say that there is no resurrection, and asked him,

24 Saying, Master, Moses said, if a man die, having no children, his brother shall marry his wife, and raise up seed unto his brother.

25 Now there were with us seven brethren: and the first, when he had married a wife, deceased, and, having no issue, left his wife unto his brother:

26 Likewise the second also, and the third, unto the seventh.

27 And last of all the woman died also.

28 Therefore in the resurrection whose wife shall she be of the seven? for they all had her.

29 Jesus answered and said unto them, Ye do err, not knowing the Scriptures, nor the power of God.

30 For in the resurrection they neither marry, nor are given in marriage, but are as the angels of God in heaven.

31 But as touching the resurrection of the dead, have ye not read that which was spoken unto you by God, saying,

32 I am the God of Abraham, and the God of Isaac, and the God of Jacob? God is not the God of the dead, but of the living.

33 And when the multitude heard *this,* they were astonished at his doctrine.

God the things that are God's. And they marveled at him.

18 Then come unto him the Sadducees, which say there is no resurrection; and they asked him, saying,

19 Master, Moses wrote unto us, If a man's brother die, and leave *his* wife *behind him,* and leave no children, that his brother should take his wife, and raise up seed unto his brother.

20 Now there were seven brethren: and the first took a wife, and dying left no seed.

21 And the second took her, and died, neither left he any seed: and the third likewise.

22 And the seven had her, and left no seed: last of all the woman died also.

23 In the resurrection therefore, when they shall rise, whose wife shall she be of them? for the seven had her to wife.

24 And Jesus answering said unto them, Do ye not therefore err, because ye know not the Scriptures, neither the power of God?

25 For when they shall rise from the dead, they neither marry, nor are given in marriage; but are as the angels which are in heaven.

26 And as touching the dead, that they rise; have ye not read in the book of Moses, how in the bush God spake unto him, saying, I *am* the God of Abraham, and the God of Isaac, and the God of Jacob?

27 He is not the God of the dead, but the God of the living: ye therefore do greatly err.

unto God the things which be God's.

26 And they could not take hold of his words before the people: and they marveled at his answer, and held their peace.

27 Then came to *him* certain of the Sadducees, which deny that there is any resurrection; and they asked him,

28 Saying, Master, Moses wrote unto us, If any man's brother die, having a wife, and he die without children, that his brother should take his wife, and raise up seed unto his brother.

29 There were therefore seven brethren: and the first took a wife, and died without children.

30 And the second took her to wife, and he died childless.

31 And the third took her; and in like manner the seven also: and they left no children, and died.

32 Last of all the woman died also.

33 Therefore in the resurrection whose wife of them is she? for seven had her to wife.

34 And Jesus answering said unto them, The children of this world marry, and are given in marriage:

35 But they which shall be accounted worthy to obtain that world, and the resurrection from the dead, neither marry, nor are given in marriage:

36 Neither can they die any more: for they are equal unto the angels; and are the children of God, being the children of the resurrection.

37 Now that the dead are raised, even Moses showed at the bush, when he calleth the Lord the God of Abraham, and the God of Isaac, and the God of Jacob.

38 For he is not a God of the dead, but of the living: for all live unto him.

39 Then certain of the scribes answering said, Master, thou hast well said.

40 And after that they durst not ask him any *question at all.*

The Greatest Commandment

Matthew 22:34-40

Now when the Pharisees heard that Jesus had silenced the Sadducees, they gathered together. And one of them, a teacher of the law, asked Jesus a question, to test him:

"Master, which is the greatest commandment in the law?"

"You shall love the Lord your God with all your heart, with all your soul, and with all your mind,' " answered Jesus. "This is the greatest and most important commandment. And there is a second one like it, 'You shall love your neighbor as yourself.' The whole of the law and the prophets rests on these two commandments."

MATTHEW 22:34-40

34 But when the Pharisees had heard that he had put the Sadducees to silence, they were gathered together.

35 Then one of them, *which was* a lawyer, asked *him a question,* tempting him, and saying,

36 Master, which is the great commandment in the law?

37 Jesus said unto him, Thou shalt love the Lord thy God with all thy heart, and with all thy soul, and with all thy mind.

38 This is the first and great commandment.

39 And the second *is* like unto it, Thou shalt love thy neighbor as thyself.

40 On these two commandments hang all the law and the prophets.

MARK 12:28-34

28 And one of the scribes came, and having heard them reasoning together, and perceiving that he had answered them well, asked him, Which is the first commandment of all?

29 And Jesus answered him, The first of all the commandments *is,* Hear, O Israel; The Lord our God is one Lord:

30 And thou shalt love the Lord thy God with all thy heart, and with all thy soul, and with all thy mind, and with all thy strength: this *is* the first commandment.

31 And the second *is* like, *namely* this, Thou shalt love thy neighbor as thyself. There is none other commandment greater than these.

32 And the scribe said unto him, Well, Master, thou hast said the truth: for there is one God; and there is none other but he:

33 And to love him with all the heart, and with all the understanding, and with all the soul, and with all the strength, and to love *his* neighbor as himself, is more than all whole burnt offerings and sacrifices.

34 And when Jesus saw that he answered discreetly, he said unto him, Thou art not far from the kingdom of God. And no man after that durst ask him *any question.*

Jesus' Unanswerable Question

Matthew 22:41-46

Now while the pharisees were assembled together, Jesus asked them a question, saying, "What do you think about the Messiah? Whose son is he?"

"The son of David," they replied.

"Then how is it," said Jesus, "that David, moved by the Spirit, calls him Lord, saying, 'The Lord said to my Lord, "Sit at my right hand until I put your enemies under your feet" '? If David calls him Lord, how can he be his son?"

And no one was able to answer him a word, and from that day, no one dared to ask him any more questions.

MATTHEW 22:41-46

41 While the Pharisees were gathered together, Jesus asked them,

42 Saying, What think ye of Christ? whose son is he? They say unto him, *The son* of David.

43 He saith unto them, How then doth David in spirit call him Lord, saying,

44 The Lord said unto my Lord, Sit thou on my right hand, till I make thine enemies thy footstool?

45 If David then call him Lord, how is he his son?

46 And no man was able to answer him a word, neither durst any *man* from that day forth ask him any more *questions.*

MARK 12:35-40

35 And Jesus answered and said, while he taught in the temple, How say the scribes that Christ is the son of David?

36 For David himself said by the Holy Ghost, The Lord said to my Lord, Sit thou on my right hand, till I make thine enemies thy footstool.

David therefore himself calleth him Lord.

37 David therefore himself calleth him Lord; and whence is he *then* his son? And the common people heard him gladly.

38 And he said unto them in his doctrine, Beware of the scribes, which love to go in long clothing, and *love* salutations in the market places,

39 And the chief seats in the synagogues, and the uppermost rooms at feasts:

40 Which devour widows' houses, and for a pretense make long prayers: these shall receive greater damnation.

LUKE 20:41-47

41 And he said unto them, How say they that Christ is David's son?

42 And David himself saith in the book of Psalms, The LORD said unto my Lord, Sit thou on my right hand,

43 Till I make thine enemies thy footstool.

44 David therefore calleth him Lord, how is he then his son?

45 Then in the audience of all the people he said unto his disciples,

46 Beware of the scribes, which desire to walk in long robes, and love greetings in the markets, and the highest seats in the synagogues, and the chief rooms at feasts;

47 Which devour widows' houses, and for a show make long prayers: the same shall receive greater damnation.

Jesus Denounces Sin

Matthew 23:1-39

Then Jesus said to the crowds and to his disciples,

"The scribes and the Pharisees sit in Moses' chair; therefore do the things they tell you to do. But do not do as they do; for they say what men should do, but do not practice what they preach. They bind heavy burdens hard to bear and lay them on men's shoulders, but they themselves will not lift a finger to move them. They do all their works only to be seen by men. They make their phylacteries broad and their tassels long, and they love the place of honor at feasts and the front seats in the synagogues, and salutations in the market places, and to have men call them 'Rabbi.'

"But as for you, my disciples, you are not to be called 'Rabbi,' for you have but one teacher, and all of you are brothers. And do not call any man on earth 'Father,' for you have but one Father, who is in heaven. And you are not to be called 'masters,' for you have but one master, the Messiah. He who is greatest among you will be your servant, but whoever exalts himself shall be humbled, and whoever humbles himself shall be exalted.

"Woe to you, scribes and Pharisees—hypocrites! For you shut the door of the kingdom of heaven against men. You do not enter yourselves, nor do you allow those who would enter to go in.

"Woe to you, scribes and Pharisees—hypocrites! For you gobble up the houses of widows and, to cover up your wickedness, pray great long prayers in public. Therefore you will receive all the more condemnation.

"Woe to you, scribes and Pharisees—hypocrites! For you travel all over the sea and the land to win a single convert, and after he is converted, you make him twice as much a son of hell as yourselves.

"Woe to you, blind guides, who say, 'If a man swears by the temple, it is nothing; but if a man swears by the gold of the temple, he is bound by his oath.' You blind fools! Which is greater, the gold, or the temple that sanctifies the gold? You also say, 'If a man swears by the altar, it is nothing; but if a man swears by the gift that is on the altar, he is bound by his oath.' You blind men! Which is greater, the gift, or the altar that sanctifies the gift? He who swears by the altar, swears by the altar and everything on it. He who swears by the temple, swears by the temple and by him who dwells in it. He who swears by heaven, swears by the throne of God and by the one who sits on it.

"Woe to you, scribes and Pharisees—hypocrites! You tithe mint and dill and cummin, but you ignore the more important matters of the law—justice, mercy, and honesty. Certainly you ought to tithe your produce, but that does not excuse you from the more important matters. You blind guides! You strain out a gnat and swallow a camel!

"Woe to you, scribes and Pharisees—hypocrites! You carefully clean the outside of the cup and the dish, and leave them full of plunder and self-indulgence. You blind Pharisee! First clean the inside of the cup and the dish, so that the outside may truly be clean.

"Woe to you, scribes and Pharisees—hypocrites! You are like whitewashed tombs which are beautiful on the outside, but inside are full of dead men's bones and all sorts of corruption. So it is with you; outwardly you appear to men to be righteous, but inside you are full of hypocrisy and wickedness.

"Woe to you, scribes and Pharisees—hypocrites! You build tombs for the prophets and decorate the monuments of the righteous and say, 'If we had lived in the days of our fathers, we would not have taken part with them in shedding the blood of the prophets.' Thus you testify against yourselves that you are the sons of those who murdered the prophets. Go ahead and finish what your fathers began.

"You serpents, you sons of vipers! How will you escape condemnation to hell? Therefore, behold, I will send you prophets and wise men and scribes. Some of them you will kill and crucify, and some you will flog in your synagogues and persecute from town to town, so that all the righteous blood shed on earth may be on your hands, from the blood of righteous Abel to the blood of Zechariah the son of Barachiah, whom you murdered between the sanctuary and the altar. I tell you truly, judgment for all these things will fall on this generation.''

"O Jerusalem, Jerusalem!—killing the prophets and stoning those who are sent to you! How often have I longed to gather your children together as a hen gathers her chicks under her wings! But you refused. Behold, your house is left to you desolate. For I tell you, you will not see me again until you say, 'Blessed is he who comes in the name of the Lord!' ''

MATTHEW 23:1-39

1 Then spake Jesus to the multitude, and to his disciples,

2 Saying, The scribes and the Pharisees sit in Moses' seat:

3 All therefore whatsoever they bid you observe, *that* observe and do; but do not ye after their works: for they say, and do not.

4 For they bind heavy burdens and grievous to be borne, and lay *them* on men's shoulders; but they *themselves* will not move them with one of their fingers.

5 But all their works they do for to be seen of men: they make broad their phylacteries, and enlarge the borders of their garments,

6 And love the uppermost rooms at feasts, and the chief seats in the synagogues,

7 And greetings in the markets, and to be called of men, Rabbi, Rabbi.

8 But be not ye called Rabbi: for one is your Master, *even* Christ; and all ye are brethren.

9 And call no *man* your father upon the earth: for one is your Father, which is in heaven.

10 Neither be ye called masters: for one is your Master, *even* Christ.

11 But he that is greatest among you shall be your servant.

12 And whosoever shall exalt himself shall be abased; and he that shall humble himself shall be exalted.

13 But woe unto you, scribes and Pharisees, hypocrites! for ye shut up the kingdom of heaven against men: for ye neither go in *yourselves,* neither suffer ye them that are entering to go in.

14 Woe unto you, scribes and Pharisees, hypocrites! for ye devour widows' houses, and for a pretense make long prayer: therefore ye shall receive the greater damnation.

15 Woe unto you, scribes and Pharisees, hypocrites! for ye compass sea and land to make one proselyte; and when he is made, ye make him twofold more the child of hell than yourselves.

LUKE 13:34-35

34 O Jerusalem, Jerusalem, which killest the prophets, and stonest them that are sent unto thee; how often would I have gathered thy children together, as a hen *doth gather* her brood under *her* wings, and ye would not!

35 Behold, your house is left unto you desolate: and verily I say unto you, Ye shall not see me, until *the time* come when ye shall say, Blessed *is* he that cometh in the name of the Lord.

Jesus Views Jerusalem. *Before the time of His arrest Jesus spent the daytime hours teaching in the temple area, but at night He stayed on the Mount of Olives east of the city. How His loving heart must have ached as He viewed the city and contemplated its fate.*

Jesus Denounces Sin (continued)

16 Woe unto you, *ye* blind guides, which say, Whosoever shall swear by the temple, it is nothing; but whosoever shall swear by the gold of the temple, he is a debtor!

17 *Ye* fools and blind: for whether is greater, the gold, or the temple that sanctifieth the gold?

18 And, Whosoever shall swear by the altar, it is nothing; but whosoever sweareth by the gift that is upon it, he is guilty.

19 *Ye* fools and blind: for whether *is* greater, the gift, or the altar that sanctifieth the gift?

20 Whoso therefore shall swear by the altar, sweareth by it, and by all things thereon.

21 And whoso shall swear by the temple, sweareth by it, and by him that dwelleth therein.

22 And he that shall swear by heaven, sweareth by the throne of God, and by him that sitteth thereon.

23 Woe unto you, scribes and Pharisees, hypocrites! for ye pay tithe of mint and anise and cummin, and have omitted the weightier *matters* of the law, judgment, mercy, and faith: these ought ye to have done, and not to leave the other undone.

24 *Ye* blind guides, which strain at a gnat, and swallow a camel.

25 Woe unto you, scribes and Pharisees, hypocrites! for ye make clean the outside of the cup and of the platter, but within they are full of extortion and excess.

26 *Thou* blind Pharisee, cleanse first that *which is* within the cup and platter, that the outside of them may be clean also.

27 Woe unto you, scribes and Pharisees, hypocrites! for ye are like unto whited sepulchres, which indeed appear beautiful outward, but are within full of dead *men's* bones, and of all uncleanness.

28 Even so ye also outwardly appear righteous unto men, but within ye are full of hypocrisy and iniquity.

29 Woe unto you, scribes and Pharisees, hypocrites! because ye build the tombs of the prophets, and garnish the sepulchres of the righteous,

30 And say, If we had been in the days of our fathers, we would not have been partakers with them in the blood of the prophets.

31 Wherefore ye be witnesses unto yourselves, that ye are the children of them which killed the prophets.

32 Fill ye up then the measure of your fathers.

33 *Ye* serpents, *ye* generation of vipers, how can ye escape the damnation of hell?

34 Wherefore, behold, I send unto you prophets, and wise men, and scribes: and *some* of them ye shall kill and crucify; and *some* of them shall ye scourge in your synagogues, and persecute *them* from city to city:

35 That upon you may come all the righteous blood shed upon the earth, from the blood of righteous Abel unto the blood of Zechariah son of Berechiah, whom ye slew between the temple and the altar.

36 Verily I say unto you, All these things shall come upon this generation.

37 O Jerusalem, Jerusalem, *thou* that killest the prophets, and stonest them which are sent unto thee, how often would I have gathered thy children together, even as a hen gathereth her chickens under *her* wings, and ye would not!

38 Behold, your house is left unto you desolate.

39 For I say unto you, Ye shall not see me henceforth, till ye shall say, Blessed *is* he that cometh in the name of the Lord.

Jesus Previews History

Matthew 24:1-14, 21-51, Mark 13:33-37, Luke 21:12-24, 34-36

Then Jesus went out, and as he was departing from the temple, his disciples came to him and began to call his attention to the buildings of the temple.

"You see all these buildings, do you not?" said Jesus. "I tell you truly, there will not be left here one stone upon another—not one stone that is not thrown down."

And as he sat on the Mount of Olives, the disciples came to him privately and said, "Tell us, when will these things be? And what will be the sign of your coming and of the end of the age?"

"Take heed that no man leads you astray," replied Jesus, "for many will come in my name, saying, 'I am the Messiah,' and will deceive many. And you will hear of wars and rumors of wars. See that you are not alarmed, for it is necessary that these things happen, but this is not yet the end of the age. For nation will rise against nation, and kingdom against kingdom, and there will be famines and earthquakes in different places. But all these things are only the beginning of the sufferings.

"Then they will hand you over to persecution and will kill you, and you will be hated by all nations for my name's sake. And in those days many will fall away and will betray one another and hate one another, and many false prophets will rise and lead many astray. And because wickedness will prevail more and more, the love of many will grow cold, but he who endures to the end will be saved. And this gospel of the kingdom will be preached throughout all the world as a testimony to all nations, and then the end will come."

"But before all these things," said Jesus, "they will lay hands on you and persecute you, handing you over to the synagogues and prisons, and you will be brought before kings and governors for my name's sake. This will be an opportunity for you to bear testimony. Settle it therefore in your hearts not to meditate beforehand how to answer, for I will give you words and wisdom that none of your adversaries will be able to withstand or contradict. But you will be betrayed even by parents, brothers, kinsmen, and friends, and they will put some of you to death. You will be hated by all men for my name's sake, but not a hair of your head will perish. By your steadfast endurance you will win your souls.

"But when you see Jerusalem surrounded by armies, then know that her desolation is at hand. Then let those in Judea flee to the mountains, let those in the city depart, and those in the country, let them not enter the city. For these are the days of vengeance, that all the things that have been written may be fulfilled. But woe to those with child and to those giving suck in those days, for there will be great distress throughout the land and wrath upon this people. And they will fall by the edge of the sword and be led away as captives among all the nations, and Jerusalem will be trampled under foot by the Gentiles until the times of the Gentiles are fulfilled."

"At that time will be great tribulation such as has not been from the beginning of the world until now, no, nor ever will be. And if those days were not shortened, no one would survive; but for the sake of the elect those days will be shortened.

"If anyone says to you in those days, 'Lo, here is the Messiah!' or 'There he is!' do not believe it. For false messiahs and false prophets will rise and show great signs and wonders to lead astray, if possible, even the elect. Behold, I have told you beforehand. Therefore, if they say to you, 'Lo, he is in the wilderness,' do not go out. If they say, 'Behold, he is in the inner chambers,' do not believe it. For as the lightning flashes out of the east and is seen in the west, so will be the coming of the Son of Man. 'Wherever the body is, there the vultures will be gathered together.'

"Immediately after the tribulation of those days, the sun will be darkened and the moon will not give her light, and the stars will fall from heaven and the powers of the heavens will be shaken. And then will the sign of the Son of Man appear in heaven, and all the nations of earth will mourn and will see the Son of Man coming on the clouds of heaven with power and great glory. And he will send forth his angels with a great trumpet call, and they will gather together his elect from the four winds, from one end of heaven to the other."

"Now learn a lesson from the fig tree," said Jesus. "As soon as its branch becomes tender and puts forth leaves, you know that summer is near. In like manner, when you see all these things, know that he is near, at the very gates. I tell you truly, this generation will not pass away till all these things are fulfilled. Heaven and earth will pass away, but my words will not pass away.

"But no one knows that day and hour, not even the angels of heaven, nor the Son, but the Father alone. But as the days of Noah, so will be the coming of the Son of Man. For as in the

Arch of Titus. *In A.D. 70 Titus, later the Roman Emperor, fulfilled Jesus' prophecy by destroying Jerusalem, beginning the Jews' tragic history. The arch was erected in Rome to celebrate Titus' victory.*

283

days before the flood they were eating and drinking, marrying and giving in marriage, until the day Noah entered the ark, and did not know until the flood came and took them all away, so will be the coming of the Son of Man. Then will two men be in the field; one will be taken, and the other left. Two women will be grinding at the mill; one will be taken, and the other left. Watch therefore, for you do not know on what day your Lord will come.

"But take heed to yourselves lest your hearts be overwhelmed with indulgence and drunkenness and the cares of life, and that day come upon you suddenly like a trap; for it will come upon all who dwell on the face of all the earth. But watch and pray continually that you may prevail to escape all these things that will come to pass, and to stand before the Son of Man.

"Take heed and watch, for you know not when the time will be. It is like a man taking a journey into another country; leaving his house in charge of his servants, each with his work, he commands the doorkeeper to keep watch. Watch therefore, for you do not know when the master of the house will come—in the evening, or at midnight, at cockcrow, or in the morning. Watch, lest he come suddenly and find you asleep. What I say to you, I say to all: Watch!

"But know this, that if the householder had known what time of night the thief was coming, he would have watched and would not have allowed his house to be broken into. Therefore you, too, must be ready, for at an hour when you do not expect him, the Son of Man will come.

"Who then is the faithful and wise servant, whom his master has placed in charge of his household, to give them their food at the proper time? Blessed is that servant whom his master, when he comes, will find doing as instructed. I tell you truly, he will place him in charge of all his possessions. But if that wicked servant says in his heart, 'My master delays,' and begins to beat his fellow servants and to eat and drink with the drunkards, the master of that servant will come on a day when he does not expect him, and at an hour of which he is unaware, and will cut him asunder and assign him his place with the hypocrites, where there will be weeping and gnashing of teeth."

MATTHEW 24:1-51 ✓

1 And Jesus went out, and departed from the temple: and his disciples came to *him* for to show him the buildings of the temple.

2 And Jesus said unto them, See ye not all these things? verily I say unto you, There shall not be left here one stone upon another, that shall not be thrown down.

3 And as he sat upon the mount of Olives, the disciples came unto him privately, saying, Tell us, when shall these things be? and what *shall be* the sign of thy coming, and of the end of the world?

4 And Jesus answered and said unto them, Take heed that no man deceive you.

5 For many shall come in my name, saying, I am Christ; and shall deceive many.

6 And ye shall hear of wars and rumors of wars: see that ye be not troubled: for all *these things* must come to pass, but the end is not yet.

7 For nation shall rise against nation, and kingdom against kingdom: and there shall be famines, and pestilences, and earthquakes, in divers places.

8 All these *are* the beginning of sorrows.

9 Then shall they deliver you up to be afflicted, and shall kill you: and ye shall be hated of all nations for my name's sake.

10 And then shall many be offended, and shall betray one another, and shall hate one another.

11 And many false prophets shall rise, and shall deceive many.

12 And because iniquity shall abound, the love of many shall wax cold.

13 But he that shall endure unto the end, the same shall be saved.

14 And this gospel of the kingdom shall be preached in all the world for a witness unto all nations; and then shall the end come.

15 When ye therefore shall see the abomination of desolation, spoken of by Daniel the prophet, stand in the holy place, (whoso readeth, let him understand,)

16 Then let them which be in Judea flee into the mountains:

17 Let him which is on the housetop not come down to take any thing out of his house:

18 Neither let him which is in the field return back to take his clothes.

19 And woe unto them that are with child, and to them that give suck in those days!

20 But pray ye that your flight be not in the winter, neither on the sabbath day:

21 For then shall be great tribulation, such as was not since the beginning of the world to this time, no, nor ever shall be.

22 And except those days should be shortened, there should no flesh be saved: but for the elect's sake those days shall be shortened.

23 Then if any man shall say unto you, Lo, here *is* Christ, or there; believe *it* not.

24 For there shall arise false Christs, and false prophets, and shall show great signs and wonders; insomuch that, if *it were* possible, they shall deceive the very elect.

25 Behold, I have told you before.

26 Wherefore if they shall say unto you, Behold, he is in the desert; go not forth: behold, *he is* in the secret chambers; believe *it* not.

27 For as the lightning cometh out of the east, and shineth even unto the west; so shall also the coming of the Son of man be.

28 For wheresoever the carcass is, there will the eagles be gathered together.

29 Immediately after the tribulation of those days shall the sun be darkened, and the moon shall not give her light, and the stars shall fall from heaven, and the powers of the heavens shall be shaken:

30 And then shall appear the sign of the Son of man in heaven: and then shall all the tribes of the earth mourn, and they shall see the Son of man coming in the clouds of heaven with power and great glory.

31 And he shall send his angels with a great sound of a trumpet, and they shall gather together his elect from the four winds, from one end of heaven to the other.

32 Now learn a parable of the fig tree; When his branch is yet tender, and putteth forth leaves, ye know that summer *is* nigh:

33 So likewise ye, when ye shall see all these things, know that it is near, *even* at the doors.

34 Verily I say unto you, This generation shall not pass, till all these things be fulfilled.

35 Heaven and earth shall pass away, but my words shall not pass away.

36 But of that day and hour knoweth no *man,* no, not the angels of heaven, but my Father only.

37 But as the days of Noah *were,* so shall also the coming of the Son of man be.

38 For as in the days that were before the flood they were eating and drinking, marrying and giving in marriage, until the day that Noah entered into the ark,

39 And knew not until the flood came, and took them all away; so shall also the coming of the Son of man be.

40 Then shall two be in the field; the one shall be taken, and the other left.

41 Two *women shall be* grinding at the mill; the one shall be taken, and the other left.

42 Watch therefore; for ye know not what hour your Lord doth come.

43 But know this, that if the goodman of the house had known in what watch the thief would come, he would have watched, and would not have suffered his house to be broken up.

44 Therefore be ye also ready: for in such an hour as ye think not the Son of man cometh.

45 Who then is a faithful and wise servant, whom his lord hath made ruler over his household, to give them meat in due season?

46 Blessed *is* that servant, whom his lord when he cometh shall find so doing.

47 Verily I say unto you, That he shall make him ruler over all his goods.

48 But and if that evil servant shall say in his heart, My lord delayeth his coming;

49 And shall begin to smite *his* fellow servants, and to eat and drink with the drunken;

50 The lord of that servant shall come in a day when he looketh not for *him,* and in an hour that he is not aware of,

51 And shall cut him asunder, and appoint *him* his portion with the hypocrites: there shall be weeping and gnashing of teeth.

Boy with the Torah. *The Bar Mitzvah ("son of the law") ceremony is an important event in the life of a Jewish boy. It occurs when he is 13 years old and signifies his assuming adulthood in regard to religious responsibilities. In the container shown here is a copy of the Pentateuch, the first five books of the Scriptures.*

Jesus Previews History (continued)

1 And as he went out of the temple, one of his disciples saith unto him, Master, see what manner of stones and what buildings *are here!*

2 And Jesus answering said unto him, Seest thou these great buildings? there shall not be left one stone upon another, that shall not be thrown down.

3 And as he sat upon the mount of Olives, over against the temple, Peter and James and John and Andrew asked him privately,

4 Tell us, when shall these things be? and what *shall be* the sign when all these things shall be fulfilled?

5 And Jesus answering them began to say, Take heed lest any *man* deceive you:

6 For many shall come in my name, saying, I am *Christ;* and shall deceive many.

7 And when ye shall hear of wars and rumors of wars, be ye not troubled: for *such things* must needs be; but the end *shall* not *be* yet.

8 For nation shall rise against nation, and kingdom against kingdom: and there shall be earthquakes in divers places, and there shall be famines and troubles: these *are* the beginnings of sorrows.

9 But take heed to yourselves: for they shall deliver you up to councils; and in the synagogues ye shall be beaten: and ye shall be brought before rulers and kings for my sake, for a testimony against them.

10 And the gospel must first be published among all nations.

11 But when they shall lead *you,* and deliver you up, take no thought beforehand what ye shall speak, neither do ye premeditate: but whatsoever shall be given you in that hour, that speak ye: for it is not ye that speak, but the Holy Ghost.

12 Now the brother shall betray the brother to death, and the father the son; and children shall rise up against *their* parents, and shall cause them to be put to death.

13 And ye shall be hated of all *men* for my name's sake: but he that shall endure unto the end, the same shall be saved.

14 But when ye shall see the abomination of desolation, spoken of by Daniel the prophet, standing where it ought not, (let him that readeth understand,) then let them that be in Judea flee to the mountains:

15 And let him that is on the housetop not go down into the house, neither enter *therein,* to take any thing out of his house:

16 And let him that is in the field not turn back again for to take up his garment.

17 But woe to them that are with child, and to them that give suck in those days!

18 And pray ye that your flight be not in the winter.

19 For *in* those days shall be affliction, such as was not from the beginning of the creation which God created unto this time, neither shall be.

20 And except that the Lord had shortened those days, no flesh should be saved: but for the elect's sake, whom he hath chosen, he hath shortened the days.

21 And then if any man shall say to you, Lo, here *is* Christ; or, lo, *he is* there; believe *him* not:

22 For false Christs and false prophets shall rise, and shall show signs and wonders, to seduce, if it *were* possible, even the elect.

23 But take ye heed: behold, I have foretold you all things.

24 But in those days, after that tribulation, the sun shall be darkened, and the moon shall not give her light,

25 And the stars of heaven shall fall, and the powers that are in heaven shall be shaken.

26 And then shall they see the Son of man coming in the clouds with great power and glory.

27 And then shall he send his angels, and shall gather together his elect from the four winds, from the uttermost part of the earth to the uttermost part of heaven.

28 Now learn a parable of the fig tree: When her branch is yet tender, and putteth forth leaves, ye know that summer is near:

29 So ye in like manner, when ye shall see these things come to pass, know that it is nigh, *even* at the doors.

30 Verily I say unto you, that this generation shall not pass, till all these things be done.

31 Heaven and earth shall pass away: but my words shall not pass away.

32 But of that day and *that* hour knoweth no man, no, not the angels which are in heaven, neither the Son, but the Father.

33 Take ye heed, watch and pray: for ye know not when the time is.

34 *For the Son of man is* as a man taking a far journey, who left his house, and gave authority to his servants, and to every man his work, and commanded the porter to watch.

35 Watch ye therefore: for ye know not when the master of the house cometh, at even, or at midnight, or at the cockcrowing, or in the morning:

36 Lest coming suddenly he find you sleeping.

37 And what I say unto you I say unto all, Watch.

Jesus Previews History (continued)

5 And as some spake of the temple, how it was adorned with goodly stones and gifts, he said,

6 *As for* these things which ye behold, the days will come, in the which there shall not be left one stone upon another, that shall not be thrown down.

7 And they asked him, saying, Master, but when shall these things be? and what sign *will there be* when these things shall come to pass?

8 And he said, Take heed that ye be not deceived: for many shall come in my name, saying, I am *Christ;* and the time draweth near: go ye not therefore after them.

9 But when ye shall hear of wars and commotions, be not terrified: for these things must first come to pass; but the end *is* not by and by.

10 Then said he unto them, Nation shall rise against nation, and kingdom against kingdom:

11 And great earthquakes shall be in divers places,and famines, and pestilences; and fearful sights and great signs shall there be from heaven.

12 But before all these, they shall lay their hands on you, and persecute *you,* delivering *you* up to the synagogues, and into prisons, being brought before kings and rulers for my name's sake.

13 And it shall turn to you for a testimony.

14 Settle *it* therefore in your hearts, not to meditate before what ye shall answer:

15 For I will give you a mouth and wisdom, which all your adversaries shall not be able to gainsay nor resist.

16 And ye shall be betrayed both by parents, and brethren, and kinsfolk, and friends; and *some* of you shall they cause to be put to death.

17 And ye shall be hated of all *men* for my name's sake.

18 But there shall not a hair of your head perish.

19 In your patience possess ye your souls.

20 And when ye shall see Jerusalem compassed with armies, then know that the desolation thereof is nigh.

21 Then let them which are in Judea flee to the mountains; and let them which are in the midst of it depart out; and let not them that are in the countries enter thereinto.

22 For these be the days of vengeance, that all things which are written may be fulfilled.

23 But woe unto them that are with child, and to them that give suck, in those days! for there shall be great distress in the land, and wrath upon this people.

24 And they shall fall by the edge of the sword, and shall be led away captive into all nations: and Jerusalem shall be trodden down of the Gentiles, until the times of the Gentiles be fulfilled.

25 And there shall be signs in the sun, and in the moon, and in the stars; and upon the earth distress of nations, with perplexity; the sea and the waves roaring;

26 Men's hearts failing them for fear, and for looking after those things which are coming on the earth: for the powers of heaven shall be shaken.

27 And then shall they see the Son of man coming in a cloud with power and great glory.

28 And when these things begin to come to pass, then look up, and lift up your heads; for your redemption draweth nigh.

29 And he spake to them a parable; Behold the fig tree, and all the trees;

Watch ye therefore, and pray always, that ye may be accounted worthy to escape all these things that shall come to pass.

---

30 When they now shoot forth, ye see and know of your own selves that summer is now nigh at hand.

31 So likewise ye, when ye see these things come to pass, know ye that the kingdom of God is nigh at hand.

32 Verily I say unto you, This generation shall not pass away, till all be fulfilled.

33 Heaven and earth shall pass away; but my words shall not pass away.

34 And take heed to yourselves, lest at any time your hearts be overcharged with surfeiting, and drunkenness, and cares of this life, and *so* that day come upon you unawares.

35 For as a snare shall it come on all them that dwell on the face of the whole earth.

36 Watch ye therefore, and pray always, that ye may be accounted worthy to escape all these things that shall come to pass, and to stand before the Son of man.

37 And in the daytime he was teaching in the temple; and at night he went out, and abode in the mount that is called *the mount* of Olives.

38 And all the people came early in the morning to him in the temple, for to hear him.

Parable of the Virgins

Matthew 25:1-13

"Then will the kingdom of heaven be like ten bridesmaids who took their lamps and went to meet the bridegroom. Five of them were foolish, and five were wise. The foolish took their lamps, but took no oil with them, but the wise took flasks of oil along with their lamps. Now as the bridegroom delayed a long while, they all became drowsy and fell asleep. But at midnight there was a shout, 'Behold, the bridegroom! Come out to meet him!'

"Then all those bridesmaids rose and trimmed their lamps. And the foolish said to the wise, 'Give us some of your oil, for our lamps are going out!'

" 'No,' replied the wise, 'for there might not be enough for us and for you. Go instead to the oil sellers and buy some for yourselves.'

"But while they went to buy more oil, the bridegroom came, and those who were ready went in with him to the wedding feast, and the door was shut. Later on, the other bridesmaids came and said, 'Lord, Lord, open to us!'

"But he replied, 'I tell you truly, I do not know you.'

"Watch therefore, for you do not know the day or the hour."

MATTHEW 25:1-13

1 Then shall the kingdom of heaven be likened unto ten virgins, which took their lamps, and went forth to meet the bridegroom.

2 And five of them were wise, and five *were* foolish.

3 They that *were* foolish took their lamps, and took no oil with them:

4 But the wise took oil in their vessels with their lamps.

5 While the bridegroom tarried, they all slumbered and slept.

6 And at midnight there was a cry made, Behold, the bridegroom cometh; go ye out to meet him.

7 Then all those virgins arose, and trimmed their lamps.

8 And the foolish said unto the wise, Give us of your oil; for our lamps are gone out.

9 But the wise answered, saying, *Not so;* lest there be not enough for us and you: but go ye rather to them that sell, and buy for yourselves.

10 And while they went to buy, the bridegroom came; and they that were ready went in with him to the marriage: and the door was shut.

11 Afterward came also the other virgins, saying, Lord, Lord, open to us.

12 But he answered and said, Verily I say unto you, I know you not.

13 Watch therefore; for ye know neither the day nor the hour wherein the Son of man cometh.

Parable of the Talents

Matthew 25:14-30

"The kingdom of heaven is like a man going on a journey who called his servants and entrusted to them his property. And to one he gave five talents, to another two, and to another one—to each man according to his ability. Then he took his journey. He who had received the five talents went at once and began to trade with them and gained five more. In like manner, he who received the two talents gained two more.

MATTHEW 25:14-30

14 For *the kingdom of heaven is* as a man traveling into a far country, *who* called his own servants, and delivered unto them his goods.

15 And unto one he gave five talents, to another two, and to another one; to every man according to his several ability; and straightway took his journey.

16 Then he that had received the five talents went and traded with the same, and made *them*

Tower of Antonia. *Stands at the north-western corner of the Temple area, about where the Fortress of Antonia was situated. Here procurators like Pilate would stay while in Jerusalem. It was in the Fortress Jesus stood on trial.*

Parable of the Talents (continued)

But he who received the one talent went away and dug a hole in the ground and hid his master's money. And after a long time the master of those servants came to settle accounts with them. Then he who received the five talents came and brought five more talents and said, 'Master, you gave me five talents. See, I have gained five more talents.'

" 'Well done, good and faithful servant,' said his master, 'you have been faithful over a few things, I will place you in charge of many things. Come and share your master's joy.'

"Then he who received the two talents came and said, 'Sir, you gave me two talents. See, I have gained two more talents.'

" 'Well done, good and faithful servant,' said his master, 'you have been faithful over a few things, I will place you in charge of many things. Come and share your master's joy.'

"Then he who had received the one talent came and said, 'Sir, I knew you to be a hard man, reaping where you did not sow and gathering where you did not winnow, and I was afraid and went and hid your talent in the ground. See, you still have what is yours.'

"Then his master answered him, 'You wicked and lazy servant! You knew, did you, that I reap where I have not sowed and gather where I have not winnowed? Then you should have deposited my money with the bankers, and at my coming I should have received what was my own with interest. Take the talent from him and give it to the man who has ten talents. For to everyone who has will more be given, and he will have an abundance, but from him who has not, even what he has will be taken away. Cast the worthless servant into the darkness outside, where there will be weeping and gnashing of teeth.' "

other five talents.

17 And likewise he that *had received* two, he also gained other two.

18 But he that had received one went and digged in the earth, and hid his lord's money.

19 After a long time the lord of those servants cometh, and reckoneth with them.

20 And so he that had received five talents came and brought other five talents, saying, Lord, thou deliveredst unto me five talents: behold, I have gained beside them five talents more.

21 His lord said unto him, Well done, *thou* good and faithful servant: thou hast been faithful over a few things, I will make thee ruler over many things: enter thou into the joy of thy lord.

22 He also that had received two talents came and said, Lord, thou deliveredst unto me two talents: behold, I have gained two other talents beside them.

23 His lord said unto him, Well done, good and faithful servant; thou hast been faithful over a few things, I will make thee ruler over many things: enter thou into the joy of thy lord.

24 Then he which had received the one talent came and said, Lord, I knew thee that thou art a hard man, reaping where thou hast not sown, and gathering where thou hast not strewed:

25 And I was afraid, and went and hid thy talent in the earth: lo, *there* thou hast *that is* thine.

26 His lord answered and said unto him, *Thou* wicked and slothful servant, thou knewest that I reap where I sowed not, and gather where I have not strewed:

27 Thou oughtest therefore to have put my money to the exchangers, and *then* at my coming I should have received mine own with usury.

28 Take therefore the talent from him, and give *it* unto him which hath ten talents.

29 For unto every one that hath shall be given, and he shall have abundance: but from him that hath not shall be taken away even that which he hath.

30 And cast ye the unprofitable servant into outer darkness: there shall be weeping and gnashing of teeth.

The Coming Judgment

"When the Son of Man comes in his glory, and all the angels with him, then he will sit on his throne of glory and all the nations will be gathered before him. And he will separate the people as a shepherd divides the sheep from the goats; he will set the sheep on his right hand, and the goats on his left.

"Then the King will say to those on his right hand, 'Come, you blessed of my Father, inherit the kingdom prepared for you from the foundation of the world. For I was hungry and you gave me food, I was thirsty and you gave me a drink. I was a stranger, and you took me in. I was naked, and you clothed me. I was sick, and you visited me. I was in prison, and you came to me.

"Then the righteous will answer him, 'Lord, when did we see you hungry and feed you, or thirsty and give you a drink? And when did we see you a stranger and take you in, or naked and clothe you? And when did we see you sick or in prison and come to you?

"And the King will answer them, 'I tell you truly, inasmuch as you did it to one of the least of these my brethren, you did it to me.'

"Then he will say to those on his left, 'Depart from me, you accursed, into everlasting fire prepared for the devil and his angels. For I was hungry and you gave me no food, I was thirsty and you gave me no drink. I was a stranger and you did not take me in, naked and you did not clothe me, sick and in prison and you did not visit me.'

"Then they too will answer, 'Lord, when did we see you hungry, or thirsty, or a stranger, or naked, or sick, or in prison, and did not minister to you?'

"Then he will answer them, 'I tell you truly, inasmuch as you did it not to one of the least of these, you did it not to me.' And these will go away into everlasting punishment, but the righteous into eternal life.''

MATTHEW 25:31-46

31 When the Son of man shall come in his glory, and all the holy angels with him, then shall he sit upon the throne of his glory:

32 And before him shall be gathered all nations: and he shall separate them one from another, as a shepherd divideth *his* sheep from the goats:

33 And he shall set the sheep on his right hand, but the goats on the left.

34 Then shall the King say unto them on his right hand, Come, ye blessed of my Father, inherit the kingdom prepared for you from the foundation of the world:

35 For I was ahungered, and ye gave me meat: I was thirsty, and ye gave me drink: I was a stranger, and ye took me in:

36 Naked, and ye clothed me: I was sick, and ye visited me: I was in prison, and ye came unto me.

37 Then shall the righteous answer him, saying, Lord, when saw we thee ahungered, and fed *thee?* or thirsty, and gave *thee* drink?

38 When saw we thee a stranger, and took *thee* in? or naked, and clothed *thee?*

39 Or when saw we thee sick, or in prison, and came unto thee?

40 And the King shall answer and say unto them, Verily I say unto you, Inasmuch as ye have done *it* unto one of the least of these my brethren, ye have done *it* unto me.

41 Then shall he say also unto them on the left hand, Depart from me, ye cursed, into everlasting fire, prepared for the devil and his angels:

42 For I was ahungered, and ye gave me no meat: I was thirsty, and ye gave me no drink:

43 I was a stranger, and ye took me not in: naked, and ye clothed me not: sick, and in prison, and ye visited me not.

44 Then shall they also answer him, saying, Lord, when saw we thee ahungered, or athirst, or a stranger, or naked, or sick, or in prison, and did not minister unto thee?

45 Then shall he answer them, saying, Verily I say unto you, Inasmuch as ye did *it* not to one of the least of these, ye did *it* not to me.

46 And these shall go away into everlasting punishment: but the righteous into life eternal.

Sheep and Goats. *In His parable Jesus illustrated the judgment of nations by the shepherds' custom of gathering both the sheep and the goats together, then separating them.*

Judas' Conspiracy

Matthew 26:1-5, 14-16

And when Jesus had finished all these sayings, he said to his disciples, "You know that after two days the Passover will come. Then the Son of Man will be delivered up to be crucified."

Then the chief priests and the elders of the people gathered together in the palace of the High Priest, Caiaphas, and discussed how they might arrest Jesus by some sort of craftiness and kill him.

"But not during the feast," they said, "or it might cause an uprising among the people."

Then one of the twelve, Judas Iscariot, went to the chief priests and said, "What will you give me if I deliver him into your hands?"

And they weighed him out thirty pieces of silver, and from that time, he watched for an opportunity to betray him.

MATTHEW 26:1-5, 14-16	MARK 14:1-2, 10-11	LUKE 22:1-6
1 And it came to pass, when Jesus had finished all these sayings, he said unto his disciples,	1 After two days was *the feast of* the passover, and of unleavened bread: and the chief priests and the scribes sought how they might take him by craft, and put *him* to death.	1 Now the feast of unleavened bread drew nigh, which is called the passover.
2 Ye know that after two days is *the feast of* the passover, and the Son of man is betrayed to be crucified.	2 But they said, Not on the feast *day*, lest there be an uproar of the people.	2 And the chief priests and scribes sought how they might kill him; for they feared the people.
3 Then assembled together the chief priests, and the scribes, and the elders of the people, unto the palace of the high priest, who was called Caiaphas,	10 And Judas Iscariot, one of the twelve, went unto the chief priests, to betray him unto them.	3 Then entered Satan into Judas surnamed Iscariot, being of the number of the twelve.
4 And consulted that they might take Jesus by subtilty, and kill *him*.	11 And when they heard *it,* they were glad, and promised to give him money. And he sought how he might conveniently betray him.	4 And he went his way, and communed with the chief priests and captains, how he might betray him unto them.
5 But they said, Not on the feast *day*, lest there be an uproar among the people.		5 And they were glad, and covenanted to give him money.
14 Then one of the twelve, called Judas Iscariot, went unto the chief priests,		6 And he promised, and sought opportunity to betray him unto them in the absence of the multitude.
15 And said *unto them,* What will ye give me, and I will deliver him unto you? And they covenanted with him for thirty pieces of silver.		
16 And from that time he sought opportunity to betray him.		

Preparing for Passover

On the first day of Unleavened Bread, when they sacrificed the passover lamb, his disciples said to Jesus, "Where do you want us to go to prepare for you to eat the Passover?"

And he sent two of his disciples, saying, "Go into the city, and a man will meet you carrying a pitcher of water. Follow him, and wherever he enters, say to the master of the house, 'The Master says, "Where is the guest chamber where I will eat the Passover with my disciples?" ' He will show you a large upper room, furnished and ready, and there you are to make preparations for us."

And the disciples left and went into the city and found things just as Jesus had told them, and prepared the Passover. And when it was evening, Jesus arrived with the twelve.

MATT. 26:17-20

17 Now the first *day* of the *feast of* unleavened bread the disciples came to Jesus, saying unto him, Where wilt thou that we prepare for thee to eat the passover?

18 And he said, Go into the city to such a man, and say unto him, The Master saith, My time is at hand; I will keep the passover at thy house with my disciples.

19 And the disciples did as Jesus had appointed them; and they made ready the passover.

20 Now when the even was come, he sat down with the twelve.

MARK 14:12-17

12 And the first day of unleavened bread, when they killed the passover, his disciples said unto him, Where wilt thou that we go and prepare that thou mayest eat the passover?

13 And he sendeth forth two of his disciples, and saith unto them, Go ye into the city, and there shall meet you a man bearing a pitcher of water: follow him.

14 And wheresoever he shall go in, say ye to the goodman of the house, The Master saith, Where is the guest chamber, where I shall eat the passover with my disciples?

15 And he will show you a large upper room furnished *and* prepared: there make ready for us.

16 And his disciples went forth, and came into the city, and found as he had said unto them: and they made ready the passover.

17 And in the evening he cometh with the twelve.

LUKE 22:7-18

7 Then came the day of unleavened bread, when the passover must be killed.

8 And he sent Peter and John, saying, Go and prepare us the passover, that we may eat.

9 And they said unto him, Where wilt thou that we prepare?

10 And he said unto them, Behold, when ye are entered into the city, there shall a man meet you, bearing a pitcher of water; follow him into the house where he entereth in.

11 And ye shall say unto the goodman of the house, The Master saith unto thee, Where is the guest chamber, where I shall eat the passover with my disciples?

12 And he shall show you a large upper room furnished; there make ready.

13 And they went, and found as he had said unto them: and they made ready the passover.

14 And when the hour was come, he sat down, and the twelve apostles with him.

15 And he said unto them, With desire I have desired to eat this passover with you before I suffer:

16 For I say unto you, I will not any more eat thereof, until it be fulfilled in the kingdom of God.

17 And he took the cup, and gave thanks, and said, Take this, and divide *it* among yourselves:

18 For I say unto you, I will not drink of the fruit of the vine, until the kingdom of God shall come.

JOHN 13:1-2

1 Now before the feast of the passover, when Jesus knew that his hour was come that he should depart out of this world unto the Father, having loved his own which were in the world, he loved them unto the end.

2 And supper being ended, the devil having now put into the heart of Judas Iscariot, Simon's *son,* to betray him;

Jesus Washes the Disciples' Feet. *It became urgent for Jesus to teach His disciples a lesson in humility. They had been arguing as to who would be the greatest. By taking the place of a servant He showed them the path to true greatness.*

296

Contending for the Highest Place

Luke 22:24-27

And there arose a dispute among the disciples as to which of them should be considered the most important. Then Jesus said to them,

"The kings of the Gentiles lord it over them, and their rulers are called 'benefactors.' But it is not to be that way among you. Instead, let the greatest among you become as the youngest, and the one who leads as one who serves. Who is the greater, the one who sits at the table, or the one who serves? Is it not the one who sits at the table? And yet I am among you as one who serves."

LUKE 22:24-30

24 And there was also a strife among them, which of them should be accounted the greatest.

25 And he said unto them, The kings of the Gentiles exercise lordship over them; and they that exercise authority upon them are called benefactors.

26 But ye *shall* not *be* so: but he that is greatest among you, let him be as the younger; and he that is chief, as he that doth serve.

27 For whether *is* greater, he that sitteth at meat, or he that serveth? *is* not he that sitteth at meat? but I am among you as he that serveth.

28 Ye are they which have continued with me in my temptations.

29 And I appoint unto you a kingdom, as my Father hath appointed unto me;

30 That ye may eat and drink at my table in my kingdom, and sit on thrones judging the twelve tribes of Israel.

Yad Vashem Inscription. *These words expressing both the hope and faith for the coming of the Messiah appear alongside a path at the Jewish memorial to the Holocaust. Jesus assured His disciples the Father had destined Him to have a kingdom for himself and His followers.*

Jesus Teaches Humility

John 13:3-20

Then Jesus, fully aware that the Father had committed all things into his hands and that he had come from God and would return to God, rose from the supper table, laid aside his garments, and took a towel and tied it around his waist. Then he poured water into a basin and began to wash the disciples' feet and to wipe them with the towel around his waist. And he came to Simon Peter.

"Lord," said Peter, "are *you* going to wash *my* feet?"

"You do not know now what I am doing," replied Jesus, "but you will understand later on."

"You shall never wash my feet!" said Peter.

"Unless I wash you," replied Jesus, "you have no part with me."

"Lord," said Simon Peter, "not just my feet, but also my hands and my head!"

He who has bathed," said Jesus, "needs only to wash his feet to be clean all over. And you are clean, though not all of you."

(For Jesus knew who was betraying him, and that is why he said, "Not all of you are clean.")

When he had washed their feet, Jesus put on his garments and sat down again and said,

"Do you understand the meaning of what I have done to you? You call me Master and Lord, and you are right, for so I am. If I therefore, your Lord and Master, washed your feet, you ought also to wash one another's feet. I have given you an example, that you should do as I have done to you. I tell you truly, a servant is not greater than his master, nor is one who is sent greater than the one who sent him. If you know these things, you are blessed if you do them.

"I am not speaking of all of you. I know whom I have chosen. But the scripture must be fulfilled, 'He who eats my bread has lifted up his heel against me.' I am telling this to you now, before it comes to pass, that when it comes to pass you may believe that I am he. I tell you truly, he who receives anyone whom I send receives me, and he who receives me receives the one who sent me."

JOHN 13:3-20

3 Jesus knowing that the Father had given all things into his hands, and that he was come from God, and went to God;

4 He riseth from supper, and laid aside his garments; and took a towel, and girded himself.

5 After that he poureth water into a basin, and began to wash the disciples' feet, and to wipe *them* with the towel wherewith he was girded.

6 Then cometh he to Simon Peter: and Peter saith unto him, Lord, dost thou wash my feet?

7 Jesus answered and said unto him, What I do thou knowest not now; but thou shalt know hereafter.

8 Peter saith unto him, Thou shalt never wash my feet. Jesus answered him, If I wash thee not, thou hast no part with me.

9 Simon Peter saith unto him, Lord, not my feet only, but also *my* hands and *my* head.

10 Jesus saith to him, He that is washed needeth not save to wash *his* feet, but is clean every whit: and ye are clean, but not all.

11 For he knew who should betray him; therefore said he, Ye are not all clean.

12 So after he had washed their feet, and had taken his garments, and was set down again, he said unto them, Know ye what I have done to you?

13 Ye call me Master and Lord: and ye say well; for *so* I am.

14 If I then, *your* Lord and Master, have washed your feet; ye also ought to wash one another's feet.

15 For I have given you an example, that ye should do as I have done to you.

16 Verily, verily, I say unto you, The servant is not greater than his lord; neither he that is sent greater than he that sent him.

17 If ye know these things, happy are ye if ye do them.

18 I speak not of you all: I know whom I have chosen: but that the Scripture may be fulfilled, He that eateth bread with me hath lifted up his heel against me.

19 Now I tell you before it come, that, when it is come to pass, ye may believe that I am *he*.

20 Verily, verily, I say unto you, He that receiveth whomsoever I send receiveth me; and he that receiveth me receiveth him that sent me.

Events at the Last Supper

Luke 22:15-16, Matthew 26:21-29, John 13:22-30

And Jesus said to them, "With great longing have I desired to eat this Passover with you before I suffer. For I tell you, I shall not eat it again until it is fulfilled in the kingdom of God."

And as they were eating, Jesus said, "I tell you truly, one of you will betray me."

And they were very sorrowful, and began to say to him, one after another, "Is it I, Lord?"

"One who has dipped his hand in the dish with me will betray me," answered Jesus. "The Son of Man will go, of course, as it was written of him; but woe to that man by whom the Son of Man is betrayed! It would have been better for that man if he had not been born."

Then Judas, who betrayed him, said, "Is it I, Master?"

"As you say," said Jesus.

The disciples looked at one another, uncertain of whom Jesus had spoken. One of his disciples, whom Jesus loved, was leaning against his breast. Simon Peter therefore beckoned to him and said, "Tell us who it is of whom he is speaking."

Leaning thus against the breast of Jesus, he asked him, "Lord, who is it?"

"It is the one to whom I give this sop after I dip it," replied Jesus.

And when he had dipped the sop, he gave it to Judas, the son of Simon Iscariot; and after Judas took the sop, Satan entered into him.

"What you are going to do, do quickly," said Jesus.

None of the others sitting at the table knew why Jesus said this to him. Because Judas had charge of the money bag, some thought that Jesus was telling him, "Buy what we need for the festival," or that he should give something to the poor. And he took the sop and went out at once, and it was night.

And as they were eating, Jesus took a loaf of bread and blessed it, and broke it and gave it to the disciples.

"Take this and eat it," he said. "This is my body."

Then he took a cup, and when he had given thanks, he gave it to them.

"All of you drink of it," he said. "This is my blood of the covenant, which is shed for many for the forgiveness of sins. I say to you, I will not drink again of this fruit of the vine until that day when I drink it new with you in my Father's kingdom."

The Cenacle. *Here the Last Supper took place according to tradition. Some believe that the outpouring of the Holy Spirit also occurred here while others think it happened in the Temple.*

Events at the Last Supper (continued)

MATT. 26:21-29 ✓	MARK 14:18-25 ✓	LUKE 22:19-23 ✓	JOHN 13:21-30 ✓
21 And as they did eat, he said, Verily I say unto you, that one of you shall betray me. 22 And they were exceeding sorrowful, and began every one of them to say unto him, Lord, is it I? 23 And he answered and said, He that dippeth *his* hand with me in the dish, the same shall betray me. 24 The Son of man goeth as it is written of him: but woe unto that man by whom the Son of man is betrayed! it had been good for that man if he had not been born. 25 Then Judas, which betrayed him, answered and said, Master, is it I? He said unto him, Thou hast said. 26 And as they were eating, Jesus took bread, and blessed *it,* and brake *it,* and gave *it* to the disciples, and said, Take, eat; this is my body. 27 And he took the cup, and gave thanks, and gave *it* to them, saying, Drink ye all of it; 28 For this is my blood of the new testament, which is shed for many for the remission of sins. 29 But I say unto you, I will not drink henceforth of this fruit of the vine, until that day when I drink it new with you in my Father's kingdom.	18 And as they sat and did eat, Jesus said, Verily I say unto you, One of you which eateth with me shall betray me. 19 And they began to be sorrowful, and to say unto him one by one, *Is* it I? and another *said, Is* it I? 20 And he answered and said unto them, *It is* one of the twelve, that dippeth with me in the dish. 21 The Son of man indeed goeth, as it is written of him: but woe to that man by whom the Son of man is betrayed! good were it for that man if he had never been born. 22 And as they did eat, Jesus took bread, and blessed, and brake *it,* and gave to them, and said, Take, eat; this is my body. 23 And he took the cup, and when he had given thanks, he gave *it* to them: and they all drank of it. 24 And he said unto them, This is my blood of the new testament, which is shed for many. 25 Verily I say unto you, I will drink no more of the fruit of the vine, until that day that I drink it new in the kingdom of God.	19 And he took bread, and gave thanks, and brake *it,* and gave unto them, saying, This is my body which is given for you: this do in remembrance of me. 20 Likewise also the cup after supper, saying, This cup *is* the new testament in my blood, which is shed for you. 21 But, behold, the hand of him that betrayeth me *is* with me on the table. 22 And truly the Son of man goeth, as it was determined: but woe unto that man by whom he is betrayed! 23 And they began to inquire among themselves, which of them it was that should do this thing.	21 When Jesus had thus said, he was troubled in spirit, and testified, and said, Verily, verily, I say unto you, that one of you shall betray me. 22 Then the disciples looked one on another, doubting of whom he spake. 23 Now there was leaning on Jesus' bosom one of his disciples, whom Jesus loved. 24 Simon Peter therefore beckoned to him, that he should ask who it should be of whom he spake. 25 He then lying on Jesus' breast saith unto him, Lord, who is it? 26 Jesus answered, He it is, to whom I shall give a sop, when I have dipped *it.* And when he had dipped the sop, he gave *it* to Judas Iscariot, *the son* of Simon. 27 And after the sop Satan entered into him. Then said Jesus unto him, That thou doest, do quickly. 28 Now no man at the table knew for what intent he spake this unto him. 29 For some *of them* thought, because Judas had the bag, that Jesus had said unto him, Buy *those things* that we have need of against the feast; or, that he should give something to the poor. 30 He then, having received the sop, went immediately out; and it was night.

Jesus to Be Forsaken, Denied

John 13:31-38, Matthew 26:30-35, Luke 22:31-38

When Judas had gone out, Jesus said, "Now the Son of Man is glorified, and God is glorified in him. And if God is glorified through him, then God will share his own glory with the Son of Man, and will glorify him soon. Little children, I will be with you only a little while longer. You will seek me; but as I said to the Jews, so I must now say to you: where I am going you cannot come.

"And now, I give you a new commandment: you are to love one another. Just as I have loved you, you are to love one another. If you love one another, all men will know by this that you are my disciples."

"Lord, where are you going?" asked Simon Peter.

"Where I am going, you cannot follow now," replied Jesus, "but you will follow me later."

"Lord," said Peter, "why can't I follow you now? I will lay down my life for you!"

"Will you indeed lay down your life for me?" replied Jesus. "I tell you truly, the cock will not crow before you disown me three times."

And after they had sung a hymn, they went out to the Mount of Olives.

Then Jesus said to them, "This night, you will all turn away from me, for it is written, 'I will smite the shepherd, and the sheep of the flock will be scattered.' But after I am raised from the dead, I will go before you into Galilee."

Then Peter said to Jesus, "Even if all the others turn away from you, I never will!"

"Simon, Simon," said Jesus, "behold, Satan wants every one of you, to sift you as wheat. But I have prayed for you, that your faith may not fail; and when you have come back, strengthen your brothers."

"Lord," said Peter, "I am ready to go with you to prison and to death!"

"I tell you, Peter," said Jesus, "the cock will not crow this day until you deny three times that you even know me."

"Even if I have to die with you, I will not disown you," said Peter. And all the disciples said the same thing.

Then Jesus said to them, "When I sent you out without purse or provision bag or sandals, did you lack anything?"

"Nothing," they replied.

"But now, let him who has a purse take it with him," said Jesus, "and also a provision bag. And let him who has no sword sell his coat and buy one. For I tell you, this that has been written must be fulfilled in me: 'And he was reckoned with the transgressors.' For the things written about me are about to be fulfilled."

"Lord, see, here are two swords," they said.

And he said to them, "That is enough."

MATT. 26:30-35	MARK 14:26-31	LUKE 22:31-38	JOHN 13:31-38
30 And when they had sung a hymn, they went out into the mount of Olives. 31 Then saith Jesus unto them, All ye shall be offended because of me this night: for it is written, I will smite the shepherd, and the sheep of the flock shall be scattered abroad. 32 But after I am risen again, I will go before you into Galilee.	26 And when they had sung a hymn, they went out into the mount of Olives. 27 And Jesus saith unto them, All ye shall be offended because of me this night: for it is written, I will smite the shepherd, and the sheep shall be scattered. 28 But after that I am risen, I will go before you into Galilee.	31 And the Lord said, Simon, Simon, behold, Satan hath desired *to have* you, that he may sift *you* as wheat: 32 But I have prayed for thee, that thy faith fail not: and when thou art converted, strengthen thy brethren. 33 And he said unto him, Lord, I am ready to go with thee, both into prison, and to death. 34 And he said, I tell thee, Peter, the cock shall	31 Therefore, when he was gone out, Jesus said, Now is the Son of man glorified, and God is glorified in him. 32 If God be glorified in him, God shall also glorify him in himself, and shall straightway glorify him. 33 Little children, yet a little while I am with you. Ye shall seek me; and as I said unto the Jews, Whither I go, ye

301

Jesus to Be Forsaken, Denied (continued)

33 Peter answered and said unto him, Though all *men* shall be offended because of thee, *yet* will I never be offended.

34 Jesus said unto him, Verily I say unto thee, That this night, before the cock crow, thou shalt deny me thrice.

35 Peter said unto him, Though I should die with thee, yet will I not deny thee. Likewise also said all the disciples.

29 But Peter said unto him, Although all shall be offended, yet *will* not I.

30 And Jesus saith unto him, Verily I say unto thee, That this day, *even* in this night, before the cock crow twice, thou shalt deny me thrice.

31 But he spake the more vehemently, If I should die with thee, I will not deny thee in any wise. Likewise also said they all.

not crow this day, before that thou shalt thrice deny that thou knowest me.

35 And he said unto them, When I sent you without purse, and scrip, and shoes, lacked ye any thing? And they said, Nothing.

36 Then said he unto them, But now, he that hath a purse, let him take *it,* and likewise *his* scrip: and he that hath no sword, let him sell his garment, and buy one.

37 For I say unto you, that this that is written must yet be accomplished in me, And he was reckoned among the transgressors: for the things concerning me have an end.

38 And they said, Lord, behold, here *are* two swords. And he said unto them, It is enough.

cannot come; so now I say to you.

34 A new commandment I give unto you, that ye love one another; as I have loved you, that ye also love one another.

35 By this shall all *men* know that ye are my disciples, if ye have love one to another.

36 Simon Peter said unto him, Lord, whither goest thou? Jesus answered him, Whither I go, thou canst not follow me now; but thou shalt follow me afterward.

37 Peter said unto him, Lord, why cannot I follow thee now? I will lay down my life for thy sake.

38 Jesus answered him, Wilt thou lay down thy life for my sake? Verily, verily, I say unto thee, The cock shall not crow, till thou hast denied me thrice.

Jesus Comforts His Disciples

John 14:1-31

"Let not your heart be troubled," said Jesus. "You believe in God, believe also in me. In my Father's house are many mansions. If it were not so, would I have told you that I go to prepare a place for you? And if I go and prepare a place for you, I will come again and receive you to myself, that where I am, there you may be also. And you know the way to where I am going."

"Lord," said Thomas, "we don't know where you are going. How can we know the way?"

"I am the way, the truth, and the life," said Jesus. "No one can come to the Father except through me. If you had truly known me, you

1 Let not your heart be troubled: ye believe in God, believe also in me.

2 In my Father's house are many mansions: if *it were* not *so,* I would have told you. I go to prepare a place for you.

3 And if I go and prepare a place for you, I will come again, and receive you unto myself; that where I am, *there* ye may be also.

4 And whither I go ye know, and the way ye know.

5 Thomas saith unto him, Lord, we know not whither thou goest; and how can we know the way?

6 Jesus saith unto him, I am the way, the truth, and the life: no man cometh unto the Father, but by me.

Jesus Comforts His Disciples (continued)

would have known my Father too. From this time on, you know him and have seen him."

"Lord," said Philip, "show us the Father, and that will be all we need."

"Have I been with you for so long a time," said Jesus, "and yet you do not know me, Philip? He who has seen me has seen the Father. How is it that you say, 'Show us the Father'? Do you not believe that I am in the Father and the Father is in me? The words I say to you I do not speak on my own authority; but the Father, dwelling in me, is performing his works. Believe me that I am in the Father and the Father in me; at least, believe me for the sake of the works themselves.

"I tell you truly, the man who believes in me will do the works I do. And he will do greater works than these, because I am going to the Father and whatever you ask in my name I will do, that the Father may be glorified through the Son. If you ask anything in my name, I will do it.

"If you love me, you will keep my commandments. And I will ask the Father, and he will give you another Comforter to be with you for ever—the Spirit of Truth, whom the world cannot receive, because it does not recognize him or know him. You know him, for he dwells with you and will be in you. I will not leave you desolate; I will come to you. Yet a little while, and the world will see me no more; but you will see me. Because I live, you too will live. In that day you will know that I am in my Father, and you in me, and I in you. He who has my commandments and keeps them is the one who loves me, and he who loves me will be loved by my Father. And I will love him and will manifest myself to him."

Judas (not Iscariot) said to him, "Lord, how is it that you will manifest yourself to us, but not to the world?"

"If a man loves me," replied Jesus, "he will obey my word, and my Father will love him, and we will come to him and dwell with him. He who does not love me does not obey my words; and the word you are hearing is not mine, but the Father's who sent me. I have told you these things while I am still with you. But the Comforter, the Holy Spirit whom the Father will send in my name, will teach you all things and

JOHN 14:1-31

7 If ye had known me, ye should have known my Father also: and from henceforth ye know him, and have seen him.

8 Philip saith unto him, Lord, show us the Father, and it sufficeth us.

9 Jesus saith unto him, Have I been so long time with you, and yet hast thou not known me, Philip? he that hath seen me hath seen the Father; and how sayest thou *then,* Show us the Father?

10 Believest thou not that I am in the Father, and the Father in me? the words that I speak unto you I speak not of myself: but the Father that dwelleth in me, he doeth the works.

11 Believe me that I *am* in the Father, and the Father in me: or else believe me for the very works' sake.

12 Verily, verily, I say unto you, He that believeth on me, the works that I do shall he do also; and greater *works* than these shall he do; because I go unto my Father.

13 And whatsoever ye shall ask in my name, that will I do, that the Father may be glorified in the Son.

14 If ye shall ask any thing in my name, I will do *it.*

15 *If* ye love me, keep my commandments.

16 And I will pray the Father, and he shall give you another Comforter, that he may abide with you for ever;

17 *Even* the Spirit of truth; whom the world cannot receive, because it seeth him not, neither knoweth him: but ye know him; for he dwelleth with you, and shall be in you.

18 I will not leave you comfortless: I will come to you.

19 Yet a little while, and the world seeth me no more; but ye see me: because I live, ye shall live also.

20 At that day ye shall know that I *am* in my Father, and ye in me, and I in you.

21 He that hath my commandments, and keepth them, he it is that loveth me: and he that loveth me shall be loved of my Father, and I will love him, and will manifest myself to him.

22 Judas saith unto him, not Iscariot, Lord, how is it that thou wilt manifest thyself unto us, and not unto the world?

23 Jesus answered and said unto him, If a man love me, he will keep my words: and my Father will love him, and we will come unto him, and make our abode with him.

Jesus Comforts His Disciples (continued)

bring to your remembrance all that I have told you.

"Peace I leave with you; my peace I give to you. Not as the world gives do I give to you. Let not your heart be troubled, neither let it be afraid. You have heard me say, 'I am going away, and I am coming back to you.' If you loved me, you would have rejoiced because I am going to the Father, for the Father is greater than I. And now I have told you before it happens, so that when it takes place, you may have faith. I will not talk with you much longer, for the prince of this world is coming. He has no power over me; but I am doing what the Father commanded me to do, that the world may know that I love the Father. Rise, let us go."

JOHN 14:1-31 ✓

24 He that loveth me not keepeth not my sayings: and the word which ye hear is not mine, but the Father's which sent me.

25 These things have I spoken unto you, being *yet* present with you.

26 But the Comforter, *which is* the Holy Ghost, whom the Father will send in my name, he shall teach you all things, and bring all things to your remembrance, whatsoever I have said unto you.

27 Peace I leave with you, my peace I give unto you: not as the world giveth, give I unto you. Let not your heart be troubled, neither let it be afraid.

28 Ye have heard how I said unto you, I go away, and come *again* unto you. If ye loved me, ye would rejoice, because I said, I go unto the Father: for my Father is greater than I.

29 And now I have told you before it come to pass, that, when it is come to pass, ye might believe.

30 Hereafter I will not talk much with you: for the prince of this world cometh, and hath nothing in me.

31 But that the world may know that I love the Father; and as the Father gave me commandment, even so I do. Arise, let us go hence.

The True Vine

John 15:1-27

"I am the true vine," said Jesus, "and my Father is the vinedresser. Every branch in me that does not bear fruit, he trims away; and every branch that bears fruit, he prunes, that it may yield more fruit. Already, you have been pruned by the teaching I have given you. Abide in me, and I in you. Just as the branch cannot bear fruit by itself without continuing in the vine, neither can you unless you abide in me. I am the vine, you are the branches. Whoever abides in me, and I in him, is the one who will bear abundant fruit. For you can do nothing severed from me.

"If a man does not abide in me, he is cast forth as a branch and withers; and such branches are

JOHN 15:1-27 ✓

1 I am the true vine, and my Father is the husbandman.

2 Every branch in me that beareth not fruit he taketh away: and every *branch* that beareth fruit, he purgeth it, that it may bring forth more fruit.

3 Now ye are clean through the word which I have spoken unto you.

4 Abide in me, and I in you. As the branch cannot bear fruit of itself, except it abide in the vine; no more can ye, except ye abide in me.

5 I am the vine, ye *are* the branches. He that abideth in me, and I in him, the same bringeth forth much fruit; for without me ye can do nothing.

6 If a man abide not in me, he is cast forth as a branch, and is withered; and men gather

Jesus Prays in Gethsemane. *The word Gethsemane means "olive press." The olives were crushed to extract the oil so needed and beneficial. Jesus endured a crushing burden as He made the consecration to bear our sins on the cross. The oil of mercy produced by His sacrifice has blessed multiplied millions of believers.*

The True Vine (continued)

gathered up and thrown into the fire and burned. If you abide in me and my words abide in you, ask whatever you wish and it will be done for you. As you bear abundant fruit, my Father will be glorified, and you will truly be my disciples.

"As the Father has loved me, so have I loved you. Continue in my love. If you keep my commandments, you will continue in my love, just as I have kept my Father's commandments and continue in his love. I have told you these things so that you may share my joy, and that your joy may be complete.

"This is my commandment, that you love one another as I have loved you. Greater love has no man than this, that a man lay down his life for his friends. You are my friends if you do what I command you. I no longer call you servants, for a servant does not know everything about his master's business. Instead, I have called you friends, because I have shared with you everything that I have heard from my Father. It is not you who chose me, but I who chose you and appointed you, that you should go and bear fruit and that your fruit should endure, and that the Father should give you whatever you ask in my name. This I command you: love one another.

"If the world hates you, just remember that it hated me before it hated you. If you belonged to the world, the world would love you as its own; but because you do not belong to the world, but I have chosen you out of the world, therefore the world hates you. Remember what I told you, 'A servant is not greater than his master.' If they have persecuted me, they will persecute you too; if they have accepted my teaching, they will accept yours too. But they will do all these things to you because you bear my name, and because they do not know the one who sent me. If I had not come and taught them, they could have continued to pretend they were without sin. But now, they have no excuse for their sin. Whoever hates me hates my Father too. If I had not done among them such works as no one else ever did, they could have gone on pretending they were without sin. But now, they have seen both me

them, and cast *them* into the fire, and they are burned.

7 If ye abide in me, and my words abide in you, ye shall ask what ye will, and it shall be done unto you.

8 Herein is my Father glorified, that ye bear much fruit; so shall ye be my disciples.

9 As the Father hath loved me, so have I loved you: continue ye in my love.

10 If ye keep my commandments, ye shall abide in my love; even as I have kept my Father's commandments, and abide in his love.

11 These things have I spoken unto you, that my joy might remain in you, and *that* your joy might be full.

12 This is my commandment, That ye love one another, as I have loved you.

13 Greater love hath no man than this, that a man lay down his life for his friends.

14 Ye are my friends, if ye do whatsoever I command you.

15 Henceforth I call you not servants; for the servant knoweth not what his lord doeth: but I have called you friends; for all things that I have heard of my Father I have made known unto you.

16 Ye have not chosen me, but I have chosen you, and ordained you, that ye should go and bring forth fruit, and *that* your fruit should remain; that whatsoever ye shall ask of the Father in my name, he may give it you.

17 These things I command you, that ye love one another.

18 If the world hate you, ye know that it hated me before *it hated* you.

19 If ye were of the world, the world would love his own; but because ye are not of the world, but I have chosen you out of the world, therefore the world hateth you.

20 Remember the word that I said unto you, The servant is not greater than his lord. If they have persecuted me, they will also persecute you; if they have kept my saying, they will keep yours also.

21 But all these things will they do unto you for my name's sake, because they know not him that sent me.

22 If I had not come and spoken unto them, they had not had sin; but now they have no cloak for their sin.

The True Vine (continued)

and my Father, and hated us both. But thus is fulfilled what is written in their own law, 'They hated me without a cause.'

"But when the Comforter comes, whom I will send to you from the Father—the Spirit of Truth who goes forth from the Father—he will bear witness of me. And you too will bear witness, because you have been with me from the beginning.

23 He that hateth me hateth my Father also.

24 If I had not done among them the works which none other man did, they had not had sin: but now have they both seen and hated both me and my Father.

25 But *this cometh to pass,* that the word might be fulfilled that is written in their law, They hated me without a cause.

26 But when the Comforter is come, whom I will send unto you from the Father, *even* the Spirit of truth, which proceedeth from the Father, he shall testify of me:

27 And ye also shall bear witness, because ye have been with me from the beginning.

Promise of the Holy Spirit

John 16:1-33

"I have told you these things so that you will not lose faith. They will exclude you from the synagogues. Indeed, the time will come when whoever kills you will think he is rendering a service to God. They will do these things because they know neither the Father nor me. But I have told you these things so that, when the time comes, you may remember that I told you about them.

"I did not tell you these things before, because I was still with you. But now, I am going away to him who sent me. Yet not one of you is asking me, 'Where are you going?' Instead, sorrow has filled your hearts because I have told you these things. But I tell you the truth, it is best for you that I go away. For unless I go away, the Comforter will not come to you; but if I go, I will send him to you. And when he comes, he will convict the world of sin, of righteousness, and of judgment: of sin, because they do not believe in me; of righteousness, because I am going away to the Father and you will no longer see me; and of judgment, because the prince of this world has been judged and condemned.

"I still have many things to tell you, but you

1 These things have I spoken unto you, that ye should not be offended.

2 They shall put you out of the synagogues: yea, the time cometh, that whosoever killeth you will think that he doeth God service.

3 And these things will they do unto you, because they have not known the Father, nor me.

4 But these things have I told you, that when the time shall come, ye may remember that I told you of them. And these things I said not unto you at the beginning, because I was with you.

5 But now I go my way to him that sent me; and none of you asketh me, Whither goest thou?

6 But because I have said these things unto you, sorrow hath filled your heart.

7 Nevertheless I tell you the truth; It is expedient for you that I go away: for if I go not away, the Comforter will not come unto you; but if I depart, I will send him unto you.

8 And when he is come, he will reprove the world of sin, and of righteousness, and of judgment:

9 Of sin, because they believe not on me;

10 Of righteousness, because I go to my Father, and ye see me no more;

11 Of judgment, because the prince of this world is judged.

Promise of the Holy Spirit (continued)

are not able to grasp them now. But when he comes—the Spirit of Truth—he will guide you into all the truth, for he will not speak on his own authority, but will speak what he hears, and will declare to you the things that are to come. He will glorify me, for he will take the things that are mine and declare them to you. All that the Father has is mine; that is why I said that he will take the things that are mine and declare them to you. A little while, and you will see me no more; again, a little while, and you will see me.''

Then some of his disciples said one to another, ''What is this that he is saying to us—'A little while, and you will not see me; and again, a little while, and you will see me'; and 'because I am going away to the Father'? What is this that he is saying—'a little while'? We do not know what he means.''

Jesus, knowing that they wanted to ask him, said to them,

''Are you asking one another about what I said—'A little while, and you will not see me; and again, a little while, and you will see me'? I tell you truly, you will weep and lament, but the world will rejoice. You will be sorrowful; but your sorrow will change to joy. When a woman is in travail, she has sorrow because her time has come. But when she brings forth the child, she no longer remembers the agony because of the joy that a child has been born into the world. And you indeed have sorrow now, but I will see you again and your hearts will rejoice, and no one will take your joy from you. And in that day, you will ask me nothing. I tell you truly, whatever you ask the Father in my name he will give you. As yet, you have not asked anything in my name. Ask, and you will receive, that your joy may be full.

''I have been speaking to you in figures, but the time is coming when I will no longer speak to you in figures, but will tell you plainly about the Father. In that day, you will pray in my name; and I need not tell you that I will pray to the Father for you, for the Father himself loves you, because you have loved me and have believed that I came forth from God. I came

12 I have yet many things to say unto you, but ye cannot bear them now.

13 Howbeit when he, the Spirit of truth, is come, he will guide you into all truth: for he shall not speak of himself; but whatsoever he shall hear, *that* shall he speak: and he will show you things to come.

14 He shall glorify me: for he shall receive of mine, and shall show *it* unto you.

15 All things that the Father hath are mine: therefore said I, that he shall take of mine, and shall show *it* unto you.

16 A little while, and ye shall not see me: and again, a little while, and ye shall see me, because I go to the Father.

17 Then said *some* of his disciples among themselves, What is this that he saith unto us, A little while, and ye shall not see me: and again, a little while, and ye shall see me: and, Because I go to the Father?

18 They said therefore, What is this that he saith, A little while? we cannot tell what he saith.

19 Now Jesus knew that they were desirous to ask him, and said unto them, Do ye inquire among yourselves of that I said, A little while, and ye shall not see me: and again, a little while, and ye shall see me?

20 Verily, verily, I say unto you, That ye shall weep and lament, but the world shall rejoice: and ye shall be sorrowful, but your sorrow shall be turned into joy.

21 A woman when she is in travail hath sorrow, because her hour is come: but as soon as she is delivered of the child, she remembereth no more the anguish, for joy that a man is born into the world.

22 And ye now therefore have sorrow: but I will see you again, and your heart shall rejoice, and your joy no man taketh from you.

23 And in that day ye shall ask me nothing. Verily, verily, I say unto you, Whatsoever ye shall ask the Father in my name, he will give *it* you.

24 Hitherto have ye asked nothing in my name: ask, and ye shall receive, that your joy may be full.

25 These things have I spoken unto you in proverbs: but the time cometh, when I shall no more speak unto you in proverbs, but I shall show you plainly of the Father.

Promise of the Holy Spirit (continued)

forth from the Father and have come into the world; again, I am leaving the world and going to the Father.''

"Now you are speaking plainly," said the disciples, "and not talking in figures. Now we know for sure that all things are known to you, for you need not wait for anyone to ask you anything! Because of this, we believe that you came forth from God.''

"Do you now believe?" replied Jesus. "The hour is coming, indeed it has already come, when you will be scattered, each to his own place, and will leave me alone. And yet I am not alone, for the Father is with me. I have told you these things so that, in me, you may have peace. In the world you will have trouble and distress; but be of good courage, I have overcome the world.''

26 At that day ye shall ask in my name: and I say not unto you, that I will pray the Father for you:

27 For the Father himself loveth you, because ye have loved me, and have believed that I came out from God.

28 I came forth from the Father, and am come into the world: again, I leave the world, and go to the Father.

29 His disciples said unto him, Lo, now speakest thou plainly, and speakest no proverb.

30 Now are we sure that thou knowest all things, and needest not that any man should ask thee: by this we believe that thou camest forth from God.

31 Jesus answered them, Do ye now believe?

32 Behold, the hour cometh, yea, is now come, that ye shall be scattered, every man to his own, and shall leave me alone: and yet I am not alone, because the Father is with me.

33 These things I have spoken unto you, that in me ye might have peace. In the world ye shall have tribulation: but be of good cheer; I have overcome the world.

Jesus Prays for His Disciples

John 17:1-26

Having said these things, Jesus raised his eyes toward heaven and said,

"Father, the hour has come! Glorify your Son, that the Son may glorify you. For you have given him authority over all mankind, to give eternal life to all whom you have given him. And this is eternal life—to know you, the only true God, and Jesus Christ whom you have sent. I have glorifed you on earth, and have finished the work you gave me to do. And now, Father, glorify me in your own presence with the glory I shared with you before the creation of the world.

"I have made your name known to the men whom you have given me out of the world. They were yours, and you gave them to me, and they have been faithful to your word. They know,

1 These words spake Jesus, and lifted up his eyes to heaven, and said, Father, the hour is come; glorify thy Son, that thy Son also may glorify thee:

2 As thou hast given him power over all flesh, that he should give eternal life to as many as thou hast given him.

3 And this is life eternal, that they might know thee the only true God, and Jesus Christ, whom thou hast sent.

4 I have glorified thee on the earth: I have finished the work which thou gavest me to do.

5 And now, O Father, glorify thou me with thine own self with the glory which I had with thee before the world was.

6 I have manifested thy name unto the men which thou gavest me out of the world: thine they were, and thou gavest them me; and they have kept thy word.

7 Now they have known that all things what-

Jesus Prays for His Disciples (continued)

now, that all the things you have given me are from you, for I have given them the words you gave me, and they have received them and have come to know for certain that I came forth from you. They have believed that you sent me.

"I pray for them. I do not pray for the world, but for those whom you have given me, for they are yours. All who are mine are yours, and all who are yours are mine, and I am glorified through them. I will no longer be in the world; they will be in the world, but I am coming to you. Holy Father, keep them in your name which you have given me, that they may be one, just as we are one. While I was with them, I kept them in your name which you have given me. I have guarded them faithfully, and not one of them has been lost except the son of perdition, that the scripture might be fulfilled. But now, I am coming to you, and I say these things while I am still in the world, so that they may fully share my joy. I have given them your word, and the world has hated them because they are not of the world, just as I am not of the world. I do not ask that you take them out of the world, but that you keep them from the evil one. They are not of the world, just as I am not of the world. Sanctify them through the truth. Your word is truth. Just as you sent me into the world, so have I sent them into the world. And for their sake I sanctify myself, that they too may be sanctified through the truth.

"I do not pray only for these, but also for those who will believe in me through their word, that they may all be one—just as you, Father, are in me, and I in you; that they too may be in us, that the world may believe that you sent me. And I have shared with them the glory which you gave me, that they may be one, just as we are one—I in them, and you in me—that they may be brought into perfect union, that the world may know that you sent me, and that you have loved them as you have loved me.

"Father, I desire that those whom you have given me may be with me where I am, that they may see my glory which you have given me because you loved me before the foundation of

 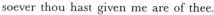

soever thou hast given me are of thee.

8 For I have given unto them the words which thou gavest me; and they have received *them,* and have known surely that I came out from thee, and they have believed that thou didst send me.

9 I pray for them: I pray not for the world, but for them which thou hast given me; for they are thine.

10 And all mine are thine, and thine are mine; and I am glorified in them.

11 And now I am no more in the world, but these are in the world, and I come to thee. Holy Father, keep through thine own name those whom thou hast given me, that they may be one, as we *are.*

12 While I was with them in the world, I kept them in thy name: those that thou gavest me I have kept, and none of them is lost, but the son of perdition; that the Scripture might be fulfilled.

13 And now come I to thee; and these things I speak in the world, that they might have my joy fulfilled in themselves.

14 I have given them thy word; and the world hath hated them, because they are not of the world, even as I am not of the world.

15 I pray not that thou shouldest take them out of the world, but that thou shouldest keep them from the evil.

16 They are not of the world, even as I am not of the world.

17 Sanctify them through thy truth: thy word is truth.

18 As thou hast sent me into the world, even so have I also sent them into the world.

19 And for their sakes I sanctify my self, that they also might be sanctified through the truth.

20 Neither pray I for these alone, but for them also which shall believe on me through their word;

21 That they all may be one; as thou, Father, *art* in me, and I in thee, that they also may be one in us: that the world may believe that thou hast sent me.

22 And the glory which thou gavest me I have given them; that they may be one, even as we are one:

Jesus Prays for His Disciples (continued)

the world. O righteous Father, the world has not known you! But I have known you, and these have known that you have sent me. I have made your name known to them, and will make it known, that the love with which you have loved me may be in them, and I in them.''

23 I in them, and thou in me, that they may be made perfect in one; and that the world may know that thou hast sent me, and hast loved them, as thou hast loved me.

24 Father, I will that they also, whom thou hast given me, be with me where I am; that they may behold my glory, which thou hast given me: for thou lovedst me before the foundation of the world.

25 O righteous Father, the world hath not known thee: but I have known thee, and these have known that thou hast sent me.

26 And I have declared unto them thy name, and will declare *it;* that the love wherewith thou hast loved me may be in them, and I in them.

Praying in Gethsemane

Matthew 26:36-46

Then Jesus came with his disciples to a place called Gethsemane and said to them, ''Sit here, while I go yonder and pray.''

And he took with him Peter and the two sons of Zebedee. And he began to be sorrowful and troubled, and said to them, ''My soul is very sorrowful, even to death. Stay here and keep watch with me.''

And he went on a little farther, and fell on his face and prayed, ''My Father, if it is possible, let this cup pass from me. Nevertheless, not as I will, but as you will.''

And he came to the disciples and found them asleep, and said to Peter, ''What! could you not keep watch with me for even an hour? Watch and pray that you may not enter into temptation. The spirit indeed is willing, but the flesh is weak.''

Again a second time, he went away and prayed, ''My Father, if this cannot pass unless I drink it, your will be done.''

And he came and found them asleep again, for their eyes were heavy. And he left them and went away again and prayed a third time, saying the same words again. Then he came to the disciples and said,

''Are you still sleeping and taking your rest? Behold, the hour is at hand, and the Son of Man is betrayed into the hands of sinners. Rise, let us go. Behold, my betrayer is at hand.''

MATTHEW 26:36-46	MARK 14:32-42	LUKE 22:39-46	JOHN 18:1
36 Then cometh Jesus with them unto a place called Gethsemane, and saith unto the disciples, Sit ye here, while I go and pray yonder. 37 And he took with him Peter and the two sons of Zebedee, and began to be sorrowful and very heavy.	32 And they came to a place which was named Gethsemane: and he saith to his disciples, Sit ye here, while I shall pray. 33 And he taketh with him Peter and James and John, and began to be sore amazed, and to be very heavy;	39 And he came out, and went, as he was wont, to the mount of Olives; and his disciples also followed him. 40 And when he was at the place, he said unto them, Pray that ye enter not into temptation. 41 And he was withdrawn from them	1 When Jesus had spoken these words, he went forth with his disciples over the brook Cedron, where was a garden, into the which he entered, and his disciples.

Praying in Gethsemane (continued)

MATTHEW 26:36-46

38 Then saith he unto them, My soul is exceeding sorrowful, even unto death: tarry ye here, and watch with me.

39 And he went a little further, and fell on his face, and prayed, saying, O my Father, if it be possible, let this cup pass from me: nevertheless, not as I will, but as thou *wilt.*

40 And he cometh unto the disciples, and findeth them asleep, and saith unto Peter, What, could ye not watch with me one hour?

41 Watch and pray, that ye enter not into temptation: the spirit indeed *is* willing, but the flesh *is* weak.

42 He went away again the second time, and prayed, saying, O my Father, if this cup may not pass away from me, except I drink it, thy will be done.

43 And he came and found them asleep again: for their eyes were heavy.

44 And he left them, and went away again, and prayed the third time, saying the same words.

45 Then cometh he to his disciples, and saith unto them, Sleep on now, and take *your* rest: behold, the hour is at hand, and the Son of man is betrayed into the hands of sinners.

46 Rise, let us be going: behold, he is at hand that doth betray me.

MARK 14:32-42

34 And saith unto them, My soul is exceeding sorrowful unto death: tarry ye here, and watch.

35 And he went forward a little, and fell on the ground, and prayed that, if it were possible, the hour might pass from him.

36 And he said, Abba, Father, all things *are* possible unto thee; take away this cup from me: nevertheless, not what I will, but what thou wilt.

37 And he cometh, and findeth them sleeping, and saith unto Peter, Simon, sleepest thou? couldest not thou watch one hour?

38 Watch ye and pray, lest ye enter into temptation. The spirit truly *is* ready, but the flesh *is* weak.

39 And again he went away, and prayed, and spake the same words.

40 And when he returned, he found them asleep again, (for their eyes were heavy,) neither wist they what to answer him.

41 And he cometh the third time, and saith unto them, Sleep on now, and take *your* rest: it is enough, the hour is come; behold, the Son of man is betrayed into the hands of sinners.

42 Rise up, let us go; lo, he that betrayeth me is at hand.

LUKE 22:39-46

about a stone's cast, and kneeled down, and prayed,

42 Saying, Father, if thou be willing, remove this cup from me: nevertheless, not my will, but thine, be done.

43 And there appeared an angel unto him from heaven, strengthening him.

44 And being in an agony he prayed more earnestly: and his sweat was as it were great drops of blood falling down to the ground.

45 And when he rose up from prayer, and was come to his disciples, he found them sleeping for sorrow,

46 And said unto them, Why sleep ye? rise and pray, lest ye enter into temptation.

JOHN 18:1

Gethsemane Olive Tree.
The Garden of Gethsemane contains 8 old olive trees. Since new shoots spring from decaying roots of old trees, these may well be traced back to Jesus' time.

313

Jesus' Betrayal and Arrest

Matthew 26:47-56

While Jesus was still speaking, Judas came— one of the twelve, along with a great crowd with swords and clubs, sent from the chief priests and elders of the people. Now the betrayer had given them a sign, saying, ''The one I shall kiss is the man. Seize him!''

And he came straight to Jesus and said, ''Hail, Master!'' and kissed him.

''Friend,'' said Jesus, ''what brings you here?''

Then the mob surrounded Jesus and laid hands on him and held him. And one of the men with Jesus drew his sword and stuck the servant of the High Priest, cutting off his ear.

''Put away your sword,'' said Jesus, ''for all who take up the sword will die by the sword. Do you think that I cannot appeal to my Father, and he will immediately send me more than twelve legions of angels? But how then should the scriptures be fulfilled, that thus it must be?''

Then Jesus said to the crowd, ''Have you come out to capture me with swords and clubs, as if I were a robber? Day after day I sat in the temple teaching, and you did not seize me. But all this has come to pass, that the scriptures of the prophets might be fulfilled.''

Then all the disciples deserted him and fled.

MATTHEW 26:47-56	MARK 14:43-52	LUKE 22:47-53	JOHN 18:2-11
47 And while he yet spake, lo, Judas, one of the twelve, came, and with him a great multitude with swords and staves, from the chief priests and elders of the people.	43 And immediately, while he yet spake, cometh Judas, one of the twelve, and with him a great multitude with swords and staves, from the chief priests and the scribes and the elders.	47 And while he yet spake, behold a multitude, and he that was called Judas, one of the twelve, went before them, and drew near unto Jesus to kiss him.	2 And Judas also, which betrayed him, knew the place: for Jesus ofttimes resorted thither with his disciples.
48 Now he that betrayed him gave them a sign, saying, Whomsoever I shall kiss, that same is he; hold him fast,	44 And he that betrayed him had given them a token, saying, Whomsoever I shall kiss, that same is he; take him, and lead *him* away safely.	48 But Jesus said unto him, Judas, betrayest thou the Son of man with a kiss?	3 Judas then, having received a band *of men* and officers from the chief priests and Pharisees, cometh thither with lanterns and torches and weapons.
49 And forthwith he came to Jesus, and said, Hail, Master; and kissed him.	45 And as soon as he was come, he goeth straightway to him, and saith, Master, Master; and kissed him.	49 When they which were about him saw what would follow, they said unto him, Lord, shall we smite with the sword?	4 Jesus therefore, knowing all things that should come upon him, went forth, and said unto them, Whom seek ye?
50 And Jesus said unto him, Friend, wherefore art thou come? Then came they, and laid hands on Jesus, and took him.	46 And they laid their hands on him, and took him.	50 And one of them smote the servant of the high priest, and cut off his right ear.	5 They answered him, Jesus of Nazareth. Jesus saith unto them, I am *he*. And Judas also, which betrayed him, stood with them.
51 And, behold, one of them which were with Jesus stretched out *his* hand, and drew his sword, and struck a servant of the high priest,	47 And one of them that stood by drew a sword, and smote a servant of the high priest, and cut off his ear.	51 And Jesus answered and said, Suffer ye thus far. And he touched his ear, and healed him.	6 As soon then as he had said unto them, I am *he*, they went backward, and fell to the ground.
	48 And Jesus answered and said unto	52 Then Jesus said unto the chief priests, and captains of the temple, and the elders, which	7 Then asked he them again, Whom seek ye?

Jesus' Betrayal and Arrest (continued)

MATTHEW 26:47-56	MARK 14:43-52	LUKE 22:47-53	JOHN 18:2-11

MATTHEW 26:47-56

and smote off his ear.

52 Then said Jesus unto him, Put up again thy sword into his place: for all they that take the sword shall perish with the sword.

53 Thinkest thou that I cannot now pray to my Father, and he shall presently give me more than twelve legions of angels?

54 But how then shall the Scriptures be fulfilled, that thus it must be?

55 In that same hour said Jesus to the multitudes, Are ye come out as against a thief with swords and staves for to take me? I sat daily with you teaching in the temple, and ye laid no hold on me.

56 But all this was done, that the Scriptures of the prophets might be fulfilled. Then all the disciples forsook him, and fled.

MARK 14:43-52

them, Are ye come out, as against a thief, with swords and *with* staves to take me?

49 I was daily with you in the temple teaching, and ye took me not: but the Scriptures must be fulfilled.

50 And they all forsook him, and fled.

51 And there followed him a certain young man, having a linen cloth cast about *his* naked *body;* and the young men laid hold on him:

52 And he left the linen cloth, and fled from them naked.

LUKE 22:47-53

were come to him, Be ye come out, as against a thief, with swords and staves?

53 When I was daily with you in the temple, ye stretched forth no hands against me: but this is your hour, and the power of darkness.

JOHN 18:2-11

And they said, Jesus of Nazareth.

8 Jesus answered, I have told you that I am *he:* if therefore ye seek me, let these go their way:

9 That the saying might be fulfilled, which he spake, Of them which thou gavest me have I lost none.

10 Then Simon Peter having a sword drew it, and smote the high priest's servant, and cut off his right ear. The servant's name was Malchus.

11 Then said Jesus unto Peter, Put up thy sword into the sheath: the cup which my Father hath given me, shall I not drink it?

St. Peter in Gallicantu (Cock-crowing) Church.
Covers the traditional site of the high priest's house, where Jesus was tried before the Sanhedrin and Peter denied his Lord.

315

Trial Before Jewish Authorities

John 18:12-13,19-24, Matthew 26:59-68, 27:1-2

Then the band of soldiers and their captain and the officers of the Jews laid hold of Jesus and bound him and led him away first to Annas, the father-in-law of Caiaphas, who was High Priest that year. The High Priest then questioned Jesus about his disciples and his teaching.

"I have spoken openly to the world," replied Jesus. "I have continually taught in synagogues and in the temple, where all the Jews gather together, and I have said nothing secretly. Why ask me? Ask those who have heard me what I told them, for they know what I have said."

Then one of the officers standing by slapped Jesus with the palm of his hand and said, "Is that the way you answer the High Priest?"

"If I have said anything wrong," replied Jesus, "bear witness to the wrong. But if I have answered well, why do you strike me?"

Then Annas sent him bound to Caiaphas, the High Priest.

Then the chief priests and the whole Council sought false testimony against Jesus so they could put him to death; but they found none, though many false witnesses came forward. But at last two of them came forward and said, "This man said, 'I can destroy the temple of God and build it in three days.' "

Then the High Priest stood up and said, "Have you no answer to offer? What is this that these men are testifying against you?"

But Jesus was silent. Then the High Priest said to him, "I charge you on oath by the living God, tell us whether you are the Messiah, the Son of God."

"I am," replied Jesus. "Hereafter, I tell you, you will see the Son of Man seated at the right hand of the Almighty and coming on the clouds of heaven."

Then the High Priest tore his robes and said, "He has spoken blasphemy! What further need have we of witnesses? You have heard the blasphemy. What is your decision?"

"He deserves death!" they replied.

Then they spat in his face and struck him. And some slapped him, saying, "Prophesy to us, Messiah! What is the name of the man who hit you?"

MATT. 26:57, 59-68	MARK 14:53, 55-65	LUKE 22:54, 63-71	JOHN 18:12-14,19-24
57 And they that had laid hold on Jesus led *him* away to Caiaphas the high priest, where the scribes and the elders were assembled. 59 Now the chief priests, and elders, and all the council, sought false witness against Jesus, to put him to death; 60 But found none: yea, though many false witnesses came, *yet* found they none. At the last came two false witnesses, 61 And said, This *fellow* said, I am able to destroy the temple of God, and to build it in three days.	53 And they led Jesus away to the high priest: and with him were assembled all the chief priests and the elders and the scribes. 55 And the chief priests and all the council sought for witness against Jesus to put him to death; and found none. 56 For many bare false witness against him, but their witness agreed not together. 57 And there arose certain, and bare false witness against him, saying,	54 Then took they him, and led *him,* and brought him into the high priest's house. And Peter followed afar off. 63 And the men that held Jesus mocked him, and smote *him.* 64 And when they had blindfolded him, they struck him on the face, and asked him, saying, Prophesy, who is it that smote thee? 65 And many other things blasphemously spake they against him. 66 And as soon as it was day, the elders of the people and the chief	12 Then the band and the captain and officers of the Jews took Jesus, and bound him, 13 And led him away to Annas first; for he was father-in-law to Caiaphas, which was the high priest that same year. 14 Now Caiaphas was he, which gave counsel to the Jews, that it was expedient that one man should die for the people. 19 The high priest then asked Jesus of his disciples, and of his doctrine. 20 Jesus answered him, I spake openly to the world; I ever taught

Trial Before Jewish Authorities (continued)

MATT. 26:57, 59-68	MARK 14:53, 55-65	LUKE 22:54, 63-71	JOHN 18:12-14, 19-24
62 And the high priest arose, and said unto him, Answerest thou nothing? what *is it which* these witness against thee?	58 We heard him say, I will destroy this temple that is made with hands, and within three days I will build another made without hands.	priests and the scribes came together, and led him into their council, saying,	in the synagogue, and in the temple, whither the Jews always resort; and in secret have I said nothing.
63 But Jesus held his peace. And the high priest answered and said unto him, I adjure thee by the living God, that thou tell us whether thou be the Christ, the Son of God.	59 But neither so did their witness agree together.	67 Art thou the Christ? tell us. And he said unto them, If I tell you, ye will not believe:	21 Why askest thou me? ask them which heard me, what I have said unto them: behold, they know what I said.
64 Jesus saith unto him, Thou hast said: nevertheless I say unto you, Hereafter shall ye see the Son of man sitting on the right hand of power, and coming in the clouds of heaven.	60 And the high priest stood up in the midst, and asked Jesus, saying, Answerest thou nothing? what *is it which* these witness against thee?	68 And if I also ask *you,* ye will not answer me, nor let *me* go.	22 And when he had thus spoken, one of the officers which stood by struck Jesus with the palm of his hand, saying, Answerest thou the high priest so?
65 Then the high priest rent his clothes, saying, He hath spoken blasphemy; what further need have we of witnesses? behold, now ye have heard his blasphemy.	61 But he held his peace, and answered nothing. Again the high priest asked him, and said unto him, Art thou the Christ, the Son of the Blessed?	69 Hereafter shall the Son of man sit on the right hand of the power of God.	23 Jesus answered him, If I have spoken evil, bear witness of the evil: but if well, why smitest thou me?
66 What think ye? They answered and said, He is guilty of death.	62 And Jesus said, I am: and ye shall see the Son of man sitting on the right hand of power, and coming in the clouds of heaven.	70 Then said they all, Art thou then the Son of God? And he said unto them, Ye say that I am.	24 Now Annas had sent him bound unto Caiaphas the high priest.
67 Then did they spit in his face, and buffeted him; and others smote *him* with the palms of their hands.	63 Then the high priest rent his clothes, and saith, What need we any further witnesses?	71 And they said, What need we any further witness? for we ourselves have heard of his own mouth.	
68 Saying, Prophesy unto us, thou Christ, Who is he that smote thee?	64 Ye have heard the blasphemy: what think ye? And they all condemned him to be guilty of death.		
	65 And some began to spit on him, and to cover his face, and to buffet him, and to say unto him, Prophesy: and the servants did strike him with the palms of their hands.		

Peter's Denial

Matthew 26:58, 69-74, Luke 22:61-62

But Peter followed him from a distance to the courtyard of the palace of the High Priest, and went in and sat down among the guards to see the outcome.

Now Peter was sitting in the courtyard, and a maid came up to him and said, "You too were with Jesus, the Galilean!"

But he denied it before them all, saying, "I don't know what you are talking about."

And he went out into the porch, and another maid saw him and said to the bystanders, "This man was with Jesus, the Nazarene!"

And again he denied it with an oath, "I don't know the man!"

A little while later the bystanders surrounded Peter and said, "You are one of them for sure, for your accent gives you away."

Then he began to curse and to swear, "I don't know the man!"

And immediately, while he was still speaking, a cock crowed. And the Lord turned and looked at Peter, and Peter remembered the word of the Lord, how he had told him, "Before the cock crows today, you will deny me three times."

And he went out and wept bitterly.

MATT. 26:58, 69-75

58 But Peter followed him afar off unto the high priest's palace, and went in, and sat with the servants, to see the end.

69 Now Peter sat without in the palace: and a damsel came unto him, saying, Thou also wast with Jesus of Galilee.

70 But he denied before *them* all, saying, I know not what thou sayest.

71 And when he was gone out into the porch, another *maid* saw him, and said unto them that were there, This *fellow* was also with Jesus of Nazareth.

72 And again he denied with an oath, I do not know the man.

73 And after a while came unto *him* they that stood by, and said to Peter, Surely thou also art *one* of them; for thy speech betrayeth thee.

MARK 14:54, 66-72

54 And Peter followed him afar off, even into the palace of the high priest: and he sat with the servants, and warmed himself at the fire.

66 And as Peter was beneath in the palace, there cometh one of the maids of the high priest:

67 And when she saw Peter warming himself, she looked upon him, and said, And thou also wast with Jesus of Nazareth.

68 But he denied, saying, I know not, neither understand I what thou sayest. And he went out into the porch; and the cock crew.

69 And a maid saw him again, and began to say to them that stood by, This is *one* of them.

70 And he denied it again. And a little after, they that stood by said again to Peter, Surely

LUKE 22:55-62

55 And when they had kindled a fire in the midst of the hall, and were set down together, Peter sat down among them.

56 But a certain maid beheld him as he sat by the fire, and earnestly looked upon him, and said, This man was also with him.

57 And he denied him, saying, Woman, I know him not.

58 And after a little while another saw him, and said, Thou art also of them. And Peter said, Man, I am not.

59 And about the space of one hour after another confidently affirmed, saying, Of a truth this *fellow* also was with him; for he is a Galilean.

60 And Peter said, Man, I know not what thou sayest. And immediately, while he yet

JOHN 18:15-18, 25-27

15 And Simon Peter followed Jesus, and *so did* another disciple: that disciple was known unto the high priest, and went in with Jesus into the palace of the high priest.

16 But Peter stood at the door without. Then went out that other disciple, which was known unto the high priest, and spake unto her that kept the door, and brought in Peter.

17 Then saith the damsel that kept the door unto Peter, Art not thou also *one* of this man's disciples? He saith, I am not.

18 And the servants and officers stood there, who had made a fire of coals, for it was cold; and they warmed themselves: and Peter stood with them, and warmed himself.

25 And Simon Peter stood and warmed

Peter's Denial (continued)

MATT.26:58, 69-75

74 Then began he to curse and to swear, *saying*, I know not the man. And immediately the cock crew.
75 And Peter remembered the word of Jesus, which said unto him, Before the cock crow, thou shalt deny me thrice. And he went out, and wept bitterly.

MARK 14:54, 66-72

thou art *one* of them: for thou art a Galilean, and thy speech agreeth *thereto*.
71 But he began to curse and to swear, *saying*, I know not this man of whom ye speak.
72 And the second time the cock crew. And Peter called to mind the word that Jesus said unto him, Before the cock crow twice, thou shalt deny me thrice. And when he thought thereon, he wept.

LUKE 22:55-62

spake, the cock crew.
61 And the Lord turned, and looked upon Peter. And Peter remembered the word of the Lord, how he had said unto him, Before the cock crow, thou shalt deny me thrice.
62 And Peter went out, and wept bitterly.

JOHN 18:15-18, 25-27

himself. They said therefore unto him, Art not thou also *one* of his disciples? He denied *it*, and said, I am not.
26 One of the servants of the high priest, being *his* kinsman whose ear Peter cut off, saith, Did not I see thee in the garden with him?
27 Peter then denied again; and immediately the cock crew.

Jesus Brought Before Pilate

Matthew 27:1-2, John 18:28-38   Mark 15:3-5, Luke 23:2, 5-7,

And when it was morning, all the chief priests and the elders of the people consulted together against Jesus to put him to death. And they bound him and led him away and handed him over to Pilate, the governor.

It was early in the morning, and the chief priests and elders did not enter the Praetorium, so that they might not be defiled, but might eat the Passover. Pilate therefore went out to them and said, "What charge do you bring against this man?"

"If he were not a criminal," they replied, "we would not have handed him over to you."

"You take him and judge him according to your law," said Pilate.

"We are not allowed to put anyone to death," said the Jews. Thus the word of Jesus was to be fulfilled which he spoke concerning the manner of death he was to die.

Then they began to accuse him, saying, "We found this man perverting our nation and forbidding people to pay taxes to Caesar, saying that he himself is the Messiah, a king."

Then Pilate entered the Praetorium again and called Jesus and said to him, "Are you the King of the Jews?"

"Are you saying this of your own accord," replied Jesus, "or did others say this to you about me?"

"Am I a Jew?" answered Pilate. "Your own nation and the chief priests have handed you over to me. What have you done?"

"My kingdom is not of this world," replied Jesus. "If my kingdom were of this world, my

Jesus Brought Before Pilate (continued)

servants would have fought to keep me from being handed over to the Jews. But my authority as king is not of earthly origin.''

"Are you indeed a king?'' said Pilate.

"You are right in saying that I am a king,'' replied Jesus. ''For this purpose I was born, and for this cause I have come into the world, to bear witness to the truth. Everyone who loves the truth listens to my voice.''

"What is 'truth'?'' said Pilate. And having said this, he went out again to the Jews and said, ''I do not find this man guilty of any crime.''

Then the chief priests began to accuse Jesus of many things.

"Have you no answer to offer?'' Pilate asked Jesus. ''See how many charges they are bringing against you!''

But Jesus made no reply, to Pilate's astonishment. Then the chief priests grew more insistent, saying, ''He is stirring up the people, teaching throughout all Judea—all the way from Galilee, where he started, even to here.''

When Pilate heard this, he asked whether the man was a Galilean; and when he learned that he belonged to Herod's jurisdiction, he sent him to Herod, who happened to be in Jerusalem at that time.

MATT 27:1-2, 11-14	MARK 15:1-5	LUKE 23:1-7	JOHN 18:28-38

MATT 27:1-2, 11-14

1 When the morning was come, all the chief priests and elders of the people took counsel against Jesus to put him to death:

2 And when they had bound him, they led *him* away, and delivered him to Pontius Pilate the governor.

11 And Jesus stood before the governor: and the governor asked him, saying, Art thou the King of the Jews? And Jesus said unto him, Thou sayest.

12 And when he was accused of the chief priests and elders, he answered nothing.

13 Then said Pilate unto him, Hearest thou not how many things they witness against thee?

14 And he answered him to never a word; insomuch that the governor marveled greatly.

MARK 15:1-5

1 And straightway in the morning the chief priests held a consultation with the elders and scribes and the whole council, and bound Jesus, and carried *him* away, and delivered *him* to Pilate.

2 And Pilate asked him, Art thou the King of the Jews? And he answering said unto him, Thou sayest *it.*

3 And the chief priests accused him of many things; but he answered nothing.

4 And Pilate asked him again, saying, Answerest thou nothing? behold how many things they witness against thee.

5 But Jesus yet answered nothing; so that Pilate marveled.

LUKE 23:1-7

1 And the whole multitude of them arose, and led him unto Pilate.

2 And they began to accuse him, saying, We found this *fellow* perverting the nation, and forbidding to give tribute to Caesar, saying that he himself is Christ a king.

3 And Pilate asked him, saying, Art thou the King of the Jews? And he answered him and said, Thou sayest *it.*

4 Then said Pilate to the chief priests and *to* the people, I find no fault in this man.

5 And they were the more fierce, saying, He stirreth up the people, teaching throughout all Jewry, beginning from Galilee to this place.

6 When Pilate heard of Galilee, he asked whether the man were a Galilean.

7 And as soon as he knew that he belonged unto Herod's jurisdiction, he sent him to Herod, who himself also was at Jerusalem at that time.

JOHN 18:28-38

28 Then led they Jesus from Caiaphas unto the hall of judgment: and it was early; and they themselves went not into the judgment hall, lest they should be defiled; but that they might eat the passover.

29 Pilate then went out unto them, and said, What accusation bring ye against this man?

30 They answered and said unto him, If he were not a malefactor, we would not have delivered him up unto thee.

31 Then said Pilate unto them, Take ye him, and judge him according to your law. The Jews therefore said unto him, It is not lawful for us to put any man to death:

32 That the saying of Jesus might be fulfilled, which he spake, signifying what death he should die.

Jesus Brought Before Pilate (continued)

MA 27:1-2, 11-14   MARK 15:1-5   LUKE 23:1-7   JOHN 18:28-38

JOHN 18:28-38

33 Then Pilate entered into the judgment hall again, and called Jesus, and said unto him, Art thou the King of the Jews?

34 Jesus answered him, Sayest thou this thing of thyself, or did others tell it thee of me?

35 Pilate answered, Am I a Jew? Thine own nation and the chief priests have delivered thee unto me: what hast thou done?

36 Jesus answered, My kingdom is not of this world: if my kingdom were of this world, then would my servants fight, that I should not be delivered to the Jews: but now is my kingdom not from hence.

37 Pilate therefore said unto him, Art thou a king then? Jesus answered, Thou sayest that I am a king. To this end was I born, and for this cause came I into the world, that I should bear witness unto the truth. Every one that is of the truth heareth my voice.

38 Pilate saith unto him, What is truth? And when he had said this, he went out again unto the Jews, and saith unto them, I find in him no fault *at all*.

Jesus Appears Before Herod

Luke 23:8-12

When Herod saw Jesus, he was delighted; for he had long wanted to see him, because he had heard about him and hoped to see him perform some miracle. And he questioned him at length, but Jesus gave him no reply. Then the chief priests and scribes, who had been standing by, began shouting accusations at Jesus. And after Herod, along with his soldiers, had mocked Jesus and shown his contempt for him, he dressed him in a gorgeous cloak and sent him back to Pilate. And Herod and Pilate became friends with each other that same day, for before this they had been at enmity with each other.

LUKE 23:8-12 ✓

8 And when Herod saw Jesus, he was exceeding glad: for he was desirous to see him of a long *season,* because he had heard many things of him; and he hoped to have seen some miracle done by him.

9 Then he questioned with him in many words; but he answered him nothing.

10 And the chief priests and scribes stood and vehemently accused him.

11 And Herod with his men of war set him at nought, and mocked *him,* and arrayed him in a gorgeous robe, and sent him again to Pilate.

12 And the same day Pilate and Herod were made friends together; for before they were at enmity between themselves.

Before Pilate Again

Matthew 23:13-16, Mark 15:6-7, Matthew 27:17-26

Then Pilate called together the chief priests and the rulers and the people and said to them,

"You brought this man to me as one who is misleading the people. After examining him before you, I have not found this man guilty of your charges against him. Nor did Herod, for he sent him back to us. He has done nothing deserving of death. I will therefore give him a flogging and release him."

Now it was the custom of Pilate at the time of the festival to release to them one prisoner, whomever they asked. And there was a man named Barabbas in custody along with some others who had taken part in a riot, and who had committed murder during their insurrection. Pilate therefore said to the crowd, "Whom do you want me to release to you—Barabbas, or Jesus who is called Messiah?"

For Pilate knew that it was because of envy that they had delivered up Jesus. Besides, while he was conducting the hearing, his wife sent word to him, "Have nothing to do with that righteous man, for I have suffered much today in a dream about him."

But the chief priests and elders persuaded the mob to ask for Barabbas and to demand the death of Jesus. But the governor responded by saying to them again, "Which of the two do you want me to release to you?"

"Barabbas!" they said.

"Then what shall I do with Jesus, who is called Messiah?" asked Pilate.

"Let him be crucified!" they all shouted.

"Just what has he done that is wrong?" asked Pilate.

But they shouted all the more, "Let him be crucified!"

When Pilate saw that he was accomplishing nothing, but a riot was developing instead, he took water and washed his hands before the crowd, saying, "I am innocent of the blood of this man. The responsibility is yours."

"His blood be on us and on our children!" all the people answered.

Then Pilate released Barabbas to them, and after flogging Jesus, handed him over to be crucified.

MATT. 27:15-26 ✓	MARK 15:6-15 ✓	LUKE 23:13-25 ✓	JOHN 18:39-40 ✓
15 Now at *that* feast the governor was wont to release unto the people a prisoner, whom they would. 16 And they had then a notable prisoner, called Barabbas. 17 Therefore when they were gathered together, Pilate said unto them, Whom will ye that I release unto you? Barabbas, or Jesus which is called Christ? 18 For he knew that for envy they had delivered him. 19 When he was set down on the judgment seat, his wife sent unto	6 Now at *that* feast he released unto them one prisoner, whomsoever they desired. 7 And there was *one* named Barabbas, *which lay* bound with them that had made insurrection with him, who had committed murder in the insurrection. 8 And the multitude crying aloud began to desire *him to do* as he had ever done unto them. 9 But Pilate answered them, saying, Will ye that I release unto you the King of the Jews? 10 For he knew that the chief priests had	13 And Pilate, when he had called together the chief priests and the rulers and the people, 14 Said unto them, Ye have brought this man unto me, as one that perverteth the people; and, behold, I, having examined *him* before you, have found no fault in this man touching those things whereof ye accuse him: 15 No, nor yet Herod: for I sent you to him; and, lo, nothing worthy of death is done unto him.	39 But ye have a custom, that I should release unto you one at the passover: will ye therefore that I release unto you the King of the Jews? 40 Then cried they all again, saying, Not this man, but Barabbas. Now Barabbas was a robber.

Before Pilate Again (continued)

MATTHEW 27:15-26

him, saying, Have thou nothing to do with that just man: for I have suffered many things this day in a dream because of him.

20 But the chief priests and elders persuaded the multitude that they should ask Barabbas, and destroy Jesus.

21 The governor answered and said unto them, Whether of the twain will ye that I release unto you? They said, Barabbas.

22 Pilate saith unto them, What shall I do then with Jesus which is called Christ? *They* all say unto him, Let him be crucified.

23 And the governor said, Why, what evil hath he done? But they cried out the more, saying, Let him be crucified.

24 When Pilate saw that he could prevail nothing, but *that* rather a tumult was made, he took water, and washed *his* hands before the multitude, saying, I am innocent of the blood of this just person: see ye *to it.*

25 Then answered all the people, and said, His blood *be* on us, and on our children.

26 Then released he Barabbas unto them: and when he had scourged Jesus, he delivered *him* to be crucified.

MARK 15:6-15

delivered him for envy.

11 But the chief priests moved the people, that he should rather release Barabbas unto them.

12 And Pilate answered and said again unto them, What will ye then that I shall do *unto him* whom ye call the King of the Jews?

...Pilate, willing to content the people, released Barabbas unto them.

---

13 And they cried out again, Crucify him.

14 Then Pilate said unto them, Why, what evil hath he done? And they cried out the more exceedingly, Crucify him.

15 And *so* Pilate, willing to content the people, released Barabbas unto them, and delivered Jesus, when he had scourged *him,* to be crucified.

LUKE 23:13-25

16 I will therefore chastise him, and release *him.*

17 (For of necessity he must release one unto them at the feast.)

18 And they cried out all at once, saying, Away with this *man,* and release unto us Barabbas:

19 (Who for a certain sedition made in the city, and for murder, was cast into prison.)

20 Pilate therefore, willing to release Jesus, spake again to them.

21 But they cried, saying, Crucify *him,* crucify him.

22 And he said unto them the third time, Why, what evil hath he done? I have found no cause of death in him: I will therefore chastise him, and let *him* go.

23 And they were instant with loud voices, requiring that he might be crucified: and the voices of them and of the chief priests prevailed.

24 And Pilate gave sentence that it should be as they required.

25 And he released unto them him that for sedition and murder was cast into prison, whom they had desired; but he delivered Jesus to their will.

JOHN 18:39-40

Jesus Mocked

Matthew 27:27-30

The governor's soldiers took Jesus into the Praetorium and assembled the whole regiment before him. And they stripped off his garments and put a scarlet robe on him, and braided a crown of thorns and put it on his head, and put a reed in his right hand. And kneeling before him, they mocked him, shouting, "Hail, King of the Jews!" Then they spat on him and took the reed and hit him on the head.

MATTHEW 27:27-30 ✓	MARK 15:16-19 ✓	JOHN 19:1-3 ✓
27 Then the soldiers of the governor took Jesus into the common hall, and gathered unto him the whole band *of soldiers.*	16 And the soldiers led him away into the hall, called Pretorium; and they call together the whole band.	1 Then Pilate therefore took Jesus, and scourged *him.*
28 And they stripped him, and put on him a scarlet robe.	17 And they clothed him with purple, and platted a crown of thorns, and put it about his *head,*	2 And the soldiers platted a crown of thorns, and put *it* on his head, and they put on him a purple robe,
29 And when they had platted a crown of thorns, they put *it* upon his head, and a reed in his right hand: and they bowed the knee before him, and mocked him, saying, Hail, King of the Jews!	18 And began to salute him, Hail, King of the Jews!	3 And said, Hail, King of the Jews! and they smote him with their hands.
30 And they spit upon him, and took the reed, and smote him on the head.	19 And they smote him on the head with a reed, and did spit upon him, and bowing *their* knees worshipped him.	

Jesus Delivered for Crucifixion

John 19:4-16

Then Pilate went out again and said to the crowd, "Behold, I am bringing him out to you so that you may know that I find him guilty of no crime."

Jesus therefore came out, wearing the crown of thorns and the scarlet robe.

"Behold, here is the man!" said Pilate.

When the chief priests and the officers saw him, they shouted, "Crucify him! Crucify him!"

"Take him and crucify him yourselves," said Pilate, "for I do not find him guilty of any crime."

"We have a law," answered the Jews, "and according to that law he should die, because he claimed to be the Son of God."

When Pilate heard this, he became even more alarmed and went into the Praetorium again and said to Jesus, "Where did you come from?"

But Jesus did not answer him. Pilate therefore said to him, "Aren't you going to speak to me? Don't you know that I have the authority to release you, and the authority to crucify you?"

"You would have no authority at all over me unless it had been given to you from above," replied Jesus. "Therefore, he who handed me over to you is guilty of the greater sin."

Hearing this, Pilate renewed his efforts to release Jesus. But the Jews shouted, "If you release this man, you are not a friend of Caesar! Everyone who sets himself up as a king proclaims treason against Caesar."

When Pilate heard these words, he brought Jesus out and sat down on the judgment seat at a place called The Pavement (in Hebrew, Gabbatha). Now it was the Preparation Day of Passover, about the sixth hour. Pilate said to the Jews, "Behold, your king!"

"Away with him, away with him, crucify him!" they shouted.

"Shall I crucify your king?" asked Pilate.

"We have no king but Caesar," answered the chief priests.

Then Pilate handed Jesus over to them to be crucified.

Jesus Delivered for Crucifixion (continued)

4 Pilate therefore went forth again, and saith unto them, Behold, I bring him forth to you, that ye may know that I find no fault in him.

5 Then came Jesus forth, wearing the crown of thorns, and the purple robe. And *Pilate* saith unto them, Behold the man!

6 When the chief priests therefore and officers saw him, they cried out, saying, Crucify *him*, crucify *him*. Pilate saith unto them, Take ye him, and crucify *him*: for I find no fault in him.

7 The Jews answered him, We have a law, and by our law he ought to die, because he made himself the Son of God.

8 When Pilate therefore heard that saying, he was the more afraid;

9 And went again into the judgment hall, and saith unto Jesus, Whence art thou? But Jesus gave him no answer.

10 Then saith Pilate unto him, Speakest thou not unto me? knowest thou not that I have power to crucify thee, and have power to release thee?

11 Jesus answered, Thou couldest have no power *at all* against me, except it were given thee from above: therefore he that delivered me unto thee hath the greater sin.

12 And from thenceforth Pilate sought to release him: but the Jews cried out, saying, If thou let this man go, thou art not Caesar's friend: whosoever maketh himself a king speaketh against Caesar.

13 When Pilate therefore heard that saying, he brought Jesus forth, and sat down in the judgment seat in a place that is called the Pavement, but in the Hebrew, Gabbatha.

14 And it was the preparation of the passover, and about the sixth hour: and he saith unto the Jews, Behold your King!

15 But they cried out, Away with *him*, away with *him*, crucify him. Pilate saith unto them, Shall I crucify your King? The chief priests answered, We have no king but Caesar.

16 Then delivered he him therefore unto them to be crucified. And they took Jesus, and led *him* away.

Judas' Remorse and Death

Matthew 27:3-10

When Judas, who betrayed him, saw that Jesus was condemned, he was filled with remorse and brought back the thirty pieces of silver to the chief priests and the elders and said, ''I have sinned by betraying innocent blood!''

''What is that to us?'' they replied. ''That is your affair.''

Throwing down the pieces of silver in the temple, Judas left and went away and hanged himself. Then the chief priests took the pieces of silver and said, ''It is unlawful to put this in the temple treasury, as this is the price of blood.''

And when they had consulted together, they used the money to buy the potter's field for a burial place for strangers. Therefore that field has been called the Field of Blood to this day. Then was fulfilled what was said by the prophet Jeremiah,

And I took the thirty pieces of silver,
the price of him on whom a price was set
  by some of the sons of Israel,
and gave them for the potter's field,
  as the Lord appointed me.

3 Then Judas, which had betrayed him, when he saw that he was condemned, repented himself, and brought again the thirty pieces of silver to the chief priests and elders,

4 Saying, I have sinned in that I have betrayed the innocent blood. And they said, What *is that* to us? see thou *to that*.

5 And he cast down the pieces of silver in the temple, and departed, and went and hanged himself.

6 And the chief priests took the silver pieces, and said, It is not lawful for to put them into the treasury, because it is the price of blood.

7 And they took counsel, and bought with them the potter's field, to bury strangers in.

8 Wherefore that field was called, The field of blood, unto this day.

9 Then was fulfilled that which was spoken by Jeremiah the prophet, saying, And they took the thirty pieces of silver, the price of him that was valued, whom they of the children of Israel did value;

10 And gave them for the potter's field, as the Lord appointed me.

Jesus Led to Calvary

Matthew 27:31-32, John 19:17, Luke 23:27-32

And after they had mocked Jesus, the soldiers stripped the robe from him and put his own garments on him, and led him away to crucify him. And he went out bearing his cross. And as they went their way, they came upon a man of Cyrene named Simon, and they compelled him to carry Jesus' cross.

And there followed him a great crowd of people, and of women who bewailed and lamented him. But Jesus turned to them and said, "Daughters of Jerusalem, do not weep for me, but weep for yourselves and for your children. For behold, the days are coming in which they will say, 'Blessed are the childless, the wombs that never bore and the breasts that never nursed.' Then they will begin to say to the mountains, 'Fall on us!' and to the hills, 'Cover us!' For if this is what they do when the wood is green, what will happen when it is dry?''

Two others also, who were criminals, were led away to be put to death with him.

MATT. 27:31-34 ✓

31 And after that they had mocked him, they took the robe off from him, and put his own raiment on him, and led him away to crucify *him*.

32 And as they came out, they found a man of Cyrene, Simon by name: him they compelled to bear his cross.

33 And when they were come unto a place called Golgotha, that is to say, a place of a skull,

34 They gave him vinegar to drink mingled with gall: and when he had tasted *thereof*, he would not drink.

MARK 15:20-23 ✓

20 And when they had mocked him, they took off the purple from him, and put his own clothes on him, and led him out to crucify him.

21 And they compel one Simon a Cyrenian, who passed by, coming out of the country, the father of Alexander and Rufus, to bear his cross.

22 And they bring him unto the place Golgotha, which is, being interpreted, The place of a skull.

23 And they gave him to drink wine mingled with myrrh: but he received *it* not.

LUKE 23:26-32 ✓

26 And as they led him away, they laid hold upon one Simon, a Cyrenian, coming out of the country, and on him they laid the cross, that he might bear *it* after Jesus.

27 And there followed him a great company of people, and of women, which also bewailed and lamented him.

28 But Jesus turning unto them said, Daughters of Jerusalem, weep not for me, but weep for yourselves, and for your children.

29 For, behold, the days are coming, in the which they shall say, Blessed *are* the barren, and the wombs that never bare, and the paps which never gave suck.

30 Then shall they begin to say to the mountains, Fall on us; and to the hills, Cover us.

31 For if they do these things in a green tree, what shall be done in the dry?

32 And there were also two others, malefactors, led with him to be put to death.

JOHN 19:17 ✓

17 And he bearing his cross went forth into a place called *the place* of a skull, which is called in the Hebrew Golgotha:

Via Dolorosa. *The "Way of Sorrows"*
along which Jesus carried His cross. Begins
at the traditional site of Pilate's tribunal and
ends at the Church of the Holy Sepulchre.

The Crucifixion

Matthew 27:39-54, Mark 15:22-37, Luke 23:34-49, John 19:19-37

And they brought Jesus to the place called Golgotha (which means the place of a skull). And they offered him wine mixed with myrrh, but he refused it. And it was the third hour when they nailed him to his cross.

"Father, forgive them," said Jesus, "for they do not understand what they are doing."

And they crucified two robbers with him, one on his right and one on his left. And Pilate wrote a title and put it on the cross: "Jesus of Nazareth, the King of the Jews." Many of the Jews read this title, for the place where Jesus was crucified was near the city. It was written in Hebrew, in Latin, and in Greek.

Then the chief priests of the Jews said to Pilate, "Do not write 'The King of the Jews'; instead, write 'This man said, I am King of the Jews.' "

"What I have written, I have written," answered Pilate.

When the soldiers had nailed Jesus to the cross, they took his garments and divided them into four parts, a part for each soldier. But his tunic was seamless, woven in one piece from top

Gordon's Calvary. *A site preferred by Protestants. In 1880's the likeness to a skull led General Charles "Chinese" Gordon to conclude this was probably the correct location of Calvary.*

The Crucifixion

to bottom. Therefore they said one to another, "Let us not tear it, but let us draw lots for it to see whose it shall be."

This was in fulfillment of the scripture,
They parted my garments among them,
and cast lots for my raiment.

And those who passed by reviled him, wagging their heads and saying, "You who would destroy the temple and build it again in three days, save yourself! If you are the Son of God, come down from the cross!"

In the same manner the chief priests, with the scribes and elders, mocked him, saying, "He saved others, but he cannot save himself! He is the King of Israel! Let him now come down from the cross, and we will believe him. He trusts in God; let God now deliver him, if he cares for him. For he said, 'I am the Son of God!' "

The soldiers also mocked him, coming up to him and offering him vinegar, and saying, "If you are the King of the Jews, save yourself!"

One of the criminals hanging there reviled him, saying, "Aren't you the Messiah? Save yourself and us!"

But the other, rebuking him, said, "Don't you even fear God—you who are receiving the same punishment? And we rightly so, for we are receiving a proper reward for what we did; but this man has done nothing wrong." And he said, "Jesus, remember me when you come into your kingdom."

"I tell you truly," said Jesus, "today you will be with me in Paradise."

Now standing by the cross of Jesus were his mother, and his mother's sister, Mary the wife of Clopas, and Mary Magdalene. When Jesus saw his mother, and the disciple whom he loved standing close by, he said to his mother, "Woman, behold your son." Then he said to the disciple, "Behold your mother." And from that hour the disciple took her into his own home.

Now from the sixth hour there was darkness over all the land until the ninth hour. And about the ninth hour Jesus cried with a loud voice, *"Eli, Eli, lama sabachthani?"* (that is, "My God, my God, why have you forsaken me?")

Some of the bystanders, hearing this, said, "This fellow is calling Elijah."

Jesus, knowing that all was now finished, said, "I thirst!"

Then one of them ran and got a sponge and filled it with vinegar, and stuck it on a reed and held it up to him to drink. But the rest said, "Wait! Let us see whether Elijah will come to save him!"

When Jesus had received the vinegar, he said, "It is finished! Father, into your hands I commit my spirit." And he bowed his head and died.

And behold, the veil of the temple was torn in two, from top to bottom. And the earth shook, rocks split asunder, and tombs were opened; and after the resurrection of Jesus, many saints who had fallen asleep in death rose and came forth from the tombs and went into the holy city and appeared to many.

When the centurion and those with him keeping guard over Jesus saw the earthquake and all that took place, they were filled with fear and exclaimed, "This man really *was* God's Son!"

And all the crowd who had gathered to see the spectacle, when they saw what happened, returned home beating their breasts. And Jesus' friends, and the women who had followed him from Galilee, stood at a distance and saw these things.

Now because it was the Preparation Day, in order that the bodies might not remain on the cross on the Sabbath (for that Sabbath was a high day), the Jews asked Pilate to have their legs broken and have them taken away. So the soldiers came and broke the legs of the first man, and of the other who had been crucified with him. But when they came to Jesus and saw that he was already dead, they did not break his legs. But one of the soldiers pierced his side with a spear, and immediately blood and water flowed out. These things took place in fulfillment of the scripture,

Not a bone of him shall be broken.
And again another scripture says,
They shall look on him whom they pierced.

The Crucifixion (continued)

35 And they crucified him, and parted his garments, casting lots: that it might be fulfilled which was spoken by the prophet, They parted my garments among them, and upon my vesture did they cast lots.

36 And sitting down they watched him there;

37 And set up over his head his accusation written, THIS IS JESUS THE KING OF THE JEWS.

38 Then were there two thieves crucified with him; one on the right hand, and another on the left.

39 And they that passed by reviled him, wagging their heads,

40 And saying, Thou that destroyest the temple, and buildest *it* in three days, save thyself. If thou be the Son of God, come down from the cross.

41 Likewise also the chief priests mocking *him,* with the scribes and elders, said,

42 He saved others; himself he cannot save. If he be the King of Israel, let him now come down from the cross, and we will believe him.

43 He trusted in God; let him deliver him now, if he will have him: for he said, I am the Son of God.

44 The thieves also, which were crucified with him, cast the same in his teeth.

45 Now from the sixth hour there was darkness over all the land unto the ninth hour.

46 And about the ninth hour Jesus cried with a loud voice, saying, Eli, Eli, lama sabachthani? that is to say, My God, my God, why hast thou forsaken me?

47 Some of them that stood there, when they heard *that,* said, This *man* calleth for Elijah.

48 And straightway one of them ran, and took a sponge, and filled *it* with vinegar, and put *it* on a reed, and gave him to drink.

49 The rest said, Let be, let us see whether Elijah will come to save him.

50 Jesus, when he had cried again with a loud voice, yielded up the ghost.

51 And, behold, the veil of the temple was rent in twain from the top to the bottom; and the earth did quake, and the rocks rent;

52 And the graves were opened; and many bodies of the saint which slept arose,

53 And came out of the graves after his resurrection, and went into the holy city, and appeared unto many.

54 Now when the centurion, and they that were with him, watching Jesus, saw the earthquake, and those things that were done, they feared greatly, saying, Truly this was the Son of God.

55 And many women were there beholding afar

(Continued on p. 332)

24 And when they had crucified him, they parted his garments, casting lots upon them, what every man should take.

25 And it was the third hour, and they crucified him.

26 And the superscription of his accusation was written over, THE KING OF THE JEWS.

27 And with him they crucify two thieves; the one on his right hand, and the other on his left.

28 And the Scripture was fulfilled, which saith, And he was numbered with the transgressors.

29 And they that passed by railed on him, wagging their heads, and saying, Ah, thou that destroyest the temple, and buildest *it* in three days,

30 Save thyself, and come down from the cross.

31 Likewise also the chief priests mocking said among themselves with the scribes, He saved others; himself he cannot save.

32 Let Christ the King of Israel descend now from the cross, that we may see and believe. And they that were crucified with him reviled him.

33 And when the sixth hour was come, there was darkness over the whole land until the ninth hour.

34 And at the ninth hour Jesus cried with a loud voice, saying, Eloi, Eloi, lama sabachthani? which is, being interpreted, My God, my God, why hast thou forsaken me?

35 And some of them that stood by, when they heard *it,* said, Behold, he calleth Elijah.

36 And one ran and filled a sponge full of vinegar, and put *it* on a reed, and gave him to drink, saying, Let alone; let us see whether Elijah will come to take him down.

37 And Jesus cried with a loud voice, and gave up the ghost.

38 And the veil of the temple was rent in twain from the top to the bottom.

39 And when the centurion, which stood over against him, saw that he so cried out, and gave up the ghost, he said, Truly this man was the Son of God.

40 There were also women looking on afar off: among whom was Mary Magdalene, and Mary the mother of James the less and of Joses, and Salome;

41 Who also, when he was in Galilee, followed him, and ministered unto him; and many other women which came up with him unto Jerusalem.

The Crucifixion (continued)

33 And when they were come to the place, which is called Calvary, There they crucified him, and the malefactors, one on the right hand, and the other on the left.

34 Then said Jesus, Father, forgive them; for they know not what they do. And they parted his raiment, and cast lots.

35 And the people stood beholding. And the rulers also with them derided *him,* saying, He saved others; let him save himself, if he be Christ, the chosen of God.

36 And the soldiers also mocked him, coming to him, and offering him vinegar,

37 And saying, If thou be the King of the Jews, save thyself.

38 And a superscription also was written over him in letters of Greek, and Latin, and Hebrew, THIS IS THE KING OF THE JEWS.

39 And one of the malefactors which were hanged railed on him, saying, If thou be Christ, save thyself and us.

40 But the other answering rebuked him, saying, Dost not thou fear God, seeing thou art in the same condemnation?

41 And we indeed justly; for we receive the due reward of our deeds: but this man hath done nothing amiss.

42 And he said unto Jesus, Lord, remember me when thou comest into thy kingdom.

43 And Jesus said unto him, Verily I say unto thee, Today shalt thou be with me in paradise.

44 And it was about the sixth hour, and there was a darkness over all the earth until the ninth hour.

45 And the sun was darkened, and the veil of the temple was rent in the midst.

46 And when Jesus had cried with a loud voice, he said, Father, into thy hands I commend my spirit: and having said thus, he gave up the ghost.

47 Now when the centurion saw what was done, he glorified God, saying, Certainly this was a righteous man.

48 And all the people that came together to that sight, beholding the things which were done, smote their breasts, and returned.

49 And all his acquaintance, and the women that followed him from Galilee, stood afar off, beholding these things.

18 Where they crucified him, and two others with him, on either side one, and Jesus in the midst.

19 And Pilate wrote a title, and put *it* on the cross. And the writing was JESUS OF NAZARETH THE KING OF THE JEWS.

20 This title then read many of the Jews; for the place where Jesus was crucified was nigh to the city: and it was written in Hebrew, *and* Greek, *and* Latin.

21 Then said the chief priests of the Jews to Pilate, Write not, The King of the Jews; but that he said, I am King of the Jews.

22 Pilate answered, What I have written I have written.

23 Then the soldiers, when they had crucified Jesus, took his garments, and made four parts, to every soldier a part; and also *his* coat: now the coat was without seam, woven from the top throughout.

24 They said therefore among themselves, Let us not rend it, but cast lots for it, whose it shall be: that the Scripture might be fulfilled, which saith, They parted my raiment among them, and for my vesture they did cast lots. These things therefore the soldiers did.

25 Now there stood by the cross of Jesus his mother, and his mother's sister, Mary the *wife* of Cleophas, and Mary Magdalene.

26 When Jesus therefore saw his mother, and the disciple standing by, whom he loved, he saith unto his mother, Woman, behold thy son!

27 Then saith he to the disciple, Behold thy mother! And from that hour that disciple took her unto his own *home.*

28 After this, Jesus knowing that all things were now accomplished, that the Scripture might be fulfilled, saith, I thirst.

29 Now there was set a vessel full of vinegar: and they filled a sponge with vinegar, and put *it* upon hyssop, and put *it* to his mouth.

30 When Jesus therefore had received the vinegar, he said, It is finished: and he bowed his head, and gave up the ghost.

31 The Jews therefore, because it was the preparation, that the bodies should not remain upon the cross on the sabbath day, (for that sabbath day was a high day,) besought Pilate that their legs might be broken, and *that* they might be taken away.

32 Then came the soldiers, and brake the legs of the first, and of the other which was crucified with him.

33 But when they came to Jesus, and saw that he was dead already, they brake not his legs:

The Crucifixion (continued)

(Continued from p. 330)

MATTHEW 27:35-56 ✓

off, which followed Jesus from Galilee, ministering unto him:

56 Among which was Mary Magdalene, and Mary the mother of James and Joses, and the mother of Zebedee's children.

JOHN 19:18-37 ✓

34 But one of the soldiers with a spear pierced his side, and forthwith came there out blood and water.

35 And he that saw *it* bare record, and his record is true; and he knoweth that he saith true, that ye might believe.

36 For these things were done, that the Scripture should be fulfilled, A bone of him shall not be broken.

37 And again another Scripture saith, They shall look on him whom they pierced.

The Burial of Jesus

Matthew 27:57, 60, Mark 15:42-47, Luke 23:50, John 19:38-41

Now when it was evening, there came a rich man from Arimathea named Joseph, who was a disciple of Jesus and was looking for the coming of the kingdom of God. He was a member of the Council, a good and righteous man, and had not consented to their decision and action. He gathered courage and went in to Pilate and asked for the body of Jesus. Pilate wondered whether Jesus were already dead, and called the centurion and asked him how long he had been dead. After learning from the centurion that he was dead, he granted the body to Joseph.

Joseph then came and took away his body. Nicodemus, who at first had come to Jesus by night, also came, bringing a mixture of myrrh and aloes—about a hundred pounds' weight. And they took the body of Jesus and bound it in linen winding cloths with the spices, according to the burial custom of the Jews, and laid it in Joseph's own new tomb which he had cut in the rock, in which no one had as yet been laid, and rolled a great stone against the door of the tomb and departed.

And Mary Magdalene and Mary, the mother of Joses, saw where he was laid.

MATT. 27:57-61 ✓

57 When the even was come, there came a rich man of Arimathea, named Joseph, who also himself was Jesus' disciple:

58 He went to Pilate, and begged the body of Jesus. Then Pilate commanded the body to be delivered.

59 And when Joseph

MARK 15:42-47 ✓

42 And now when the even was come, because it was the preparation, that is, the day before the sabbath,

43 Joseph of Arimathea, an honorable counselor, which also waited for the kingdom of God, came, and went in boldly unto Pilate, and craved the body of Jesus.

LUKE 23:50-56 ✓

50 And, behold, *there was* a man named Joseph, a counselor; *and he was* a good man, and a just:

51 (The same had not consented to the counsel and deed of them:) *he was* of Arimathea, a city of the Jews; who also himself waited for the kingdom of God.

JOHN 19:38-42 ✓

38 And after this Joseph of Arimathea, being a disciple of Jesus, but secretly for fear of the Jews, besought Pilate that he might take away the body of Jesus: and Pilate gave *him* leave. He came therefore, and took the body of Jesus.

39 And there came also Nicodemus, which

The Burial of Jesus (continued)

had taken the body, he wrapped it in a clean linen cloth,

60 And laid it in his own new tomb, which he had hewn out in the rock: and he rolled a great stone to the door of the sepulchre, and departed.

61 And there was Mary Magdalene, and the other Mary, sitting over against the sepulchre.

—

44 And Pilate marveled if he were already dead: and calling *unto him* the centurion, he asked him whether he had been any while dead.

45 And when he knew *it* of the centurion, he gave the body to Joseph.

46 And he bought fine linen, and took him down, and wrapped him in the linen, and laid him in a sepulchre which was hewn out of a rock, and rolled a stone unto the door of the sepulchre.

47 And Mary Magdalene and Mary *the mother* of Joses beheld where he was laid.

—

52 This *man* went unto Pilate, and begged the body of Jesus.

53 And he took it down, and wrapped it in linen, and laid it in a sepulchre that was hewn in stone, wherein never man before was laid.

54 And that day was the preparation, and the sabbath drew on.

55 And the women also, which came with him from Galilee, followed after, and beheld the sepulchre, and how his body was laid.

56 And they returned, and prepared spices and ointments; and rested the sabbath day according to the commandment.

—

at the first came to Jesus by night, and brought a mixture of myrrh and aloes, about a hundred pound *weight*.

40 Then took they the body of Jesus, and wound it in linen clothes with the spices, as the manner of the Jews is to bury.

41 Now in the place where he was crucified there was a garden; and in the garden a new sepulchre, wherein was never man yet laid.

42 There laid they Jesus therefore because of the Jews' preparation *day;* for the sepulchre was nigh at hand.

Guards Stationed at the Tomb

Matthew 27:62-66

Now on the next day, following the Preparation Day, the chief priests and the Pharisees gathered before Pilate and said,

"Sir, we remember that while he was still alive, that impostor said, 'After three days I will rise again.' Therefore, command that the tomb be made secure until the third day, lest his disciples come and steal him away and say to the people, 'He has risen from the dead,' and the last fraud will be worse than the first."

"You shall have a guard," said Pilate. "Go make it as secure as you can."

And they went and made the tomb secure, sealing the stone and stationing a guard of soldiers.

62 Now the next day, that followed the day of the preparation, the chief priests and Pharisees came together unto Pilate,

63 Saying, Sir, we remember that that deceiver said, while he was yet alive, After three days I will rise again.

64 Command therefore that the sepulchre be made sure until the third day, lest his disciples come by night, and steal him away, and say unto the people, He is risen from the dead: so the last error shall be worse than the first.

65 Pilate said unto them, Ye have a watch: go your way, make *it* as sure as ye can.

66 So they went, and made the sepulchre sure, sealing the stone, and setting a watch.

Jesus Rises from the Dead

Matthew 28:2-4, 8, Mark 16:1-7, Luke 24:1-11, John 20:2

And behold, there was a great earthquake; for an angel of the Lord descended from heaven and came and rolled back the stone and sat down on it. His appearance was like lightning, and his garments were white as snow. And for fear of him the guards trembled and became as dead men.

Now when the Sabbath was past, Mary Magdalene, Mary the mother of James, and Salome bought spices, that they might go and anoint Jesus. And on the first day of the week, at early dawn, they went to the tomb, taking the spices they had prepared. And as they went, they said, "Who will roll away the stone for us from the door of the tomb?" (for it was very large). But when they came within sight of the tomb, they saw that the stone had been rolled back. And they went in and found not the body of the Lord Jesus.

Then Mary Magdalene hurried away to Simon Peter and to the other disciple, the one whom Jesus especially loved, and said, "They have taken away the Lord out of the tomb, and we know not where they have laid him!"

And the other women entered the tomb and saw a young man dressed in a white robe sitting over on the righthand side, and they were amazed and alarmed.

"Do not be afraid," he said. "You are looking for Jesus of Nazareth, who was crucified. He has risen, and is not here. See, here is the place where they laid him. But go and tell his disciples, and Peter, that he will go ahead of you into Galilee, and you will see him there, as he told you."

While they were still amazed by all of this, behold, two men stood by them in dazzling garments; and the women were afraid and bowed their faces to the ground. But the men said to them,

"Why are you seeking the living among the dead? He is not here, but has risen. Remember how he told you, while he was still in Galilee, that the Son of Man must be delivered into the hands of sinful men and be crucified, and on the third day rise."

And they remembered his words, and departed quickly from the tomb with fear and great joy.

And they returned from the tomb and told all these things to the eleven and to all the others. It was Mary Magdalene, Joanna, Mary the mother of James, and the other women with them who told these things to the apostles. But their words seemed to them as an idle tale, and they did not believe them.

Rolling Stone. *The stone used to seal Jesus' tomb was not a rock but a chiseled stone made so it could be rolled along a groove.*

Jesus Rises from the Dead (continued)

1 In the end of the sabbath, as it began to dawn toward the first day of the week, came Mary Magdalene and the other Mary to see the sepulchre.

2 And, behold, there was a great earthquake: for the angel of the Lord descended from heaven, and came and rolled back the stone from the door, and sat upon it.

3 His countenance was like lightning, and his raiment white as snow:

4 And for fear of him the keepers did shake, and became as dead *men*.

5 And the angel answered and said unto the women, Fear not ye: for I know that ye seek Jesus, which was crucified.

6 He is not here: for he is risen, as he said. Come, see the place where the Lord lay.

7 And go quickly, and tell his disciples that he is risen from the dead; and, behold, he goeth before you into Galilee; there shall ye see him: lo, I have told you.

8 And they departed quickly from the sepulchre with fear and great joy; and did run to bring his disciples word.

1 And when the sabbath was past, Mary Magdalene, and Mary the *mother* of James, and Salome, had bought sweet spices, that they might come and anoint him.

2 And very early in the morning, the first day of the week, they came unto the sepulchre at the rising of the sun.

3 And they said among themselves, Who shall roll us away the stone from the door of the sepulchre?

4 And when they looked, they saw that the stone was rolled away: for it was very great.

5 And entering into the sepulchre, they saw a young man sitting on the right side, clothed in a long white garment; and they were affrighted.

6 And he saith unto them, Be not affrighted: ye seek Jesus of Nazareth, which was crucified: he is risen; he is not here: behold the place where they laid him.

7 But go your way, tell his disciples and Peter that he goeth before you into Galilee: there shall ye see him, as he said unto you.

8 And they went out quickly, and fled from the sepulchre; for they trembled and were amazed: neither said they any thing to any *man;* for they were afraid.

1 Now upon the first day of the week, very early in the morning, they came unto the sepulchre, bringing the spices which they had prepared, and certain *others* with them.

2 And they found the stone rolled away from the sepulchre.

3 And they entered in, and found not the body of the Lord Jesus.

4 And it came to pass, as they were much perplexed thereabout, behold, two men stood by them in shining garments:

5 And as they were afraid, and bowed down *their* faces to the earth, they said unto them, Why seek ye the living among the dead?

6 He is not here, but is risen: remember how he spake unto you when he was yet in Galilee,

7 Saying, The Son of man must be delivered into the hands of sinful men, and be crucified, and the third day rise again.

8 And they remembered his words,

9 And returned from the sepulchre, and told all these things unto the eleven, and to all the rest.

10 It was Mary Magdalene, and Joanna, and Mary *the mother* of James, and other *women that were* with them, which told these things unto the apostles.

11 And their words seemed to them as idle tales, and they believed them not.

1 The first day of the week cometh Mary Magdalene early, when it was yet dark, unto the sepulchre, and seeth the stone taken away from the sepulchre.

2 Then she runneth, and cometh to Simon Peter, and to the other disciple, whom Jesus loved, and saith unto them, They have taken away the Lord out of the sepulchre, and we know not where they have laid him.

Peter and John Run to the Tomb

John 20:3-10

Peter and the other disciple set out for the tomb, hurrying along together. But the other disciple outran Peter and, arriving first at the tomb, peered inside and saw the linen winding cloths lying there, but did not go in. Then Simon Peter arrived and went inside the tomb and saw the linen winding cloths lying there, and the napkin which had been around his head—not lying with the linen winding cloths, but wrapped round and round and lying in a separate place. Then the other disciple, who had arrived at the tomb first, went inside and saw these things and believed (for as yet they had not understood the scripture, how that it was necessary for Jesus to rise from the dead). Then the disciples returned to their homes.

LUKE 24:12

12 Then arose Peter, and ran unto the sepulchre; and stooping down, he beheld the linen clothes laid by themselves, and departed, wondering in himself at that which was come to pass.

JOHN 20:3-10

3 Peter therefore went forth, and that other disciple, and came to the sepulchre.

4 So they ran both together: and the other disciple did outrun Peter, and came first to the sepulchre.

5 And he stooping down, *and looking in,* saw the linen clothes lying; yet went he not in.

6 Then cometh Simon Peter following him, and went into the sepulchre, and seeth the linen clothes lie,

7 And the napkin, that was about his head, not lying with the linen clothes, but wrapped together in a place by itself.

8 Then went in also that other disciple, which came first to the sepulchre, and he saw, and believed.

9 For as yet they knew not the Scripture, that he must rise again from the dead.

10 Then the disciples went away again unto their own home.

The Women See Jesus

Matthew 28:9-10, Mark 16:11, John 20:11-18

But Mary stood before the tomb and wept. And as she wept, she peered inside the tomb and saw two angels in white, sitting where the body of Jesus had lain—one at the head, and one at the feet.

"Woman," they said, "why are you weeping?"

"Because they have taken away my Lord," said Mary, "and I know not where they have laid him."

Then she turned around and saw Jesus standing there, but was not aware that it was Jesus.

"Woman," said Jesus, "why are you weeping? Whom are you seeking?"

"Sir," said Mary (supposing him to be the gardener), "if you have carried him away, tell me where you have laid him, and I will take him away."

"Mary!" said Jesus.

Mary turned to Jesus and cried, "Rabboni!"

The Women See Jesus (continued)

(that is to say in Hebrew, "Master!").

"Do not hold me," said Jesus, "for I have not yet ascended to the Father. But go to my brethren and tell them, 'I am ascending to my Father and your Father, and to my God and your God.'"

Then Mary Magdalene went away to the disciples and said, "I have seen the Lord!" and told them the things he said to her. When they heard that he was alive and that she had seen him, they did not believe it.

As the women went to bring his disciples word, behold, Jesus met them, saying, "Hail!" And they came and clasped his feet and worshipped him.

"Do not be afraid," said Jesus. "Go and tell my brethren that they are to go to Galilee, and there they will see me."

MATTHEW 28:9-10

9 And as they went to tell his disciples, behold, Jesus met them, saying, All hail. And they came and held him by the feet, and worshipped him.

10 Then said Jesus unto them, Be not afraid: go tell my brethren that they go into Galilee, and there shall they see me.

MARK 16:9-11

9 Now when *Jesus* was risen early the first *day* of the week, he appeared first to Mary Magdalene, out of whom he had cast seven devils.

10 *And* she went and told them that had been with him, as they mourned and wept.

11 And they, when they had heard that he was alive, and had been seen of her, believed not.

JOHN 20:11-18

11 But Mary stood without at the sepulchre weeping: and as she wept, she stooped down, *and looked* into the sepulchre,

12 And seeth two angels in white sitting, the one at the head, and the other at the feet, where the body of Jesus had lain.

13 And they say unto her, Woman, why weepest thou? She saith unto them, Because they have taken away my Lord, and I know not where they have laid him.

14 And when she had thus said, she turned herself back, and saw Jesus standing, and knew not that it was Jesus.

15 Jesus saith unto her, Woman, why weepest thou? whom seekest thou? She, supposing him to be the gardener, saith unto him, Sir, if thou have borne him hence, tell me where thou hast laid him, and I will take him away.

16 Jesus saith unto her, Mary. She turned herself, and saith unto him, Rabboni; which is to say, Master.

17 Jesus saith unto her, Touch me not; for I am not yet ascended to my Father: but go to my brethren, and say unto them, I ascend unto my Father, and your Father; and *to* my God, and your God.

18 Mary Magdalene came and told the disciples that she had seen the Lord, and *that* he had spoken these things unto her.

The Garden Tomb. *Excavations made nearby after General Gordon's discovery of Calvary revealed a first-century tomb—empty—which seems to fit the descriptions found in the Gospels.*

The Report of the Guards

MATTHEW 28:11-15

Matthew 28:11-15

Some of the guard went into the city and told the chief priests what had taken place. And when the priests had assembled with the elders and had taken counsel, they gave a large sum of money to the soldiers and said, "Tell people, 'His disciples came at night and stole him away while we were asleep.' And if the governor hears of it, we will satisfy him so that you will have nothing to worry about."

And they took the money and did as they were instructed, and this report has been circulated among the Jews to this day.

MATTHEW 28:11-15

11 Now when they were going, behold, some of the watch came into the city, and showed unto the chief priests all the things that were done.

12 And when they were assembled with the elders, and had taken counsel, they gave large money unto the soldiers,

13 Saying, Say ye, His disciples came by night, and stole him *away* while we slept.

14 And if this come to the governor's ears, we will persuade him, and secure you.

15 So they took the money, and did as they were taught: and this saying is commonly reported among the Jews until this day.

The Emmaus Road Appearance

Luke 24:13-35

On the same day, two disciples were on their way to the village of Emmaus, about sixty furlongs from Jerusalem, and were talking together about all the things that had happened. And while they were talking and discussing together, Jesus himself drew near and began walking along with them, but they were prevented from recognizing him.

"What is this discussion you are having as you walk along?" said Jesus.

They halted, looking very sad. Then one of them, whose name was Cleopas, said, "You must be the only stranger in Jerusalem who has not known the things that have happened there in these days."

"What things?" asked Jesus.

"The things concerning Jesus of Nazareth," they said, "a man who was a prophet mighty in deed and word before God and all the people, and how the chief priests and our rulers handed him over to be condemned to death and crucified him. But we were hoping that he was the one who is to redeem Israel. And besides all this, it is now the third day since these things happened.

MARK 16:12-13

12 After that he appeared in another form unto two of them, as they walked, and went into the country.

13 And they went and told *it* unto the residue: neither believed they them.

LUKE 24:13-35

13 And, behold, two of them went that same day to a village called Emmaus, which was from Jerusalem *about* threescore furlongs.

14 And they talked together of all these things which had happened.

15 And it came to pass, that, while they communed *together* and reasoned, Jesus himself drew near, and went with them.

16 But their eyes were holden that they should not know him.

17 And he said unto them, What manner of communications *are* these that ye have one to another, as ye walk, and are sad?

18 And the one of them, whose name was Cleopas, answering said unto him, Art thou only a stranger in Jerusalem, and hast not known the things which are come to pass there in these days?

19 And he said unto them, What things? And they said unto him, Concerning Jesus of

The Emmaus Road Appearance (continued)

Furthermore, some women of our company caused us much astonishment: they were at the tomb early this morning and did not find his body, and came back saying that they had seen a vision of angels who said that he is alive. Then some of them who were with us went to the tomb and found it just as the women said, but they did not see *him*."

"O foolish men, and slow of heart to believe all that the prophets have spoken!" said Jesus. "Was it not necessary for the Messiah to suffer these things before entering into his glory?"

And beginning with Moses and all the prophets, he explained to them the things concerning himself in all the scriptures. And they drew near to the village to which they were going, and Jesus appeared to be going on. But they constrained him, saying, "Abide with us, for the evening is at hand and the day is far spent."

And he went in to abide with them. And as he sat at table with them, he took the bread and blessed it, and broke it and gave it to them. And their eyes were opened and they recognized him, and he vanished from their sight.

Then they exclaimed one to another, "Did not our hearts burn within us as he spoke to us along the way and opened up the scriptures to us?"

And they got up from the table at once and hurried back to Jerusalem and found the eleven gathered together, and others with them, who exclaimed, "The Lord has risen indeed, and has appeared to Simon!"

Then the two told what had happened on the road, and how they recognized Jesus when he broke the bread.

Nazareth, which was a prophet mighty in deed and word before God and all the people:

20 And how the chief priests and our rulers delivered him to be condemned to death, and have crucified him.

21 But we trusted that it had been he which should have redeemed Israel: and beside all this, today is the third day since these things were done.

22 Yea, and certain women also of our company made us astonished, which were early at the sepulchre;

23 And when they found not his body, they came, saying, that they had also seen a vision of angels, which said that he was alive.

24 And certain of them which were with us went to the sepulchre, and found *it* even so as the women had said: but him they saw not.

25 Then he said unto them, O fools, and slow of heart to believe all that the prophets have spoken:

26 Ought not Christ to have suffered these things, and to enter into his glory?

27 And beginning at Moses and all the prophets, he expounded unto them in all the Scriptures the things concerning himself.

28 And they drew nigh unto the village, whither they went: and he made as though he would have gone further.

29 But they constrained him, saying, Abide with us; for it is toward evening, and the day is far spent. And he went in to tarry with them.

30 And it came to pass, as he sat at meat with them, he took bread, and blessed *it,* and brake, and gave to them.

31 And their eyes were opened, and they knew him; and he vanished out of their sight.

32 And they said one to another, Did not our heart burn within us, while he talked with us by the way, and while he opened to us the Scriptures?

33 And they rose up the same hour, and returned to Jerusalem, and found the eleven gathered together, and them that were with them,

34 Saying, The Lord is risen indeed, and hath appeared to Simon.

35 And they told what things *were done* in the way, and how he was known of them in breaking of bread.

The Emmaus Road. *A short distance from Jerusalem is the site of the town to which Jesus traveled with two disciples the day of His resurrection. Some of the original pavement still exists.*

SAMARIA

Jordan River

Ein Kerem

JERUSALEM

Bethany

Bethlehem

Jericho

Hebron

Mt. Nebo

DEAD SEA

Machaerus

Masada

E

Here can be seen the places where events occurred during the week of Jesus' Passion: The Triumphal Entry starting from Bethany.

Jesus Appears to the Disciples

Luke 24:36-49, John 20:21-23

And as they were telling these things, Jesus himself stood in their midst and said, "Peace be to you."

But they were startled and frightened, and thought they were seeing a spirit.

"Why are you troubled," asked Jesus, "and why do doubts arise in your hearts? Behold my hands and my feet, that it is I myself. Handle me and see, for a spirit does not have flesh and bones as you see that I have."

And when he had said this, he showed them his hands and his feet. And while they still could not believe for joy, overcome by the wonder of it all, Jesus said, "Have you anything here to eat?"

And they gave him a piece of broiled fish, and he took it and ate before them. Then he said to them, "These are the things I told you while I was still with you, that all the things written about me in the law of Moses and in the prophets and psalms must be fulfilled."

Then he opened their understanding, that they might understand the scriptures, and said to them, "Thus it is written, that the Messiah should suffer and on the third day rise from the dead, that repentance and forgiveness of sins should be preached in his name to all nations, beginning at Jerusalem. You are witnesses of these things. And behold, I will send the promise of my Father upon you; but tarry in the city until you are clothed with power from above."

Then Jesus said to them again, "Peace be to you. As the Father sent me, so do I send you."

And when he had said this, he breathed on them and said, "Receive the Holy Spirit. Whose sins you forgive, they are forgiven them; whose sins you retain, they are retained.

MARK 16:14

14 Afterward he appeared unto the eleven as they sat at meat, and upbraided them with their unbelief and hardness of heart, because they believed not them which had seen him after he was risen.

LUKE 24:36-49

36 And as they thus spake, Jesus himself stood in the midst of them, and saith unto them, Peace *be* unto you.

37 But they were terrified and affrighted, and supposed that they had seen a spirit.

38 And he said unto them, Why are ye troubled? and why do thoughts arise in your hearts?

39 Behold my hands and my feet, that it is I myself: handle me, and see; for a spirit hath not flesh and bones, as ye see me have.

40 And when he had thus spoken, he showed them *his* hands and *his* feet.

41 And while they yet believed not for joy, and wondered, he said unto them, Have ye here any meat?

42 And they gave him a piece of a broiled fish, and of a honeycomb.

43 And he took *it,* and did eat before them.

44 And he said unto them, These *are* the words which I spake unto you, while I was yet with you, that all things must be fulfilled, which were written in the law of Moses, and *in* the prophets, and *in* the psalms, concerning me.

45 Then opened he their understanding, that they might understand the Scriptures,

46 And said unto them, Thus it is written, and thus it behooved Christ to suffer, and to

JOHN 20:19-23

19 Then the same day at evening, being the first *day* of the week, when the doors were shut where the disciples were assembled for fear of the Jews, came Jesus and stood in the midst, and saith unto them, Peace *be* unto you.

20 And when he had so said, he showed unto them *his* hands and his side. Then were the disciples glad, when they saw the Lord.

21 Then said Jesus to them again, Peace *be* unto you: as *my* Father hath sent me, even so send I you.

22 And when he had said this, he breathed on *them,* and saith unto them, Receive ye the Holy Ghost:

Jesus Appears to the Disciples (continued)

	LUKE 24:36-49	JOHN 20:19-23
	rise from the dead the third day:	23 Whosesoever sins ye remit, they are remitted unto them; *and* whosesoever *sins* ye retain, they are retained.
	47 And that repentance and remission of sins should be preached in his name among all nations, beginning at Jerusalem.	
	48 And ye are witnesses of these things.	
	49 And, behold, I send the promise of my Father upon you: but tarry ye in the city of Jerusalem, until ye be endued with power from on high.	

Thomas Sees Jesus and Believes

John 20:24-31

But Thomas, one of the twelve, called the Twin, was not with them when Jesus came. The other disciples therefore said to him, "We have seen the Lord!"

But Thomas said, "Unless I see in his hands the mark of the nails and put my finger where the nails were and put my hand into his side, I will not believe."

And after eight days, his disciples were again in the house, and Thomas with them. The doors were shut, but Jesus came and stood in the midst and said, "Peace be to you."

Then he said to Thomas, "Place your finger here; behold my hands. Take your hand and put it in my side. Do not be faithless, but believe."

"My Lord, and my God!" cried Thomas.

"Because you have seen me, you have believed," said Jesus. "Blessed are those who have not seen me, and yet have believed."

And Jesus did many other signs in the presence of the disciples which are not written in this book. But these are written that you may believe that Jesus is the Messiah, the Son of God, and that believing, you may have life through his name.

24 But Thomas, one of the twelve, called Didymus, was not with them when Jesus came.

25 The other disciples therefore said unto him, We have seen the Lord. But he said unto them, Except I shall see in his hands the print of the nails, and put my finger into the print of the nails, and thrust my hand into his side, I will not believe.

...because thou hast seen me, thou hast believed: blessed are they that have not seen, and yet have believed.

26 And after eight days again his disciples were within, and Thomas with them: *then* came Jesus, the doors being shut, and stood in the midst, and said, Peace *be* unto you.

27 Then saith he to Thomas, Reach hither thy finger, and behold my hands; and reach hither thy hand, and thrust *it* into my side; and be not faithless, but believing.

28 And Thomas answered and said unto him, My Lord and my God.

29 Jesus saith unto him, Thomas, because thou hast seen me, thou hast believed: blessed *are* they that have not seen, and *yet* have believed.

30 And many other signs truly did Jesus in the presence of his disciples, which are not written in this book:

31 But these are written, that ye might believe that Jesus is the Christ, the Son of God; and that believing ye might have life through his name.

343

Jesus Appears by Galilee

John 21:1-23

After these things, Jesus again appeared to the disciples at the Sea of Tiberius, in this way. Simon Peter, Thomas (called the Twin), Nathaniel of Cana of Galilee, the sons of Zebedee, and two others of his disciples were together, and Simon Peter said, "I'm going fishing."

"We'll go with you," they replied.

They went out and got into the boat, and during the night caught nothing. And at daybreak, Jesus stood on the shore, but the disciples did not know it was Jesus.

"Lads, do you have any fish?" asked Jesus.

"No," they replied.

"Cast the net on the right side of the boat and you will catch some," said Jesus.

So they cast the net, and were unable to draw it in because of the great number of fish. Then that disciple whom Jesus especially loved said to Peter, "It is the Lord!"

When Simon Peter heard that it was the Lord, he put on his outer cloak (for he was wearing only a waistcloth) and jumped into the water. But the other disciples came in the boat, towing the net full of fish (they were not far from land, about two hundred cubits). When they came ashore, they saw a fire of coals with fish roasting on it, and bread.

"Bring some of the fish you just caught," said Jesus.

Simon Peter went aboard and drew the net ashore, full of large fish—a hundred and fifty-three. Although there were so many, the net was not torn.

"Come and have breakfast," said Jesus.

None of the disciples ventured to ask "Who are you?" for they knew it was the Lord. Jesus came and took the bread and gave it to them, and also the fish. This was now the third time that Jesus appeared to the disciples after he had risen from the dead.

Now when they had finished breakfast, Jesus said to Simon Peter, "Simon, son of John, do you love me more than these?"

"Yes, Lord," replied Peter, "you know that I love you."

"Then feed my lambs," said Jesus.

A second time Jesus said to him, "Simon, son of John, do you love me?"

"Yes, Lord," replied Peter, "you know that I love you."

"Then tend my sheep," said Jesus.

Jesus said to him the third time, "Simon, son of John, do you love me?"

Peter was grieved because Jesus asked him the third time, "Do you love me?" And he said, "Lord, you know everything; you know that I love you!"

"Then feed my sheep," said Jesus. "I tell you truly, when you were young, you girded yourself and walked wherever you pleased; but when you are old, you will stretch forth your hands and someone else will gird you and carry you where you do not wish to go."

Jesus said this to show by what kind of death Peter should glorify God. And after saying this, he said to him, "Follow me."

Peter turned and saw following them the disciple whom Jesus especially loved, who had leaned against his breast at the supper and had said, "Lord, who is it that is going to betray you?" When he saw him, Peter said to Jesus, "Lord, what about this man?"

"If it is my will that he remain until I come," replied Jesus, "what is that to you? Follow me."

Then word spread abroad among the brethren that that disciple would not die. But Jesus did not say that he would not die, but rather, "If it is my will that he remain until I come, what is that to you?"

Jesus Appears by Galilee (continued)

1 After these things Jesus showed himself again to the disciples at the sea of Tiberias; and on this wise showed he *himself.*

2 There were together Simon Peter, and Thomas called Didymus, and Nathanael of Cana in Galilee, and the *sons* of Zebedee, and two other of his disciples.

3 Simon Peter saith unto them, I go a fishing. They say unto him, We also go with thee. They went forth, and entered into a ship immediately; and that night they caught nothing.

> *...when the morning was now come, Jesus stood on the shore; but the disciples knew not it was Jesus.*

4 But when the morning was now come, Jesus stood on the shore; but the disciples knew not that it was Jesus.

5 Then Jesus saith unto them, Children, have ye any meat? They answered him, No.

6 And he said unto them, Cast the net on the right side of the ship, and ye shall find. They cast therefore, and now they were not able to draw it for the multitude of fishes.

7 Therefore that disciple whom Jesus loved saith unto Peter, It is the Lord. Now when Simon Peter heard that it was the Lord, he girt *his* fisher's coat *unto him,* (for he was naked,) and did cast himself into the sea.

8 And the other disciples came in a little ship, (for they were not far from land, but as it were two hundred cubits,) dragging the net with fishes.

9 As soon then as they were come to land, they saw a fire of coals there, and fish laid thereon, and bread.

10 Jesus saith unto them, Bring of the fish which ye have now caught.

11 Simon Peter went up, and drew the net to land full of great fishes, a hundred and fifty and three: and for all there were so many, yet was not the net broken.

12 Jesus saith unto them, Come *and* dine. And none of the disciples durst ask him, Who art thou? knowing that it was the Lord.

13 Jesus then cometh, and taketh bread, and giveth them, and fish likewise.

14 This is now the third time that Jesus showed himself to his disciples, after that he was risen from the dead.

15 So when they had dined, Jesus saith to Simon Peter, Simon *son* of Jonas, lovest thou me more than these? He saith unto him, Yea, Lord; thou knowest that I love thee. He saith unto him, Feed my lambs.

16 He saith to him again the second time, Simon, *son* of Jonas, lovest thou me? He saith unto him, Yea, Lord; thou knowest that I love thee. He saith unto him, Feed my sheep.

17 He saith unto him the third time, Simon, *son* of Jonas, lovest thou me? Peter was grieved because he said unto him the third time, Lovest thou me? And he said unto him, Lord, thou knowest all things; thou knowest that I love thee. Jesus saith unto him, Feed my sheep.

18 Verily, verily, I say unto thee, When thou wast young, thou girdedst thyself, and walkedst whither thou wouldest: but when thou shalt be old, thou shalt stretch forth thy hands, and another shall gird thee, and carry *thee* whither thou wouldest not.

19 This spake he, signifying by what death he should glorify God. And when he had spoken this, he saith unto him, Follow me.

> *And he said unto him, Lord, thou knowest all things; thou knowest that I love thee. Jesus saith unto him, Feed my sheep.*

20 Then Peter, turning about, seeth the disciple whom Jesus loved following; which also leaned on his breast at supper, and said, Lord, which is he that betrayeth thee?

21 Peter seeing him saith to Jesus, Lord, and what *shall* this man *do?*

22 Jesus saith unto him, If I will that he tarry till I come, what *is that* to thee? follow thou me.

23 Then went this saying abroad among the brethren, that that disciple should not die: yet Jesus said not unto him, He shall not die; but, If I will that he tarry till I come, what *is that* to thee?

Jesus Returns to Heaven. *The last moments
with a loved one are precious. The disciples who
watched their beloved Master ascend never forgot
that moment nor the commission He had given
them to take His gospel to the ends of the earth.*

346

Jesus Commissions His Disciples

Matthew 28:16-20, Mark 16:15-18

Then the eleven disciples went into Galilee to the mountain where Jesus had appointed them. And when they saw him, they worshipped him; but some doubted. And Jesus came and said,

"All authority in heaven and on earth has been given to me. Go therefore and make disciples of all nations, baptizing them in the name of the Father and of the Son and of the Holy Spirit, teaching them to observe all the things that I have commanded you. And lo, I am with you always, to the end of the age."

"Go into all the world and preach the gospel to all mankind. He who believes and is baptized will be saved, and he who does not believe will be condemned. And these signs will accompany those who believe: in my name they will cast out demons; they will speak in new tongues; they will take up serpents, and if they drink anything deadly it will not hurt them; they will lay hands on the sick, and they will recover."

MATTHEW 28:16-20 ✓

16 Then the eleven disciples went away into Galilee, into a mountain where Jesus had appointed them.

17 And when they saw him, they worshipped him: but some doubted.

18 And Jesus came and spake unto them, saying, All power is given unto me in heaven and in earth.

19 Go ye therefore, and teach all nations, baptizing them in the name of the Father, and of the Son, and of the Holy Ghost:

20 Teaching them to observe all things whatsoever I have commanded you: and, lo, I am with you alway, *even* unto the end of the world. Amen.

MARK 16:15-18

15 And he said unto them, Go ye into all the world, and preach the gospel to every creature.

16 He that believeth and is baptized shall be saved; but he that believeth not shall be damned.

17 And these signs shall follow them that believe; In my name shall they cast out devils; they shall speak with new tongues;

18 They shall take up serpents; and if they drink any deadly thing, it shall not hurt them; they shall lay hands on the sick, and they shall recover.

Jesus' Ascension

Acts 1:3-11, Luke 24:50-53

To his apostles, Jesus showed himself alive after his sufferings by many infallible proofs, appearing to them from time to time during forty days and talking about the kingdom of God. And while he was together with them, he instructed them not to depart from Jerusalem, but to wait for the Father's promise—"of which you have heard me speak," he said. "For John baptized with water, but you shall be baptized with the Holy Spirit not many days from now."

And he led them out as far as Bethany. While they were together, they asked him, "Lord, are you going to restore the kingdom to Israel at this time?"

"It is not for you to know the times or seasons which the Father has determined by his own authority," replied Jesus. "But you will receive power when the Holy Spirit has come upon you, and you shall be my witnesses in Jerusalem and in all Judea and Samaria, and to the ends of the earth."

And he lifted up his hands and blessed them; and while he was blessing them, he was parted from them and carried up into heaven, and a

Jesus' Ascension (continued)

cloud received him out of their sight. And while they were gazing toward heaven as he went up, behold, two men dressed in white stood by them and said,

"Men of Galilee, why do you stand gazing toward heaven? This same Jesus who was taken up from you into heaven will come again in the same manner in which you saw him go into heaven."

And they worshipped him, and returned to Jerusalem with great joy, and were continually in the temple praising God.

MARK 16:19-20

19 So then, after the Lord had spoken unto them, he was received up into heaven, and sat on the right hand of God.

20 And they went forth, and preached every where, the Lord working with *them*, and confirming the word with signs following. Amen.

LUKE 24:50-53

50 And he led them out as far as to Bethany, and he lifted up his hands, and blessed them.

51 And it came to pass, while he blessed them, he was parted from them, and carried up into heaven.

52 And they worshipped him, and returned to Jerusalem with great joy:

53 And were continually in the temple, praising and blessing God. Amen.

ACTS 1:3-11

3 To whom also he shewed himself alive after his passion by many infallible proofs, being seen of them forty days, and speaking of the things pertaining to the kingdom of God:

4 And, being assembled together with *them*, commanded them that they should not depart from Jerusalem, but wait for the promise of the Father, which, *saith he*, ye have heard of me.

5 For John truly baptized with water; but ye shall be baptized with the Holy Ghost not many days hence.

6 When they therefore were come together, they asked of him, saying, Lord, wilt thou at this time restore again the kingdom to Israel?

7 And he said unto them, It is not for you to know the times or the seasons, which the Father hath put in his own power.

8 But ye shall receive power, after that the Holy Ghost is come upon you: and ye shall be witnesses unto me both in Jerusalem, and in all Judaea, and in Samaria, and unto the uttermost part of the earth.

9 And when he had spoken these things, while they beheld, he was taken up; and a cloud received him out of their sight.

10 And while they looked stedfastly toward heaven as he went up, behold, two men stood by them in white apparel;

11 Which also said, Ye men of Galilee, why stand ye gazing up into heaven? this same Jesus, which is taken up from you into heaven, shall so come in like manner as ye have seen him go into heaven.

John's Epilogue

JOHN 21:24-25

24 This is the disciple which testifieth of these things, and wrote these things: and we know that his testimony is true.

25 And there are also many other things which Jesus did, the which, if they should be written every one, I suppose that even the world itself could not contain the books that should be written. Amen.

The Greatest Life Ever Lived

BIOGRAPHICAL PANORAMA

Biographical Panorama

When the Son of God invaded history, He made an impact which has continued to the present day. Spread before you in the pages which follow is the narrative of that remarkable life.

1. The Family and Genealogy of Jesus

The entrance of Jesus Christ into the human family took place by a divine miracle of creation. The virgin Mary, the mother of Jesus, became pregnant through the power of the Holy Spirit (Luke 1:26-38; Matthew 1:18-25). By this means Jesus, the eternal Son of God, became human, the Son of Man, but without partaking of the sin of the human race. Because He is the Holy One (Luke 1:35), He was qualified for His supreme duty as the perfect Saviour of the race—Immanuel, "God with us" (Matthew 1:18-23).

An absolute qualification for the Messianic claims and ministry of Jesus himself, as well as for faith in Him as the promised Messiah, Saviour, in the Old Testament, was that He should descend from David and Abraham. The Gospels contain two genealogies, both of which, in different ways, prove this.

In his Gospel Matthew proves this through Joseph, the foster-father. As a result of the child's connection with him from a legal point of view, Jesus was considered to be his son and thus belonging to the family of David (Matthew 1:2-17).

The Gospel of Luke deals with the matter from the point of view of Mary, showing her genealogy. This leads back to David also. As the son of Mary, according to the flesh, Jesus had a legitimate royal relationship with David (Luke 3:22-38). If these facts are correct, Jesus was the son of David on His mother's side as well as His father's, so the heir to the throne of Israel and its royal power. See the information concerning the genealogy of Jesus in the *Introductory Survey* for Matthew.

Jesus was also the son of Abraham. It is through him that all the promises of God concerning salvation and blessing for all races of the earth will be realized (Matthew 1:1). "The ripe fruit of the theocratical particularity becomes the seed of the universality which is the final goal ever since the beginning." —F. Godet.

2. The Birth and Childhood of Jesus

According to Micah the prophet, the Messiah was to be born in Bethlehem, the home city of David's family (Micah 5:2 ff.). A decree from Augustus Caesar, who reigned 13 B.C. to A.D. 14, brought this to pass. The decree required a common census all over the Roman Empire and in the subkingdoms (and Judea was counted among these at this time) thus forcing Mary and her fiance Joseph to go to Bethlehem in order to be registered there, since they belonged to the family of David.

They had to find shelter in a stable where animals were usually kept, possibly in a cave. It was under circumstances like this that the Saviour of the world entered human life. His first resting place was in a manger (Luke 2:1-7), and a multitude of angels proclaimed His coming to the shepherds in a field near the town (Luke 2:8-20).

Jesus' birth occurred during the reign of King Herod, shortly before he died in the spring of the year 750 after the founding of Rome, that is, about four or five years before our Christian era began.

Eight days after the child's birth, He was circumcised and by this became a member of the theocracy, partaking of the covenant but also subject to the Law of Moses during His entire life (see Galatians 4:4). At that time He received the name which God through the angel had told Mary of before His birth; namely,

Jesus. This was the Greek form of the Hebrew Yeshua, "the salvation of Jehovah" (Luke 2:21, 22). When the purification period for Mary after the birth of the male child was finished (compare Leviticus 12:2 ff), the parents brought Him to the Temple in Jerusalem.

As the firstborn child, Jesus belonged to God in a special way, with the duty of serving all His life in the Temple. However, this duty was reserved for the tribe of Levi, so a provision was made of redemption for firstborn males. This was done with Mary's firstborn (Luke 2:22, 23). At the same time, on her own behalf Mary offered a sacrifice which the Law required for the mother who was poor (Luke 2:24). Two representatives of the true, spiritual theocracy, Simeon and Anna, the prophetess, paid homage to the child as the promised Messiah (Luke 2:25-38).

The parents returned to Bethlehem with the child, perhaps with the intention of having Him grow up in the town of His ancestor David. But Wise Men from the East came to Jerusalem. A new star had been a sign to them that the expected King of the Jews had been born. Astonished by their questions, King Herod sought the advice of the scribes and learned from them where Messiah was to be born. He sent the Wise Men to Bethlehem, commanding them to return with full details, though actually he intended to do away with his supposed rival.

At their journey's end, the Wise Men paid homage to the child but took another route back to their native country (Matthew 2:1-12). That same night Joseph fled to Egypt with the child and His mother, after being warned in a dream by an angel of the Lord (Matthew 2:13-15). Herod then instituted a massacre of all the male children of two years of age and under in the small area around Bethlehem, to make sure this newborn pretender to the throne was eliminated (Matthew 2:16-18).

After the death of the king some months later, the family returned again to their own land, according to the commandment of the Lord. They settled down in Nazareth, which would be more hidden and safe than Bethlehem (Matthew 2:19-23; Luke 2:39). Here the boy spent His childhood, going through a normal human development—physically, intellectually and spiritually (Luke 2:40).

Toward the end of His twelfth year Jesus entered a new period of His life. Like all Jewish boys, at the age of 13 He was obliged to observe the regulations of the Mosaic Law, becoming a "Son of the Law." Therefore, in the Passover Feast of the year A.D. 8, Jesus went with His parents up to Jerusalem.

What the young boy experienced at that time made an indelible mark on His soul. He became intensely aware of His intimate, personal relationship with Jehovah, whom He knew to be His Father. As Jesus left the Temple in the Holy City (Luke 2:41-50) He was prepared to dedicate himself completely to serving God's interests on earth. He went back with His parents to the small town of Nazareth in order to be matured for His high calling through 18 silent years of fulfilling His duty as the son of a carpenter (Luke 2:51, 52).

3. Transition from Private Life to the Messianic Ministry

This was accomplished by two decisive events: The Baptism of Jesus and His Temptation. It was in the twelfth year of the reign of the Emperor Tiberius; that is, about the year 26 of our Christian era, that John the Baptist began his ministry in late fall. He was preparing the way for the promised Messiah, who would soon appear.

Jesus came to John in order to be baptized. At this time He was about 30 years old, an age which the ancients considered to be the apex of human life from a physical and intellectual viewpoint. It seems that John, who had lived since his youth in the wilderness, did not know Jesus personally.

We are told that those who wanted to be baptized confessed their sins to John. We cannot help but wonder what the confession of Jesus contained. Certainly, He had no sin of His own. Perhaps vicariously He assumed the sin of the world, which already weighed on His heart and which He began to feel as His own. We can understand then how John later on could present Jesus as the Lamb of God who would take away the sin of the world. This also explains why John spontaneously exclaimed: "I need to be baptized by you, and you come to me." However, at Jesus' insistence he baptized Him.

At the time of the baptism, the Heavenly Father confirmed Jesus to be the Son of God in an absolute and unique way. Jesus' own development as man also reached its perfection at that time. Thirty years of unceasing voluntary subjection to the influence and guidance of the Holy Spirit reached its natural climax in an indissolvable union between the Spirit and the Person of Jesus.

At the baptism Jesus dedicated himself to His Messianic ministry as the Redeemer and Saviour of the race. The voice of the Father from Heaven, and the descent of the Holy Spirit, who remained upon Jesus, was God's public installation of His Son in His high office, and the provision of supernatural power which His ministry would demand. John saw and heard all that now took place between the Father and Son and from then on could with full certainty carry through his assignment of confessing Jesus to be the Messiah (Matthew 3:13-17; Mark 1:11; Luke 3:21, 22).

Jesus received not only divine empowerment but also clear directions for the way to minister as the Son of God and yet be truly man.

Just as Adam, the first man, was asked to consecrate to God in obedience and humility the powers he possessed, so Jesus as head of the new spiritual race had to come to the decision not to rely upon His supernatural powers and His position as Son of God. But in order for this consecration to be both voluntary and conscious, Jesus must have the opportunity to use His powers for His own benefit. The trial which the head of the new spiritual race faced was a Messianic struggle in the true sense of the word. The result of this struggle would decide whether the kingdom of God here on earth could exist at all. Here the future ruler, for whom the world was intended, fought a spiritual battle for that territory with Satan, who up to that time had maintained control (John 12:31, 32).

After 40 days of fasting and internal conflicts, Jesus met the tempter on the three main arenas of human life—the phsyical, mental and spiritual. The victory He won here formed the basis of all His future ministry (Luke 4:11-13; Matthew 4:1-11; Mark 1:12, 13).

After the period of time spent in the wilderness, Jesus returned to the Jordan River where John was continuing his ministry. The Baptist denied he himself was the Messiah but explained at the same time that this One had already come (John 1:19-28). The following day when Jesus approached, John observed Him and testified of His being the Son of God and the Redeemer of the world. The following day he repeated His testimony, with the result that two of his disciples began to follow Jesus (John 1:29-37).

4. The Early Ministry of Jesus

Jesus began His ministry as the Messiah by gathering around himself His first followers. He revealed His glory to the first of them by demonstrating His supernatural knowledge of them (John 1:38-50). When He returned to Galilee (John 1:43) He participated in a wedding festival in Cana. Here He revealed His supernatural power by changing water into wine. This, His first miracle, strengthened and deepened the disciples' faith in Him (John

2:1-11). Then He continued His journey to Nazareth and made a short visit to Capernaum (John 2:12).

Jesus went up to Jerusalem for the Feast of Passover. Here He began His public Messianic ministry by purifying the Temple, causing a great sensation (see Malachi 3:1-3).

His action in cleansing the Temple produced a two-way effect: His disciples remembered the prophetic word concerning the Messiah and were strengthened in their faith that He was the One to come. For their part the Jews showed symptoms of unbelief, asking for a sign of His authority to undertake ministry which only the Messiah would do (John 2:13-25).

After the opposition Jesus met in the Temple, He continued His ministry in Jerusalem, where many believed in Him after seeing His miracles. But most of them lacked the faith that results in full surrender to the Lord. So Jesus did not trust their faith (John 2:23-25).

Nicodemus was an encouraging exception to this attitude. A Pharisee and a ruler of the Jews, he came to confer with Jesus by night. Jesus explained the nature of the heavenly kingdom to him, its qualification and advantages, as well as the importance of His own ministry to the world (John 3:1-21). The later history of Nicodemus confirmed that this contact had been successful (John 7:50-51; 19:39).

From the Temple in the capital city of Jerusalem, Jesus turned His attention to the province of Judea. His activity here was similar to that of John and took place not far from where John was ministering (John 3:22-24). At this time the Baptist proclaimed that which has been characterized as the last message of the Old Covenant. It is characterized by the announcement of judgment for unbelief concerning the Messiah whom John had served and about whom he had preached (John 3:25-36).

5. Jesus' Ministry in Galilee

From the Feast of Passover in April until the month of December (John 4:35), Jesus ministered in Judea with a varying degree of success. Because of the religious leaders' negative reaction, He found it best to withdraw rather than become involved in inevitable controversies at this early point in time. At this time also He learned about the imprisonment of John the Baptist (Matthew 4:12; Mark 1:14; Luke 3:19, 20).

Leaving Judea, Jesus started on the journey to Galilee which had now become the stage for His ministry (John 4:1-3). While resting at Jacob's well outside the town of Sychar in Samaria, Jesus revealed himself to a woman as the promised Messiah. She and a great multitude of Samaritans became believers (John 4:4-42).

After two days in Samaria, Jesus continued His journey to Galilee where He received a warm welcome. The report of Jesus' ministry in Judea had preceded Him.

In Cana He once more had the opportunity to reveal His supernatural power. He healed the son of a nobleman just by His word, for the son was in Capernaum a long distance away (John 4:45-54).

In the power of the Spirit Jesus returned once more to His home town of Nazareth. Immediately He became engaged in a multi-faceted ministry, teaching in the synagogues and performing signs and wonders. The report of His activities spread out over the entire territory (Luke 4:14, 15). His sermon, indicating a claim to be the Messiah, brought about a crisis. He was taken out of the synagogue and the town, and the crowd purposed to throw Him over the nearby cliff. But the Bible says He walked through the crowd and went on His way (Luke 4:16-30).

A change now occurred in His base of operations. He took up His residence in Capernaum (compare with Matthew 4:13). This city was situated beside the great highway, the Via Maris, leading from the interior of Asia, the Mesopotamian Valley, to the Mediterranean Sea, and Egypt. It gave Jesus a more central location for His ministry in Galilee, and at the same time fulfilled the Messianic prophecy (compare Matthew 4:13-16 and Luke 4:31). His ministry continued in the same pattern: He taught, cast out evil spirits, healed multitudes of sick people, and was so overwhelmed with work that He scarcely had time for rest (Luke 4:31-44; compare with Matthew 8:14-17; Mark 1:2-31).

The ministry of Jesus increased rapidly and made necessary a certain change in procedure. Up to this time Jesus had been followed by an often-changing crowd of occasional listeners. Now He established a group of disciples who would follow Him constantly and assist Him in His work. His first four co-workers were Andrew and Peter and the two sons of Zebedee, James and John (Matthew 4:18-21; Luke 5:1 ff.; Mark 1:16-20).

At this period in time Jesus healed a man who was a leper (Luke 5:12-16; Matthew 8:2-4; Mark 1:40-45).

Several days later Jesus healed a paralyzed man, carried to Him by four friends (Luke 5:17-26; Mark 2:1-12; Matthew 9:1-8). In connection with this deed there were signs of opposition. The Pharisees and scribes had come in order to spy on Jesus (Luke 5:17, 30). They accused Him openly of blasphemy, because He pronounced the man's sins forgiven. However, Jesus just let the miracle speak for itself.

Contrary to the principles of the spiritual leaders of that time, Jesus called Levi (Matthew), the publican, as His disciple and co-worker (Luke 5:27, 28; Matthew 9:9). At the feast which Levi provided for Him, Jesus took the opportunity to defend His attitudes toward publicans and sinners and to compare His new system of the gospel with the old system of the Law (Luke 5:29-39).

At the Feast of Purim, in March, A.D. 28, Jesus once more went up to Jerusalem. Beside the Pool of Bethesda, by the sheepgate northeast of the Temple, He healed a man who had been sick for 38 years (John 5:1-15). The miracle aroused the hatred of the Jews, partly because it was done on the Sabbath Day and partly because in His sermon which defended His action Jesus called God His Father, saying that their work was similar (John 5:15-18).

In His defense Jesus pointed to the fact that in His ministry He depended upon the Father (John 5:19-30). God himself endorsed Jesus' ministry (John 5:31-40). The unbelief and hatred of His opponents was caused by their own faulty attitude toward God; in fact; Moses to whom they appealed, was their judge (John 5:41-47).

When Jesus returned to Galilee, the Pharisees criticized His disciples because on the Sabbath Day, while they walked between two fields, they picked heads of grain and ate the kernels. Jesus rejected that accusation, using the Scriptures to support His claim that He himself as the Son of Man is Lord of the Sabbath (Luke 6:1-5; Mark 2:23-28; Matthew 12:1-8). On another Sabbath Day the Lord healed a man with a paralyzed hand in the synagogue. And there was discussion on how to get rid of Him (Luke 6:6-11; Matthew 12:9-14; Mark 3:1-6).

The ministry of Jesus in Galilee had now reached an important turning point. Persistent opposition made it impossible to avoid conflict with those who held to the Mosaic Law, which was to be replaced by the gospel. Faced with this situation, Jesus did two things that made His purpose clear:

First, after a night in prayer on a mountain, from the group of disciples He chose twelve men to be apostles. We might say they were to be the twelve patriarchs of the new Israel, which came into existence. They took the place of the older ones (Luke 6:12-16; Mark 3:13-19; Matthew 10:2-4).

Next, surrounded by the Twelve, including those of the inner circle, Peter, James and John, Jesus ascended to a small mountaintop just west of the Sea of Galilee. Here, to the apostles, disciples and the rest of the people, He announced the laws of His kingdom which were so different from the legalism of the Pharisees and the other religious leaders (Matthew, chapters 5-7; Luke 6:20-49). On the way back to Capernaum, He healed the servant of a centurion (Luke 7:1-10; Matthew 8:5-13), then just outside the town of Nain raised to life the only son of a widow (Luke 7:11-17).

From His prison, John the Baptist sent a delegation to Jesus, to quiet some of his doubts as to whether Jesus was fulfilling the Messianic qualifications. This question Jesus answered by referring to His work as fulfilling the prophecies concerning the Messiah. When John's messengers had left, the Lord greatly praised John and rebuked the places which had not received the message of God (Luke 7:18-35; Matthew 11:2-30).

Surprisingly, a Pharisee invited Jesus to dinner with him. While he was there, a woman notorious for her sins, who had been forgiven and cleansed by Jesus earlier, came to where Jesus was. Weeping, she wet his feet with her tears and wiped them with her hair, then poured an aromatic ointment over them. The Pharisee observed all this with scorn, but Jesus defended His actions by telling the parable about two debtors, saying that the one who had the greatest sense of forgiveness had the greatest love.

In this jewel among the stories in the Gospels, two major features of New Testament salvation clearly appear: It is undeserved and therefore universal (Luke 7:36-50).

Another turning point now occurred in Jesus' ministry. He no longer used Capernaum as the center of His activity. Instead, He moved from town to town, giving each place special care, teaching and preaching the message of grace. He was accompanied not only by the Twleve but by some women who had experienced His healing power and wanted to show their gratitude by ministering to the group (Luke 8:1-3).

A great change also took place in the teaching ministry of Jesus. Until this time He had used parables in a casual sort of way (Luke 5:36-39; 6:39-49). Now parables became His most common type of teaching.

This was because of the attitudes He faced. As in the case of His forerunner John, Jesus found that most of the people had not responded to His message. However, a considerable number had believed and followed Him. So He now let those who rejected His message continue in their unbelief, while He led those who believed deeper into the secrets of the kingdom of heaven.

For this purpose a parable became the clearest type of teaching. It illuminated and emphasized the truth for honest listeners, while the truth remained hidden to the careless, shallow sinner. In eight parables Jesus described the heavenly kingdom; its appearance, its mysterious growth, struggle and opposition, its transforming and expanding power, also its immeasurable value and how men determine their own destiny by their reaction to the message of the kingdom (Luke 8:4-18; Matthew 13:1-53; Mark 4:1-34).

Even Jesus' brothers and His nearest relatives were skeptical of Him. Concerned about what He was doing, they interrupted some of His teaching. But Jesus let it be known that He was not bound by earthly ties and that the relationship of the great spiritual family of believers was the most important of all (Luke 8:19-21); Matthew 12:46-50).

While Jesus traveled to the territory on the eastern side of the Sea of Galilee in order to preach the gospel (the Decapolis, a territory comprised of ten Gentile cities), the revelation of His divine power reached a climax: He showed himself to be Lord of the powers of nature (Luke 8:22-25); of the powers of the spiritual world (Luke 8:26-39); and of life and death (Luke 8:40-56). The blind received their sight. The deaf and dumb heard and spoke (Matthew 9:27-34). Back in Nazareth, Jesus gave the citizens a last opportunity but once again met only scorn and unbelief (Matthew 13:54-58; Mark 6:1-6).

The work of Jesus in Galilee now entered its final stage. He sent out the Twelve to give through them a final powerful appeal to this area, which soon He would leave forever (Luke 9:1-6). Even Herod heard about the mighty miracles of the Lord and thought it might be John, whom he had beheaded, now risen from the dead (Luke 9:7-9; Matthew 14:1-12; Mark 6:14-29).

Jesus then withdrew with His disciples. Partly, it was because He wanted to rest and discuss with them their experiences (Luke 9:10-11; Mark 6:30-34); partly, He was deeply moved by the news that John was dead (Matthew 14:13, 14). But great multitudes still followed Him. His loving care for them was proved, among other ways, by the miraculous feeding of 5,000 men besides women and children (Luke 9:10-17; Matthew 14:15-23; Mark 6:30-46; John 6:1-15). Excited by this, the shallow Galileans tried to make Jesus King, but in His sermon in the synagogue at Capernaum Jesus revealed His real mission on earth was to give the world life and show them the way to receive it. The sermon precipitated a crisis among His followers as well as among the general population in Galilee, though the faith of the more spiritual ones was strengthened (John 6:16-71). This took place in Capernaum. In Judea He could no longer appear in public because of the hatred of His enemies (John 7:1).

Jesus next went northwest toward Phoenicia, near the cities of Tyre and Sidon. There He healed the daughter of a woman of Canaan (Matthew 15:21-28; Mark 7:24-30). His return trip took them through the area in the eastern part of the upper reaches of the River Jordan, an area which He had not visited up to this time. Here He healed a man who was both deaf and dumb (Matthew 15:29-31; Mark 7:31-37). Still east of the Sea of Galilee, Jesus fed a multitude of 4,000 persons by a miracle (Matthew 15:32-38; Mark 8:1-9). He also rejected a request for signs (Matthew 15:3 to 16:12; Mark 8:10-21). Near Bethsaida He healed a blind man (Mark 8:22-26).

In order to be alone with the disciples and to prepare them for His coming suffering, Jesus moved them northward from the Sea of Galilee to the sources of the River Jordan. Caesarea-Philippi was located near there, and in the vicinity of this city Jesus heard the testimony of His disciples, through Peter, that they believed Him to be the Son of God and the Messiah. With this as a background, Jesus began to teach them concerning the necessity of His death in Jerusalem which would take place very soon (Luke 9:18-27; Matthew 16:16-30; Mark 9:27-50).

Six days later Jesus experienced the Transfiguration in the presence of His three most intimate apostles on a high mountain (Matthew 17:1-13). After they had returned to the other disciples at the foot of the mountain, He healed a boy, a lunatic (Matthew 17:14-21). As they returned toward the south, for the second time Jesus foretold His suffering (Luke 9:43, 44).

Back at Capernaum, by a miracle Jesus provided for himself and Peter the Temple tax (found in the mouth of a fish!).

When the disciples raised the question as to who would be the greatest in the kingdom, Jesus seized the opportunity to teach about the need for proper relationships in the Body of Christ (Matthew, chapter 18). When the disciples reported about a person who worked in the name of Jesus but did not follow Him, the Master spoke of the need for tolerance (Luke 9:49-50; Mark 9:38-50).

In the fall of A.D. 29, Jesus started His journey to Jerusalem to the Feast of Tabernacles. He avoided traveling with the multitudes because of the critical situation but went in secret (John 7:3-13). However, in the middle of the Feast Jesus entered the Temple area, where He openly spoke to the people concerning His doctrine (John 7:14-24) His divine origin (John 7:25-30), and His approaching death and its significance (verses 31-36).

The Feast featured a ceremony commemorating the miracle during Israel's wandering in the wilderness when water came out of the rock. Jesus used this to refer to himself as the spiritual fountain of life (John 7:37-39). His sermon aroused great discussions among the listeners and in the Sanhedrin (verses 40-52).

The next morning the scribes and Pharisees brought before Jesus a woman taken in the very act of adultery. They asked Him to pronounce judgment so they could bring a charge against Him. But when Jesus invited the one who was without sin to begin the stoning ordered in the Law, all of the woman's accusers disappeared, and Jesus let her go, assuring her of the forgiveness of sins but also admonishing her not to sin any more (John 7:53 to 8:11).

Two new sermons in the Temple brought on Jesus the hatred of the Jews (John 8:12-59). Then a man who was born blind was healed by the power of Jesus and was hated when he fearlessly testified about it (John 9:1-41). In this connection (in John 10:1-18) Jesus showed that He is the One by whom people can be saved and that He is the Shepherd and preserver of those who are saved. After the Feast of Tabernacles Jesus returned once again to Galilee.

6. Jesus' Journey to Jerusalem

Jesus' ministry in Galilee had come to a close, but before He left Galilee to go to Jerusalem where the Great Sacrifice was to be offered, He wished to visit the southern parts of the province on the border of Samaria. The people there had not heard the words of life nor seen Jesus personally. Also He wanted to visit Perea, where descendants of the tribes of Gad, Reuben and Manasseh lived, and where He had been only once on a casual visit. The trip to Jerusalem lasted from the fall of A.D. 29 until the Passover Feast in Jerusalem in April of A.D. 30 (Luke 9:51).

At the very first town of the Samaritans Jesus received an unfriendly welcome and had to seek shelter for the night in a neighboring Jewish town (Luke 9:52-56).

In order to prepare for His coming Jesus sent 70 disciples to the places He intended to visit. They returned with good news (Luke 10).

During His journey Jesus met a scribe who asked Him concerning eternal life. Jesus pointed out that love was the way to meet the claims of the Law and in order to correct the scribe's understanding told the parable about the Good Samaritan (Luke 10:25-37).

Jesus made a short visit to Jerusalem at the Feast of Dedication in the winter of A.D. 29 (John 10:22-39) and at the same time visited the home of Lazarus in Bethany (Luke 10:38-42). This visit interrupted the long missionary journey of Jesus; however, He soon returned to Perea to continue His ministry.

Following one of His private prayer times, at the request of His disciples concerning how they should pray, Jesus taught them what is known as the Lord's Prayer (Luke 11:1-13).

A man in the crowd appealed for help in settling an inheritance dispute. In response Jesus began to teach concerning the proper attitude of believers about material things (Luke 12:13-59).

Two traumatic incidents had occurred: the massacre of worshippers from Galilee in the Temple at the instigation of Pilate; and the fall of the Tower of Siloam which fell, killing eighteen people of Jerusalem. In these incidents Jesus saw a prelude to the terrible events which would take place 40 years later when the Roman armies destroyed the city of Jerusalem. He made an earnest appeal for repentance to the entire nation (Luke 13:1-9).

In a synagogue He healed a woman from a sickness she had suffered for eighteen years and then added teaching concerning the true nature of the kingdom of God (Luke 13:10-22).

While Jesus continued His journey a man asked Him whether many would be saved. Jesus replied by warning believers against overconfidence and predicting the rejection of Israel and the Gentiles' part in redemption (Luke 13:23-30).

Some Pharisees warned Jesus about Herod's bloody plans, but Jesus saw through their trickery, understanding that this plan was projected by Herod himself who wanted Jesus to leave his domain—though he really wanted nothing to do with Jesus because he remembered very well the reaction of the people at the murder of John the Baptist.

The Lord sent word to the king letting him know He had seen through his cunning and that He was guided by much higher principles in His work. He himself would decide when He should leave the territory of the king and approach death in Jerusalem. As He thought of the sin of the holy city and its destruction, an exclamation of pain and prophetic vision came from the lips of the Son of God (Luke 13:31-35).

While a guest in the house of a Pharisee, Jesus had the opportunity to correct some wrong behavior and used it to teach those present concerning true humility. He also likened salvation to a great feast and the need for accepting the invitation (Luke 14:1-24). Recognizing that, though great multitudes followed Him, many did not understand what it really meant to be His disciple, He had to explain what it means to be a true follower (Luke 14:25-35).

Jesus was criticized because of His loving attitude toward publicans and sinners. He replied by describing His motives in three parables (Luke 15:1-32): (1) like a lost sheep, man is helpless in himself to find salvation (verses 3-7); (2) like a woman's wedding jewelry our soul is very precious (verses 8-10); (3) the

way to God is the route followed by the lost son (verses 11-32).

In Luke 16 Jesus taught His disciples the relationship between the proper use of earthly goods and man's destiny in eternity. He commended the wise actions of the steward (verses 1-13) but condemned the faulty selfishness of the rich man (verses 14-31).

While He continued His journey toward Jerusalem, Jesus healed ten leprous men, only one of whom returned to give God the glory (Luke 17:11-19).

Jesus was asked when the kingdom of God would be revealed. He explained that in a sense it was already at hand, though invisible. He continued teaching about how the kingdom would become visible at the return of the Lord (Luke 17:20 to 18:8). In the parable concerning the Pharisee and the publican He pointed out an important spiritual truth: those who elevate themselves will be humbled while true humility will be honored (Luke 18:9-14). While they were passing through a town, the mothers brought their children to Jesus who blessed them (Luke 18:15-17).

Some Pharisees tried to trap Him but He replied with a thorough teaching about the holiness of marriage and the dangers in its dissolution (Matthew 19:1-12). A rich young ruler who was instructed concerning the right road to follow to eternal life went sadly away because he would not accept the terms which Jesus announced (Luke 18:18-30). Jesus then used this occasion to describe the rewards of wholeheartedly following Him but at the same time warned them against being proud of their relationship to Him (Matthew 19:23 to 20:16).

As he traveled in Perea, Jesus learned His friend Lazarus was sick. He waited two days, then knowing by divine knowledge Lazarus had died, He started up the road toward Bethany in spite of the obvious risks which this involved. By a miracle Jesus raised him to life again. The miracle caused many to believe, but conversely the religious leaders decided to get rid of the Lord. Therefore He withdrew to the town of

Ephraim, north of Jerusalem (John 11:1-54). Here He foretold for the third time His approaching death (Luke 18:31-34; Mark 10:32-34; Matthew 20:17-19). Amazingly, the disciples seemed to understand nothing of what He told them. They probably believed that this referred to a short and temporary hindrance before Jesus would take over the kingdom. The two sons of Zebedee, through their mother, asked to receive a throne in His kingdom. Jesus sharply rebuked them (Matthew 20:20-28; Mark 10:35-45).

The Passover of the Jews was at hand and the "hour" Jesus had talked about would soon arrive (John 2:4; 7:6-8). He decided to enter Jerusalem in the most public way possible, appearing before the people and the leaders as the king of Israel. Therefore He went down into the Jordan valley and joined with the pilgrims from Galilee who were traveling through Perea to the capital. Just outside Jericho He healed the blind man Bartimaeus (Luke 18:35-43). He also met Zacchaeus the publican, who received Him joyfully (Luke 19:1-10).

As Jesus continued His journey up to Jerusalem He tried to disillusion the multitudes in their shallow expectations that soon the kingdom would be established at Jerusalem. In telling the parable about the pounds He tried to make them understand a long period would elapse before He returned, and that personal faithfulness during this time would decide the rewards they would receive in the kingdom (Luke 19:11-27).

It would take quite a while to walk from Jericho to Bethany, over 3,000 feet higher in altitude. Jesus and His disciples stopped there the day before the Sabbath, Friday the seventh day of the month Nisan.

On the evening of the next day the thankful people of Bethany arranged a feast for Jesus. They remembered very well the miracle of Lazarus' resurrection. During the meal, his sister Mary annointed the feet of Jesus with pure, costly spikenard ointment as a preparation for His burial (Matthew 26:6-13; Mark 14:3-9; and John 12:1-8).

7. Jesus' Last Ministry in Jerusalem

On the day after the Sabbath, Sunday, the ninth day of Nisan, the Lord made His solemn entrance into Jerusalem, while the disciples and the multitudes of people shouted joyfully. In contrast, the Pharisees and religious leaders protested furiously. When the procession reached a spot where they caught a glimpse of the city and the Temple, Jesus began weeping, lamenting because of the inevitable catastrophe which would be visited upon them (Luke 19:29-44; Matthew 21:1-11; Mark 11:1-11; John 12:12-19). After a short visit to the Temple, together with the Twelve, Jesus returned to Bethany, about two miles away (Matthew 21:17; Mark 11:11).

The next morning, on His way to Jerusalem, Jesus cursed a fig tree which had leaves but no fruit—in Jesus' view a symbol of the hypocrisy and empty worship of God's chosen people (Matthew 21:18, 19; Mark 11:12-14).

In the Temple, once more Jesus' anger was aroused by the dishonest traffic in sacrificial animals and money which took place in the court of the Gentiles, where they came in order to worship the God of Israel. With Messianic authority, Jesus cleansed the sanctuary (Matthew 21:12-17; Mark 11:15-19; Luke 19:45, 46).

By now the leaders of the people had decided to get rid of Jesus, but they were powerless because of the multitude's great admiration for Him (Luke 19:47, 48).

As the group went from Bethany to the city on Tuesday morning, the disciples expressed their surprise because they noticed that the fig tree Jesus had cursed already was totally dried up against the usual course of nature, even from the root. Jesus used this occasion to teach them concerning the miraculous power of faith (Matthew 21:18-22; Mark 11:20-26).

As He entered the Temple, Jesus was confronted by the high priest and scribes, demanding an explanation for His conduct in cleansing the Temple the day before. They recognized this to be an action only the Messiah would take, as well as a proof of His authority (Matthew 21:23-27; Mark 11:27-33; Luke 20:1-8). Jesus' answer, in the form of a question, was a counterattack which exposed their incompetence to judge His actions.

Jesus related several parables by which He rebuked their impenitent attitude, beginning with the parable concerning the two sons. Their rejection of the divine message stood in strong contrast to the humble, attitudes of the publicans and sinners (Matthew 21:28-32).

In the parable concerning the husbandmen, Jesus unveiled the real reason for their hostility and foretold their criminal action toward Him as well as the rejection and that they would be replaced by others as the people of God (Matthew 21:33-46; Mark 12:1-12).

In the parable concerning the marriage of the king's son Jesus pinpointed the disobedience of the nation in rejecting God's offering of grace, and the national catastrophe which would result, and the calling of the Gentiles instead of the chosen people (Matthew 22:1-14).

Trying to trap Jesus, the Pharisees presented a political-religious question concerning payment of taxes to the emperor. Jesus' reply showed a wisdom which filled even His opponents with wonder (Matthew 22:15-22; Mark 12:13 ff.). Then the Sadducees who denied the resurrection of the body, the immortality of the soul, and any kind of life after death, by the help of a fictitious story tried to place the resurrection in a ridiculous light. Jesus' reply shut their mouths also (Matthew 22:23-33; Mark 12:18 ff.; Luke 20:27 ff.).

Jesus also responded to a question by a Pharisee about which was the most important commandment in the Law (Matthew 22:34-40).

Then Jesus made a further counterattack with the question concerning whose son Messiah is. With their knowledge of the prophecies, the only reply they could give was that He was the Son of God. But to say this would have deprived them of any possibility of accusing and judging Jesus of blasphemy that He had said He was the Son of God. Therefore, they preferred to remain silent (Matthew 22:41-46). Jesus used this occasion to call attention to their hypocrisy when they should have been spiritual leaders. They emphasized small details of the Law but ignored its basic principles. And once again He foretold the judgment which would come upon the people and the land (Matthew 23:1-39). Significantly, Jesus then left the Temple.

A group of Greeks sought to see Jesus. At this point, like a flash of lightning, the sequence of coming events became crystal clear to Jesus: His painful death would be the means of salvation for many. A preview of the agony He later experienced at Gethsemane flashed through His mind and soul. But He received special consolation from the Father (John 12:20-36).

With His disciples Jesus next went to the Mount of Olives. Here He gave an outline of history, foretelling the conditions in the world from His death until His return (Matthew 24 and 25; Mark 13; and Luke 21:5-38). Once more Jesus spoke of His coming suffering, now with a definite knowledge concerning the time (Matthew 26:1, 2).

Wednesday seems to have been a day of rest and quietness as far as Jesus was concerned, probably spent in Bethany. But during this time the leaders were seeking a suitable occasion to get rid of Him. Unexpectedly, they received help from one of the Twelve, Judas Iscariot (Matthew 26:1-5, 14-16; Mark 14:1, 2, 10, 11; Luke 22:1-6).

On Thursday morning Jesus sent two of His disciples into Jerusalem to prepare the Passover meal, and at early evening the Lord and the Twelve sat down to eat. As a final proof of His love to His disciples the Lord washed their feet, taking the place of a lowly slave. Then He instituted the ordinance of the Lord's Supper. When the disciples began to argue as to who would be greatest, Jesus ended the argument by referring to His own example, saying that the one who wanted to be greatest should be the servant of all.

As they conversed, Jesus announced that one of the Twelve would betray Him. He clearly identified Judas, who immediately left the group and parted from his Lord forever. Jesus also foretold the flight of the disciples and the three-fold denial of Peter.

Finishing the supper with a hymn of praise, the party started on their way to a well-known place in the Garden of Gethsemane at the lower extremity of the Mount of Olives (Matthew 26:17-35; Mark 14:12-26; Luke 22:7-39).

While they were on their way, Jesus continued teaching the disciples: in the parable of the Vine and Branches, the spiritual union between believers and Christ (John 15:1-17); about the hostile attitude of the world toward them (John 15:18 to 16:4); and concerning the victorious ministry they would have through the guidance of the Holy Spirit (John 16:5-15). Finally, He spoke of the events which would soon transpire—difficult, it seems, for the disciples to understand (John 16:16-33).

Just before crossing the brook Kidron, Jesus stopped, looked toward heaven and as the great High Priest prayed the greatest prayer ever addressed to the Father (John 17). First, Jesus prayed for himself to whom had been assigned the work of redemption (verses 1-5); then He prayed for the apostles who would be given the work of continuing His ministry (verses 6-19); and last He prayed for the entire family of believers that they would be unified in spreading the gospel message (verses 20-26).

8. The Suffering and Death of Jesus

As Jesus entered the Garden of Gethsemane, He became involved in a very intense spiritual battle. The Prince of Darkness made his last attack with all his demonic forces, trying, if possible, to keep Jesus from fulfilling the work of redemption. Physical signs of the trauma now beginning became apparent as blood oozed out of the pores of His skin. Strengthened by an angel from heaven, Jesus made the great commitment and was ready to endure the agonies awaiting Him (Matthew 26:30, 36-46; Mark 14:26, 32-42; Luke 22:39-46).

Headed by the betrayer Judas, a band of armed soldiers forced their way into the Garden together with a servant of the high priest. Judas identified Jesus to the soldiers by kissing His cheek and they immediately seized and bound the Lord. Swinging his sword wildly, Peter cut off the ear of the high priest's servant Malchus, but Jesus healed him immediately (Matthew 26:47-56; Mark 14:43-52; Luke 22:47-53; John 18:1-11).

From the Garden Jesus was led directly to the high priest Annas for the preliminary examination (John 18:12-14, 19-23). Before Caiaphas and those members of the Sanhedrin who could be gathered at his place, there was later on that same night another informal examination. Here Jesus was sentenced to death because of blasphemy, since He had claimed to be the Son of God (Matthew 26:57, 63-65; John 18:24). However, at neither of these meetings was it legal to pass sentence, either according to Jewish custom or the Roman law, because it took place during the night.

A third examination therefore was needed. This occurred during the early morning of Friday in the usual place of trial near the Temple. All the Sanhedrin had now gathered (Matthew 27:1; Mark 15:1; Luke 22:66-71).

Here the death sentence was ratified and there was discussion about how to proceed in order to obtain the confirmation and action by the Roman authorities.

However, there was not complete agreement during this meeting. Joseph of Arimathea, who had not been present at the meeting held during the night at Caiaphas' house and was now participating for the first time, did not agree with the decision which had been made (compare Luke 23:51). While these discussions were going on, Peter had three times denied his Lord in the courtyard of the high priest's palace, saying that he did not know the prisoner (Matthew 26:58, 69-75; Mark 14:54, 66-72; Luke 22:54-62; John 18:15-18, 25-27).

It was now Friday morning, and the Sanhedrin took their prisoner to Pilate. To him a religious accusation meant nothing, so they produced a political one. A witness testified that Jesus had claimed to be the Messiah, implying this meant Jesus was the leader of a revolt against the Romans. Pilate saw through their scheme, however. Examining Jesus, he was convinced of His innocence.

Sensitive to the attitudes of the Jews, and trying to escape making the decision without antagonizing them, he used the pretext that Jesus was from the district of Herod, who happened to be in Jerusalem at this time (Matthew 27:2, 11-18; Mark 15:1-5; Luke 23:1-7; John 18:33-38). Herod was glad because he had hoped to see Jesus work a miracle, but was very chagrined because Jesus remained absolutely silent before him. Angered, Herod and his soldiers ridiculed and mocked Jesus and sent Him back to Pilate.

Pilate used all the arguments possible to secure Jesus' release then tried to satisfy their hatred by having Jesus flogged before He was sentenced and presenting Him to the multitude bleeding and exhausted. Even this approach was without effect and the Governor succumbed to the pressure. He confirmed the sentence of death and commanded that it be done immediately (Matthew 27:15-30; Mark 15:6-19; Luke 23:13-25; John 18:39 to 19:16).

Jesus was immediately brought to the place of the skull, Calvary, outside the city, the usual place of execution. He was forced to carry His own cross until, exhausted, He could carry it no longer. The Romans then forced a man, Simon from Cyrene, who happened to pass by, to take the disgraceful load (Matthew 27:31-34; Mark 15:20-23; Luke 23:26-33; John 19:15, 16, 17).

Though the Roman soldiers performed their brutal work of nailing His hands and feet to the rough, wooden cross, the Son of God in love and mercy cried out, "Father, forgive them, they know not what they do."

At 9 o'clock Friday morning the three crosses, of Jesus and the two thieves, were erected. On them was placed an inscription in the three universal languages of Greek, Latin and Hebrew, giving the name and the crime of which the prisoner was accused. At the foot of the cross the soldiers cast lots for the few personal effects.

All around stood the multitudes, the soldiers and the rulers, and in the beginning the thieves on either side of Jesus sneered at Him, insulting Him. Gradually, however, one of the thieves changed his attitude, rebuked the other one and prayed to the Son of God, "Remember me when thou comest into thy kingdom." Even in His agony Jesus would show mercy, "Verily I say unto thee: Today thou shalt be with me in Paradise!" And even when dying He thought of His mother. Seeing her and the disciple whom He loved, Jesus left the care of Mary to John with the words, "Woman, behold thy son." "Behold thy mother." (Matthew 27:35-44; Mark 15:24-32; Luke 23:33-43; John 19:27, 28).

At the sixth hour, that is 12 o'clock noon, suddenly intense darkness spread over the entire land, lasting until the ninth hour, 3 o'clock in the afternoon. With a feeling of abandonment, Jesus cried out: "My God, my God, why hast thou forsaken me?" A little later He exclaimed, "I thirst!" Then, after they had brought some vinegar on a sponge, placed on a branch of hyssop, Jesus exclaimed triumphantly, "It is finished!" And with a loud voice cried out, "Father, into thy hands I commend my spirit." Then he bowed His head and gave up the ghost.

This, the most important event in the history of the world, was finished on Friday the 14th day of Nisan in the year 783 after the founding of Rome; that is, the 7th day of April in A.D. 30, at 3 o'clock in the afternoon. The redemption of all mankind had been obtained (Matthew 27:45-50; Mark 15:33-37; Luke 23:44-46; John 19:28-30).

The death of Christ was followed by three great miraculous events: (1) In the world of nature, the ancient mountains trembled and shook; (2) In the realm of the dead, the doors were opened, the spirits of the righteous dead re-entered their bodies, and the dead arose and entered the city; (3) In the spiritual world the veil in the Temple was rent in two, showing that the way to God was open to mankind (Matthew 27:51-56; Mark 15:38-41; Luke 23:45, 47-56).

Because the Jews were anxious to have the bodies of these men removed before the Passover feast, now close at hand, they asked Pilate that death be hastened and the crosses removed. Usually death did not occur in the case of crucifixion until after 24 to 48 hours of struggle. In fact, there have been cases when death took place after as long as three to six days. In order to hasten death, the soldiers broke the legs of the two thieves but finding that Jesus already was dead after only six hours, they did not break His legs. Instead, one of them thrust a spear into the side of Jesus. Blood and water came out showing that death had indeed occurred.

In order to have complete proof of Jesus' death, Pilate checked with the centurion, who confirmed it to be so. The body was surrendered to Joseph of Arimathea. Loving hands took it down from the cross, wrapped it with spices in a clean linen cloth and placed it in Joseph's new tomb.

When the day had ended, the Son of God was resting after His completed work and according to the law of the Sabbath (Matthew 27:57-60; Mark 15:42-46; Luke 23:50-54; John 19:31-42). At the request of the Jews, a band of Roman soldiers was sent to guard the sealed tomb (Matthew 27:62-66).

9. The Resurrection of Jesus

On Sunday, the 16th day of Nisan; that is, April 9, early in the morning there was an earthquake as an angel of God descended and removed the stone from the tomb, and Jesus emerged as the Prince of Life (Matthew 28:1-4). Some women came to the grave early that morning and were informed by angels about what had taken place (Matthew 28:5-8; Mark 16:2-8; Luke 24:1-8; John 20:1).

During the forty days after His resurrection, Jesus was seen by the disciples and followers on various occasions, giving them definite proof that He was indeed alive. On the morning of the Resurrection Mary Magdalene was the first to meet the risen Christ (Mark 16:9-11; John 20:11-18). The other women met Him also.

The information about the resurrection of Jesus was a difficult one for the Jewish authorities to handle. When the Roman guards reported what had happened, the authorities took action. They gave the guards a large sum of money to spread the rumor that the disciples had stolen the body of Jesus (Matthew 28:11-15).

Others saw the risen Christ. Peter met Him (Luke 24:34; 1 Corinthians 15:7). Later that day, two disciples walking to Emmaus met Jesus (Luke 24:12-35; Mark 16:12, 13). That same day, in the evening, through closed doors Jesus entered the room where ten of His disciples were gathered (Luke 24:36 ff; John 20:19-23). And a week later, Thomas, absent the first time, was with the other apostles when they met Jesus again (John 20:26-29).

Seven of Jesus' apostles had an interesting experience. After fishing all night on the Sea of Galilee without any result, they found Jesus awaiting them on the shore. When they cast the net on the right side of the boat, they caught 153 fish. And Jesus had prepared breakfast for them (John 21:1-24).

The 11 remaining apostles gathered on a mountain in Galilee where Jesus had asked them to meet Him and there He gave them the Great Commission (Matthew 28:16-20; Mark 16:15, 16). It may have been on this occasion that 500 other believers saw Him (1 Corinthians 15:6).

The Scripture tells us that James, the brother of Jesus, the leader of the original Jerusalem church, had a personal meeting with the resurrected Christ (1 Corinthians 15:7). An unconfirmed tradition asserts that this event took place on the morning of the Resurrection. The last meeting between Jesus and His disciples took place on the Mount of Olives, near Bethany, from which He ascended in the clouds to heaven (Mark 16:19, 20; Luke 24:50-53; Acts 1:9-11).

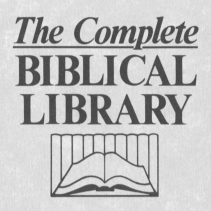

The Complete BIBLICAL LIBRARY

The Greatest Life Ever Lived

PICTORIAL PANORAMA

The Artist and His Work

William Hole, the artist whose paintings adorn this book, was born in Edinburgh in 1846. At the beginning of the 20th Century, he conceived the idea of producing a series of pictures to illustrate the earthly life of Jesus.

Hole was a perfectionist and determined to produce a work which would be authentic. For this reason he traveled to Palestine to recapture, as nearly as possible, the environment and customs of the first century times in which Jesus lived.

It must have been difficult for the artist to recapture the landscape as it had appeared in the time of Jesus, but on one point William Hole found a favorable circumstance. Despite the waves of conquest which have swept over Palestine, the customs, architecture and dress of the Middle East have changed very little over the centuries.

This is especially true of the noble city of Jerusalem, sitting serenely like a queen on its superb site, about 2,500 feet above sea level. It provides a magnificent panorama, viewed from the Mount of Olives across the narrow Kidron Valley.

The paintings reveal the meticulous skill with which William Hole worked. Strongly believing in the authenticity and authority of the four Gospels, he strove to duplicate details of life in the first century.

William Hole died in 1917 but left behind a legacy in art which pictures the greatest life ever lived. Through an intricate chain of circumstances, the artwork made its way to Norway, where the book *Det Evige Motiv (The Eternal Theme)* was produced. These pictures have now been made available for our HARMONY.

The Message to Mary

The words of the Apostolic Creed state that Jesus Christ was born of the Virgin Mary by the power of the Holy Spirit. The artist has chosen to show Mary kneeling and facing the angelic messenger. The angel is depicted as a figure surrounded by light and glory. Mary is shown as an ordinary young Jewish woman dressed in peasant garments.

Luke 1:26-35
And in the sixth month the angel Gabriel was sent from God unto a city of Galilee, named Nazareth, To a virgin espoused to a man whose name was Joseph, of the house of David; and the virgin's name was Mary. And the angel came in unto her, and said, Hail, thou that art highly favored, the Lord is with thee: blessed art thou among women. And when she saw him, she was troubled at his saying, and cast in her mind what manner of salutation this should be. And the angel said unto her, Fear not, Mary: for thou hast found favor with God. And, behold, thou shalt conceive in thy womb, and bring forth a son, and shalt call his name JESUS. He shall be great, and shall be called the Son of the Highest; and the Lord God shall give unto him the throne of his father David: And he shall reign over the house of Jacob for ever; and of his kingdom there shall be no end. Then said Mary unto the angel, How shall this be, seeing I know not a man? And the angel answered and said unto her, The Holy Ghost shall come upon thee, and the power of the Highest shall overshadow thee: therefore also that holy thing which shall be born of thee shall be called the Son of God.

No Room in the Inn

The artist shows the innkeeper as he says there is no room available. An Oriental inn of that time possessed none of the privacy we usually associate with a hotel or inn. There was no furniture. The place to recline was a sort of platform raised slightly above ground level. The animals and people occupied the same quarters.

Luke 2:1-7

And it came to pass in those days, that there went out a decree from Caesar Augustus, that all the world should be taxed. (And this taxing was first made when Cyrenius was governor of Syria.) And all went to be taxed, every one into his own city. And Joseph also went up from Galilee, out of the city of Nazareth, into Judea, unto the city of David, which is called Bethlehem, (because he was of the house and lineage of David,) To be taxed with Mary his espoused wife, being great with child. And so it was, that, while they were there, the days were accomplished that she should be delivered. And she brought forth her firstborn son, and wrapped him in swaddling clothes, and laid him in a manger; because there was no room for them in the inn.

A Great Joy

It is in harmony with the heart of the Christian message when Luke tells about the shepherds receiving the angelic message about the child who had been born. God prized that which was of little value in the eyes of man. The task of being a shepherd was assigned to the most poor, to slaves and younger sons.

Luke 2:8-14

And there were in the same country shepherds abiding in the field, keeping watch over their flock by night. And, lo, the angel of the Lord came upon them, and the glory of the Lord shone round about them; and they were sore afraid. And the angel said unto them, Fear not: for, behold, I bring you good tidings of great joy, which shall be to all people. For unto you is born this day in the city of David a Saviour, which is Christ the Lord. And this shall be a sign unto you; Ye shall find the babe wrapped in swaddling clothes, lying in a manger. And suddenly there was with the angel a multitude of the heavenly host praising God, and saying, Glory to God in the highest, and on earth peace, good will toward men.

371

The Wise Men Pay Homage to Jesus

For many centuries it has been assumed there were three Wise Men, and that they were kings. In fact, however, we do not know if they were kings or from which countries they came. We can consider them as representing the vast heathen world where some were searching for reality and God. By the dim light of the knowledge they had received they found their way to Bethlehem.

Matthew 2:7-12

Then Herod, when he had privily called the wise men, inquired of them diligently what time the star appeared. And he sent them to Bethlehem, and said, Go and search diligently for the young child; and when ye have found him, bring me word again, that I may come and worship him also. When they had heard the king, they departed; and, lo, the star, which they saw in the east, went before them, till it came and stood over where the young child was. When they saw the star, they rejoiced with exceeding great joy. And when they were come into the house, they saw the young child with Mary his mother, and fell down, and worshipped him: and when they had opened their treasures, they presented unto him gifts; gold, and frankincense, and myrrh. And being warned of God in a dream that they should not return to Herod, they departed into their own country another way.

At the Age of Twelve

This is the only view of Jesus the Gospels afford us, between His infant days and His emergence on the public scene at the age of 30. What was the subject matter of those discussions in the Temple? It does not appear that the child Jesus was teaching the doctors of the Law during this time. This was a quest for knowledge. He was "hearing and asking them questions." The astonishment of those gathered there was evoked by the deep understanding He demonstrated of spiritual principles, His awareness of God and His purposes, and His answers to their questions.

There is no definite knowledge available as to the architectural style of the Temple's interior at that time. The artist has, to a large extent, adapted the leading features from the Dome of the Rock, which occupies the same site.

Luke 2:41-49

Now his parents went to Jerusalem every year at the feast of the passover. And when he was twelve years old, they went up to Jerusalem after the custom of the feast. And when they had fulfilled the days, as they returned, the child Jesus tarried behind in Jerusalem; and Joseph and his mother knew not of it. But they, supposing him to have been in the company, went a day's journey; and they sought him among their kinsfolk and acquaintance. And when they found him not, they turned back again to Jerusalem, seeking him. And it came to pass, that after three days they found him in the temple, sitting in the midst of the doctors, both hearing them, and asking them questions. And all that heard him were astonished at his understanding and answers. And when they saw him, they were amazed: and his mother said unto him, Son, why hast thou thus dealt with us? behold, thy father and I have sought thee sorrowing.

At Home in Nazareth

Mark states that people asked, "Is not this the carpenter?" Because of this we may well infer that as Jesus increased in wisdom and stature, He also learned the trade of a carpenter. This shows that Jesus was truly man as well as truly God.

The artist shows in this picture all we know of Jesus' entire life from 12 to 30 years of age when He began His public ministry. Most certainly He received His education at home. Joseph was a carpenter who made simple furniture and farm equipment: for example, the wooden plow which continued in use in Palestine for many years after Jesus' time on earth.

Luke 2:51,52
And he went down with them, and came to Nazareth, and was subject unto them: but his mother kept all these sayings in her heart. And Jesus increased in wisdom and stature, and in favor with God and man.

The Baptism of Jesus

Jesus was baptized by John, His forerunner. This was the last great presentation for the Old Testament covenant and the first great proclamation of the Kingdom of God. Three of the Gospels state that John the Baptist saw the heavens opened and the Holy Ghost descending upon Jesus like a dove. The artist pictures the River Jordan where the baptism took place.

Matthew 3:13-17

Then cometh Jesus from Galilee to Jordan unto John, to be baptized of him. But John forbade him, saying, I have need to be baptized of thee, and comest thou to me? And Jesus answering said unto him, Suffer it to be so now: for thus it becometh us to fulfil all righteousness. Then he suffered him. And Jesus, when he was baptized, went up straightway out of the water: and, lo, the heavens were opened unto him, and he saw the Spirit of God descending like a dove, and lighting upon him: And lo a voice from heaven, saying, This is my beloved Son, in whom I am well pleased.

John 1:32-34

And John bare record, saying, I saw the Spirit descending from heaven like a dove, and it abode upon him. And I knew him not: but he that sent me to baptize with water, the same said unto me, Upon whom thou shalt see the Spirit descending, and remaining on him, the same is he which baptizeth with the Holy Ghost. And I saw, and bare record that this is the Son of God:

The Woman at the Well

Jesus rested at Jacob's well while traveling through Samaria. The well is near to the village of Sychar, a little south of Shechem (modern Nablus), at the foot of Mount Gerizim where the surviving Samaritans still observe the Passover. The well was deep (over 100 feet) and probably had steps leading down to it.

The picture shows the Samaritan woman coming down the stairs. It was to her that Jesus spoke and told her of water that was not in the well—the water of life.

John 4:3-10

He left Judea, and departed again into Galilee. And he must needs go through Samaria. Then cometh he to a city of Samaria, which is called Sychar, near to the parcel of ground that Jacob gave to his son Joseph. Now Jacob's well was there. Jesus therefore, being wearied with his journey, sat thus on the well: and it was about the sixth hour. There cometh a woman of Samaria to draw water: Jesus saith unto her, Give me to drink. (For his disciples were gone away unto the city to buy meat.) Then saith the woman of Samaria unto him, How is it that thou, being a Jew, askest drink of me, which am a woman of Samaria? for the Jews have no dealings with the Samaritans. Jesus answered and said unto her, If thou knewest the gift of God, and who it is that saith to thee, Give me to drink; thou wouldest have asked of him, and he would have given thee living water.

The Great Catch of Fish

Like all the other miracles of Jesus, the draught of fish had a specific purpose—to enlist Peter as a great fisher of men. This is the type of boat that was still being used by fishermen in the early years of this century. The artist shows this as the kind of craft used by Peter.

Luke 5:1-7

And it came to pass, that, as the people pressed upon him to hear the word of God, he stood by the lake of Gennesaret, And saw two ships standing by the lake: but the fishermen were gone out of them, and were washing their nets. And he entered into one of the ships, which was Simon's, and prayed him that he would thrust out a little from the land. And he sat down, and taught the people out of the ship. Now when he had left speaking, he said unto Simon, Launch out into the deep, and let down your nets for a draught. And Simon answering said unto him, Master, we have toiled all the night, and have taken nothing: nevertheless at thy word I will let down the net. And when they had this done, they inclosed a great multitude of fishes: and their net brake. And they beckoned unto their partners, which were in the other ship, that they should come and help them. And they came, and filled both the ships, so that they began to sink.

The First Disciples

It is a dramatic sequence. John the Baptist is standing with two of his disciples, sees Jesus and exclaims, "Behold, the Lamb of God." Immediately, it seems, the two men leave him and follow Jesus. The picture portrays the scene as Jesus talks with them. With his customary humility John names one of the two men as Andrew, but leaves himself nameless. They were the first of a long line who have chosen to follow the Son of God.

John 1:35-42

Again the next day after, John stood, and two of his disciples; And looking upon Jesus as he walked, he saith, Behold the Lamb of God! And the two disciples heard him speak, and they followed Jesus. Then Jesus turned, and saw them following, and saith unto them, What seek ye? They said unto him, Rabbi, (which is to say, being interpreted, Master,) where dwellest thou? He saith unto them, Come and see. They came and saw where he dwelt, and abode with him that day: for it was about the tenth hour. One of the two which heard John speak, and followed him, was Andrew, Simon Peter's brother. He first findeth his own brother Simon, and saith unto him, We have found the Messias, which is, being interpreted, the Christ. And he brought him to Jesus. And when Jesus beheld him, he said, Thou art Simon the son of Jona: thou shalt be called Cephas, which is by interpretation, A stone.

The Sermon on the Mount

We do not know the exact location where Jesus gave this great message, later named *The Sermon on the Mount*. The artist has pictured the masses of people together with the disciples. In this scene they are gathered at a hilly location called the *Horns of Hattin*, one of the sites suggested by tradition as the possible place. A more popular site, nearer the sea, is dominated by the Church of the Beatitudes, erected in honor of the event.

Matthew 5:1-12
And seeing the multitudes, he went up into a mountain: and when he was set, his disciples came unto him: And he opened his mouth, and taught them, saying, Blessed are the poor in spirit: for theirs is the kingdom of heaven. Blessed are they that mourn: for they shall be comforted. Blessed are the meek: for they shall inherit the earth. Blessed are they which do hunger and thirst after righteousness: for they shall be filled. Blessed are the merciful: for they shall obtain mercy. Blessed are the pure in heart: for they shall see God. Blessed are the peacemakers: for they shall be called the children of God. Blessed are they which are persecuted for righteousness' sake: for theirs is the kingdom of heaven. Blessed are ye, when men shall revile you, and persecute you, and shall say all manner of evil against you falsely, for my sake. Rejoice, and be exceeding glad: for great is your reward in heaven: for so persecuted they the prophets which were before you.

Jesus Walks on the Water

This incident took place immediately after the miracle in which Jesus fed 5,000 men, besides women and children, with 5 loaves and 2 fishes. He sent His disciples to the other side of the Sea of Galilee while He went to pray. A mighty storm arose, but Jesus came walking to them upon the water, and when He reached their boat the storm ceased. Matthew's account (chapter 14) tells of Peter's attempt to walk on the water too. John's Gospel (chapter 6) says that as soon as Jesus got in the boat, "immediately the ship was at the land whither they went."

Mark 6:45-52

And straightway he constrained his disciples to get into the ship, and to go to the other side before unto Bethsaida, while he sent away the people. And when he had sent them away, he departed into a mountain to pray. And when even was come, the ship was in the midst of the sea, and he alone on the land. And he saw them toiling in rowing; for the wind was contrary unto them: and about the fourth watch of the night he cometh unto them, walking upon the sea, and would have passed by them. But when they saw him walking upon the sea, they supposed it had been a spirit, and cried out: For they all saw him, and were troubled. And immediately he talked with them, and saith unto them, Be of good cheer: it is I; be not afraid. And he went up unto them into the ship; and the wind ceased: and they were sore amazed in themselves beyond measure, and wondered. For they considered not the miracle of the loaves; for their heart was hardened.

The Woman Who Touched Jesus

The artist shows here a typical Palestine town at the turn of the century. Notice the narrow street and the gateway. It may have looked a good deal like this in the time of Christ. The woman who touched Jesus is seen kneeling before Him.

The astonishment of the disciples at Jesus' question, "Who touched me?" is understandable. As Mark points out, "Much people followed him and thronged him." But Jesus knew someone had touched Him in a special way. It was an act of faith, the kind that always brings results.

Mark 5:22-34

And, behold, there cometh one of the rulers of the synagogue, Jairus by name; and when he saw him, he fell at his feet, And besought him greatly, saying, My little daughter lieth at the point of death: I pray thee, come and lay thy hands on her, that she may be healed; and she shall live. And Jesus went with him. And much people followed him, and thronged him. And a certain woman, which had an issue of blood twelve years, And had suffered many things of many physicians, and had spent all that she had, and was nothing bettered, but rather grew worse, When she had heard of Jesus, came in the press behind, and touched his garment. For she said, If I may touch but his clothes, I shall be whole. And straightway the fountain of her blood was dried up; and she felt in her body that she was healed of that plague. And Jesus, immediately knowing in himself that virtue had gone out of him, turned him about in the press, and said, Who touched my clothes? And his disciples said unto him, Thou seest the multitude thronging thee, and sayest thou, Who touched me? And he looked round about to see her that had done this thing. But the woman fearing and trembling, knowing what was done in her, came and fell down before him, and told him all the truth. And he said unto her, Daughter, thy faith hath made thee whole; go in peace, and be whole of thy plague.

Jairus' Daughter

The Gospels record three times when Jesus raised a person from the dead: One, Lazarus, was an older man. The son of the widow of Nain was a youth. Jairus' daughter was a child, 12 years old.

The girl is pictured lying on her bed, a mattress upon the floor, the type of bed used at that time.

The Aramaic expression, "Talitha cumi," or "Damsel, I say unto thee arise," is said to have a special meaning. It is the way a father would awaken a much-loved little girl in the morning: "Darling, it's time to get up."

To Jesus, death was only a sleep.

Mark 5:35-43

While he yet spake, there came from the ruler of the synagogue's house certain which said, Thy daughter is dead; why troublest thou the Master any further? As soon as Jesus heard the word that was spoken, he saith unto the ruler of the synagogue, Be not afraid, only believe. And he suffered no man to follow him, save Peter, and James, and John the brother of James. And he cometh to the house of the ruler of the synagogue, and seeth the tumult, and them that wept and wailed greatly. And when he was come in, he saith unto them, Why make ye this ado, and weep? the damsel is not dead, but sleepeth. And they laughed him to scorn. But when he had put them all out, he taketh the father and the mother of the damsel, and them that were with him, and entereth in where the damsel was lying. And he took the damsel by the hand, and said unto her, Talitha cumi; which is, being interpreted, Damsel, (I say unto thee,) arise. And straightway the damsel arose, and walked; for she was of the age of twelve years. And they were astonished with a great astonishment. And he charged them straitly that no man should know it; and commanded that something should be given her to eat.

Five Thousand Are Fed

Like many other sites in the Holy Land, the exact place where Jesus fed 5,000 men, plus women and children, is open to question. Tradition suggests two places: (1) on the northeast shore of the Sea of Galilee, near Bethsaida; (2) Tabgha, on the northwestern shore of the Lake. What matters is that this outstanding miracle, the only one recorded by all four Evangelists, marked the high point of Jesus' popularity, when a demand arose to make Him king. When Jesus rejected the offer, His favor with the people began to decline.

Mark 6:35-44

And when the day was now far spent, his disciples came unto him, and said, This is a desert place, and now the time is far passed: Send them away, that they may go into the country round about, and into the villages, and buy themselves bread: for they have nothing to eat. He answered and said unto them, Give ye them to eat. And they say unto him, Shall we go and buy two hundred pennyworth of bread, and give them to eat? He saith unto them, How many loaves have ye? go and see. And when they knew, they say, Five, and two fishes. And he commanded them to make all sit down by companies upon the green grass. And they sat down in ranks, by hundreds, and by fifties. And when he had taken the five loaves and the two fishes, he looked up to heaven, and blessed, and brake the loaves, and gave them to his disciples to set before them; and the two fishes divided he among them all. And they did all eat, and were filled. And they took up twelve baskets full of the fragments, and of the fishes. And they that did eat of the loaves were about five thousand men.

The Thankful Leper

A 10 percent response is not very much, but that is all Jesus received in the way of thanks after healing 10 lepers. Only one turned back and thanked the Master after being healed. Luke points out that the one thankful enough to express it was a Samaritan, a group often despised by the Jews.

Luke 17:11-19

And it came to pass, as he went to Jerusalem, that he passed through the midst of Samaria and Galilee. And as he entered into a certain village, there met him ten men that were lepers, which stood afar off: And they lifted up their voices, and said, Jesus, Master, have mercy on us. And when he saw them, he said unto them, Go show yourselves unto the priests. And it came to pass, that, as they went, they were cleansed. And one of them, when he saw that he was healed, turned back, and with a loud voice glorified God, And fell down on his face at his feet, giving him thanks: and he was a Samaritan. And Jesus answering said, Were there not ten cleansed? but where are the nine? There are not found that returned to give glory to God, save this stranger. And he said unto him, Arise, go thy way: thy faith hath made thee whole.

Jesus Raises Lazarus

Jesus raised to life three people, according to the Gospel records: a child, the daughter of Jairus; a young man, son of the widow of Nain; and an older person, Lazarus. The child had been dead a short time, the young man perhaps a day, and Lazarus four days. According to John, this miracle was the event which precipitated the Triumphal Entry. Martha had faith for the past—"If thou hadst been here, my brother had not died." She had faith for the future—"I know he shall rise again in the resurrection." But Jesus told her, "I am (present tense) the Resurrection and the Life." It is a lesson for us to learn.

John 11:1, 5-7, 17, 32-44
Now a certain man was sick, named Lazarus, of Bethany, the town of Mary and her sister Martha. Now Jesus loved Martha, and her sister, and Lazarus. When he had heard therefore that he was sick, he abode two days still in the same place where he was. Then after that saith he to his disciples, Let us go into Judea again. Then when Jesus came, he found that he had lain in the grave four days already. Then when Mary was come where Jesus was, and saw him, she fell down at his feet, saying unto him, Lord, if thou hadst been here, my brother had not died. When Jesus therefore saw her weeping, and the Jews also weeping which came with her, he groaned in the spirit, and was troubled. And said, Where have ye laid him? They say unto him, Lord, come and see. Jesus wept. Then said the Jews, Behold how he loved him! And some of them said, Could not this man, which opened the eyes of the blind, have caused that even this man should not have died? Jesus therefore again groaning in himself cometh to the grave. It was a cave, and a stone lay upon it. Jesus said, Take ye away the stone. Martha, the sister of him that was dead, saith unto him, Lord, by this time he stinketh: for he hath been dead four days. Jesus saith unto her, Said I not unto thee, that, if thou wouldest believe, thou shouldest see the glory of God? Then they took away the stone from the place where the dead was laid. And Jesus lifted up his eyes, and said, Father, I thank thee that thou hast heard me. And I knew that thou hearest me always: but because of the people which stand by I said it, that they may believe that thou hast sent me. And when he thus had spoken, he cried with a loud voice, Lazarus, come forth. And he that was dead came forth, bound hand and foot with graveclothes; and his face was bound about with a napkin. Jesus saith unto them, Loose him, and let him go.

Healing of Bartimeus

The incident occurred at Jericho, the oasis in the Jordan Valley, about 20 miles slightly northeast of Jerusalem, about 800 feet below sea level. Matthew (chapter 20) says another unnamed blind man was also healed, and Luke's account (chapter 18) does not name the beggar. Bartimeus was desperate, and in spite of the efforts of those nearby to silence him, he persisted until he gained Jesus' attention. Then in only a few moments he received his sight.

Mark 10:46-52

And they came to Jericho: and as he went out of Jericho with his disciples and a great number of people, blind Bartimeus, the son of Timeus, sat by the highway side begging. And when he heard that it was Jesus of Nazareth, he began to cry out, and say, Jesus, thou Son of David, have mercy on me. And many charged him that he should hold his peace: but he cried the more a great deal, Thou Son of David, have mercy on me. And Jesus stood still, and commanded him to be called. And they call the blind man, saying unto him, Be of good comfort, rise; he calleth thee. And he, casting away his garment, rose, and came to Jesus. And Jesus answered and said unto him, What wilt thou that I should do unto thee? The blind man said unto him, Lord, that I might receive my sight. And Jesus said unto him, Go thy way; thy faith hath made thee whole. And immediately he received his sight, and followed Jesus in the way.

The Last Supper

In this scene Jesus is establishing the ordinance of Communion. They were celebrating the Jewish Passover in remembrance of the deliverance from Egypt, when a lamb's blood, sprinkled on the lintel and doorposts, saved them from the avenging sword of the angel of death. From this time on, however, believers would observe this ordinance to be reminded of the death of a greater sacrifice, the Lamb of God whose blood insures deliverance from judgment.

Luke 22:14-20
And when the hour was come, he sat down, and the twelve apostles with him. And he said unto them, With desire I have desired to eat this passover with you before I suffer: For I say unto you, I will not any more eat thereof, until it be fulfilled in the kingdom of God. And he took the cup, and gave thanks, and said, Take this, and divide it among yourselves: For I say unto you, I will not drink of the fruit of the vine, until the kingdom of God shall come. And he took bread, and gave thanks, and brake it, and gave unto them, saying, This is my body which is given for you: this do in remembrance of me. Likewise also the cup after supper, saying, This cup is the new testament in my blood, which is shed for you.

Arrested in Gethsemane

Since the word *Gethsemane* means "olive press," the "Garden" was probably an oliveyard. The eight old olive trees standing at the present site are of great antiquity. Historians tell us that Titus destroyed all the trees in his siege of Jerusalem in A.D. 70, but since olive tree roots rarely die, and new shoots grow out of them, the ancient ones still there possibly trace their ancestry to the time of Jesus. In this scene Jesus has said, "It is I," acknowledging His identity, and His would-be captors, overwhelmed by the divine presence, are falling to the ground. Judas the traitor is standing at Jesus' side.

John 18:3-6

Judas then, having received a band of men and officers from the chief priests and Pharisees, cometh thither with lanterns and torches and weapons. Jesus therefore, knowing all things that should come upon him, went forth, and said unto them, Whom seek ye? They answered him, Jesus of Nazareth. Jesus saith unto them, I am he. And Judas also, which betrayed him, stood with them. As soon then as he had said unto them, I am he, they went backward, and fell to the ground.

Matthew 26:48-56

Now he that betrayed him gave them a sign, saying, Whomsoever I shall kiss, that same is he; hold him fast, And forthwith he came to Jesus, and said, Hail, Master; and kissed him. And Jesus said unto him, Friend, wherefore art thou come? Then came they, and laid hands on Jesus, and took him. And, behold, one of them which were with Jesus stretched out his hand, and drew his sword, and struck a servant of the high priest, and smote off his ear. Then said Jesus unto him, Put up again thy sword into his place: for all they that take the sword shall perish with the sword. Thinkest thou that I cannot now pray to my Father, and he shall presently give me more than twelve legions of angels? But how then shall the Scriptures be fulfilled, that thus it must be? In that same hour said Jesus to the multitudes, Are ye come out as against a thief with swords and staves for to take me? I sat daily with you teaching in the temple, and ye laid no hold on me. But all this was done, that the Scriptures of the prophets might be fulfilled. Then all the disciples forsook him, and fled.

Before the Sanhedrin

It was a hastily convened tribunal and an unjust trial before the Sanhedrin, the rulers of Israel. Carefully formulated laws had been prepared for conducting this kind of trial, but nearly every one of them was flagrantly violated. No witnesses were summoned to speak for Jesus. No advocate was appointed to plead His case. It was held in the dead of night. It was a pre-arranged condemnation.

Matthew 26:57-66

And they that had laid hold on Jesus led him away to Caiaphas the high priest, where the scribes and the elders were assembled. But Peter followed him afar off unto the high priest's palace, and went in, and sat with the servants, to see the end. Now the chief priests, and elders, and all the council, sought false witness against Jesus, to put him to death; But found none: yea, though many false witnesses came, yet found they none. At the last came two false witnesses, And said, This fellow said, I am able to destroy the temple of God, and to build it in three days. And the high priest arose, and said unto him, Answerest thou nothing? what is it which these witness against thee? But Jesus held his peace. And the high priest answered and said unto him, I adjure thee by the living God, that thou tell us whether thou be the Christ, the Son of God. Jesus saith unto him, Thou hast said: nevertheless I say unto you, Hereafter shall ye see the Son of man sitting on the right hand of power, and coming in the clouds of heaven. Then the high priest rent his clothes, saying, He hath spoken blasphemy; what further need have we of witnesses? behold, now ye have heard his blasphemy. What think ye? They answered and said, He is guilty of death.

The Jews Accuse Jesus

The Jewish authorities entertained no scruples about bringing false witnesses to testify against Jesus and breaching other laws in the religious trial, but they held to their rules of behavior when they brought Jesus before Pilate to ask for His death. To go inside the judgment hall would have rendered them ritually unclean, so they stayed outside.

The Romans often conducted their trials in the open air, by the city gate, in the marketplace, or even by the roadside, so all could see and hear. The palace of Herod, now Pilate's official residence, evidently offered a permanent provision for this custom. In the center of the Gabbatha ("Pavement"), just before the judgment hall was a slightly raised platform. On it was the chair of the procurator, with seats for other officials. Here Jesus was brought to trial before the Roman governor.

John 18:28-29
Then led they Jesus from Caiaphas unto the hall of judgment: and it was early; and they themselves went not into the judgment hall, lest they should be defiled; but that they might eat the passover. Pilate then went out unto them, and said, What accusation bring ye against this man?

Luke 23:2
And they began to accuse him, saying, We found this fellow perverting the nation, and forbidding to give tribute to Caesar, saying that he himself is Christ a king.

Jesus Crucified

Probably no event in history has been written about, discussed or spoken about more than the crucifixion of Jesus Christ. It furnished the prime subject for literature and art. The danger is that "familiarity breeds contempt," or at least indifference. Only the Great Author of the Book, the Holy Spirit, can stimulate us to understand all the harrowing details and stir us not merely to know but also to appreciate all that Jesus' death means to us nearly two thousand years later.

> A Christless cross no refuge were
>   for me,
> A crossless Christ my Saviour could
>   not be,
> But, oh Christ crucified, I rest in
>   thee.

John 19:17-22
And he bearing his cross went forth into a place called the place of a skull, which is called in the Hebrew Golgotha: Where they crucified him, and two others with him, on either side one, and Jesus in the midst. And Pilate wrote a title, and put it on the cross. And the writing was JESUS OF NAZARETH THE KING OF THE JEWS. This title then read many of the Jews; for the place where Jesus was crucified was nigh to the city: and it was written in Hebrew, and Greek, and Latin. Then said the chief priests of the Jews to Pilate, Write not, The King of the Jews; but that he said, I am King of the Jews. Pilate answered, What I have written I have written.

The Empty Tomb

After Peter and John's race to the tomb, their subsequent actions depict three kinds of vision. The younger man, John, arrived first and with physical eyesight peered in and in the dim light saw the clothes lying. Bold Peter, arriving, brushed past John and went inside. There, his mental vision perceived the situation, especially noticing the folded napkin (an important point; it had not been an hurried exit, executed by grave robbers or a person who had swooned and revived). Then came John who not only viewed the tomb but with spiritual sight comprehended the truth of the Resurrection.

John 20:3-10

So they ran both together: and the other disciple did outrun Peter, and came first to the sepulchre. And he stooping down, and looking in, saw the linen clothes lying; yet went he not in. Then cometh Simon Peter following him, and went into the sepulchre, and seeth the linen clothes lie, And the napkin, that was about his head, not lying with the linen clothes, but wrapped together in a place by itself. Then went in also that other disciple, which came first to the sepulchre, and he saw, and believed. For as yet they knew not the Scripture, that he must rise again from the dead. Then the disciples went away again unto their own home.

Jesus on the Shore

What a mundane thing for the risen Lord to do—prepare a breakfast on the beach. But it was practical. His seven followers had toiled all night and caught nothing, reminiscent of the time recorded in Luke 5, when He first called them to be fishers of men. They were hungry, discouraged. As before, there was a great catch of fish—then a renewed call. The traditional site is located on the northwestern shore of the Sea of Galilee.

John 21:4-14

But when the morning was now come, Jesus stood on the shore; but the disciples knew not that it was Jesus. Then Jesus saith unto them, Children, have ye any meat? They answered him, No. And he said unto them, Cast the net on the right side of the ship, and ye shall find. They cast therefore, and now they were not able to draw it for the multitude of fishes. Therefore that disciple whom Jesus loved saith unto Peter, It is the Lord. Now when Simon Peter heard that it was the Lord, he girt his fisher's coat unto him, (for he was naked,) and did cast himself into the sea. And the other disciples came in a little ship, (for they were not far from land, but as it were two hundred cubits,) dragging the net with fishes. As soon then as they were come to land, they saw a fire of coals there, and fish laid thereon, and bread. Jesus saith unto them, Bring of the fish which ye have now caught. Simon Peter went up, and drew the net to land full of great fishes, a hundred and fifty and three: and for all there were so many, yet was not the net broken. Jesus saith unto them, Come and dine. And none of the disciples durst ask him, Who art thou? knowing that it was the Lord. Jesus then cometh, and taketh bread, and giveth them, and fish likewise. This is now the third time that Jesus showed himself to his disciples, after that he was risen from the dead.